The Economics of Tourism Destinations

The measurement of tourism, for example analysing competitiveness and evaluating tourism projects, is not an easy task. Now in its third edition, *The Economics of Tourism Destinations*: *Theory and Practice* provides a succinct guide to the economic aspects of tourism for students and practitioners alike to decipher the methods of measurement of supply, demand, trends and impacts. This new edition has been revised and updated to include:

- Three new chapters: Tourism as a development strategy, Tourism export-led growth, and a dedicated chapter on Macro-evaluation of tourism projects and events, including the travel cost method and the contingent valuation method.
- New case studies from emerging destinations in Asia, Australia and America to show theory in practice.
- New and updated data throughout.

Each chapter combines theory and practice and is integrated with international case studies. Combining macro- and micro-aspects of economics to the tourism destination, this is an invaluable resource for students learning about this subject, as well as being aimed at tourism researchers and policy-makers.

Norbert Vanhove (PhD Economic Sciences, Erasmus University, Rotterdam) started his career in tourism at WES Research & Strategy (Bruges) and is co-founder and honorary president of TRC (Tourism Research Center). He is one of the founding fellows of IAST (International Academy for the Study of Tourism) and has been vice-president of AIEST for over ten years. He has been visiting professor (1967–2001) and later treasurer at the College of Europe. Since 2002 he has been part-time professor at KU Leuven (Tourism). In the years 1979–2000 he was general director of the Regional Development Authority of West-Flanders and of WES Research & Strategy.

The Economics of Tourism Destinations

Theory and Practice

Third edition

Norbert Vanhove

Routledge
Taylor & Francis Group

LONDON AND NEW YORK

Third edition published 2018
by Routledge
2 Park Square, Milton Park, Abingdon, Oxon, OX14 4RN

and by Routledge
711 Third Avenue, New York, NY 10017

Routledge is an imprint of the Taylor & Francis Group, an informa business

© 2018 Norbert Vanhove

First edition published by Elsevier 2005
Second edition published by Elsevier 2011

British Library Cataloguing-in-Publication Data
A catalogue record for this book is available from the British Library

Library of Congress Cataloging-in-Publication Data
Names: Vanhove, Norbert, author.
Title: The economics of tourism destinations : theory and practice / Norbert Vanhove.
Description: Third edition. | New York : Routledge, 2018. | Includes bibliographical references and index.
Identifiers: LCCN 2017033827 (print) | LCCN 2017046354 (ebook) | ISBN 9781351263801 (Master ebook) | ISBN 9781351263795 (Web pdf) | ISBN 9781351263788 (epub3) | ISBN 9781351263771 (Mobipocket) | ISBN 9781138578760 (Hardback : alk. paper) | ISBN 9781138578791 (Paperback : alk. paper) | ISBN 9781351263801 (Ebook)
Subjects: LCSH: Tourism.
Classification: LCC G155.A1 (ebook) | LCC G155.A1 V365 2018 (print) | DDC 338.4/791—dc23
LC record available at https://lccn.loc.gov/2017033827

ISBN: 978-1-138-57876-0 (hbk)
ISBN: 978-1-138-57879-1 (pbk)
ISBN: 978-1-351-26380-1 (ebk)

Typeset in Sabon and Frutiger
by Keystroke, Neville Lodge, Tettenhall, Wolverhampton

In memory of Prof. Dr. Olivier Vanneste and Professor S. Medlik

This third edition is dedicated to the memory and support of two figures who are indirectly at the basis of all three editions. Professor Vanneste (1930–2014) was the founding director of WES in Bruges. He created a new department, 'tourism research', in 1962, and introduced me to this new field. This third edition is also dedicated to the memory and support of Professor S. Medlik (1928–2007). In the early 1990s Professor Medlik suggested that I should myself write a handbook on the economics of tourism. It was many years before I responded. This book celebrates their memory.

Contents

Figures

Tables

Foreword

Economics can be credited for presenting tourism as an important sector or industry, and this as early as the 1950s and 1960s, with its socio-cultural and related dimensions coming to the surface in the following decade. Much of the initial coverage of the economics of tourism was limited to quantifying arrivals, sometimes grouping them, and assessing monetary incomes from tourism, often expressed in export earnings and number of jobs generated. With the passage of time, the supply side received more attention, gradually leading to the realization that tourism is an essentially socio-economic phenomenon, recognizing that its economics relate to and depend on many other factors often discussed within the realms of anthropology, ecology, political science, psychology, religion, sociology, and more. This led to the stand that the economics of tourism can best be understood if it is unfolded and interpreted beyond its disciplinary limits.

This volume, *The Economics of Tourism Destinations: Theory and Practice,* conveys the broader yet integrative contexts of the economics of tourism, without detailing the outlying texts. Prof. Dr. Norbert Vanhove theorizes, applies and explains the economics of tourism comprehensively and engagingly. This third edition casts a wider net than its earlier versions, offers micro and macro views, and opts for regional economics and policy, while zigzagging between theory and practice. The latter connects to my evolved stand in the field which in 2009 resulted in the *Bridging Tourism Theory and Practice* book series and to the establishment of the Tourism Intelligence Forum (the t-Forum) in 2015, set to transfer knowledge or intelligence to and within tourism. These further connect to a thesis which I wrote years earlier on the socio-economic role of tourism in developing countries.

Economics of Tourism Destinations: Theory and Practice, capturing the 'economic reality' of tourism, is set to educate students, inform researchers, and guide policy makers who are learning about the role that tourism can play in inclusive development processes at national and regional levels. I am looking forward to the next contribution of Prof. Dr. Vanhove which will further advance our knowledge in this field.

Jafar Jafari, Professor Emeritus
University of Wisconsin-Stout, USA

Preface to the third edition

In the preface to the first edition (2005), I focussed on the origins of this book. That was my research in tourism at WES (West Flemish Study Office) and my teaching task in the 1990s at RUCA (Rijks Universitair Centrum Antwerpen, now incorporated in Antwerp University). Between the preface to the first and the second edition six years passed. Six years is not that long. Nevertheless, it is astonishing to see the many changes and above all the many new publications about economics in tourism. The third edition comes another six years later. My teaching post at the KU Leuven was inspiring for the second as well as for the third edition.

The new edition differs from the second one in several aspects. Firstly, the title of the book has changed. A subtitle is added: 'Theory and Practice'. One of the characteristics of the publication is the link to the real tourism world. Many examples and case studies illustrate the reality of tourism. The change of title should also avoid any confusion with another publication. Secondly, data have changed. We are living in a rapidly changing world. But there is more. My colleague Douglas Frechtling of George Washington University formulated a number of suggestions for the second edition and advised me to give more examples and cases from outside Europe. Thus America, Australia and Asia are even more present in the third edition. Fourthly, a number of new topics were added to existing chapters. Tourism is more than ever before considered as a vehicle of economic development. Two new chapters are related to this topic. The original chapter 'Micro-and Macro-Evaluation of Projects in the Tourism and Hospitality Industry' has been split into two separate chapters. One deals with micro evaluation and the second is focussed on project evaluation from the macro point of view. One problem of most cost–benefit applications is the absence of a price for non-marketable products. The theory on willingness to pay is very helpful in solving some of these problems. Therefore, special attention is given to two well-known methods; the travel cost method and the contingent valuation method.

The basic structure of the book has not changed very much. The first chapter covers the up-to-date definition of tourism and provides a review of the economic characteristics of tourism. Measurement of tourism is not an easy task. In the last decade there has been a growing interest in the tourism world and new methods to measure demand and supply of tourism. Tourism information and management systems, Tourism Satellite Account, tourism surveys, production indexes and tourism barometers are exponents of these research efforts. They are presented in Chapter 2. The economics of tourism implies particular attention to demand and supply. Tourism demand focusses on four main subjects: determinants of tourism demand, trends in tourism demand, the evolution of holiday participation in a number of European tourism generating countries, and the phenomenon of seasonality.

The chapter concerning supply pays particular attention to the market structures in tourism and new supply trends. Price mechanism and taxation in tourism are combined in one chapter. This is the content of the new Chapter 5. Chapter 6 on competition is an extension of the supply side. In this chapter the focus is on the 'tourism destination'. The economic literature on tourism during the last decade is characterized by many publications dealing with competitiveness of destinations. This chapter tries to give an insight into the complexity of competition in tourism and to bring a synthesis of the different developed models. A central point of this chapter is the so-called 'ten key factors for a competitive destination'. Besides the conceptual models a couple of tourism benchmarking models are incorporated.

The next chapter is an extension of the third chapter. It is surprising how many publications are related to forecasting of tourism demand. Forecasting of tourism demand is not an easy task. There is not only a certain lack of reliable data, but also apart from economic factors many other determinants particularly influence tourism demand. Therefore it is necessary to make a distinction between qualitative and quantitative methods of forecasting.

Chapter 8 'Tourism as a development strategy' and Chapter 9 'Tourism export-led growth' are new. Both chapters are complementary. The value chain is the starting point of Chapter 8. The focus is, however, on tourism as a strategic option for regional development based on the theory of 'basic and non-basic activities' and the comparative advantages and other benefits of tourism. Tourism as a strategic vehicle in developed and less developed countries is the key question. The eight case studies on 'tourism export-led growth' dealt with in Chapter 9 should give empirical evidence of the thesis developed in the preceding chapter.

The economic impact of tourism is treated in Chapter 10. Several impact facets come under discussion: tourism as a strategic dimension of economic development, economic disadvantages, balance of payments aspects, employment characteristics and the magic tourism multiplier. The main focus is, however, on the methods of measuring the income and employment generation of tourism expenditure. At the end of this important chapter these methods are compared and contrasted with the Computable General Equilibrium models applied in tourism. Evaluation of tourism projects is a central point of tourism policy.

Chapters 11 and 12 are dedicated to the micro- and macro-evaluation of tourism project investment. The description of micro-evaluation deals with the scientific discounting methods. Macro-evaluation is of great importance in tourism and is directly related to cost–benefit analysis. I develop a systematic approach to measuring the economic return of projects and events.

The philosophy of this publication is to serve as a handbook for students studying the economic aspects of tourism at university level. However, the book is also addressed to researchers and people involved in tourism policy and destination management.

Dr. Norbert Vanhove
Professor KU Leuven
Director of the Board WES Research & Strategy
July 2017

Acknowledgements

We are indebted to WES, UNWTO and many TRC colleagues for the documentation and data provided. I would like to thank especially Mrs B. Declercq, librarian at WES. Thanks to my colleague Professor Douglas Frechtling of the George Washington University for the many suggestions in the preparation of the second edition. I wish to express my warm gratitude to Mr M. Cumberlege and Mrs Angela O' Neill for polishing the English with much care. I also thank J. Bisschop who assisted me by drawing the figures. Finally, I am grateful to my wife Elisabeth for her encouragement and support during the process of producing the third edition of this book.

Abbreviations

ACC	Annual capital charge
ACP	Africa, Caribbean, Pacific
AGE	Applied general equilibrium
AIEST	Association Internationale d'Experts Scientifiques du Tourisme
ARMA/ARIMA	Autoregressive Integrated Moving Average
ATC	Australian Tourist Commission
BCG	Boston Consulting Group
BL	Inter-sectoral backward
BoP	Balance of Payments
BOTA	Best of the Alps
CAPI	Computer Assisted Personal Interviewing
CBA	Cost–benefit analysis
CES	Constant Elasticity of Substitution
CET	Constant Elasticity of Transformation
CGE	Computable General Equilibrium
CPI	Consumer Price Index
CRS	Central Reservations System
CVM	Contingent Valuation Method
DCF	discounted cash flow
DEA	Data envelopment analysis
DM	Destination Management
DMIS	Destination Management Information System
DMO	Destination Management Organization
DMO	Direct Marketing Organization
DMUs	Decision Making Units
DPPD	Destination policy, planning and development
ECM	Error correction model
EIU	Economist Intelligence Unit
ELVS	English Leisure Visits Survey
EPI	Event Performance Index
ETC	European Travel Commission
ETIP	English Tourism Intelligence Partnership
ETIS	European Tourism Indicator System
f.o.b.	free on board
FC	Flag Companies

Abbreviations

FISIM	Financial intermediation services indirectly measure
FL	Inter-sectoral forward
FMOLS	Fully modified ordinary least squares
GATT	General Agreement on Tariffs and Trade
GBDVS	Great Britain Day Visit Survey
GBTS	Great Britain Tourism Survey
GC	Gini coefficient
GDP	Gross Domestic Product
GDS	Global Distribution System
GMM	Generalized method of moments
GOP	Gross operational profit
GVA	Gross Value Added
I–O	Input–output
IAST	International Academy for the Study of Tourism
IATA	International Air Transport Association
ICP	International Comparison Programme
II	Interval International
ILO	International Labour Organization
IMF	International Monetary Fund
IPA	Importance-Performance Analysis
IPS	International Passenger Survey
IRR	Internal rate of return
IRTS	International Recommendations for Tourism Statistics
ITCM	Individual travel cost method
IUCN	International Union for Conservation of Nature
IUOTO	International Union of Official Travel Organizations
LCC	Low Cost Carriers
LDC	Less developed country
MICE	Meetings, Incentives, Conferences and Exhibitions
MMRF	MONASH Multi Regional Forecasting
NAT	New Age of Tourism
NIEIR	National Institute of Economic and Industry Research
NNI	Net national income
NPISH	Non-profit institutions serving households
NPV	Net present value
OECD	Organization for Economic Co-operation and Development
OLS	(method) Ordinary least square
ONS	Office for National Statistics
ONSCE	Office for National Statistics Centre for Demography
P2P	peer-to-peer
PEST	Political, Economic, Socio-cultural, Technological
PII	Price Competitiveness Indices
PMC	Passenger Movement Charge
PPP	Purchasing Power Parities
RCI	Resort Condominiums International
ROI	Return on Investment
SAM	Social accounting matrix
SICTA	Standard International Classification of Tourism Activities

SME	Small and medium-sized enterprises
SNA	System of National Accounts
SOC	Social opportunity cost
STBT	Sustainable tourism benchmarking tool
STP	Social time preference
SWOT	Strengths, Weaknesses, Opportunities, Threats
TA/TA_P	Tourist arrivals per capita
TALC	Tourist Area Lifecycle
TCM	Travel cost method
TD/TE_P	Tourist expenditure per capita
TDM	Tourism Destination Management
TEA	Themed Entertainment Association
TEIM	Travel Economic Impact Model
TGDP	Tourism Gross Domestic Product
TGVA	Tourism Gross Value Added
TIA	Travel Industry Association of America
TIM	Tourism income multiplier
TIS	Tourism Information System
TLG	Tourism export-led growth
TLGH	Tourism-led growth hypothesis
TourMIS	Tourism Marketing Information System
TPD	Tourism Product Development
TPI	Tourism Performance Index
TRC	Tourist Research Centre
TSA	Tourism Satellite Account
TTCI	Travel and Tourism Competitiveness Index
TVA	Tourism Value Added
UKTS	United Kingdom Tourism Survey
UN	United Nations
UNCTAD	United Nations Conference on Trade and Development
UNWTO	World Tourist Organization
VAR	(model) Vector Autoregression
VAT	Value Added Tax
VCA	Value Chain Analysis
VFR	Visits to Friends and Relatives
WEF	World Economic Forum
WES	Westvlaams Economisch Studiebureau
WTO	World Trade Organization
WTP	Willingness to pay
WTTC	World Travel and Tourism Council
WTTOUR	World Trade Tourism Model
ZTCM	Zonal travel cost method

Chapter 1

The economic characteristics of the tourism sector

The purpose of this first chapter is to focus on a number of economic characteristics of the tourism sector. These characteristics are fundamental to many aspects of the economics of tourism and they will be referred to throughout this book. However, before starting with an overview of the economic characteristics, it is important to define what we understand by 'tourism' and what do we *not* consider to be tourism.

What is tourism?

What is tourism? This is not such a simple question as it seems. Colloquially, free time, leisure, recreation, travel and tourism are used synonymously and are almost interchangeable. However, from a scientific and practical point of view, the reality is quite different. The case of Austria is a simple illustration. In 1999, based on the Tourism Satellite Account (TSA), tourism represented, in terms of value added (direct and indirect effect), 8.7 per cent of GDP (Gross Domestic Product). However, tourism and recreation together make up a total of 15.5 per cent of GDP (Franz *et al.*, 2001). The difference is clear.

In the tourism literature, a distinction is made between conceptual and statistical (technical or operational) definitions of tourism.

Conceptual definitions

One of the oldest conceptual definitions of tourism was given by two pioneers of tourism research, Hunziker and Krapf (1942), who defined tourism as being 'a sum of relations and phenomena resulting from travel and stay of non residents, in so far as a stay does not lead to permanent residence and is not connected with any permanent or temporary earning activity'. For a considerable time this definition was generally accepted – including by the AIEST (Association Internationale d'Experts Scientifiques du Tourisme) – although it had more than one shortcoming. For example, a stay in a hospital could be considered to be tourism, and a business trip would be excluded as being related to an earning activity. Moreover, under this definition non-residents were identified with foreigners – in other words, domestic tourism was totally excluded.

The AIEST discussed the definition once again on the occasion of their annual congress in Cardiff in 1981. This congress accepted the following definition: 'The entirety of interrelations and phenomena which result from people travelling to and stopping at places which are neither their main continuous domiciles nor places of work either for leisure or in the context of business activities or study'.

A clearer definition can be found at the British Tourism Society, which in 1979 adopted a definition based upon the work of Burkart and Medlik (1974): 'Tourism is deemed to include any activity concerned with the temporary short-term movement of people to destinations outside the places where they normally live and work, and their activities during the stay at these destinations'.

Within this definition we can identify the inclusion of those activities that are involved in the stay or visit to the destination. There is no insistence on overnight stays or foreign visits, and it allows for domestic as well as day visits (Gilbert, 1990).

According to Burkart and Medlik (1974) – and this still applies today – conceptually, tourism has five characteristics:

1   Tourism is an amalgam of phenomena and relationships rather than a single one.
2   These phenomena and relationships arise from a movement of people to, and a stay in, various destinations; there is a dynamic element (the journey) and a static element (the stay).
3   The journey and stay are to and in destinations outside the normal place of residence and work, so that tourism gives rise to activities which are distinct from those of the resident and working populations of the places through which tourists travel and of their destinations.
4   The movement to the destinations is of a temporary, short-term character.
5   Destinations are visited for purposes not connected to paid work – that is, not to take up employment.

A conceptual definition that deserves special attention is the one given by Gilbert (1990) and proposed for a social understanding of tourism: 'Tourism is one part of recreation which involves travel to a less familiar destination or community, for a short-term period, in order to satisfy a consumer need for one or a combination of activities'.

The merits of this definition are several. It places tourism in the overall context of recreation; retains the need for travel outside the normal place of work habitation, and focusses on the reasons for travel.

Operational or technical definitions

The main practical need for exact definitions of tourism and the tourist has arisen from the necessity to establish adequate statistical standards (Mieczkowski, 1990). Furthermore, many people, including tourism experts, have difficulty in considering business trips and vocational travel as tourism activities. They are often included with tourism because they respond to the characteristics described in the preceding section, and their economic significance is also the same (see Burkart and Medlik, 1974). Business travellers are pure consumers, and it is difficult or impossible in practice to separate them from those travelling for pleasure. The main difference is purpose, but most hoteliers or accommodation providers are unable to make a distinction between holidaymakers and business travellers.

In the opinion of Burkart and Medlik (1974), a technical definition of tourism must:

●   Identify the categories of travel and visits that are and are not included;
●   Define the time element in terms of length of stay away from home (i.e. the minimum and maximum period);
●   Recognize particular situations (e.g. transit traffic).

A well-known definition is the one recommended on the occasion of the United Nations Conference on Travel and Tourism held in Rome in 1963, although it should be recognized that the UN definition was not the first (see Committee of Statistical Experts of the League of

Nations, ETC, IUOTO, OECD and IMF, in Gilbert, 1990). The UN Conference recommended the following definition of 'visitor' in international statistics: 'For statistical purposes, the term *visitor* describes any person visiting a country other than that in which he has usual place of residence, for any reason other than following an occupation remunerated from within the country visited'. This definition covers:

- *Tourists*, i.e. temporary visitors staying at least 24 hours in the country visited and the purpose of whose journey can be classified under the headings of either (a) leisure (recreation, holiday, health, study, religion, and sport) or (b) business, family, mission, meeting.
- *Excursionists*, i.e. temporary visitors staying less than 24 hours in the country visited (including travellers on cruises).

The statistics should not include travellers who, in the legal sense, do not enter the country (for example, air travellers who do not leave an airport's transit area, and similar cases).

Later, the phrase '24 hours' became a point of discussion, and was replaced by 'overnight' (United Nations Statistical Commission of 1967 and the IUOTO (International Union of Official Travel Organizations) meeting of 1968, in Gilbert, 1990). This precision does correspond better to the reality (a trip with an overnight stay may last less than 24 hours), but is after all of minor importance.

The UN definition refers to international tourism (visiting a country other than that in which a traveller usually resides), but there is no reason to neglect domestic tourism. A person travelling from New York to California to visit the city of San Francisco (domestic tourism) is no less a tourist than is a Belgian visiting Paris (international tourism). The 1980 Manilla Declaration of the WTO (World Trade Organization) extends the definition implicitly to all tourism, both domestic and international. Excluded from the definition are returning residents, immigrants, migrants (temporary workers staying less than one year), commuters, soldiers, diplomats and transit passengers.

This was the standard definition for a long time, although it was not applied in all countries. In that respect, the USA is a typical example. Even within the USA the definition of tourism and tourists varies from state to state (De Brabander, 1992).

There was, however, still no common language of tourism statistics. Many scientists and organizations were aware of the problem, and the early 1990s saw a long period of discussion and negotiation, in which several international organizations participated (Eurostat, OECD, WTO and UN Statistic Division), in an attempt to solve it. The conclusion, in 2000, was the adoption by the United Nations Statistical Commission of the *Tourism Satellite Account: Recommended Methodological Framework* (Eurostat *et al.*, 2001). The Vancouver Conference of 2001 was a celebration of ten years of scientific and intellectual international cooperation leading to a consensus on the development of the TSA. This remarkable achievement by the tourism industry was the culmination of the life's work of the late Enzo Paci – the WTO's former chief of statistics (see Enzo Paci World Conference on the Measurement of the Economic Impact of Tourism, Nice, 1999, in Eurostat *et al.*, 2001). At the same time, it was a reformulation of a technical definition of tourism which was (or should have been) accepted worldwide:

> Tourism comprises the activities of persons travelling to and staying in places outside their usual environment for not more than one consecutive year for leisure, business and other purposes not related to the exercise of an activity remunerated from within the place visited, where the persons referred to in the definition of tourism are termed 'visitors', a visitor being defined as: Any person travelling to a place other than that of his/her usual environment for less than twelve months and whose main purpose of trip is other than the exercise of an activity remunerated from within the place visited.

This definition differs in two respects from the former UN description: first, the maximum duration of stay (one consecutive year) outside the usual place of residence is determined; and secondly, 'usual place of residence' is replaced by the term 'usual environment'.

In the new definition, 'usual environment' is a key element. In the *Tourism Satellite Account: Recommended Methodological Framework* (Eurostat *et al.*, 2001), this corresponds to the geographical boundaries within which an individual moves during his or her regular routine of life. The usual environment of a person therefore consists of the direct vicinity of his or her home place of work or study and other places frequently visited, and has several dimensions:

● Frequency – places that are frequently visited by a person (on a routine basis) are considered as part of the usual environment even though these places may be located at a considerable distance from the place of residence.
● Distance – places located close to the place of residence of a person are part of the usual environment even if the actual spots are rarely visited.
● Time – how much time does the visitor spend between leaving the place of residence and returning home?
● Definition – the definition of places where people perform routine activities (homework, shopping, study, etc.).

To determine the usual environment, there are two different approaches in survey research: endogenous and exogenous. In the endogenous approach, the researcher has to define distance and time thresholds and must indicate what is 'frequent'. The available international applications show how different the interpretations of the above-mentioned dimensions are. Many factors are influential, including the size of the country, population density, spreading of regional city centres, etc. In rural areas, the usual environment can be quite large, whereas in an urban centre the people living in one part of the city might never (or seldom) visit another part although the distance between them is relatively small.

In the exogenous approach, visitors are supposed to indicate themselves if the place visited is within their usual environment. The latter method is preferred by the WTTC (World Travel and Tourism Council), but it is a very dangerous path because the interpretation of individuals is very subjective.

There seems to be no general agreement on what is meant by 'usual environment'. The researcher has to be very pragmatic. There is always a grey line between tourism and recreational activities, and between tourism and routine activities. In practice, this will not greatly influence research results.

In the framework of definitions we should make reference to an important publication, *International Recommendations for Tourism Statistics 2008* (IRTS, 2008), adopted by the United Nations Statistical Commission and prepared by UNWTO experts from different countries with the assistance of the OECD, WTTC and ILO. It presents a system of definitions, concepts, classifications and indicators that are internally consistent and facilitate the link to the TSA (see Chapter 2). There are minor differences, none of which are essential. Thus tourism is defined as:

> Specific types of trips: those that take a traveller outside his/her usual environment for less than a year and for a main purpose other than to be employed by a resident entity in the place visited.
>
> (Frechtling, 2009)

And in IRTS (2008) 'visitor' is defined as:

> A traveller taking a trip to a main destination outside his/her usual environment, for less than a year, for any main purpose (business, leisure or other personal purpose) other

than to be employed by a resident entity in the country or place visited. These trips taken by visitors qualify as tourism trips. Tourism refers to the activity of visitors.

Travellers can be classified in several groups (see Figure 1.1 referring to inbound travellers). The key concept in these definitions is 'usual environment of an individual', defined as the geographical area (though not a contiguous one) within which an individual conducts his/her regular life routines. The following clarification is important:

> The usual environment of an individual includes the place of usual residence of the household to which he/she belongs, his/her place of work or study and any other place that he/she visits regularly and frequently, even when this place is located far away from his/her place of usual residence or in another locality, except for vacation homes.
>
> (IRTS, 2008)

Here there is full correspondence with what has been said above about usual environment.

Most of the economic activities associated with visitors occur while they are outside their usual environment and have effects on local or national economies different from that of their usual environment. Nevertheless, the TSA also includes consumption that normally happens within the usual environment; for instance, that of potential visitors in anticipation of trips (such as the acquisition of small items to take along to use or give away, or purchases of camping gear, luggage or travel insurance, travel agency services, or transportation services from the usual environment to the place visited).

Special attention must be given to vacation homes. Each household has a principal dwelling, usually defined with reference to the time spent there, whose location determines the country of residence and place of usual residence of this household and all of its members. All other dwellings (owned or leased, medium- or long-term by the households) are considered as secondary dwellings. *International Recommendations for Tourism Statistics 2008* explicitly excludes secondary dwellings used as vacation homes (those visited mainly for recreation purposes) from the usual environment, regardless of how close they are to the usual place of residence, the frequency of the visits and duration of stay.

Dimensions of travel and tourism

Notwithstanding the many international and/or scientific definitions of tourism, there seems not to be a universally accepted definition. There is, however, more agreement on the dimensions of tourism. De Brabander (1992) makes a distinction between the 'travel' and 'stay' dimensions. As far as the 'travel' component is concerned, he refers to three sub-dimensions:

1 Distance – short-, medium- and long-haul.
2 Origin – domestic and international.
3 Mode of transport – car, coach, train, plane, boat and other.

For the 'stay' dimension, there are another three classifications:

1 Duration – less than 24 hours (excursions) and more than 24 hours; for the latter group a further distinction is very often made between short holidays (one to three nights) and holidays (four nights or more). In IRTS (2008) a distinction is made between a tourist (or overnight visitor) and a same-day visitor (or excursionist).
2 Purpose – leisure, business, congress and personal (family, religion, health, education).
3 Accommodation – hotel, boarding house, camping, holiday village, rented apartment or villa, cruise, farm and other.

It is evident that excursions do not involve an overnight stay.

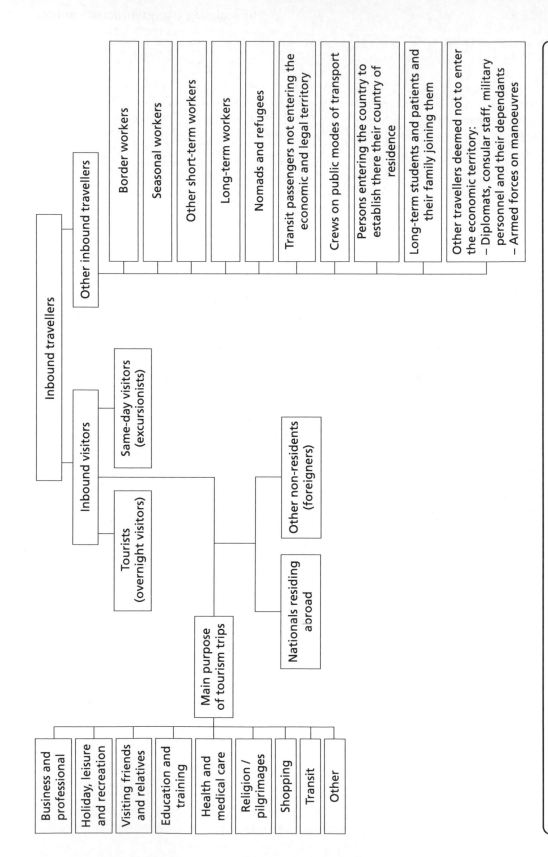

Figure 1.1 Classification of inbound travellers (IRTS, 2008)

Types of tourism

It is important to locate the tourist (and related consumption) geographically in order to analyse the impacts on a country of reference. This applies not only when statistics are established at the national level, but even more when they are compiled at the regional level. In the TSA, tourism is divided into the following categories (taking France as an example):

- Domestic tourism – the tourism of residents of a country visiting destinations in their own country. The TSA makes a distinction between resident visitors travelling only within their country and resident visitors with a final destination outside the country (e.g. a French visitor from Paris travelling to Madrid and spending one night in Montpellier). In other words, domestic tourism comprises the activities of a resident visitor within the country of reference, either as part of a domestic tourism trip or part of an outbound tourism trip (IRTS, 2008).
- Inbound tourism – the tourism of non-resident visitors within the country.
- Outbound tourism – tourism of nationals (e.g. French) visiting destinations in other countries. UNWTO is more precise: outbound tourism comprises the activities of a resident visitor outside the country of reference, either as part of an outbound tourism trip or as part of a domestic tourism trip (IRTS, 2008).
- Internal tourism – the combination of domestic and inbound tourism.
- National tourism – the tourism of resident visitors (e.g. French) within and outside the economic territory of the country of reference (France).
- International tourism – the combination of inbound and outbound tourism.

Based on the types and categories of tourism, and taking into account that consumption is an activity of visitors, the following aggregates for visitor consumption can be derived:

- Domestic tourism consumption – the consumption of resident visitors within the economy of reference; for example, France.
- Inbound tourism consumption – the consumption of non-resident visitors within the country of reference and/or of goods and services provided by residents.
- Outbound tourism consumption – the consumption of resident visitors outside the country of reference and/or of goods and services provided by non-residents.
- Internal tourism consumption – the consumption of both resident and non-resident visitors within the country of reference and/or or goods and services provided by residents.
- National tourism consumption – the consumption of resident visitors within and outside the country of residence.

IRTS (2008) makes a distinction between tourism expenditure and tourism consumption. Tourism expenditure is the amount paid for the acquisition of consumption goods and services, as well as valuables, for personal use or to give away, for and during tourism trips. It includes expenditure by visitors themselves as well as expenses that are paid for or reimbursed by others.

Tourism consumption has the same formal definition as tourism expenditure. Nevertheless, the concept of tourism consumption used in the TSA (see Chapter 2) goes beyond that of tourism expenditure. Besides the amount paid for the acquisition of consumption goods and services, as well as valuables for personal use or to give away, for and during tourism trips (corresponding to monetary transactions, which is the focus of tourism expenditure), it also includes services associated with vacation accommodation, tourism social transfers in kind and other imputed consumption. These transactions need to be estimated using sources different from information collected directly from the visitors, such as reports on home exchanges, estimations of rents associated with vacation homes, and calculations of financial intermediation services indirectly measured. More precisely, beyond acquisitions already included in tourism expenditure, it includes imputed consumption and other adjustments. These are, in particular:

a   The imputed value of barter transactions (for example, temporary exchange of dwellings for vacation purposes);
b   The imputed value of goods (vegetables, fruits, game, fish, etc.) produced by the tourists themselves from the vacation home or resulting from recreation activities (gardening, hunting, fishing, etc.) outside the usual environment;
c   The value of services (either market or for own final use) associated with vacation accommodation on own account (secondary dwellings for vacation purposes and all other types of non-traditional vacation home ownership);
d   The value of FISIM (financial intermediation services indirectly measured) included in any interest paid by visitors on tourism expenditure;
e   The net cost for hosts of receiving visitors in terms of increased expenditure on food, utilities, invitations, presents, etc.;
f   The cost for producers (businesses, governments and non-profit institutions serving households, or NPISH) of expenditure by employees on business trips that do not involve a monetary disbursement by the employee (transportation services provided free of charge or at subsidized price to their employees by carriers, accommodation or meals provided free of charge or at subsidized price to employees by hotels, etc.);
g   The net cost (that is net of employees' out of pocket payments) for producers of additional services provided to their employees and their families as visitors beyond those already included in tourism expenditure, such as: cost of free or employer-subsidized transportation, cost of accommodation in vacation centres, etc.;
h   The part of the value of what the System of National Accounts 2008 qualifies as government consumption expenditure on individual non-market services on products such as education, social services, health, museums, recreation services, etc. that can be considered as benefiting visitors and that System of National Accounts 2008 describes as social transfers in kind.

Although tourism consumption will be dealt with in greater detail in Chapter 2, a number of remarks should be made with respect to some of the above-mentioned categories of consumption. First, with regard to domestic consumption, the final destination of the visitor might be within or outside the country of reference (e.g. France), but the consumption activity that is referred to must take place within that country. In other words, the domestic portion of outbound tourism consumption is part of domestic tourism consumption (see the example above regarding the French tourist travelling from Paris to Madrid with a visit to Montpellier).

Secondly, inbound consumption does not include purchases that took place in other countries (such as an air transport provided by a foreign company, or a bottle of whisky bought in the tax-free airport shop). However, goods and services purchased in the destination country may have been imported.

Thirdly, outbound tourism consumption does not include the goods and services acquired before and after the trip and within the country of residence, which is traditionally identified as the domestic portion of outbound tourism consumption.

Fourthly, inbound tourism consumption is an 'export' for the country concerned, whereas outbound tourism consumption is an 'import'.

Tourism and related concepts

Tourism should be seen in relationship with and distinguished from a number of related concepts. The first of those concepts is 'free time' – i.e. the time available to the individual, after completing necessary work and other survival activities and duties, to be spent at his or her own discretion (Miller and Robinson, 1963; Mieczkowski, 1990). In other words, free time can be defined as 'empty time'.

The second concept is 'leisure'. Leisure time is 'part of free time devoted to activities undertaken in pursuit of leisure, which may, through recreative processes and playful activities, or may not, be attained' (Cooper *et al.*, 2008). Leisure is time filled with specific kinds of activities. There is, however, another wider and more pragmatic understanding of the term, identifying it with free (uncommitted, discretionary) time as contrasted to work, work-related and subsistence time, called by some authors 'existence time' (Clawson and Knetsch, 1964; Mieczkowski, 1990). The relationship between the two notions remains hazy, and there is a grey transition zone between them. Fully committed time is, for example, essential sleep, eating, travelling to work and essential shopping; highly committed time concerns activities such as child-raising, religion, house repairs and overtime work. Therefore there is nowadays a general agreement that leisure should be described as the time available to an individual when work, sleep and other basic needs have been met (Cooper *et al.*, 2008).

'Recreation' is the third concept. According to Cooper *et al.* (2008), 'Recreation can be thought of as the pursuits engaged in during leisure time, and an activity spectrum can be identi-fied from recreation around the home, at one end of the scale, through to tourism where an overnight stay is involved, at the other'. As we have seen in the preceding section, day trips outside the usual environment are also a tourism activity.

Essential and/or possible characteristics of leisure are:

- The revitalizing function for work (may be old fashioned)
- That it is a non-working activity engaged in for pleasure
- Its voluntary character without external compulsion.

Mieczkowski makes it very clear when he states that 'In leisure the emphasis is on the time element where recreation refers to the content, to the way leisure time is spent'. Most authors express the opinion that recreation consists of 'activities' (Clawson and Knetsch, 1964; Mieczkowski, 1990; Cooper *et al.*, 2008). The latter make a distinction between home-based recreation (gardening, watching TV, reading, etc.), daily leisure (visiting sports events, visiting restaurants, etc.), day trips (visiting attractions, theme parks or beaches, etc.), and tourism.

However, not all tourism is carried out during leisure time; business tourism takes place during work time. Indeed, part of tourism is associated particularly with working time, including business meetings and conventions (see Figure 1.2).

The last related concept is 'travel'. On the one hand, travel is more than tourism – it may also be undertaken for such reasons as commuting, migration and other movements of people which are beyond the scope of tourism. However, it is also possible to defend the thesis that tourism is more than travel, for travel constitutes only one component of tourism.

Colloquially, travel is often used as a substitute for tourism – indeed, Mieczkowski (1990) makes the humorous remark that a WTO publication is called 'World Travel' in English, and

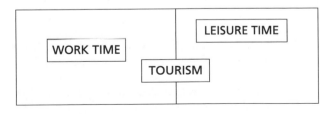

Figure 1.2 Tourism, work and leisure time

'Tourisme Mondiale' in French. The term 'tourism' is more frequently used in Europe, whereas in the United States the more common term is 'travel'. Two of the oldest tourism scientific journals are *Tourism Review* (AIEST, and more European-based) and the *Travel Research Journal* (American-based). However, in IRTS (2008), a distinction is made between tourism and travel. Trips taken by visitors are tourism trips. Travel refers to the activity of travellers. A traveller is someone who moves between different geographic locations for any purpose and any duration.

The economic characteristics of tourism

Tourism has a number of typical economic characteristics which influence to a large extent the economics of tourism or lead to special methods of measurement and economic impact analysis. This section deals with the most relevant points.

Is there a tourism industry?

In reports, speeches, articles and publications in general, the expression 'the tourism industry' is commonly used. Nevertheless, there is an ongoing debate in the literature regarding whether tourism constitutes an industry or a sector in its own right (Wahab, 1971; Burkart and Medlik, 1974; Chadwick, 1981; Jefferson and Lickorish, 1988; Medlik, 1988).

What is an industry? An industry or an economic sector in general comprises firms that produce the same products or services, or the same group of products and services, and/or are based on the same raw materials (leather, rubber, etc.). The System of National Accounts defines 'industry' as groups of establishments engaged in the same kind of productive activities.

A tourist travelling abroad buys services provided by the travel trade, transportation services, accommodation, foods and drinks, souvenirs of all kinds, entertainment services, etc. Clearly all these commodities and services do not belong to the same category of products or services, and this explains why there is not a sector in the national accounts called tourism. The hotel and catering industry (*horéca* in French) can hardly be considered as a substitute, as it is only a part of the total tourism sector. On the other hand, many firms in the catering industry have no or few links with tourists.

Nevertheless, Burkart and Medlik (1974) defend the thesis of the existence of a tourism industry based on the idea that all the components mentioned above have the one common function of supplying tourist needs:

> Although it is difficult to apply to these services the normal concept of an industry – in view of the special nature and complexity of their respective contributions to the tourist product – they may be described as the *tourist industry*: they include that part of the economy which has a common function of supplying tourist needs. This enables us to link demand and supply in tourism and to analyse the impact of tourism on the economy.

This is in any case a strong argument.

Smith (1988) also agrees with the notion of a tourism industry and, like Medlik (1988), has formulated an operational measurement for tourism industry activity. In his supply-side view he makes a distinction between firms that serve tourists exclusively (e.g. hotels) and a second group that serves a mix of tourists and local residents (e.g. a restaurants or pubs).

The fact that in reality the components of a tourist product belong to different sectors of national accounts, and that some firms serve exclusively tourists and others serve tourists as well as non-tourists, makes it difficult to measure the real significance of tourism. All this created the need for a Tourism Satellite Account (TSA).

The International Conference on Travel and Tourism Statistics held by the WTO in Ottawa in 1991 was the culmination of the great efforts made in the late 1970s and in the 1980s by international organizations (United Nations, WTO, OECD), tourism experts and countries (Canada and France) in the measurement of the economic impact of tourism. The United Nations (through its statistical commission), Eurostat, the OECD and the WTO are the international organizations that have established a set of definitions and classifications for tourism, the well-known Tourism Satellite Account (Eurostat *et al.*, 2001). There were two main purposes for this; first, the achievement of international comparability, and secondly, to serve as a guide to countries for the introduction of a statistical system for tourism.

How can the TSA be defined? We find a very good description of the philosophy in Franz *et al.* (2001):

> Countries measure economic activities – GDP, employment or demand – on the basis of internationally agreed standards for national accounts (NA). As part of the overall economy tourism is already represented in NA; the respective commodities produced by suppliers and purchased by visitors are also included in the core accounts. However, they are not visible as such because tourism is not identified as a separate activity, and the commodities produced and consumed by tourism demand are buried in other elements of the core accounts. In the overall national accounts framework there is little room for analysis by function. In order to overcome this problem, satellite accounts are proposed which are conceptually based on the same core accounts, able to highlight a particular aspect of the economy at the same time. The basic NA concepts are applied to tourism as well, taking into account those industries supplying tourism output and which are identified in the production account; at the same time these industries determine demand characteristics of tourism (e.g. visitors), which are identified by function.

More generally speaking, 'satellite account' is a term developed by the United Nations to measure the size of economic sectors that are not included in their own right in national accounts. The basic content of the TSA is dealt with in Chapter 2 of this book.

In the framework of the TSA, the tourism industries comprise all establishments for which the principal activity is a tourism characteristic activity (see Chapter 2). The term 'tourism industries' is equivalent to tourism characteristic activities and the two terms are sometimes used synonymously in IRTS (2008). The five main sectors of the tourism industry are:

1 The attraction sector

- natural attractions
- cultural attractions
- theme parks
- museums
- national parks
- wildlife parks
- gardens
- heritage sites
- entertainment
- events

2 The accommodation sector

- hotels
- motels
- bed and breakfast

- Airbnb
- guest houses
- apartments, villas and flats
- condominium timeshares
- campsites
- touring caravans
- holiday villages
- marinas
- cruises

3 The transport sector

- airlines
- railways
- bus and coach operators
- car rental operators
- shipping lines

4 The travel organizer sector

- tour operators
- travel agents
- incentive travel organizers, etc.

5 The destination organization sector

- national tourist offices
- regional tourist offices
- local tourist offices
- tourism associations.

The tourist product is an amalgam

A tourist product can have a very different meaning, depending on whether the viewpoint is that of the supplier or that of the visitor. For the hotel owner the hotel room is the product; the air carrier supplies seats, and the restaurateur sells meals. These are the products that are supplied to the holidaymaker. In the narrow sense, the tourist product consists of what the tourist buys.

In fact, the tourist buys much more. The holidaymaker purchases a holiday experience – or everything from the moment he leaves home until he returns (the experience chain). That is the meaning in the wider sense – 'The tourist product is an amalgam of what he does at the destination and the services he uses to make it possible' (Burkart and Medlik, 1974). Attractions, accessibility, amenities at the destination (accommodation, catering, entertainment, internal transport and communication, incoming tour operators, etc.) and many intangible elements (such as atmosphere, ambience and friendliness of the local population) are the components of the amalgam, and these components complement each other. For Gilbert (1990), a tourism product is 'an amalgam of different goods and services offered as an activity experience to the tourist'. The composer of the product can be the tour operator, a travel agency, the accommodation sector, the destination management organization, other organizers or, last but not least, the individual tourist.

Nulty and Cleverdon (2011) use the expression 'fragmentation of supply'. The fragmented nature of supply on the one hand and the demand for a combined set of products on the other, creates the challenge for destinations to achieve coordination and integration of all components across all sub-sectors of the tourism industry.

Tourism is a service activity

Earlier in this chapter tourism was considered as a sector in its own right, but it is not an industry in the strict sense of the word. Tourism has all the characteristics of services. Middleton, in the excellent book *Marketing in Travel and Tourism* (Middleton *et al.*, 2009), mentions a number of characteristics that distinguish services from goods. For the sake sof this book, three characteristics of services are of great significance.

First, all tourism services are *intangible*. In terms of international trade and balance of payments, inbound and outbound tourism are invisible exports and imports respectively (see Chapter 10).

The *inseparability* of tourism services is a second important characteristic. Production and consumption take place on the premises or in the equipment of the producer (e.g. aircraft), and not in the residence of the tourist. As a consequence, the staff of tourism suppliers have some consumer contact and are seen by the tourists to be an inseparable aspect of the service product. Whereas commodities can be tested and guaranteed, and product performance can be enforced by consumer protection laws; this is much more difficult with tourism services (see Table 1.1). The performance in an aircraft or a hotel is determined by the attitude of the staff, and normal guarantees or legal enforcement cannot be expected. The inseparability has direct consequences not only for tourism marketing but also in managing the competitive position of a tourism provider or destination (see Chapter 6).

Indeed, the attitude of the staff (e.g. friendliness, helpfulness) is often a vital element in delivering tourism products. Human beings are not machines, and one group of hotel tourists may be very satisfied with the staff's behaviour whereas another group arriving a week later may have a lot of complaints – perhaps owing to the staff's pressure of work. Together with climate, attitude is to a large extent responsible for the heterogeneity of performance. Heterogeneity is directly related to the characteristic of inseparability.

For our purpose, *perishability* is the most important character of services with respect to tourism. For this reason, the following subsection is dedicated to this characteristic.

Table 1.1 Generic characteristics distinguishing services from goods

Source: Middleton *et al.* (2009), *Marketing in Travel and Tourism*, published by Butterworth–Heinemann and reproduced with kind permission.

Goods	*Services*
• are manufactured	• are performed
• are made on premises not normally open to customers (separable)	• are performed on the producer's premises, often with full customer participation (inseparable)
• are delivered to places where customers live	• customers travel to places where the services are delivered
• purchase conveys ownership and right to use at own convenience	• purchase confers temporary right to access at a prearranged place and/or time
• possess tangible form at the point of sale and can be inspected prior to sale	• are intangible at the point of sale, and often cannot be inspected
• stocks of product can be created and held for future sale	• are perishable; services can be inventoried but stocks of product cannot be held

Tourism products are perishable

The perishability of tourism products can best be illustrated by a practical example. A hotel with 100 rooms has a production capacity of 100 rooms for rent every day, and the hotelier will try to sell this full capacity every day. On most days of the year he will not be successful. Unlike goods, the hotelier cannot save the unsold rooms in stock for the next day or week, and nor can he reduce the capacity. Supply in tourism is relatively inflexible, and rooms that are not rented on the day of the performance are totally lost – or 'perishable'. All hotels with a fixed number of rooms (which is the normal case) and transport operators with a fixed number of seats (railway, air carrier, bus/coach companies, etc.) face identical situations of matching perishable supply to the available demand. The production capacity that is not sold on a particular day is lost and can never be recovered.

As a direct consequence of perishability, it is not possible to create a stock of hotel rooms or train seats. However, this is not a phenomenon specific to the tourism sector. Many service industries with fixed capacity are confronted with the same problem. To cope with the perishable character of tourism products, many hoteliers, air carriers and railway companies apply more and more price differentiation and yield management. Yield management is a method for managing capacity profitably, and has gained widespread acceptance, particularly in the airline and hotel industries, over the last two decades. Yield management is a method that can help a firm to sell the right inventory unit to the right customer, at the right time, and for the right price (Kimes, 1999). In Chapter 5 we will see that a number of necessary conditions should be fulfilled for yield management – a firm should have a fixed capacity, high fixed costs, low variable costs, a segmented market, time-varied demand and similarity of inventory units.

The seasonality of tourism demand

Demand for tourism products is characterized by an unequal temporal distribution. Annually, there are weeks and months with a great demand and others with a low demand. This temporal peaking pattern is called seasonality. This uneven distribution is different from receiving country to receiving country, and from destination to destination. Some regions have a high season of a maximum of six weeks, whereas for other destinations high season lasts several months. There are also regions that attract tourists all year round, although with some months of lower occupancy rate. The peaking pattern is not necessarily restricted to one peak – for example, many Alpine regions have two peaks (see Figure 1.3). The tourism sector refers to two seasons; however, there are not only seasonal but also weekend peaks. The relationship between 'seasonality' and 'perishability' is quite evident.

The main factor responsible for the seasonal peaks is climate. Residents of northern Europe, for example, tend to take their main holidays in the summer period of June to mid-September. However, in the Pacific, Mediterranean or Caribbean tourist destinations, where the climatic variations are less important, there is also a seasonal pattern of demand. Two factors are responsible for this. The first is the organization of the school holidays in the main generating markets. Many people are involved in education-related activities – children, students, the parents of those children and students, teachers and school-related persons – and in developed countries this group constitutes a high percentage of the population.

The second factor also has an institutional origin. The organization of annual paid leave in business is well defined in several generating markets. Many firms in Europe are closed during the annual period of paid leave, while others work at a reduced capacity. The choice of the period of paid leave is also influenced by the annual school summer holidays.

This appears to be a self-reinforcing system, because many people without links to school or business prefer to take holidays in the peak season – perhaps because of a psychological 'vacation pressure', or in some cases because people may prefer to take holidays when their neighbours are away from home (Vanhove, 1974).

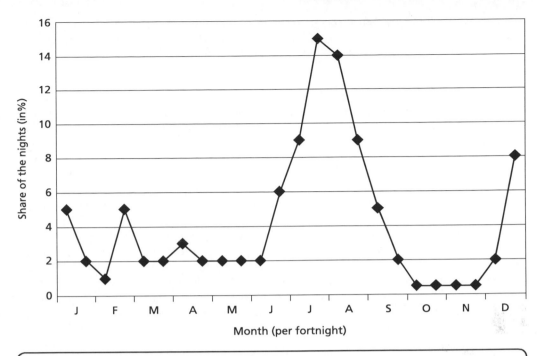

Figure 1.3 A possible seasonal pattern of tourism demand in a tourist destination

Seasonality has a number of unpleasant economic and ecological consequences for tourist destinations:

1   The seasonal pattern of demand affects the occupancy rate of accommodation providers, and it is impossible to run a hotel in a profitable way with only 100 days of operation. This is a typical example of underutilization of resources.
2   The general tourism infrastructure (manmade attractions, beach equipment, parking, roads, marinas, etc.) is under-occupied at certain times. This is a typical example of wrong (or partly wrong) use of capital.
3   To cope with the peaks, the public sector is confronted with high operational costs (police force, fire brigade, hospital capacity, etc.). These cost are not restricted to the high season, but have repercussions all year round.
4   In many tourism regions, seasonality leads to seasonal employment, and the correlative seasonal unemployment can cause welfare problems. Clearly the reality is a little bit more complex. During the season working hours are sometimes very long, and during the off-season unemployment benefit for tourist workers is in some tourism regions more or less 'institutionalized', or a blind eye is turned.
5   The tourist as a consumer is confronted with high prices, over-concentration, traffic congestion and very often low service performance during the high season. This causes dissatisfaction on the part of the tourists.
6   The concentration of demand in a few weeks in many cases provokes ecological dangers or leads to exceeding the carrying capacity of natural or cultural attractions.

It is therefore not surprising that several countries are making efforts to achieve better management of tourism demand by staggering holidays (see Stäblein, 1994, and Chapter 3).

The general trend in most generating countries is to take more than one holiday a year, with a reduction in the duration of the main holiday and a growing demand for short breaks (one to three nights), and this has flattened the seasonal pattern in many destinations.

Interdependence of tourism products

Interdependence of tourism products is a direct consequence of the characteristics mentioned earlier – a tourist product is an amalgam. Even an individual tourist buys a whole set of products supplied by different firms – the attractions have no economic value without the necessary accommodation, but the latter cannot function properly without the supporting factors and resources: infrastructure, accessibility, facilitating resources and hospitality (Ritchie and Crouch, 2003). A destination is a cluster of activities, and a bad performance by one sub-sector influences the profitability of the other sectors of the cluster. A destination's reputation can be set by the weakest link in the tourist product chain (Nulty and Cleverdon, 2011). Different suppliers always benefit from combining their respective efforts.

In a wider sense, there can be an interdependence of destinations and/or resorts. The benefits offered by two neighbouring destinations are more than the sum of the two individual destinations. Bruges as a cultural destination is a real support for the seaside resorts at the Belgian coast and for the other cities of culture in Belgium, and *vice versa*. This has encouraged the Flemish cultural cities to organize their promotion partly together.

Rigidity of supply

It is not evident to make rapid adjustments to the supply of tourism products to variations in demand. A hotel cannot add or remove capacity in line with demand. This limited flexibility has a serious impact on the operation and financial results. When demand falls below capacity, the production factors labour and capital are underutilized; when it exceeds capacity, the tourism industry fails to maximize its revenue (Nulty and Cleverdon, 2011).

Relatively low investment costs but high fixed cost of operation

It may be hard to prove that the tourism sector has low investment costs, as low investment cost is a relative notion. Comparisons must be made with other sectors, and the tourism sector itself does not exist in the strict sense of the word as it is composed of many sub-sectors. However, there are several indicators that support the thesis of low investment costs. The investment per person employed in the accommodation sector (e.g. a hotel) and other facilities is relatively low. Many natural attractions are free goods, or only need marginal investments to make them operational. Most cultural attractions, such as churches, castles, abbeys and museums, were built for non-tourism purposes, and only later became tourism attractions.

Not all tourism investments have relatively low investment costs. Airports, aircraft, highways, railways, cruise ships, cruise terminals, waterworks and cable railways all require high investment costs. However, some of them not only serve the tourism sector but also other activities in the national economy.

More important are the high fixed costs of operation. The cost for a firm can be divided into fixed and variable costs. Fixed costs are costs that are independent of the number of customers and must be paid anyhow, whereas variable costs are costs that are incurred as a function of the number of customers received at any given time.

A hotel, an air charter or a tourism attraction has in any case to finance the following costs in order to be open and to receive customers (Middleton with Clarke, 2001):

- Depreciation of premises and equipment
- Maintenance

- Energy and utilities
- Insurance
- Property taxes
- Wages and indirect salary costs for full-time employees
- Overheads
- Marketing costs.

The point is that these costs are mostly committed in advance for the whole year, and have to be met whether the hotel or air charter draws few or many visitors. It is a general rule that a hotel cannot be profitable with an occupancy rate of less than 60 per cent, and air charters should have a load factor of more than 90 per cent. Owing to the relatively high fixed costs of operations, many holiday villages offer off-season or mid-week arrangements at very low prices, which cover the variable costs and provide a little surplus to contribute to the payment of the annual fixed costs.

As a consequence of the typical cost structure, many tourist firms make substantial and fast-growing profits once they exceed the break-even point but make great and increasing losses when they stay below that breakeven.

Tourism is a growth sector but with declining growth rates

During the second half of the last century, tourism became one of the most important and rapidly growing sectors in the world economy. Figure 1.4 shows the evolution of international tourist arrivals worldwide during the period 1970–2015, and a forecast up to the year 2025.

During the 1970s the average world annual growth rate of tourism in terms of arrivals amounted to about 5.5 per cent, but this decreased to 5.2 per cent in the 1980s and 5.0 per cent in the 1990s. After the millennium, the growth declined to 3.9 per cent during the period 2000–2015. There was even an absolute decline by the end of the first decade of this century.

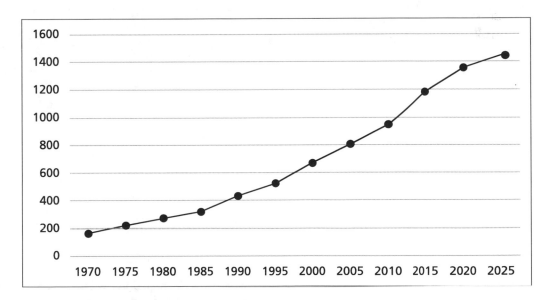

Figure 1.4 International tourist arrivals, 1970–2025 (x1,000)

Source: UNWTO

Table 1.2 Annual growth rate in international tourist arrivals, 2005–2015 and 2020–2030

Source: UNWTO

Period	2005–2015	2020–2030
Europe	3.0	1.8
Asia/Pacific	6.1	4.2
(South-East Asia)	7.9	4.3
Americas	3.7	2.2
Africa	4.4	4.6
Middle East	4.7	4.0
World	3.9	2.9

For the next 15 years (2015–2030) the UNWTO foresees an annual growth rate of international arrivals of about 3.6 per cent (2.9 per cent for the period 2020–2030).

During the period 2000–2015 the international tourism receipts increased at a lower rate than the international arrivals (3.2 per cent). This was not the case in previous decades. It is important to notice that all regions register a very positive declining growth rate (see Table 1.2).

High income-elasticity

The relatively high growth rate of tourism demand is partly the result of the high income-elasticity of international arrivals and receipts. Demand for tourism reveals a high degree of sensitivity to changes in incomes – i.e. it is generally considered to be income-elastic. What does this mean? Income-elasticity is the reaction of demand to rising or falling incomes, and is measured as a ratio between changes in demand and corresponding changes in income. For example, if a 1 per cent increase in income causes a 1.5 per cent growth in tourism demand, then the income-elasticity of tourism demand is equal to 1.5. The coefficient of elasticity can be expressed as the following formula:

$$E_Y = \frac{\Delta D/D}{\Delta Y/Y} \qquad (1.1)$$

where

E_Y = coefficient of income-elasticity
ΔD = change of tourism demand
D = tourism demand
ΔY = change of income
Y = income

A tourism demand is considered to be income-elastic when E_Y is bigger than 1; an E_Y value of between 0 and 1 is an indication of an inelastic demand.

Tourism income-elasticity varies from country to country and from period to period. Smeral (2012) calculated the income- and price-elasticity for the outbound tourism (imports) of a number of countries over the period 1977–2012 (see Table 1.3).

For all five destinations in Table 1.3, income-elasticity is greater than 1. However, the coefficients differ from country to country.

Table 1.3 Income- and price-elasticity for real tourism imports, by country
Source: Smeral (2012)

	Income-elasticity	Price-elasticity
Australia	1.90	−0.93
EU15	2.08	−1.12
Japan	2.95	−0.80
USA	2.48	−0.86
Canada	1.00	−1.42

Smeral (2010) measured the income-elasticity of the outbound tourism (period 1978–2008) for five generating markets (see also Chapter 7). The highest income elasticities were measured for the United States (3.4) and Japan (3.3). For EU15 (the 15 member countries of the European Union at that moment) and Australia, the elasticity of tourism import with respect to changes in GDP amounted to about 2.

As well as income-elasticity, price-elasticity is very important in the tourism sector. This is the reaction of demand to changes in price, and is calculated in a similar way to income-elasticity. Smeral's exercise shows that tourism demand is sensitive to price variations, and the price-elasticity is higher than commonly stated. The tourism business is highly competitive. It is clear that coefficients of price-elasticity have a negative sign. When the independent variable of 'price' increases, a decrease in tourism demand (dependent variable) can be expected, and *vice versa* – when prices decrease, demand will increase. Results of recent research work by Smeral (2010) are in line with previous price elasticities. The estimation results for elasticities of tourism imports with respect to changes in relative prices were in most cases similar and amounted to about −1.

It is important to notice that income elasticities are declining and that they are influenced by the business cycle (see Chapter 3, Smeral, 2012). For the measurement of coefficients of elasticity, refer to Chapter 7.

Predominance of SMEs

Another economic feature of tourism is the predominance of small and medium-sized enterprises (SMEs) in the tourism industry. Middleton (1998) has estimated the number of SMEs in the UK alone to be 170,000 (he uses the term 'micro-businesses'), and these comprise some 95 per cent of all the enterprises providing tourism services. In many well-known tourism countries, the hotel sector is no exception. Cooper *et al.* (2008) made a comparison between the USA and Europe with respect to rooms owned by publicly quoted companies. Although the 1991 data are no longer very current, they are illustrative. The share of rooms in so-called quoted companies varied from 30 per cent in the USA, 23.5 per cent in the UK and 20.4 per cent in the Netherlands to 3.2 per cent in Spain, 1.7 per cent in Italy and 1.0 per cent in Greece. Although not fully comparable, Marvel (2004) has recently published data regarding the chain penetration (chains are hotel groups with at least ten properties) as a percentage of total hotel stock. These data confirm the above-mentioned differences. In 2004, branded rooms represent 65 per cent of the total hotel stock in North America and only 25 per cent of that in Europe (11 EU countries plus Switzerland); the penetration (in 2003) varied from 37 per cent in France and 32 per cent in the UK to 8 per cent in Switzerland and 6 per cent each in Italy and Austria. It should be emphasized that the chain penetrations are much lower in terms of hotel units.

In Europe, the 87 brands with at least ten properties represent no more than 6 per cent of the total stock.

Middleton with Clarke (2001) lists a number of economic advantages and disadvantages of these micro-businesses:

- The money earned by micro-businesses tends to stay in the local community – they typically purchase locally and are part of the fabric of the local money circulation cycle.
- They are a vital element in job creation in rural areas and less developed regions in general.
- They do not have the commercial rationale that dominates big enterprises.
- Typically, 'Numbered in their hundreds of thousands, micro-businesses are unique as individual enterprises and they cannot be standardized – to attempt to do so would destroy their contribution. Unfortunately this makes them amorphous and difficult to measure and "badge" as a coherent sector.'

It should be recognized that in many developing countries tourism is a gateway to 'entrepreneurship', and this is considered to be one of the positive points of tourism in the development process of many countries and regions (Mathieson and Wall, 1982; Vanhove, 1986).

The characteristics dealt with in this first chapter should be seen as an introduction to the more 'economic' chapters of this book.

What is a tourism destination?

The title of this book is *The Economics of Tourism Destinations*. What do we understand by 'destinations'? Many people think in terms of countries. In tourism, country destinations are not that evident. Very often a tourist visits a town (or towns) or a region (or regions). For this reason, Professor D. Frechtling, fellow colleague in the International Academy for the Study of Tourism (IAST), suggested a destination be described as 'A specific geographic area under one or more government authorities that draws visitors from a substantial distance away by its attractions and provides paid accommodation facilities'. Indeed we speak of the Rocky Mountains, Sicily, Venice, Isfagan, etc. This is an indication that the optimum level for destination management in most countries is below the national level.

The UNWT0 (2007) defines a local tourism destination as:

> A physical space in which a tourist spends at least one overnight. It includes tourism products such as support services and attractions and tourist resources within one day's return travel time. It has physical and administrative boundaries defining its management, and images and perceptions defining its market competitiveness. Local destinations incorporate various stakeholders often including a host community, and can nest and network to form larger destinations.

They could be on any scale, from a whole country (e.g. Australia), a region (such as the Spanish 'Costas') or island (e.g. Bali), to a village, town or city, or a self-contained centre (e.g. Center Parcs or Disneyland). We come back to the concept of a tourism destination and destination management in Chapter 6. Economic impact is measured at the destination level.

This final consideration does not mean that this publication is exclusively focussed on destinations. Some chapters are more destination oriented, while others deal with tourism economics in general with attention paid to the micro- and macro-level.

References and further reading

Boniface, B., and Cooper, C. (1987). *The Geography of Travel and Tourism*. London: Heinemann.

Burkart, A.J., and Medlik, S. (1974). *Tourism: Past, Present and Future*. London: Heinemann.

Chadwick, R.A. (1981). Some notes on the geography of tourism: a comment. *Canadian Geographer, 25*.

Chadwick, R.A. (1994). Concepts, definitions and measures used in travel and tourism research. In J.R. Brent Ritchie and Ch. R. Goeldner (eds), *Travel, Tourism, and Hospitality Research*. New York: John Wiley & Sons.

Clawson, M., and Knetsch, J.L. (1964). *Economics of Outdoor Recreation*. Baltimore, MD: Johns Hopkins Press.

Cooper, C., Fletcher, J., Gilbert, D., and Wanhill, S. (2008). *Tourism: Principles & Practice*. Horlow, FT: Prentice Hall.

De Brabander, G. (1992). *Toerisme en economie*. Leuven: Garant.

Eurostat, OECD, WTO and UN Statistics Division (2001). *Tourism Satellite Account: Recommended Methodological Framework*. Luxembourg: UN.

Franz, A., Laimer, A., and Smeral, E. (2001). *A Tourism Satellite Account for Austria*. Vienna, Statistik Austria and WIFO.

Frechtling, D. (2009). The Tourism Satellite Account. A Primer. *Annals of Tourism Research, 1*.

Gilbert, D.C. (1990). Conceptual issues in the meaning of tourism. In C.P. Cooper (ed.), *Progress in Tourism, Recreation and Hospitality Management, Vol. 2*. London: Pitman Publishing.

Hunziker, W., and Krapf, K. (1942). *Grundriss der Algemeinen Fremdenverkehrslehre*. Zurich: Polygraphisher Verlag.

IRTS (2008). See: United Nations Statistics Division and UNWTO (2008). *International Recommendations for Tourism Statistics 2008*. Madrid: UNWTO.

Jefferson, A., and Lickorish, L. (1988). *Marketing Tourism: A Practical Guide*. Harlow: Longman.

Kimes, S. (1999). Yield management: an overview. In I. Yeoman and A. Ingold (eds), *Yield Management: Strategies for the Service Industries*. London: Cassell.

Lockwood, A., and Medlik, S. (2001). *Tourism and Hospitality in the 21st Century*, Oxford: Butterworth-Heinemann.

Marvel, M. (2004). European hotel chain expansion. *Travel & Tourism Analyst*, Mintel, May.

Mathieson, A., and Wall, G. (1982). *Tourism: Economic, Physical and Social Impacts*. London: Longman.

Medlik, R. (1988). *What is Tourism? Teaching Tourism into the 1990s*. Guildford: University of Surrey.

Middleton, V.T.C. (1998). SMEs in European tourism: the context and a proposed framework for European action. *Revue de Tourisme, 4*.

Middleton, V.T.C. with Clarke, J. (2001). *Marketing in Travel and Tourism*, 3rd edn. Oxford: Butterworth-Heinemann.

Middleton, V.T.C., Fyall, A., Morgan, M., and Ranchhod, A. (2009). *Marketing in Travel and Tourism*, 4th edn. Oxford: Butterworth-Heinemann.

Mieczkowski, Z. (1990). *World Trends in Tourism and Recreation*. New York: Peter Lang.

Miller, N., and Robinson, D. (1963). *The Leisure Age: Its Challenge in Recreation*. Belmont: Worldworth Publishing Company.

Nulty, P., and Cleverdon, R. (2011). *Handbook on Tourism Product Development*. Madrid: UNWTO-ETC.

Ritchie, J.R.B., and Crouch, G. (2003). *The Competitive Destination*. Wallingford: CABI Publishing.

Rogers, J. (2002a). Crossing an administrative boundary: a new approach to leaving the usual domestic environment. *Enzo Paci Papers on Measuring the Economic Significance of Tourism, Vol. 2*. Madrid: WTO.

Rogers, J. (2002b). Have you crossed the line? A discussion of measurement challenges in leaving the usual domestic environment. *Proceedings of the 33rd Annual TTRA Conference*. Boise: Travel and Tourism Research Association.

Smeral, E. (1994). *Tourismus 2005*. Vienna: Ueberreuter.

Smeral, E. (2010). Impacts of the world recession and economic recession and economic crises on tourism: forecasts and potential risks. *Journal of Travel Research*, 1.

Smeral, E. (2012). International tourism demand and the business cycle. *Annals of Tourism Research*, 39.

Smith, S. (1988). Defining tourism: a supply side view. *Annals of Tourism Research*, 15 (2).

Smith, S. (1997). *Tourism Analysis: A Handbook*, 2nd edn. Edinburgh: Longman.

Stäblein, F. (1994). School holidays. Presentation of an experience: rolling system of school holidays. *Conference on Staggering of Holidays*. Düsseldorf. Hannover: Niedersächsisches Kultusministerium.

United Nations Statistics Division and UNWTO (2008). *International Recommendations for Tourism Statistics 2008*. Madrid: UNWTO. (Herein referred to as 'IRTS 2008'.)

UNWTO (2007). *A practical Guide to Tourism Destination Management*. Madrid: UNWTO.

UNWTO (2011). *Tourism Towards 2030: Global Overview*. Madrid: UNWTO.

UNWTO (2016). *Tourism Highlights*. Madrid: UNWTO.

Vanhove, N. (1974). *Vakantiespreiding. Een nieuw voorstel voor België*, No. 6. Brugge: Facetten van West-Vlaanderen.

Vanhove, N. (1986). Tourism and regional economic development. In J.H.P. Paelinck (ed.), *Human Behaviour in Geographical Space: Essays in Honour of Leo H. Klaassen*. Aldershot: Gower.

Wahab, S. (1971). An introduction to tourism theory. *Travel Research Journal*, 1.

WTO (1998). *Tourism: 2020 Vision*. Madrid: WTO.

Chapter 2

Measuring tourism

Introduction

Measurement of tourism activity is important for both public and private sectors. Without reliable data it is impossible to demonstrate the economic importance of the sector in terms of value added, employment, exports and imports. In many countries the amount of tourism activity is still underestimated due to a lack of correct statistical information. An efficient policy also requires data on the supply and demand structure and the development of the sector. Furthermore, a good information system is the basis for a good planning process at the local and regional levels. Strategic planning (both marketing and physical) begins with a situation analysis – which are the priority markets, what is the necessary capacity of hospitals, parking, waste treatment installations, police force, etc.?

The characteristics dealt with in Chapter 1 already provide an indication that it is not easy to measure tourism activity in particular countries or regions. What is the tourism demand and supply of a country? This is a very important question, as the answer provides the basis for the economic impact analysis.

At the risk of oversimplification, until recently tourism supply was defined only in terms of the numbers of beds, rooms, camping places, etc., and tourism demand was expressed only in the numbers of arrivals and nights. From Chapter 1 it is evident that the numbers of rooms and arrivals provide a poor indicator of the tourism activity of a country. These statistics are useful, but far from complete. This explains the numerous efforts, mainly over the last decade, by scientists and regional, national and international organizations to improve the tourism data system.

This chapter focusses on a number of measurement systems applied in practice. They can be classified in six groups:

1 A general tourism information system
2 Measurement of day tourists
3 The Tourism Satellite Account
4 Tourism and holiday surveys
5 The tourism production index
6 The tourism barometer.

All these systems have different objectives and are as such not comparable, sometimes being complementary. Besides these instruments, each country has its own (sometimes updated) registration system.

A tourism information system or destination management information system

A tourism information system (TIS) or destination management information system (DMIS), also called tourism marketing information system (TourMIS), can be described as a system used to collect, in a permanent and systematic way, the tourism supply and demand data at the destination level (national, regional or local) necessary for an efficient management and tourism policy (e.g. general policy, tourism marketing, physical planning). The elements of the TIS depend largely on the content of the tourism policy. All stakeholders of a destination need and benefit from a good TIS or DMIS. Wöber (2003) states:

> In order to solve complex problems, decision-makers need to have a factual knowledge of the industry (declarative knowledge) and the methodology used (procedural knowledge). The wealth of knowledge is drawn from two pools; that obtained from the 'storage' of already existing experiences, and by generating knowledge in the respective field. Combining these two pools creates an arena for problem solving.

Table 2.1 shows the possible content of such a system. A clear distinction is made between the demand items and the supply elements. The demand and supply categories are further divided into 'basic' and 'secondary' items. In the context of a TIS, 'basic' items are the foundation of recording tourism in a destination; it does not exclude the fact that for marketing purposes some secondary items are also important. Table 2.1 is only a possible example, and its contents are not exhaustive. It can be adapted according to the purpose of the policy being researched. A destination marketing information system will have a different outlook (Ritchie and Ritchie, 2002).

The preparation and the upkeep of a TIS is demanding and expensive, but the cost can be reduced if the following suggestions are taken into consideration. First, for several elements it is not necessary to repeat the measurement annually – for example, the expenditure pattern of visitors to a destination is unlikely to change fundamentally from one year to the next. Secondly, for several items costs can be saved by working with a representative sample – a good sample gives better results than a poor exhaustive inquiry. In sampling, particular attention should be paid to three areas:

1 The sample method (random sampling, systematic sampling, stratified sampling, cluster sampling, quota sampling or random walk)
2 The method of delivering the survey (personal interviews, telephone surveys, postal surveys or the internet)
3 Questionnaire design (phrasing and content of questions) (Cooper et al., 1993; Smith, 1997).

A number of macro-indicators can be derived directly from the TIS. This is the case with tourism turnover and occupancy rates at the destination level.

According to Wöber (2003) the major aim of TourMIS is an optimal information supply and decision support for the tourism industry. The first step is to provide online tourism survey data, as well as evaluation programmes to transform data into precious management information. An efficient TourMIS predominantly comprises:

1 A database containing tourism market research data; the national guest survey is one of the most important sources (declarative knowledge)
2 Various program modules (method-base, procedural knowledge) converting acknowledged methods/models into simple surfaces
3 Various administrative programmes which assist the maintenance of the database and track and control the information search behaviour of users.

Table 2.1 Primary and secondary items of a TIS or DMIS at destination level

Type	Items	Frequency	Method of data collection
Actual demand	Basic items • number of arrivals • number of nights • period • origin of arrivals • purpose of trip	yearly	exhaustive survey or representative sample
	• accommodation • final destination • combination of duration – purpose/origin/ accommodation		
	• expenditure per person and per family • breakdown of expenditure per major category • combination of expenditure and other attributes	every three years	sample
Actual demand	Secondary items • family size • age • profession • travel organization • transport • first or repeat visitor • information gathering • activities on the destination (visits to ...) • evaluation	every three to four years	representative sample
Potential demand	• socio-economic trends in generating markets • tourism trends in generating markets • awareness of the destination in generating and potential markets • potential demand in a number of countries or regions • image of the destination • strengths with respect to main competitors	every three years	survey desk research and information from the trade

Table 2.1 continued

Type	Items	Frequency	Method of data collection
Other marketing information	• choice of distribution channel (independent, trade) • use of the internet; consultation of the web-site • ecological indicators • target groups and communication instruments • efficiency of the communication instruments of the destination • price level in competitive destinations	every three years yearly	sample desk research sample
Day tourism	• number • expenditure (type of expenditure) • origin • profile (transport, age etc.)	yearly or every two years	sample
Supply	Basic items • number of units per accommodation type • commercial and non-commercial accommodation • location • price level • operational periods • capacity per accommodation type (beds, rooms, sites etc.) • characteristics of the accommodation (hotel classification; classification of camping sites, apartments and other) • employment and type of employees • cultural attractions	yearly	permanent inventory
Supply	Secondary items • restaurants and cafés • recreational facilities • capacity recreation facilities • sports facilities • shopping facilities • health care • meeting facilities (capacity)	every three years	desk research

Austria makes good use of a TourMIS. It makes the monthly projections of 'Statistics Austria' available within only a few seconds to all regional managers of the Austrian National Tourist Office regardless of whether they are located in New York, Sydney or Paris.

Measurement of day visitors

One of the major problems in a TIS is the measurement of excursionists. Many destinations have no or only a vague knowledge of the number of day visitors. The measurement of day tourists is not an easy task, if not impossible. But sometimes a special feature shared by many destinations can be helpful. This special feature is the passing through of a well-known narrow street by a large share of excursionists. In the WES study (1992) about the economic importance of tourism in Bruges, a method was developed to measure the excursionists. The relevant street in Bruges is the well-known 'Blind Donkey' street connecting two important tourist places in the town. The method is composed of several steps.

Step 1: Counting the number of pedestrians in the 'Blind Donkey' street during the sampling days. This counting can be manual and/or electronic. This step allows us to calculate the average number of passers-by per day. We call that number P.

Step 2: On the sampling days every n^{th} person is asked the question 'Are you an excursionist, an overstay tourist or a local person?' With this knowledge it is possible to calculate the average number of excursionists per day passing through 'Blind Donkey' street. This number is s (e.g. 60 per cent).

Step 3: On the sampling days excursionists are also interviewed at the moment they leave the town. These interviews take place at coach and car parks at the edge of the town and in the railway station. Excursionists are asked the following questions: Did you go through 'Blind Donkey' street? (b; e.g. 50 per cent). How often did you go through 'Blind Donkey' street to-day? (d; e.g. 1.5 times). This is also an opportunity to get information from excursionists about their expenditure in Bruges on various categories of products.

Step 4: Calculation of the number of excursionists on an average day in Bruges.

- Firstly, we divide the average number of excursionists who passed through 'Blind Donkey' street by the average number of times they passed through (d).
- Secondly, we multiply the number obtained by the inverse of the percentage of the total day visitors who passed through 'Blind Donkey' street or value q and q = 1/b.

Step 5: Calculation of the number of excursionists (E) per year.

$$E = (P \times s \times q \times 365)/d$$

where

E = number of day visitors per year
P = average number of passers by ('Blind Donkey' street) (e.g. 12,000)
s = percentage of excursionists among passers-by (e.g. 60 per cent)
q = inverse of the percentage of day visitors who passed through 'Blind Donkey' street (e.g. 50 per cent of day visitors passed through 'Blind Donkey' street)
d = average times excursionists passed through 'Blind Donkey' street

$$E = (12,000 \times 0.60 \times 2 \times 365)/1.5 = 3,504,000$$

This method can be simplified in cases where one makes use of data directly related to day visitors. In Bruges this can be the number of tickets sold for boat trips, for example. We call this approach the 'boat trip method'.

The starting point is the number of tickets sold for a boat trip on the canals in Bruges. That number is known and is reliable. In this case the different steps are:

Step 1: Number of boat trip tickets sold per year. This number is known.
Step 2: Which percentage of the tickets for the boat trips is sold to day visitors? This percentage is obtained via samples on the boats.
Step 3: Application of step 3 in the original approach. In this case the question becomes: 'Did you make a boat trip on the canals of Bruges today?'
Step 4: Calculation of the number of excursionists or application of the parameters obtained in steps 2 and 3.

It is clear that in most cases this approach cannot be applied. However, where a reference base is available, this method can be very helpful.

In coastal regions (e.g. Costa Blanca in Spain), day visitors can be measured via an analysis of the passenger traffic – mainly train traffic and road traffic (car, public transport and touring cars) – to the coastal areas during reference dates in the tourist season and on some reference dates in the off-season period. The latter is the passenger traffic that in any case would be created without any tourism activity. We call it functional traffic. The day visitors per day can be measured in a very simple way, by reducing the total passengers by the functional traffic. The total number of day visitors for a tourism season of the coastal area is the sum of the day passengers per day. This approach presupposes the knowledge of the average passengers per car for tourism and non-tourism traffic. WES applied this method already in the beginning of the 1960s in the framework of the 'Tourism Production Index – WES' (see page 51).

Mobile phone technology opens new possibilities to measure day visitors in many destinations (cities, coastal regions, events, etc.). The application is based on Mobile Network Signalling (MSN) data. This technology is applicable all over the world where the mobile phone has a high degree of penetration. Hendrickx (2017) makes use of MSN data to measure the day visitors at the Belgian Coast. This methodology does not only make it possible to reveal the number of day visitors but also the average duration of stay per region of origin. This technology also allows one to measure other types of tourism.

The Tourism Satellite Account

Background

It is important to understand that this section is restricted to a description of the conceptual framework of the TSA. For an extensive description of the methodology and technical aspects, we refer to the present bible on the topic, *Tourism Satellite Account: Recommended Methodological Framework 2008* (United Nations *et al.*, 2010) and to the specialized reports and manuals on the subject listed under References and Further Reading at the end of this chapter.

The *Tourism Satellite Account: Recommended Methodological Framework 2008* is the culmination of many years of effort by numerous institutions (United Nations, The Organisation for Economic Co-operation and Development, OECD, Eurostat and World Tourism Organisation, UNWTO), countries and individuals to integrate the measurement of tourism as an economic phenomenon within the mainstream of macro-economic statistics. Its history and development are strongly related to that of the *International Recommendations for Tourism Statistics 2008* (see IRTS, 2008).

The OECD Tourism Committee had worked to advance recognition of the scope, nature and role of tourism in the OECD economies and demonstrated the importance of tourism statistics for policy making. In the late 20th century the OECD worked on the integration of tourism within broader statistical instruments, such as the System of National Accounts.

The International Conference on Travel and Tourism Statistics, held by UNWTO in Ottawa (1991), was the culmination of efforts made in the second half of the 1970s and in the 1980s, not only by international organizations (especially the United Nations, UNWTO and OECD) but also by a number of countries, among which, in addition to Canada, France deserves special mention as a pioneer in the measurement of the economic importance of tourism. Since the Ottawa Conference, implementation has begun on many of the initiatives presented, and the number of countries developing a Tourism Satellite Account has increased. In 1994, the United Nations and UNWTO published *Recommendations on Tourism Statistics*, which comprised (a) the recommendations on tourism statistics proposed by UNWTO as a follow-up to the Ottawa Conference, and (b) the Standard International Classification of Tourism Activities (SICTA), a provisional classification of productive activities related to tourism that should guide countries in the compilation of supply-side statistics, an aspect that had not been previously considered systematically within tourism statistics.

In 1999, UNWTO convened the Enzo Paci World Conference on the Measurement of the Economic Impact of Tourism in Nice, France, where UNWTO unveiled its work on a tourism satellite account proposal (Enzo Paci, UNWTO, assumed from the very beginning the role of promoter of the TSA). The framework was approved in principle by the Conference, which recommended its use as a platform to achieve consensus with other international organizations. An agreement was reached, which constitutes the content of the *Tourism Satellite Account: Recommended Methodological Framework 2000*. As a result of the process, each organization now promotes TSA implementation in their member countries. The *Tourism Satellite Account: Recommended Methodological Framework 2008* (TSA: RMF 2008) is basically an update that takes into account the *International Recommendations on Tourism Statistics 2008*, the updates of other macro-economic-related frameworks, and the experience of member countries in implementing the Tourism Satellite Account.

Definition and objectives

A TSA is quite different from a general information system. The concept is on the one hand much wider, and on the other far narrower. This will become clear in the following paragraphs. Spurr (2006) explains why the term 'satellite account' is used. These accounts sit outside, or rather alongside, the tables of the classical System of National Accounts (SNA). Much of the data that satellite accounts contain already exist within the SNA under existing classifications. Thus tourism expenditure on meals consumed in restaurants appears within the existing SNA classification for restaurants or horeca (the hotels, restaurants and catering industry). The term 'account' in the acronym TSA refers to a set of tables (see TSA tables in this chapter). Satellite accounts refers to activities which are not separately identified in the conventional national accounts. They are an extension of national accounts for selected areas of interest such as tourism. In a TSA all tourism activities are identified in a separate but related account. So it is an account which is a satellite of the core national accounts. Dwyer *et al.* (2010) put it as follows:

> TSA are based on the accounts for industries which are reported in the national accounts. It is argued that tourism accounts for the proportion of the outputs of a range of industries which are explicitly recorded in the accounts. The basic procedure in satellite accounting is to claim a 'share' of sales of each commodity or industry to tourism. TSA use these estimates of tourist expenditure and then allocate tourism expenditure to different industries.

Thus tourism might account for 99 per cent of sales expenditure in 'accommodation', 80 per cent in 'air transport' and say 5 per cent in 'retail trade', for example. The outputs of all these industries which can be attributed to tourism are estimated and aggregated to obtain the output of tourism, TGVA (Tourism Gross Value Added) and TGDP (Tourism Gross Domestic Product). (For the definitions of a number of basic aggregates of national accounts, see Appendix 2.1.)

Statistics regarding tourism have often been restricted to data on the volumes of arrivals, number of nights, length of stay, purpose of visit, type of accommodation, origin of visitors and their socio-economic profile, accommodation capacity and corresponding occupancy rate, and a few other elements. It should not be difficult to make the link to the basic items of the TIS of the preceding section. These are still elements of the TSA, but the latter offers much more. However, elements that are important for an environmental or marketing policy are not retained in the TSA.

How can we define a TSA? According to the WTO (2000), 'A TSA is no more than a set of definitions, classifications integrated into tables, organized in a logical, consistent way, which allows one to view the whole economic magnitude of tourism in both its aspects of demand and supply'. It uses the same concepts, definitions and classifications as national accounts and is the internationally recognized framework for measuring tourist activity and the importance of tourism to national or regional economies. While traditional tourism statistics focus primarily on 'flows' (number of visitors, number of overnight stays, etc.), a TSA can tell us how much tourism contributes to an economy and how many jobs it creates.

As explained in Chapter 1, the 'satellite account' was developed by the United Nations to measure the size of economic sectors that are not included in their own right in national accounts. In other words, it is a system of tourism information integrated with the system of national accounts. Contrary to the production-oriented sectors such as textiles, food and many others, the structure of the tourism industry is determined by tourist consumption, and as a result tourism is not counted as a separate sector in the national accounts (Smeral, 2005).

Many organizations and tourism scientists felt, in the 1990s, the need for a comprehensive tourism measurement system. Many were frustrated because of a real underestimation of the sector. This is well expressed in a WTO brochure (WTO, 2001): 'Tourism is an activity that many in the world participate in, but which few appreciate beyond its abilities to delight the traveller and facilitate business'.

Why is the TSA needed? Governments often underestimate the economic benefits that tourism provides because it is not visible in the same way as industries such as machine construction and textiles. Business enterprises often fail to realize the role tourism plays in their success, and they do not take full advantage of opportunities in this growing area of activity because it is not measured in the same way as other industries. Citizens, too, may not seriously consider the job opportunities that tourism provides. Tourism activity generates substantial amounts in personal spending, business receipts, employment, value-added creation and government revenue. Only a small part of tourism spending takes place in what are normally considered to be tourism industries (hotels and trade), and in fact a very large part takes place outside the classical tourism industries such as in self-catering, museums, retail shops, public transport, etc. However, until now there has been insufficient attention given to measuring these economic benefits on an equal footing with other sectors such as machine construction, textiles or insurance.

The objectives of tourism satellite accounting are very diverse, and include the following (United Nations *et al.*, 2001):

● To describe the structure of a country's or region's tourism activity
● To provide macro-economic aggregates to describe the size and the economic importance of tourism, such as tourism value-added and tourism GDP
● To provide detailed data on tourism consumption and how this is met by domestic supply and imports
● To provide detailed production accounts of the tourism industries, data on employment, linkages with other productive activities and capital formation
● To provide a link between economic data and the basic items of TIS.

The purposes of TSAs are threefold (Eurostat, 2017):

● To analyse in detail all aspects of demand for goods and services associated with the activity of visitors
● To observe the operational interface with the supply of such goods and services within the economy
● To describe how this supply interacts with other economic activities.

Dwyer *et al.* (2007) make a clear distinction between the function of TSA and Computable General Equilibrium (CGE) models. TSA is used to provide the database to measure the profitability and productivity of the tourism sector in a country. CGE models involve measuring the yield of different types of tourists to the tourism industry and the economy as a whole. Furthermore, TSA provides an appropriate technique to estimate yield at the industry level, while the CGE approach is used to estimate the yield to the economy as a whole.

Designed with a view to its subject as well as its purposes, according to Franz *et al.* (2001), the TSA is not just a set of statistical tables but a self-contained, comprehensive system of specific definitions, with interrelating numbers, compilations and analyses. However, this perception of the TSA is still only half the story; the other half is its being embedded in the greater context of the overall national accounts system of a country. Franz *et al.* (2001) call it the 'holistic' view.

Dwyer et al (2010) consider TSA from two perspectives: (a) as a *statistical tool* that complements those concepts, definitions, aggregates and classifications already presented in the international recommended tourism statistics (IRTS, 2008) and articulates them into analytical tables and (b) as a *framework* to guide countries in the development of their system of tourism statistics, with the TSA as ultimate main objective.

Tourism as a demand-side phenomenon refers to the activities of visitors and their role in the acquisition of goods and services. It can also be viewed from the supply side, and tourism will then be understood as the set of productive activities that cater mainly to visitors.

The fundamental structure of the TSA is based on the general balance existing within an economy between the demand of goods and services generated by tourism and their supply. The idea behind the TSA is to analyse in detail all the aspects of demand for goods and services which might be associated with tourism within the economy, to observe the operational interface with the supply of such goods and services within that economy, and to describe how this supply interacts with other activities (Eurostat *et al.*, 2001).

The demand and supply perspectives are the subject of the next two sections.

The demand perspective

Two key elements of the demand perspective are the 'visitor' and 'tourism consumption'. The term 'visitor' (tourist and excursionist) was defined in Chapter 1. A visitor is 'a traveller taking a trip to a main destination outside his/her usual environment, for less than a year, for any main purpose (business, leisure or other personal purpose) other than to be employed by a resident entity in the country or placed visited'. Based on their main purpose, trips made by tourists and same-day visitors may be classified (see IRTS, 2008) in the following categories:

1 Personal

 ● Holidays, leisure and recreation
 ● Visiting friends and relatives
 ● Education and training
 ● Health and medical care

- Religion/pilgrimages
- Shopping
- Transit
- Other

2 Business and professional

Tourism consumption is the central element of the system and the basis for the economic impact analysis of tourism. The WTO and OECD use the following definition: 'expenditure made by, or on behalf of, the visitor before, during and after the trip and which expenditure is related to that trip and which trip is undertaken outside the usual environment of the user'. It is important to notice that some expenditure before the trip (e.g. passports, inoculation, small items to be brought along as gifts) and afterwards (e.g. printing and storing photos) is included, as long as its usage is clearly directed to the trip.

In IRTS 2008 tourism expenditure refers to the amount paid for the acquisition of consumption goods and services, as well as valuables, for own use or to give away, for and during tourism trips. It includes expenditure by visitors themselves, as well as expenses that are paid for or reimbursed by others. It excludes the acquisition of certain items such as social transfers in kind that benefit visitors, the imputation of accommodation services from owned vacation homes and financial intermediation services indirectly measured. These are included in the more inclusive concept of tourism consumption in the TSA (see Figure 2.1).

The different aggregates or categories of tourism consumption (domestic, inbound, outbound, internal and national) are linked to visitors, and were dealt with in Chapter 1. These aggregates of tourism consumption go far beyond visitors' purchases on the trip. They also encompass all expenditures on goods and services by other institutional units on behalf of

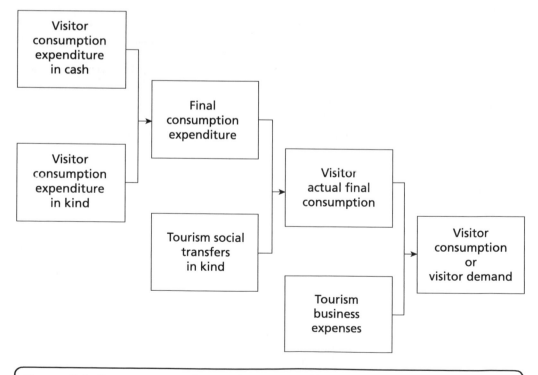

Figure 2.1 Components of visitor consumption

visitors. If cash or financial assets are transferred to the visitor to finance the trip, the purchases funded by these are included in visitor consumption. Along with this are all forms of transfers in kind and other transactions benefiting visitors where it is not cash or financial assets that are provided to the visitor but goods and services themselves.

The components of visitor consumption are shown in Figure 2.1. There are four main categories:

1 Visitor final consumption expenditure in cash
2 Visitor final consumption expenditure in kind
3 Tourism social transfers in kind
4 Tourism business expenses.

These categories and Figure 2.1 need explanation.

Visitor final consumption expenditure in cash covers what is usually meant by 'visitor expenditure', and is part of the final demand in input–output terms. It always represents the most important component of total consumption. Here, special attention should be paid to consumer durable goods. With respect to tourism, a distinction should be made between 'tourism single-purpose goods', which are goods used exclusively on trips (e.g. skiing equipment, camping equipment, luggage, etc.) and 'multipurpose consumer durable goods', which are used on holidays but also within the usual environment (such as cameras and cars). In the framework of the TSA convention, a different treatment of both categories of durables is seen. Tourism single-purpose durable goods are always included, whether purchased before, during or after a trip, or even outside the context of a specific trip. Multipurpose consumer durables are only included if purchased during a holiday.

Visitor final consumption expenditure in kind consists of non-monetary transactions, and includes barter transactions (exchange of a residence for holiday purposes), production for own final use (e.g. second homes on own account or free of charge), and income in kind (holidays offered by the employer).

Tourism social transfers in kind relate to non-market services provided by governmental organizations or non-profit institutions serving households (NPISH). Examples of these non-market services are health services provided to visitors (e.g. spas), and activities such as museum visits, where the total costs may not be fully attributed to the tourist. The charges for museums paid for by the tourist are included in visitor consumption in cash.

The definition of visitors covers not only individuals who travel for personal reasons but some who travel for business purposes as well. The consumption of these visitors can be paid for totally or partially by businesses, by government, or by NPISH that employ them or on whose behalf they are travelling. Such payments may be made through different procedures: either paying the providers directly for their consumption, being the provider of such services, or allocating a lump sum to the employee for travel to cover these additional costs, or a combination of the three. In some cases, in particular for transportation and accommodation expenditure, the System of National Accounts 2008 considers this expenditure as part of the intermediate consumption of the producing unit irrespective of the procedure used for its acquisition. As a consequence, this consumption does not fall under the System of National Accounts concept of household final/actual consumption expenditure, although in tourism statistics it is part of tourism consumption because it is considered as the acquisition of services associated directly with the activities of a visitor on his/her trip. This difference in scope should not be forgotten when trying to compare aggregates related to tourism consumption with aggregate household final consumption, as the scope of tourism consumption extends beyond that of household final consumption, so that tourism consumption is not always part of household final consumption of the corresponding individuals.

Besides visitor consumption, attention should also be paid to tourism collective consumption. In the case of tourism, collective services refer (among other things) to the provision of legislation and regulations regarding tourism, the promotion of tourism by public agencies, the maintenance of order and security, and the maintenance of the public domain. So far, tourism collective consumption is not a part of the TSA and remains as the actual final consumption of general government. However, in the TSA system, a table of tourism collective consumption is foreseen.

A special category is 'tourism gross fixed capital formation'. This is important for tourism because the existence of a basic infrastructure in terms of attractions, transport, accommodation, airports, public utilities and so on determines the nature and intensity of tourist flows. Furthermore, it requires a large amount of investment from the public as well as from the private sector. The System of National Accounts 2008 considers as part of the gross fixed capital formation of households the acquisition of dwellings (main and others) as well as all major maintenance and repairs attached to these assets. Tourism statistics and the TSA follow similar rules (see IRTS, 2008). As a consequence, this expenditure, as well as the expenditure associated with the acquisition and major repair of innovative types of vacation home ownership such as timeshare, etc., is to be excluded from tourism consumption but will be part of tourism gross fixed capital formation.

Tourism-driven investment can be roughly classified into three main categories, as follows:

- Tourism-specific fixed assets (e.g. railway passenger coaches, cruise ships, sightseeing buses, hotel facilities, convention centres, marinas, ski lifts, etc.).
- Investment by the tourism industries in non-tourism-specific fixed assets. They are investments in fixed assets considered as tourism-related not because of the nature of the assets themselves, but because of the use which is made of them by a tourism industry. This category includes, for example, hotel or travel agency computer systems, hotel laundry facilities, etc.
- Tourism-related infrastructure. Tourism-related infrastructure presents particular features:
  o The asset might have been produced or acquired with the purpose of being exclusively or principally used by visitors (e.g. the development of beach or ski sites especially oriented towards visitors).
  o At the time the investment was made and decided, it might have been done with a view to its exclusive or principal use by visitors in a specific moment in time (as in the case of public investments for a special event, such as an international sports event like the Olympic games, soccer or cricket World Cup, or an important international meeting), but a later non-tourism use has also been taken into consideration in approving this investment (future use of sport, transport or accommodation facilities by the usual residents).
  o It might be directed generally to all activities and in addition have positive effects on tourism (as in the case with an airport open to all types of traffic, a non-toll road or a hospital in a region occasionally used by visitors) because in its absence, tourism would probably be of lesser intensity.

Tourism expenditure does not include other types of payments that visitors might make that do not correspond to the acquisition of goods or services, such as payment of taxes, interest, purchase of financial and non-financial assets, etc.

The final remarks at the end of this section concern the estimation of expenditure. This is a very important and delicate point, especially when a breakdown per category of tourist expenditure is necessary. The guidelines for developing the TSA give an overview of applied expenditure estimation methods (WTO, 2000; Terrier, 2006). We refer in particular to Frechtling (2006): 'An assessment of visitor expenditure methods and models'. The expenditure estimation methods are of a very varied nature and include:

1 Existing data (Country's National Statistical Office)
2 Household surveys
3 Visitor surveys

  - diary surveys
  - surveys at accommodation establishments
  - surveys at border entry/exit points
  - surveys on board transport vehicles
  - surveys at popular visitor places

4 Tourism establishment surveys – interviews with selected guests, or giving questionnaires to selected guests
5 Central bank data
6 Expenditure models

  - expenditure ratio model
  - cost factor expenditure model (a hybrid of household surveys and establishment surveys)

Many countries make use of household surveys. They are an efficient and reliable instrument for measuring domestic tourism expenditure. The advantage of household surveys is the daily registration of expenditure. This increases the accuracy of the results.

Three of the methods listed above need further explanation. The central bank data method only provides information about inbound and outbound tourism. It is well known that central banks have real problems in estimating the amount of national currency sold to visitors; and what can we say about a German or Spanish tourist travelling within the eurozone?

The expenditure ratio model is based on a foundation of certain expenditure-related data that are readily available and reliable. A constant ratio between these readily available data and the total expenditure is assumed. Frechtling (2006) describes the method in four steps. In the first step data on hotel accommodation room receipts in the destination is gathered. The data can be based on sales tax or VAT (Value Added Tax) on these receipts. The second step is to conduct a survey among the tourists of the destination to obtain estimates of the total amount spent in the destination and expenditure on accommodation in hotels in particular. In the third step the ratio between expenditure on accommodation and total estimated expenditure is calculated. In the final step that ratio is applied to the hotel accommodation receipts obtained in the first step. The leverage associated with this approach can be high when hotel accommodation is not dominant. The validity of this method depends on the accuracy of the first and second steps. Due to tax considerations, the first step sometimes underestimates reality.

The cost factor model is applied in the USA. According to Frechtling (1996), the most prominent example is the Travel Industry Association of America's (TIA) Travel Economic Impact Model (TEIM). He describes the model as follows:

> In this model, travel expenditures are estimated for 19 different items in six basic expenditure categories: public transportation, auto transportation, lodging, food, entertainment and recreation, and incidental purchases. The expenditure component of the TEIM comprises a set of equations for each state in which the independent variables are the volumes of various travel activities (e.g. miles traveled by automobile, nights spent in hotels), the coefficients are the cost per unit of each activity (called per-unit cost factors) and the dependent variables are travel expenditures for certain categories of

travel-related goods and services (expenditure items). Estimates of the activity volumes are derived from TIS's monthly travel survey, whereas per-unit cost factors are obtained from respected industry and government sources. The model allocates travel expenditures among areas by simulating where the exchange of money for goods or services actually took place.

This model seems to give acceptable results.

The supply perspective

Tourism-specific products

The economic analysis of tourism requires the identification of tourism-specific products – i.e. the resources used by tourists on their holiday, their consumption of goods and services – and therefore the identification of the economic units that provide those goods and services. General economic classifications of activities are established from the point of view of supply by producers and from the characteristics of the production process, but for tourism some adaptation of these classifications is required. Indeed, tourism is a phenomenon that was originally defined from the point of view of demand.

The starting point is the classification of goods and services. Not all goods have the same relevance for the estimation of tourism consumption. The level and structure of an individual's consumption at home is not the same as when that individual is away from the usual environment. This has the consequence that classifications that are meaningful for the description of household consumption in general may not be so meaningful when the focus is specifically on tourism (Eurostat *et al.*, 2001).

The 1993 System of National Accounts (SNA) suggests a number of steps in the identification of different groups of products (see Figure 2.2).

In the TSA concept, production can be split into three categories. The first is tourism-characteristic goods and services – those products which, in most countries, would cease to exist in meaningful quantity (or the consumption of which would be significantly reduced) in the absence of tourism, and for which it should be possible to obtain statistical information

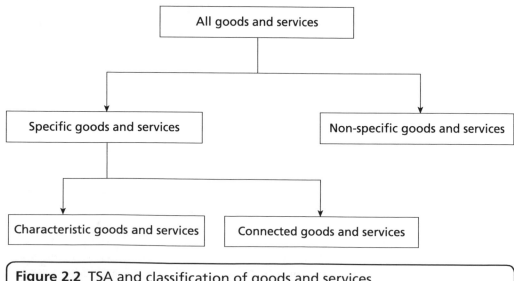

Figure 2.2 TSA and classification of goods and services

(e.g. accommodation, travel services, cable cars, etc.). TSA tables make a distinction between 12 groups – each subdivided – of tourism-characteristic products:

1   Accommodation services for visitors
2   Food- and beverage-serving services
3   Railway passenger transport services
4   Road passenger transport services
5   Water passenger transport services
6   Air passenger transport services
7   Transport equipment rental services
8   Travel agencies and other reservation services
9   Cultural services
10 Sports and recreational services
11 Country-specific tourism-characteristic goods
12 Country-specific tourism-characteristic services.

The classification of products has been developed in *International Recommendations for Tourism Statistics 2008*. In addition to consumption products, it includes all other products that circulate in the economy and have some relationship with tourism. Of these products, two main subgroups are defined: consumption products and non-consumption products. The non-consumption products category includes all products that by their nature cannot be consumption goods and services and, therefore, can neither be a part of tourism expenditure, nor a part of tourism consumption, except for valuables that might be acquired by visitors on their trips. Two subcategories are defined:

- Valuables, i.e. produced goods of considerable value that are not used primarily for purposes of production or consumption but are held as stores of value over time (see IRTS, 2008).
- Other non-consumption products comprising those products associated with tourism gross fixed capital formation and collective consumption.

IRTS (2008) tries to give a more precise definition of tourism-characteristic products. According to IRTS (2008) tourism-characteristic products are those that satisfy one or both of the following criteria:

a   Tourism expenditure on the product or service should represent a significant share of total tourism expenditure (share-of-expenditure/demand condition).
b   Tourism expenditure on the product should represent a significant share of the supply of the product in the economy (share-of-supply condition). This criterion implies that the supply of a tourism-characteristic product would cease to exist in meaningful quantity in the absence of visitors.

The second category consists of tourism-related or connected goods and services – those products which are consumed by tourists in volumes significant to the visitor and/or the provider but are not included in the list of tourism-characteristic products (e.g. taxicab transportation, currency exchange). Tourism-characteristic and tourism-related goods and services together are called 'tourism-specific products'. The significance of tourism-connected products within tourism analysis for the economy of reference is recognized, although their link to tourism is very limited worldwide. Consequently, lists of such products are country-specific (IRTS, 2008).

The third category consists of non-specific or non-tourism-characteristic production, in the TSA framework 2008 called 'non-tourism-related consumption products'. They comprise all other consumption goods and services that do not belong to the previous categories (e.g. toothpaste and, in general, most retail trade).

Smeral uses a slightly different terminology (Smeral, 2005). According to him, TSA makes a distinction between 'tourism-specific' (e.g. accommodation), 'tourism-related' (e.g. restaurants), and 'non-tourism-specific' goods and services (e.g. retail). In practice, the borderline between the different groups is not always clear. In the Austrian TSA, tourism-connected and non-characteristic products are combined into one group.

The treatment of the reservation services provided by travel agencies, tour operators and other providers needs special attention. The total amount paid in fees or commissions by visitors for services they intermediate are split into two parts:

- One part corresponds to the value of the travel agency (or reservation) service (the gross margin, i.e. the fee or commission earned).
- The other part corresponds to the value of the intermediated tourism services (the revenue of the producer net of the commission paid to the provider of reservation services).

In the case of package tours, three levels of services should be unbundled: the services themselves (for example, transport, accommodation), the services provided by the tour operator, and the margin of the travel agency (usually different from the tour operator) selling the tour.

This treatment usually requires the transformation of the basic statistical information obtained from the visitors by travel agencies and tour operators and from the activities that use them to market their products in order to generate a data set that conforms to this perspective.

This treatment has important consequences for the precise content of domestic tourism consumption, inbound tourism consumption and outbound tourism consumption because the country of residence of the visitor, of the travel agency or provider of reservation services, of the tour operator and of the provider of the tourism service might differ.

Tourism-specific activities

The activities in which the above-mentioned tourism-characteristic products originate are called 'characteristic activities'. The 1993 SNA emphasizes the analysis of characteristic *producers*: 'In a satellite account the main emphasis when looking at production is on the analysis of characteristic activities and producers'.

To assure international comparability, a list of tourism-characteristic activities has been defined. The production accounts of the TSA retain 12 tourism-characteristic activities (see annex 3, IRTS, 2008):

1 Accommodation for visitors
2 Food and beverage serving activities
3 Railway passenger transport
4 Road passenger transport
5 Water passenger transport
6 Air passenger transport
7 Transport equipment rental
8 Travel agencies and other reservation services activities
9 Cultural services
10 Sports and recreational activities
11 Retail trade and country-specific tourism-characteristic goods
12 Other country-specific tourism-characteristic activities.

Categories 1 to 10 comprise the core of international comparison. The two other categories are country-specific.

One important feature of tourism-characteristic activities is the direct contact between the consumer and the provider of the products. Some activities may be considered to be characteristic of tourism because of the importance of their products and services for the tourist, although the major part of their typical output is not sold to tourists. This is the case for transport services and restaurants (restaurant meals are consumed by visitors and non-visitors alike).

TSA tables

The next step is the integration of the demand and the supply side into tables. This allows examination of the magnitude of tourism in both demand and supply aspects. The tables of the TSA are derived from or related to the tables of the 1993 SNA that concern supply and the use of goods and services. The TSA consists of a set of ten tables:

- Table 1: Inbound tourism consumption. This describes inbound visitor final consumption expenditure in cash by type of products purchased.
- Table 2: Domestic tourism consumption. This table also shows expenditure by residents that is associated with outbound travel.
- Table 3: Outbound tourism consumption.
- Table 4: Internal tourism consumption. This combines all visitor final consumption expenditure associated with inbound and domestic tourism and all non-monetary tourism consumption (e.g. tourism in kind).
- Table 5: Production accounts of tourism industries. This presents the production accounts of tourism-characteristic industries, tourism-connected industries and non-specific industries which makes possible the conciliation with tourism consumption.
- Table 6: This makes the link between internal tourism consumption and domestic supply. It is the core of the TSA system where the link between supply and demand takes place. This table leads to the calculation of TGVA and TGDP.
- Table 7: Employment in the tourism industries.
- Table 8: Tourism gross fixed capital formation.
- Table 9: Tourism collective consumption.
- Table 10: Quantitative indicators without monetary expression (e.g. number of arrivals, nights, or establishments).

To illustrate the content of Tables 1–6, the Austrian TSA tables, in a condensed form, are shown as an example. Table 2.2 is a condensed form of the Austrian TSA Tables 1, 2 and 4. Table 2.3 relates to TSA Tables 5 and 6 (also in a condensed form).

Note that in the TSA Table 5, every tourism industry is listed vertically in rows and every product is recorded horizontally in columns. Each cell of the spreadsheet provides the value of a specific product produced in a given year by a given tourism industry (called the make matrix). TSA Table 5 (production account or supply) provides the data basis for TSA Table 6 (demand and supply). This table presents an overall illustration of internal tourism consumption with domestic supply, from which tourism value added and the GDP generated by internal tourism consumption can be derived. This table is the core element of the TSA system. In Table 2.3 only one tourism industry – 'accommodation for visitors' – is explicitly retained. All industries are grouped in the second column 'total tourism industries'.

We find a good schematic presentation of the different tables in Frechtling (2009). A modified and simplified scheme is given in Figure 2.3.

The internal tourism consumption (see the final column of Table 2.2) is integrated into Table 2.3 (TSA Table 6), and allows us to calculate the 'tourism ratio' of supply. For each variable of supply in the TSA, the tourism ratio is the ratio between the total value of tourism share and total value of the corresponding variable in the TSA. 'Tourism share' is the share of

Table 2.2 TSA tables 1, 2 and 4: results for Austria 2014, in condensed form (millions €)

Source: Statistics Austria

Products	Tourism expenditure			Internal tourism TSA 4	Other components of tourism consumption	Internal tourism consumption
	Inbound tourism TSA 1	Domestic tourism TSA 2				
A. consumption products (*)	17.090	14.837		31.927	1.122	33.049
A.1 Tourism characteristic products	15.103	12.122		27.227	–	27.227
1-Accommodation for visitors	6.891	2.774		9.665	–	9.665
1.a-accommodation visitors other than 1.b	6.824	2.730		9.554		9.554
1.b-all types of vacation home ownership	66	45		111		111
2-Food and beverage serving activities	4.973	4.344		9.317		9.317
3-Railway passenger transport	258	754		1.012		1.012
4-Road passenger transport	15	548		562		562
5- Water passenger transport	12	33		45		45
6-Air passenger transport	1.480	2.080		3.560		3.560
7-Transport equipment rental	4	222		225		225
8-Travel agencies and other reservation services	0.1	9		9		9
9-Cultural services	656	994		1.650		1.650
10-Sports and recreational services	816	366		1.182		1.182
11-Country-specific tourism characteristic goods	–	–		–		–
12-Country-specific tourism characteristic services	–	–		–		–
A.2 Other consumption products (a)	1.986	2.715		4.700	1.122	5.822
B.1 Valuables	275	56		331		331
Total	**17.365**	**14.893**		**32.258**	**1.122**	**33.380**

* Consumption products is net of the gross service charges paid to travel agencies, tour operators and other reservation services.

Table 2.3 TSA tables 5 and 6: results for Austria 2014, in condensed form (millions €)

Source: Statistics Austria

Product	TSA table 5: production account of tourism industries and other industries					TSA table 6: domestic supply and internal tourism consumption by products				
	Accommodation for visitors	Total tourism industries	Other industries	Output of domestic producers (at basic prices) GROSS	Output of domestic producers (at basic prices) NET	Imports	Taxes less subsidies on products nationally produced and imported	Domestic supply (at purchasers' prices)	Internal tourism consumption	Tourism ratio (%)
A. Consumption products (*)	26.954	52.210	592.544	644.755	644.723	102.671	35.857	843.283	33.048	3.9
A.1 Tourism characteristic products	26.013	49.311	5.902	55.214	55.181	2.574	265	58.052	27.226	46.9
1-Accommodation for visitors	25.848	25.992	7	25.999	28.020	–	151	28.171	18.982	67.4
1.a-Accommodation for visitors other than 1.b	23.859	24.003	7	24.010	26.031	–	151	26.182	18.870	72.1
1.b-All types of vacation home ownership	1.989	1.989	–	1.989	1.989			1.989	111	5.6
2-Food and beverage serving activities	–	–	–	–	–	–	–	–		
3-Railway passenger transport	–	3.114	–	3.114	3.209	187	160	3.236	1.012	31.3
4-Road passenger transport	40	4.566	41	4.606	4.657	27	351	4.333	562	13.0
5-Water passenger transport	–	98	–	98	388	–	–	388	45	11.5
6-Air passenger transport	–	3.460	10	3.470	3.565	1.218	101	4.885	3.560	72.9
7-Transport equipment rental services	–	2.147	5.636	7.783	7.783	–	–	7.783	225	2.9
8-Travel agencies and other reservation services	15	2.623	20	2.643	9	–	0.2	9	9	100.0
9-Cultural services	8	3.980	35	4.015	4.064	63	45	4.173	1.650	39.5

Table 2.3 continued

Product	TSA table 5: production account of tourism industries and other industries					TSA table 6: domestic supply and internal tourism consumption by products				
	Accommodation for visitors	Total tourism industries	Other industries	Output of domestic producers (at basic prices) GROSS	Output of domestic producers (at basic prices) NET	Imports	Taxes less subsidies on products nationally produced and imported	Domestic supply (at purchasers' prices)	Internal tourism consumption	Tourism ratio (%)
10-Sports and recreational services	102	3.332	152	3.484	3.484	1.078	479	5.041	1.182	23.4
11-Country-specific tourism characteristic goods	–	–	–	–				–	–	–
12-Country-specific tourism characteristic services	–	–	–	–				–	–	–
A.2 Other consumption products	940	2.899	586.642	589.542	589.542	160.097	35.592	785.231	5.822	0.3
B. Non-consumption products	–	–	662	662	662	–	–	662	330	50.0
B.1 Valuables	–	–	662	662	662	–	–	662	330	50.0
B.2 Other non-consumption products	–	–	–	–	–	–	–	–	–	
Total output (at basic prices)	26.954	52.210	593.207	645.417	645.417	162.671	35.857	843.945	33.380	4.0
Total intermediate consumption (at purchasers' prices)	4.342	17.833	298.288	316.121	316.121	–				
Total gross value added (at basic prices)	22.612	34.378	294.918	329.296	329.296	162.671				
Tourism ratio (%)	67.4	–	0.3							
Tourism direct gross value added (at basic prices)	15.236		885	19.584						

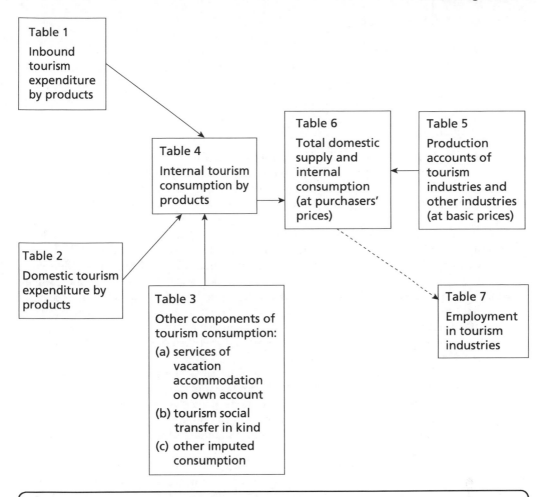

Figure 2.3 Relationship between TSA tables

the corresponding fraction of internal tourism consumption in each component of supply. For each industry, the tourism share of output (in value), is the sum of the tourism share corresponding to each product component of its output.

To calculate the tourism ratio of any given supply of commodities, the amount purchased by tourists is related to the total supply of the respective commodity. For Austria, the tourism ratio of the industry 'Accommodation for visitors' amounts to 46.9 – or in other words, 46.9 per cent of the domestic supply is consumed by domestic and inbound tourists. These tourism ratios vary from product to product. For hotel services this ratio is very high, but for railway passenger transport it only amounts to 31.3 per cent. This is an indication that a relatively high proportion of supply is used by non-tourists.

These tourism ratios, applied to the gross value added (GVA) of the symmetrically corresponding industry in TSA Table 5, result in the direct tourism value added (TVA) of each industry. The total TVA of the 12 tourism industries is related to the overall GDP, which leads to the share of tourism in the total GDP.

The valuation principles applied in TSA Tables 5 and 6 need clarification. In the TSA, the valuation principles are essentially the same as those advocated by SNA 93. 'Use' (TSA Table 6) is valued at purchasers' prices, while 'production' (TSA Table 5) is valued at basic prices.

The SNA defines basic value as:

> The amount receivable by the producer from the purchaser for a unit of good or service produced as output minus any tax payable, and plus subsidy receivable, on that unit as a consequence of its production or sale. It excludes any transport charges invoiced separately by the producer.

Purchasers' prices are defined as (OECD, 2000):

> The amount paid by the producer, excluding deductible VAT or similar deductible tax, in order to take delivery of a unit of a good or service at the time and place required by the purchaser. The purchasers' price of a good includes any transport charges paid separately by the producer to take delivery at the required time and place.

One remark is important. As we have seen in Figure 2.1, TSA allocates business expenditure to overall tourism demand; as a consequence they add value to the value added of the sector. But when comparing the TSA value added to the overall value added (all sectors) an adjustment is necessary, especially for business trips by the residents (Smeral, 2005). Intermediate consumption is not considered in GDP calculation. Intermediary consumption is treated as an intermediary input of other sectors. Therefore this consumption needs to be deducted from the tourist consumption of the residents. Analogously, in the case of an application at regional level, business trips from other regions and from abroad are taken into account, while business trips by residents of the region are ignored.

So far, this provides the conceptual framework of the TSA. The TSA is an ideal instrument to measure a number of macro-economic aggregates, We agree with Ahlert (2007) in saying: 'The TSA framework is a great step forward in quantifying the direct economic impact of tourism on the basis of a clearly understandable, uniform, internationally binding accounting system'. In this sentence the word 'direct' is very important; TSA measures only direct effects (Smeral, 2006).

Nearly 20 years after the Vancouver conference, TSA has not had the success expected. Not all countries committed to TSA and from those that are committed many are not able to apply the procedure. TSA has the greatest success in EU countries. However, the success is very relative. In 2016 Eurostat organized an inquiry in the 28 EU members and four other European countries on 50 TSA indicators (Eurostat, 2017). The result is not encouraging. Only 50 per cent of these countries could provide data on 30 or more indicators. TSA Tables 1 to 6 (see above) and Table 10 are relatively well covered. This is not the case for Table 7 on employment. The least complete TSA tables are Tables 8 and 9. Only 11 countries make use of more or less full TSA. According to the 17th meeting of the Committee on Statistics and Tourism Satellite Accounts, the TSA application rate is far lower in non-OECD countries. We find a confirmation of the relative success of the application of TSA with Frent and Frechtling (2015):

> In principle, all countries producing a TSA or planning a TSA exercise must conform to the United Nations standards presented in TSA (2010) and IRTS (2010) in order to truthfully claim to have such an account. While more than 60 countries have conducted a TSA exercise in the last two decades, there is no evidence that these efforts conform to the United Nations standards or to each other.

The two sources indicate that not only is there a low participation in TSA application but that the TSA standard rules are not applied.

Although TSA applications are confronted with many problems (the lack of enough data sources available to ensure statistical reliability; high costs and lack of experts in TSA) there are interesting applications at regional level – city-state of Vienna (Smeral, 2008), Upper

Austria, Rhode Island (Tyrrell, 2002) and Südtirol (Castlunger, 2009) – and in tourism-supplying sectors such as yachting in Greece (Diakomihalis and Lagos, 2008).

TSA and Tourism Value Added

The basic methodology underlying the estimation of the tourism value added (see TSA Table 6) is equation (2.1) (OECD, 2000):

$$TVA_{ij} = (GO_{ij} - II_{ij}) TS_{ij} \qquad (2.1)$$

where

TVA_{ij} = tourism value added for the ith commodity of the jth industry
GO_{ij} = gross output of the ith commodity of the jth industry
II_{ij} = intermediate inputs for the ith commodity of the jth industry
TS_{ij} = tourism share of the output of the ith commodity of the jth industry

The TSA Table 6 shows the domestic supply and internal consumption by products. The rows detail output by tourism characteristic product and enhancing services. Total output of an activity (in a column) is obtained as the sum of its outputs by product. The rest of the block of rows shows intermediate consumption by product, and a total. The difference between total output (at basic prices) and total input (at purchaser's prices) provides value added at basic prices. The last block of rows presents the components of value added.

The columns are first organized by productive activities, with emphasis on the tourism industries. The supply by domestic producers is first added over activities to obtain the aggregate value of total output of domestic producers at basic prices. This column is then added to imports, which represent supply within the domestic economy of imported products, and a column recording taxes less subsidies on products concerning domestic output and imports to obtain 'total domestic supply at purchaser's price'. This total domestic supply is systematically compared to internal tourism consumption product by product (on each row). For most of the variables presented in columns, a column for tourism share is presented (how much of the value of the variable is attributable to internal tourism consumption).

How do we establish tourism shares? This is based on direct information from suppliers or visitors (surveys of expenditure by product) and the opinion of experts. With the tourism shares established for output, it is possible to estimate, for each activity, a tourism share to be applied to the components of intermediate consumption. From the difference between the values of output attributable to visitor consumption and to intermediate consumption, the value added generated by visitor consumption can be computed. For each activity, an estimate of value added can be established. Adding across all activities, it is possible to obtain the total value corresponding to that variable.

The calculation of tourism GDP is more problematic: the difference between TVA and tourism GDP consists mainly of taxes and subsidies. These items are not necessary as connected to the production of tourism products as in the case with intermediate consumption and output. To obtain the GDP generated by internal tourism consumption, to the value added we must add taxes less subsidies on products and imports related to tourism products, whose value corresponds mathematically to the difference between this variable valued at purchaser's prices and at basic prices, since distribution margins have already been given the appropriate treatment.

It is very important to notice that equation (2.1), and the TSA approach in general, provides only the direct income effect and not the indirect effect. The latter should be estimated with the input–output method.

In Table 2.3 the tourism value added – direct effects – for Austria was estimated at €19,584 million or 5.9 per cent of GDP (in 2008 that share was 5.3 per cent). This is the sum of the value added of all the tourism industries and the connected and non-specific industries.

There is a reason for the distinction made in the Austrian case between inclusive or exclusive 'business travel'. In the TSA approach, business travel is considered as part of total tourism demand and has an impact on value added on the satellite level. When comparing TSA value added with the value added of the whole economy, it has to be adjusted. Indeed, on the macro-economic level the intermediate consumption – in this case business trips of residents – is considered as input and has to be deducted from the residents' tourism consumption calculated in the TSA. In other words, double counting should be avoided (Smeral, 2005).

WTO tourism statistics

The WTO is not only active in the field of TSA, but is also primarily known for a very comprehensive database of tourism statistics worldwide. It offers a selection of statistics and corresponding analysis on inbound tourism (tourist arrivals, tourism receipts, travel by purpose and means of transport) and outbound tourism (outbound tourism by region of origin and tourism expenditure), as well as on the WTO's long-term prospects – *Tourism 2020 Vision* (WTO, 1998) and *Tourism Towards 2030* (UNWTO, 2011).

In the publication *World and Country Trends*, produced annually by the WTO, we find comprehensive, comparable and up-to-date sources for an assessment of world tourism statistics by country, region and sub-region. It provides an analysis of international tourist arrivals, international tourism receipts, region of origin of arrivals, purpose of visit, means of transport, international tourism expenditure, etc. (See *Yearbook of Tourism Statistics*, published annually by the WTO.) Country data are also available on the WTO website 'Tourism Factbook'. This gives the latest and most up-to-date statistics for all the countries around the world, easily accessed by either alphabetical or geographical selection.

For the quality of the data, the WTO depends on the national data providers. A critical attitude towards some country data is recommended. The WTO is more a coordinator of tourism data than a data collector. As coordinator, it helps national and regional authorities to collect the data (see *The Technical Manuals Set*, published by the WTO). This package provides all the knowledge needed for the collection, interpretation and presentation of tourism statistics. It contains general concepts and definitions as well as technical guidelines and methods for different users and various segments of tourism research. The package includes volumes 1–4, respectively titled *Concepts, Definitions and Classifications for Tourism Statistics; Collection of Tourism Expenditure Statistics; Collection of Domestic Tourism Statistics;* and *Collection and Compilation of Tourism Statistics*.

In 2003, the WTO started using the WTO world tourism barometer, with the aim of monitoring the short-term evolution of tourism in order to provide the tourism sector with adequate and timely information. The WTO world tourism barometer is scheduled to be published several times a year. At the outset it contained three permanent elements: an overview of short-term tourism data from destination countries and air transport; the WTO Panel of Tourism Experts with a retrospective and prospective evaluation of tourism performance; and selected economic data relevant for tourism. It is remarkable how close the curve of the reality is to the curve of the expectations of the WTO panel during the period the barometer was introduced. The objective for future editions is to extend the content and improve coverage gradually over time.

The new UNWTO publication, mentioned in the previous section, *International Recommendations for Tourism Statistics 2008* is very important and is supported by several other organizations. This document should provide a common reference framework for countries to use in the compilation of tourism statistics (Frechtling, 2009).

Tourism and/or holiday surveys

Tourism and holiday surveys are of a completely different nature, and have different objectives to TSAs. They are mainly used to provide a view of the holiday pattern of a country's population. However, there are also surveys that focus on incoming tourism, and these surveys can be useful sources in the preparation of a TSA – especially for the demand side.

Typical surveys in the UK

The UK uses a number of typical tourism surveys and has a long tradition in the matter. They are from the methodological viewpoint an example that most countries could follow. The main surveys in the UK are:

- The International Passenger Survey (IPS)
- The Great Britain Tourism Survey (GBTS) or the former United Kingdom Tourism Survey (UKTS)
- The Great Britain Day Visit Survey (GBDVS), formerly the England Leisure Visits Survey (ELVS).

All three can be seen in relationship to the TSA, although the origin of each of these surveys has nothing to do with TSA.

The International Passenger Survey

The International Passenger Survey (IPS) started in 1961. Its inception was reported in the then *Board of Trade Journal* as follows:

> A new regular sample survey of sea and air passengers travelling between the United Kingdom and the continent of Europe, and on the long air routes beyond Europe, was introduced by the Government Social Survey on behalf of the Board of Trade during 1961 and 1962. This new system of interviewing a small proportion (up to 4 per cent on some routes) of travellers has enabled the important contribution made by tourist and other travellers to the balance of payments to be measured without interfering with the free flow of passengers at our sea and air ports. Nine out of ten of those approached attempted to give all the information asked of them, and more than 80 per cent were able to make an estimate of their expenditure whilst abroad. Over 150,000 successful interviews were made during the year.
> (International Passenger Survey, Overseas Travel and Tourism, User Guide, Vol 1, Background & Methodology, 2014: www.ons.gov.uk/ peoplepopulationandcommunity/leisureandtourism/topicspecificmethodology)

Since then, the IPS has been, and continues to be, a key source of primary data related to international travel. It is a dual purpose continuous sample survey carried out by the Office of National Statistics (ONS) designed to collect information about UK inbound and outbound migration, and data about UK international travel and tourism. The survey collects information about passengers entering and leaving the UK at all major airports and sea routes, at Eurostar terminals and on Eurotunnel shuttle trains.

The User Guide provides background information for users of the IPS Overseas Travel and Tourism data. The key elements of the methodology are:

> Interviewing is carried out throughout the year. In total, between 700,000 and 800,000 interviews are conducted each year for migration purposes and a subset of approximately 250,000 interviews forms the basis of the Overseas Travel and Tourism estimates.
> Data collected include: country of visit (for UK residents), country of residence and region of the UK visited (for overseas residents), purpose of visit, length of stay, expenditure, age group, gender, mode of transport, and UK port of entry or departure.
> The IPS data are weighted to produce national estimates of all international travellers to and from the UK on a quarterly basis. The calculation of the weights for the IPS takes

into account its complex sample design and information provided from other sources on total passenger traffic for all sampled and non-sampled routes and time periods.

The IPS estimates feed into the Travel Account of the Balance of Payments (BoP) and provide information on international travel and tourism (that is, visits between the UK and abroad of less than 12 months), and provide a primary source of data on long- and short-term migrants, that can be used by Office for National Statistics Centre for Demography (ONSCD) in the provision of migration and population estimates.

Provisional monthly Overseas Travel and Tourism estimates are available six weeks after the end of the fieldwork month; quarterly datasets are available four months after the end of the quarter; and annual datasets are available approximately five months after the end of the year. Annual national estimates are created by combining the four quarters of the year together. The monthly estimates provide a limited overview of the number of visits to and from the UK and the expenditure associated with these visits. However, a single quarter is the minimum period over which most detailed analyses of the data can be made. The monthly and quarterly releases are provisional estimates because the data is subject to revision during the quarterly and annual production (see the IPS revisions policy for more details).

(ibid.)

A breakdown of spending by overseas visitors is collected from a subsample from time to time. Information was collected in respect of 16 categories such as accommodation, meals out, taxi/ car hire, hair and beauty treatments, etc. The knowledge of these data is very useful in the preparation of the TSA table inbound tourism consumption.

The Great Britain Tourism Survey

A second UK source is The Great Britain Tourism Survey (GBTS). The GBTS is designed as a continuous measurement of the volume and value of overnight tourism by residents of Great Britain, in such a way as to provide absolute estimates at any point in its currency, and relative change over time. Three separate but associated measurements are required from the survey:

- The number of trips (including child trips) taken by GB residents
- The number of bed nights (including child nights) on those trips
- The value of spending on those trips.

The most important methodological aspects are summarized as follows:

The GBTS survey is conducted continuously throughout the year, using face-to-face CAPI interviewing, as part of the TNS in-home omnibus surveys. Weekly omnibus surveys are conducted with a representative sample of 2,000 adults aged 16 and over within GB. Respondents are asked whether they have taken trips in the UK in the previous four calendar weeks that involved at least one night away from home.

When such trips are reported, further questions are asked about a maximum of three trips – the most recent three trips – with a core set of questions for all three trips and additional questions for the most recent trip. The questionnaire is thus designed to maximise accuracy of recall, whilst minimising the task for those who have undertaken more than one trip.

The requirement is for a complete dataset for each of the three most recent trips. Therefore, some imputation is necessary and that imputation covers data not collected, or otherwise missing.

The results are reported in terms of total GB population values. Therefore the data are weighted to correct for differences between the sample distribution and that of the population and also to gross the sample values up to the population.

Since 2016 the survey is running in parallel online, with a view to transitioning the whole survey online in 2018 or 2019.

(See Great Britain Tourism Survey 2015, Methods & Performance Report: www.visitbritain.org/sites/default/files/vb-corporate/Documents-Library/ documents/England-documents/gbts_2015_-_methods_performance_report_fv.pdf)

A wide range of data are collected in the survey (e.g. purpose, accommodation, organization of trip, type of location stayed in, booking in advance and method of booking, transport, etc.). Information on expenditure is collected in nine categories such as package trip, accommodation (non-package trip), buying clothes, eating or drinking, etc.

The Great Britain Day Visit Survey

The third important tourism survey reports day visits. The Great Britain Day Visit Survey (GBDVS) was commissioned jointly by VisitEngland (VE), VisitScotland (VS) and Visit Wales (the Tourism Department of the Welsh Government). Tourism day trips are considered to be a sub-set of leisure visits. The day trips are defined as round trips which start from and return to home for leisure purposes, last at least three hours, and are not taken regularly. What is the aim and the procedure of the GBDVS?

The survey aims to measure the volume, value and profile of Tourism Day Visits taken by GB residents to destinations in England, Scotland, Wales and Northern Ireland. Fieldwork is undertaken on a weekly basis, commenced in January 2011 and will continue until at least the end of December 2019.

While previous surveys have been conducted with similar objectives (most recently the 2005 England Leisure Visits Survey and 2002/3 GB Day Visits Survey), the new survey represented a significant change in terms of the survey methods used and the approach followed to define a Tourism Day Visit.

Prior to the start of GBDVS fieldwork in 2011, during 2009 and 2010 VisitEngland and the English Tourism Intelligence Partnership (ETIP) commissioned a series of pilot surveys which aimed to determine the best approach for a new Tourism Day Visits Survey.

This pilot exercise involved the parallel testing of identical question-sets through the TNS in-home, telephone and online omnibus surveys. Fieldwork was conducted over identical periods allowing a direct comparison of the results collected using each mode. Alternative question wording was also used to test the impacts of asking respondents about alternative time periods and using different question wording.

Following this piloting, it was recommended that an online data collection approach would represent a cost effective yet suitably robust approach for a future longitudinal survey of Tourism Day Visits. During 2015, a total of 35,664 interviews were conducted online during 52 weeks of surveying, just over the target sample of 35,000.

A rigorous, multi-stage weighting process is applied to ensure that the final dataset was made nationally representative in terms of the key demographics, and that trip data was representative of all trips taken over the time period.

Besides the classical data, the survey collects information on nine expenditure categories such as purchase of petrol/diesel on the trip, fares on bus/coach/train, parking charges, admission tickets, etc.

(The GB Day Visitor Statistics 2015: www.visitbritain.org/sites/ default/files/vb-corporate/Documents-Library/documents/England documents/gbdvs_2015_methods_and_performance.)

All three surveys give a substantial amount of information on the volume and value of tourism expenditure by UK residents and overseas visitors to the UK, and on UK residents travelling abroad. However, there are a number of discrepancies for TSA applications: (a) variation in the questions used to solicit information on the breakdown of expenditure between the different surveys; (b) the depth of information on expenditure breakdown available and (c) the limited data on day business trips (Allin, 1998).

Holiday surveys

Most European countries perform a holiday survey. A few examples of reliable holiday surveys are:

- In Austria, the Urlaubsreisen der Österreicher – Statistik Austria
- In Belgium, the Belgisch vakantieonderzoek – WES
- In France, the Déplacements touristiques des Français
- In Italy, the Viaggi e vacanze ('Holiday and trip' survey) – ISTAT
- In Germany, the Reiseanalyse – Forschungsgemeinschaft Urlaub und Reisen (FUR)
- In the Netherlands, the ContinuVakantieOnderzoek – CVO
- In Norway, the Holiday Survey – Statistics Norway
- In Spain, the Familitur (Movimientos Turisticos de los Españoles) – IET
- In the USA, D K Shfflet & Associates Ltd – Travel Performance:/Monitor.

Among these holiday surveys, the Belgian holiday survey (WES) is well known and can be considered as an example. It covers the period 1966–2016, and relates to holidays (four nights or more) and short holidays (one to three nights). For more than 30 years the Belgian holiday survey has been conducted in a similar way, based on two samples of 6,000 persons each. The persons selected are the same in both samples. A first sample covers the summer holidays (April–September) and the second covers the winter holidays (October–March).

The survey is based on a two-stage stratified sample. In the first stage there is double stratification, first by province. The number of sampling points (600 in total) and interviews per province is proportional to the population of each region. Within each stratum, further selection is based on a self-weighting stratification per size class of villages and towns. In the second stage the selection of the interviewees is based on a quota sample, with ten people per sampling point. The interviewees are selected per street, sex, age and profession.

Holiday surveys provide a lot of information about the holiday behaviour of a country's population. Holiday participation is one of these behaviours. A distinction is made between net and gross holiday participation, where net participation expresses the number of holiday-takers in one year per 100 inhabitants and gross participation gives the number of holidays taken in one year per 100 inhabitants. Chapter 3 shows the results for a number of countries.

It is worth making one statistical note here. All these surveys are based on samples. Very often questions are raised such as: 'How reliable are the results based on a sample?' and 'How big should the sample size be?' The following test provides a reliable guideline. The best sampling method is undoubtedly a random sample, where each person has the same chance of being selected. In tourism surveys at a national level, a 100 per cent pure random sample is seldom or never applied because of the high costs. In cases of random sampling, the following formula is applicable (with a 95 per cent confidence level):

$$P_S - 1.96\sqrt{\frac{P_S(1-P_S)}{n-1}}\sqrt{\frac{N-n}{N-1}} \leq P_P \leq P_S + 1.96\sqrt{\frac{P_S(1-P_S)}{n-1}}\sqrt{\frac{N-n}{N-1}} \tag{2.2}$$

where

P_p = population proportion (the real value in the universe)
P_s = sample proportion
N = population size
n = sample size

Table 2.4 Error terms (with a 95 per cent confidence level) in function of sample proportion P$_s$ and sample size N

Sample size N	Sample proportion P$_s$ in %						
	5	10	20	25	30	40	50
	95	90	80	75	70	60	50
100	4.3	5.9	7.9	8.5	9.0	9.7	9.8
200	3.0	4.2	5.6	6.0	6.4	6.8	6.9
500	1.9	2.6	3.5	3.7	4.0	4.3	4.4
1000	1.4	1.9	2.5	2.7	2.8	3.0	3.1
2000	1.0	1.3	1.8	1.9	2.0	2.1	2.2
5000	0.6	0.8	1.1	1.2	1.3	1.4	1.4
6000	0.6	0.8	1.0	1.1	1.2	1.2	1.3
10000	0.4	0.6	0.8	0.8	0.9	1.0	1.0

Applied to the net participation rate of the Belgian population in the holiday survey for the year 2014, using the hypothesis of a random sample (which is not the case), and where P$_s$ = 0.58, N = 10,000,000 inhabitants and n = 6,000, the P$_p$ value varies (with a 95 per cent confidence level) between 56.8 and 59.2 per cent – indeed, the corresponding error term or confidence interval amounts to 1.2 (see Table 2.4). A confidence level of 95 per cent (i.e. it is accurate 19 times out of 20) is standard in most tourism research, and gives a very reliable result. The problem is that most surveys are not based on a random sample but, as in the UK surveys, on a stratified random sample or a quota sample (or a combination of both). In that case a more complex statistical formula should be applied. However, the formula applicable for a random sample can be used as a proxy, although it is important to be aware that in such a case the error term will be slightly higher.

Table 2.4 provides details of error terms with varying sample proportions and sample size, and with a 95 per cent confidence level. If in the Belgian case P$_s$ takes a value of 0.50 and the sample size is reduced to 1,000, the P$_p$ will take a value of (50 ± 3.1) – i.e. 46.9 per cent and 53.1 per cent (see Table 2.4).

Regarding the above formula, another point should be noted. For most samples from big populations, the factor $\sqrt{(N-n)/(N-1)}$ equals 1. This implies that the error term is independent of the population size – i.e. a sample size of 6,000 from a population of 10 million has the same value as a sample of 6,000 from 100 million people. This is a very important conclusion. The sample size should consider carefully the possible breakdowns (e.g. result per region). The more breakdowns, the larger the sample required.

The tourism production index – WES

Tourism arrivals or nights are, for many regions, not a good indicator for the tourism performance, as such destination data are very often unreliable or only relate to hotel nights. Camping, rented apartments, second homes and other forms of accommodation are very often not considered. It is also well known that official tourism data totally neglect day visitors. Furthermore, the official data are only available long after the tourism activity took place.

These are the reasons why the WES started in 1962 to design a tourism production index for the West-Flanders region in Belgium (coastal region, Bruges and hinterland area). It had a dual aim: to collect data covering all aspects of the tourism business in the region, and to provide information rapidly about the performance of the tourism sector. Table 2.5 gives the components of the WES tourism index, which can be compared with an index of manufacturing production.

Each category of the index was given a certain weight factor, and within each category a weight was attributed to the components of the category. The number and variety of the components was such as to guarantee coverage of all measurable aspects of the tourism activity of the region. The results were published no later than four weeks after each month of tourism production, and this was possible due to a successful data collection system, high participation of the sector and the use of a representative sample in the major components.

The WES index was produced monthly for the months April–September of each year from 1962 to 2001. Although the index was considered to be the only reliable method of measurement

Table 2.5 Components of the WES tourism index (TI)

Tourism categories (j)	Components (i)	Weight	
		Component i	Category j
Accommodation	● hotel		
	● rented apartment/villas		
	● camping		
	● social tourism		
Traffic	● rail transport		
	● road traffic		
	● road accidents		
	● road assistance		
Trade	● turnover retail trade		
	● fuel consumption cars		
Attractions	● theme parks		
	● museums		
	● ticketing swimming pools		
	● visits to casinos		
Consumption public utilities	● water consumption		
	● waste collection		
	● telephone communications		
	● post traffic		
	● patients in coastal hospitals		
	● information provided by local tourism offices		
Tourism activity Bruges	● information tourism office		
	● boat trips on the canals		
	● nights		
Tourism activity hinterland	● nights		
	● recreation		

of the performance of the sector in the region, production stopped in 2001 for financial reasons. The concept provides an example for many other tourism regions.

The 'tourism index' (TI) is an application of the following formula:

$$TI = \sum_{j=1}^{j=n} \left[\sum_{i=1}^{i=n} [w_i \Delta comp.i] \right] w_j \tag{2.3}$$

where

Δ comp.i = change component i with respect to the reference period
w_i = weight component i within the corresponding category
w_j = weight of each category j

Taking into account that data are collected monthly and the high season months are more important than off-peak periods, weight should be given to the individual months.

The Swiss tourism barometer

The Swiss tourism barometer, designed by Müller and Schmid (Müller and Schmid, 2003; Schmid, 2003) is, like the WES tourism index, a reaction to the problem of lack of reliable data in the tourism sector. It was inspired by the remarks of tourism professionals and scientists who criticized various aspects of tourism statistics for the following reasons:

● The focus is too narrow because it pays too much attention to accommodation.
● The production period is excessively long.
● Data on self-catering accommodation are poor or inexistent.
● The method of data collection does not use modern technology.
● Present statistics focus on physical data and neglect largely monetary aspects.

A tourism barometer in its generic form was not new. The term 'tourism barometer' had already been used in Voralberg, Austria (the Voralberger Tourismus-barometer) since 1981 and in the Côte d'Azur, France since 1987. In former Eastern Germany the East German Savings Bank Association started the Sparkassen-Tourismusbarometer in 1998 with very specific content for the new Federal States and with scientific support of DWIF. Later on the application field was extended to other German Federal States (die Länder Schleswig-Holstein, Niedersachsen, Saarland and Rhineland-Palatinate). Since 2008 there has been a national Sparkassen-Tourismusbarometer. The barometers are financed by the national and regional Savings Banks Associations, partly co-financed by tourism organizations and/or ministries of the Federal States. A few years ago the UNWTO started to produce a periodical publication: *WTO Barometer on Travel and Tourism*.

The concept of the Swiss tourism barometer is in several respects original, and it deserves special attention as a tourism monitoring system. The Swiss started trials in 2001 in two regions (Berner Oberland and Grisons). However, due to financial constraints the barometer is not yet operational at a national level. The barometer is based on voluntary cooperation of the following sectors:

● Hotels
● Youth hostels
● Weekend homes
● Camping firms
● Restaurants
● Cableways

- Sports (ski and sport schools), culture and entertainment enterprises
- Tourism organizations.

The participating firms of each branch report physical and monetary data on a monthly basis. Only one important sector (rented apartments and holiday homes in general) is not included. Tourism organizations are asked to report on information provided to tourists, and provide estimates of excursionists and bed-nights in private weekend houses.

The Swiss tourism barometer is composed of three parts. The first is systematic monitoring of relevant factors influencing tourism demand. Income and price are very important indicators, but national instruments on income and prices are not published on a monthly basis and are not adapted to the tourism sector. Therefore, more specific indicators are used as a substitute:

- The consumer climate index, published every three months, represents income.
- The price for overnight visitors was based on the Swiss Consumer Price Index (only items relevant to tourists are included).
- Price movements in competing destinations were based on the price of package tours.
- The rate of exchange of a basket of the currencies of the main countries of origin.
- The number of hours of sunshine per month (for day visitors).

For each of these items the changes are registered with regard to the same month of the previous year.

The second part concerns the above-mentioned branches of the industry. For each branch, a frequency indicator (e.g. number of overnight stays), a turnover indicator and one to three specific indicators (hotels: average turnover per night; restaurants: average turnover per seat; cableways: first entrances, etc.) are calculated.

To calculate frequency changes per branch, the following formula is applied:

$$\Delta \text{Freq}_t = \frac{\sum_{i=1}^{n} \text{Freq}_{i,t,cy} - \sum_{i=1}^{n} \text{Freq}_{i,t,py}}{\sum_{i=1}^{n} \text{Freq}_{i,t,py}} \tag{2.4}$$

where

ΔFreq_t = change frequency (e.g. overnights) in the month t compared with the same month of previous year

$\sum_{i=1}^{n} \text{Freq}_{i,t,cy}$ = sum of the frequency of the individual enterprises i for the month t during the current year

$\sum_{i=1}^{n} \text{Freq}_{i,t,py}$ = sum of frequency of the individual enterprises i for the month t during the previous year

The changes in turnover are not based on an absolute figure but on relative data (turnover month t compared with the same month of previous year). For the result of any branch, the individual results ΔTo_t are weighted with the turnover of each participating enterprise.

$$\Delta \text{To}_t = \sum_{i=1}^{n} w_i \Delta \text{To}_{i,t} \tag{2.5}$$

where

$$\sum_{i=1}^{n} w_i = 1$$

To = turnover

$\Delta \text{To}_{i,t}$ = turnover change of enterprise i in month t over previous year

The third part is an aggregation of the results of the branches to give a tourism performance index (TPI). This aggregation is based on turnover data, as not all branches can provide frequency data. The TPI is obtained using the formula:

$$TPI_t = \sum_{i=1}^{n} w_i \Delta To_{i,t} \qquad (2.6)$$

The weighting of each branch corresponds to its contribution to tourism value added.

Such a tourism barometer not only allows monitoring of the tourism performance of the individual branches and the region as a whole, but also provides an explanation for the positive or negative results. Participating firms can compare their performance with the enterprises of their sector.

References and further reading

Ahlert, G. (2007). Methodological aspects of preparing the German TSA, empirical findings and initial reactions. *Tourism Economics*, 2.

Ahlert, G. (2008). Estimating the economic impact of an increase in inbound tourism on the German economy using TSA results. *Journal of Travel Research*, 7.

Allin, P. (1998). *A Feasibility Study for Compiling a Tourism Satellite Account for the UK*. London: The Department for Culture, Media and Sport.

Araña, J., León, C., Carballo, M., and Gil, S. (2016). Designing tourism information offices: the role of the human factor. *Journal of Travel Research*, 6.

Aroca, P., Brida, J., and Volo, S. (2017). Tourism statistics: correcting data inadequacy. *Tourism Economics*, 1.

Blanc, J-M. (2006). L'observation, un outil de stratégie touristique. *Les Cahiesr Espaces*, 90.

Castlunger, L. (2009). Das Tourismus-Satelliten-Konto für Südtirol. *Asta Schriftenreihe collana*, 148.

Cooper, A., and Wilson, A. (2002). Extending the relevance of TSA research for the UK: general equilibrium and spillover analysis. *Tourism Economics*, 1.

Cooper, C., Fletcher, J., Gilbert, D., and Wanhill, S. (1993). *Tourism: Principles & Practice*. London: Pitman Publishing.

Delisle, J. (1999). The Canadian national tourism indicators: a dynamic picture of the satellite account. *Tourism Economics*, 5.

Diakomihalis, M.N., and Lagos, D. (2008). Estimation of the economic impacts of yachting in Greece via the tourism satellite account. *Tourism Economics*, 4.

Dwyer, L., Forsyth, P., and Spurr, R. (2007). Contrasting the uses of TSAs and CGE models: measuring tourism yield and productivity. *Tourism Economics*, 4.

Dwyer, L., Forsyth, P., and Dwyer, W. (2010). *Tourism economics and policy*. Bristol: Channel View Publications.

Eurostat (1998). *Community Methodology on Tourism Statistics*. Luxembourg: Eurostat.

Eurostat (2017). *Tourism Satellite Accounts (TSA) in Europe*. Luxembourg: Eurostat.

Eurostat, OECD, WTO and UN Statistics Division (2001). *Tourism Satellite Account: Recommended Methodological Framework*. Luxembourg: Eurostat.

Franz, A., Laimer, A., and Smeral, E. (2001). *A Tourism Satellite Account for Austria*. Vienna: Statistik Austria and WIFO.

Franz, A., Laimer, P., and Manente, M. (2002). *European Implementation Manual on Tourism Satellite Accounts*. Luxembourg: Eurostat.

Frechtling, D. (1996). *Practical Tourism Forecasting*. Oxford: Butterworth-Heinemann.

Frechtling, D. (2006). An assessment of visitor expenditure methods and models. *Journal of Travel Research*, 45.

Frechtling, D. (2009). The Tourism Satellite Account. A primer. *Annals of Tourism Research*, 1.

Frechtling, D. (2011). *Exploring the Full Economic Impact of Tourism for Policy Making: Extending the Use of Tourism Satellite Account through Macroeconomic Analysis Tools.* Madrid: World Tourism Organization.

Frent, C. (2009). The economic importance of vacation homes from the Tourism Satellite Account (TSA) perspective. *Tourism Review, 2.*

Frent, C., and Frechtling, D. (2015). Assessing a Tourism Satellite Account: a programme for ascertaining conformance with United Nations standards. *Tourism Economics, 3.*

Heerschap, N.M. (1999). The employment module for the Tourism Satellite Account of the OECD. *Tourism Economics, 5.*

Heerschap, N., De Boer, B., Hoekstra, R., Van Loon, A., and Tromp, L. (2005). A Tourism Satellite Account for the Netherlands: approach and results. *Tourism Economics, 3.*

Hendrickx, L. (2017). *Vergelijkende analyse van technieken voor het meten van dagtoerisme. Gevalstudie: de Belgische Kust.* Leuven: KU Leuven.

IRTS (2008). See: United Nations Statistics Division and UNWTO (2010). *International Recommendations for Tourism Statistics 2008.* Madrid: UNWTO.

Laimer, P., and Smeral, E. (2012). *Ein Tourismus-Satellitenkonto für Österreich. Methodik, Ergebnisse und Prognosen für die Jahre 2000 bis 2013.* Wien: WIFO.

Libreros, M., Massieu, A., and Meis, S. (2006). Progress in Tourism Satellitte Account implementation and development. *Journal of Travel Research, August.*

Lickorish, L.J. (1997). Travel statistics – the slow move forward. *Tourism Management, 18.*

Maschke, J. (2000). *Das Sparkassen-Tourismus-Barometer 2000.* Yearly Report. Ostdeutscher Sparkassen-und Giroverband.

Meis, S. (1999). The Canadian experience in developing and using the Tourism Satellite Account. *Tourism Economics, 5.*

Müller, H., and Schmid, F. (2003). Tourism barometer – developing and testing an instrument for monitoring the tourism market in Switzerland. *Tourism Review, 3.*

OECD (2000). *Measuring the Role of Tourism in OECD Economies. The OECD Manual on Tourism Satellite Accounts and Employment.* Paris: OECD.

Plaza, B., Galvez-Galvez, C., and Gonzales-Flores, A. (2011). Testing the employment impact of the Guggenheim Museum Bilbao via TSA. *Tourism economics, 1.*

Ritchie, J.B., and Ritchie J.R.B. (2002). A framework for an inquiry supported destination marketing information system. *Tourism Management, 23.*

Rubben, M., and Verhaeghe, A. (2002). *Ontwikkeling van een toeristisch informatiesysteem op Vlaams niveau.* Antwerp: University Antwerpen and Katholieke Hogeschool, Mechelen.

Schmid, F. (2003). *Tourismusbarometer.* Bern: FIF.

Smeral, E. (2005). The economic impact of tourism: beyond satellite accounts. *Tourism Analysis, 10.*

Smeral, E. (2006). Tourism Satellite Accounts: A critical assessment. *Journal of Travel Research, August.*

Smeral, E. (2008). *Application of the TSA in a regional context – the case of Vienna.* Kiel: TRC paper.

Smith, S. (1997). *Tourism Analysis: A Handbook,* 2nd edn. Edinburgh: Longman.

Spurr, R. (2006). Tourism Satellite Accounts. In L. Dwyer and P. Forsyth (eds), *International Handbook on the Economics of Tourism.* Cheltenham: Edward Elgar.

Terrier, C. (2006). Flux et afflux de touristes. Les instuments de mesure. In *Observation & tourisme. Les Cahiers Espaces, vol 90.*

Tyrrell, T. (2002). *A Tourism Satellite Account for Rhode Island.* Arlington: TTRA annual conference.

United Nations, Organisation for Economic Co-operation and Development, Eurostat and World Tourism Organisation (2001). *Tourism Satellite Account: Recommended Methodological Framework.* Madrid: WTO.

United Nations, Organisation for Economic Co-operation and Development, Eurostat and World Tourism Organisation (2010). *Tourism Satellite Account: Recommended Methodological Framework 2008*. Madrid: WTO.

United Nations Statistics Division and UNWTO (2010). *International Recommendations for Tourism Statistics 2008*. Madrid: UNWTO. (Herein referred to as 'IRTS 2008'.)

UNWTO (2011). *Tourism Towards 2030: Global Overview*. Madrid: UNWTO.

Vukasovic, S. (2017). The significance of TSA application in the economic policy of Serbia. *Tourism Economics, 1*.

WES (1992). *De Economische Betekenis van het Toerisme te Brugge*. Brugge: Facetten van West-Vlaanderen, n° 37.

WES (2002). *Toeristische Index WES-Kust, Brugge en Achterland*. Brugge: WES.

Wöber, K. (2003). Information supply in tourism management by marketing decision systems. *Tourism Management, 24*.

WTO (1998). *Tourism: 2020 Vision*. Madrid: WTO.

WTO (2000). *General Guidelines for Developing the Tourism Satellite Account, Measuring Total Tourism Demand*. Madrid: WTO.

WTO (2001). *The Economic Impact of Tourism*. Madrid: WTO

Appendix 2.1 Basic notions National Accounts

Gross Value Added (GVA)

Monetary market value of the amount of goods and services that have been produced during one year, less the cost of all inputs and raw materials that are directly attributable to that production.

Gross Domestic Product (GDP)

Monetary market value of all final goods and services produced in a country during one year period.

Final goods and services:

1 for consumption (households and public sector)
2 investments (households, companies and public sector), and
3 exports.

Gross National Product (GNP)

Market value of all the products and services produced in one year by production factors supplied by the citizens of a country. Unlike GDP, which defines production based on the geographical location of production, GNP indicates allocated production based on location of ownership.

Difference between GDP and GNP: net factor incomes received from abroad

GNP equals GDP plus factor incomes of citizens and companies of a country earned abroad (e.g. received dividends from abroad or salaries received from frontier workers) minus factor incomes of citizens, companies and public sector paid to abroad (e.g. paid dividends to abroad or salaries paid to frontier workers).

GDP at factor costs = GDP at market prices minus net indirect taxes (indirect taxes minus grants)

Gross National Income = GNP minus indirect taxes and plus grants

Net National Income = Gross National Income minus depreciation

Disposable income

1 Labour income households
2 Plus capital income households (e.g. dividends, interests, rents)
3 Plus net receipts transfers

    a Receipts transfers from the public sector (pensions, family allowances and employment benefits)
    b Minus payments social security by households and employers and transfer payments to abroad (e.g. gifts)

4 Minus direct income taxes.

Tourism (direct) Gross Value Added (TGVA)

Monetary market value of the amount of goods and services that have been produced in 'tourism industry' during one year, less the cost of all inputs and raw materials that are directly attributable to that production. Tourism Gross Value Added adds the parts of gross value added generated by tourism industries and other industries of the economy that directly serve visitors in responding to internal tourism consumption. The use of the term 'direct' in this aggregate refers to the fact that the TSA measures only that part of value added (by tourism industries and other industries) due to consumption by visitors and leaves aside the indirect and induced effects that such consumption might generate. The latter is a very important remark.

Tourism Gross Domestic Product (TGDP)

TGDP equals TGVA plus net taxes on tourism products (calculated using visitor expenditures as a proportion of total expenditures).

Chapter 3

Tourism demand

Determinants of tourism demand

The determinants of tourism demand are those factors at work in any society that drive and set limits to the volume of a population's demand for holiday and travel (Burkart and Medlik, 1981). The determinants of tourism demand explain why the population of some countries has a high propensity to participate in tourism whereas that of other countries shows a low one.

These determinants should be distinguished from motivations and buyer behaviour. Burkart and Medlik (1981) describe motivations as 'the internal factors at work within individuals, expressed as the needs, wants and desires that influence tourism choices'. Marketing managers should know why and how consumers make their holiday choices, but it is also necessary to understand how internal psychological processes influence individuals in choosing between different holiday destinations and particular types of product. These processes are known within marketing as aspects of buyer behaviour (Middleton *et al.*, 2009). Here, only determinants are discussed.

Middleton summarizes the determinants under ten headings:

1   Economic factors and comparative prices
2   Demographic factors
3   Geographic factors
4   Socio-cultural attitudes to tourism
5   Mobility
6   Government/regulatory
7   Media communications
8   Information and communication technology
9   Environmental concerns and demand for more sustainable forms of tourism
10 International political developments and terrorist actions.

However, tourism demand is also sensitive to changes in the supply of products and the capacity of supply. As an example, owing to excellent fast train connections the city of Lyon has become a short-break destination for Belgians. Demand and supply interact.

Economic factors: income, time and price

Probably the most important group of determinants is the one covering economic factors, and more particularly the income (or specifically the disposable income) of the population of the generating markets (Martins *et al.*, 2017). According to Middleton, in the late 1990s there were 30 countries of origin that accounted for over 90 per cent of world international travel spending. The concentration of the demand is even more remarkable when it is noted that the top ten countries alone account for some two-thirds of international tourism spending. Under these circumstances, it is quite logical that most destinations are fishing in the same ponds.

In the relationship between tourism and income, the latter can be measured in different ways – for example, by GDP, personal income or disposable income. Disposable income is the most adequate independent variable. Discretionary income (or the income that is left after all necessary expenditure) would be an even better variable. In periods of rising oil prices, discretionary income is under high pressure and so is tourism demand, but unfortunately there are no data available regarding this possible variable (Crouch *et al.*, 2007). A notion directly derived from the relationship between tourism demand and income is income-elasticity, or the change in tourism demand relative to a change in income. In Chapter 1 we saw that outbound tourism shows a high income-elasticity – in other words, when income increases by 1 per cent, tourism demand increases by more than 1 per cent.

With respect to the income factor, there are two significant points that should be noted. First, disposable income per capita is an average, and as such this indicator neglects the personal income distribution within the country. It is well known that, particularly in some Middle Eastern countries, the higher incomes are concentrated in the hands of just a few people.

Secondly, there can be a time lag between tourism expenditure and the availability of additional income. More evident, however, is the possible 'time lead'. Consumers very often anticipate income expectations; they can be optimistic or pessimistic, and sometimes a positive or negative over-reaction is the result (Song and Lin, 2009).

There are no holidays without time available for travel. For many years, the free time available was a major determinant. This is no longer the case in many developed economies, where employees have four to six weeks of paid leave each year and the number of working hours per annum is not higher than 1,700–2,100. For a long time, increased paid leave has enhanced holiday participation, especially the second holiday and the short breaks phenomena. However, at present additional free time no longer has such a great impact. Marginal utility is decreasing, and many people don't have the money to take more (short) holidays a year. However, more flexible working time has an impact on off-peak holidays and stimulates the staggering of holidays.

Free time is, however, still a determinant factor in developing countries, and even in many developed countries, such as Japan and the USA, not all populations have 30 days of paid leave each year.

Table 3.1 compares the situation in a number of countries at very different stages of development and from different continents. The data in Table 3.1 are minima and in many countries those minima vary from sector to sector and from age group to age group. The differences in paid holidays between the countries mentioned in Table 3.1 are significant. It is remarkable that the present situation of paid holidays per year does not differ much from the situation two decades ago.

European Union legislation mandates that all 28 member countries must by law grant all employees a minimum of four weeks of paid vacation. In the USA such a statutory right does not exist. In practice, however, the majority of employees in the USA benefit from paid leave. In some countries (e.g. the UK), paid public holidays are part of public leave.

The introduction of a second week of paid leave in the Republic of China in the late 1990s, linked to the National Holiday, created a travel boom in the first week of October. The Great Wall of China became very overcrowded during that week, and a visit there was not without danger. A third and fourth week off in China would open a very important market for many destinations in the world. In reality, there is a dichotomy between the money rich/time poor and the time rich/money poor.

Table 3.1 Minimum annual paid leave and public holidays, per country (2016)

Source: International Labour Organization

Country	Paid leave (days)	Public holidays
EU	20	
Austria	25	13
France	25	11
Finland	25	11
Germany	20	9
Italy	20	12
Poland	20	13
Sweden	25	9
UK	28	0
Russia	20	11
South Africa	15	12
China	10	7
Malaysia	7	19
Japan	10–20	0
Australia	20	10
Canada	10	6
USA	(10)	(8)

A factor that is often overlooked is the age of retirement and early retirement. The lowering of retirement age is another factor that has increased the amount of free time available, and as such has stimulated tourism demand. However, owing to the ageing population and the costs of retirement, in some countries the value of pensions is being reduced and the retirement age raised over a transitional period in several European countries.

Price is a third important economic determinant. The relationship between tourism demand and price leads to price-elasticity. In Chapter 1 we noted that price-elasticity is very often close to −1. In other words, when the price of a tourist product in a destination increases by 1 per cent, the demand in the generating country decreases by about 1 per cent. This is classic price-elasticity. However, price elasticities vary across different dimensions: business or leisure, reservations made a long time before departure or reservations made a few days before departure, departures occurring on weekends or on a working day (Morlotti *et al.*, 2017).

Due to economies of scale, technological improvements in transport and communication, deregulation in air transport and stronger competition, prices of tourism products have not followed the general inflation rate. This movement has stimulated the tourism purchasing power of potential travellers and made travel more accessible.

Price is a complicated issue. It is not only the absolute amount that should be considered but also the relative price of a tourist product against other similar products, as this will be a key factor in tourism demand. Indeed, tourism demand can also be influenced by the price of a competitive or complementary product. In such cases we are confronted with cross-elasticity, or the responsiveness of the demand for one commodity (e.g. a holiday in Italy) to changes in the price of another commodity (e.g. a holiday in Spain). In mathematical form, this can be considered as:

$$E_{cr} = \frac{\dfrac{\Delta D}{D}}{\dfrac{\Delta P_c}{P_c}} \tag{3.1}$$

where

E_{cr} = cross-elasticity
ΔD = change of demand
ΔP_c = change of price of a competitive (complementary) product

Returning to the Spanish–Italian example, a price increase of 10 per cent in Spain can lead to an increase in demand for a similar Italian tourism product of 7 per cent. In this case, the cross-elasticity equals 0.7. Competitive or substitute products always show a positive sign. Complementary products show a negative cross-elasticity – for example, an increase in the price of charter flights to Spain will lead to a decrease of demand for hotel rooms in Spain.

A comparison between prices should be based on similar products. Seaside destinations can be compared, but the sun and a beach in Rimini cannot be compared with a cultural tourism product in Tuscany. If the products are very similar, there are two other important price components in international tourism: the inflation rate in the generating and receiving countries, and the relative exchange rates between the generating country's currency and that of the receiving destination. In Europe, before the introduction of the euro Spain suffered much more from inflation than its competitors in the Mediterranean area. A switch in demand to the competitors of the region was the logical consequence, followed by devaluation of the Spanish peseta. As a member of the European Monetary Union, Spain now has to respect the famous Maastricht norms and can no longer devaluate the national currency which no longer exists. In the 1980s and 1990s, devaluation of the peseta was the weapon used to keep the Spanish tourism sector competitive.

This brings us to the second important price component in international tourism: the real exchange rate between generating and receiving countries. Prices should be adjusted for the exchange rate (see Chapter 6, and Dwyer et al., 2000). Exchange rates are highly variable. This can be illustrated with the evolution of the relationship of the euro to the US dollar the during the period 1999–2017 (see Figure 3.1).

With such variability in exchange rates, it is not surprising that tourism flows between the USA and the eurozone are fluctuating. In 2002 a German tourist received $0.88 for €1: in 2008 the exchange rate was $1.47:€1 or he received $1.47 for €1. All things being equal, travelling to the USA for Europeans became expensive in the beginning of the century. The situation changed after 2004. In the period 2004 up to 2014, due to a weaker dollar, Europeans from the eurozone were stimulated to travel to the USA. US tourism products were again cheap for the Europeans. An unfavourable change in the exchange rate means less travel abroad, travel to different locations, a reduction in expenditure and/or length of stay, and possibly changes in the mode of transport. In the recent past, two interesting papers have dealt with the short- and long-term effects of income and exchange rates. The first paper relates to US tourism (Chi, 2015). The second study examines the effects of the exchange rate and income on the Turkish tourism trade balance (Akay et al., 2017). It is important to notice that in both studies income has more impact on the trade balance than the exchange rate in the long run. Cheng et al. (2013) studied the relationship between the exchange rate and the US tourism trade for the period 1973–2007. Their conclusion is very nuanced:

> Depreciation raises the US tourism trade balance with a unit elastic effect after six quarters with no evidence of J-curve behavior. Only export revenue is marginally sensitive to the exchange rate. Foreign travel is a luxury good for US tourists, while travel to the USA is a normal good for foreign tourists.

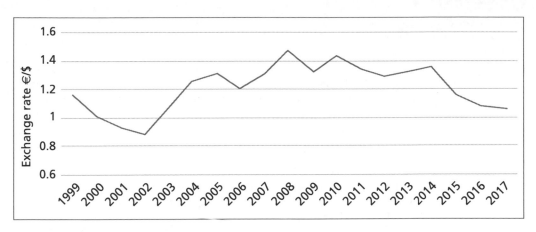

Figure 3.1 Relationship of the € to the $, 1999–2017 (exchange rates in month 1)

(In economics, the 'J curve' refers to the trend of a country's trade balance following a devaluation or depreciation under a certain set of assumptions.)

The research on the influence of exchange rate regimes on tourism is interesting. Santana-Gellego *et al.* (2010) came to the following conclusion with regards to exchange rate regimes:

> On the contrary, empirical research suggests a big positive impact of a common currency on trade, while its effect on tourism needs to be investigated further. On the basis of a gravity equation, we estimate a sizeable effect of a currency union on international tourism of almost 12%. This may add an additional argument to the debate on the benefits and drawbacks of a currency union. Also, we analyse the impact of several de facto exchange rate arrangements on international tourism. We have found that other intermediate exchange rate regimes, between completely fixed and completely flexible, promote tourism. The results show that less flexibility in the exchange rate arrangements generates a positive effect on tourism and that the less flexible the exchange regime is, the greater the impact on tourism.

A special relationship between tourism and exchange rate is the 'Dutch Disease' (referring to the influence of natural gas on the Dutch economy). Industries in an economy are interdependent on each other. This relationship is not always positive. A good example is the mining boom in Australia. This boom had adverse effects on many other industries, including tourism, through a strong appreciation of the exchange rate (Pham *et al.*, 2015).

The combination of exchange rates and price evolution leads to the important notion of 'real exchange rates'. Real exchange rates are based on market rates of exchange between each origin country's currency and each destination country's currency, adjusted by the relative price levels between the origin country and each destination. In other words, to calculate the trend in real exchange rates, the index of market rates is adjusted by an index of relative inflation rates between the origin country and each of the various destinations (Economist Intelligence Unit, 1995).

A practical fictional example makes it clear. We take Germany as the origin country and the USA as the destination country with the following data:

- Exchange rate: € in $ in year t: 1.3
- Exchange rate: € in $ in year t+1: 1.6
- CPI (consumer price index), USA year t: 100

- CPI, USA year t+1: 100
- CPI, Germany year t: 120
- CPI, Germany year t+1: 130

The real exchange rate can be calculated in two different ways: (1) the price of the destination's currency in terms of the origin's currency or (2) the price of the origin's currency in terms of the destination's currency.

1. $RP_{it} = (CPI_{it}/CPI_{jt}) \times ER_{ij}$ (3.2)

   - RP_{It} = relative price variable in destination i (USA) in period t
   - CPI_{it} = consumer price index in destination i in period t
   - CPI_{jt} = consumer price index in origin j (Germany) in period t
   - ER_{ij} = exchange rate US\$ in terms of € in period t

   An application of the formulae to year t leads to:
   RP = 0.77 * 100/120 = 0.58
   The application to year t+1 leads to:
   RP = 0.62 * 100/130 = 0.48
   A lower value of the real exchange rate in year t+1 means more purchasing power for German tourists in the USA.

2. $RP_{it} = (CPI_{jt}/CPI_{it})*ER_{ij}$ (3.3)

   - CPI_{jt} = consumer price index in origin country j (Germany) in period t
   - CPI_{it} = consumer price index in destination country i in period t
   - ER_{ij} = exchange rate of € in terms of US\$

   The application to the year t results in a RP value of:
   1.3 * 120/100 = 1.56
   The same application to the year t+1 equals:
   1.6 * 130/100 = 2.08
   In this case a higher RP value means more purchasing power for the German tourists in the USA.

The real exchange rate (REX) is often used as a proxy for prices in tourism demand models. However, Seetaram *et al.* (2016) are more restrained in the use of the real exchange rate. They posit that REX is often a valid proxy for prices in models of inbound tourism but it fares poorly in models of outbound tourism. Their argument is that REX does not measure the relative prices of the different destinations but only changes in prices.

The price of oil is or will become an important component of the price of some tourism products. Increase in oil prices will influence some tourism flows. There is a good illustration in Becken and Lennox (2012). These authors analysed the consequences of an increase of oil prices on the inbound tourism of New Zealand. They observed that with changes in global oil price came a real reduction in tourists from the United Kingdom.

A special feature of price is the 'perceived costs'. Special attention will be paid to this aspect in Chapter 6.

Tourism relative to other products must also be considered (Holloway, 1992). For an individual consumer, tourism competes with other products or services (such as a personal computer, home improvements or fitness services) for a share of the budget. A widespread reaction to special offers on the occasion of a national car fair can lead to a shift in demand in that country. An Australian study (Crouch *et al.*, 2007) aimed to identify how tourism competes against six other main categories of discretionary expenditure (see Table 3.2). This is based on a survey in Australia with more than 1,000 participants. The marginal

Table 3.2 Total versus marginal discretionary spending
Source: Crouch *et al.* (2007) p. 253

Category	Per cent of marginal discretionary spending	Per cent of total discretionary spending
Reducing household debt	44.6	18.6
Financial investment	12.5	32.2
Home improvement	11.0	13.7
Home entertainment equipment	6.0	5.0
Leisure activities	3.4	8.8
Domestic vacation	9.3	5.4
Overseas vacation	11.3	6.4
Donation to charity	2.0	2.8
Total	100.0	100.0

discretionary spending is based on a A$2,000 windfall. The results indicate that about one-fifth of marginal discretionary income would be spent on vacations. Domestic and overseas vacations represent 11.8 per cent of total discretionary income.

Economic determinants alone, however, cannot explain tourism demand in its entirety (see Crouch, 1992). Many other factors influence the volume of holidays and limits to travel.

Other determinants

First among other determinants are demographic factors. The size or volume and the growth of the population of the generating markets are very important. In many cases it is not the total population but the size of the relevant market segments that counts. This brings us to the age structure of the population of several generating markets. In Europe and the USA, the ageing population has become a real challenge (Müller, 2001), and for the tourism sector this is providing threats but also opportunities. The senior market is growing very fast. This segment has the purchasing power and time to travel, and travel experience. Moscardo (2006) speaks of 'third-age tourism' and gives examples of companies providing senior tourism services: Elderhostel, 50Plus Expeditions (USA), Odyssey travel (Australia), Travel & Learn (New Zealand) and Saga holidays (UK). The ageing of the population creates opportunities in the health market. On the other hand, it should be noted that in many developed countries some age segments are declining.

The question arises as to how long some Western economies can go on with retirement at the age of 55–58, or even earlier. Owing to the disequilibria in the age structure, in the near future the active population will be obliged to work for longer. Countries with developed economies are confronted with other demographic trends: one-person and two-person households have emerged, smaller households are the rule, and divorce and remarriage have become common. EU countries are confronted with the Lisbon Treaty (minimal activity rates). In several EU member countries early retirement is discouraged and decreasing.

With respect to geographical factors (e.g. climate, urbanization, etc.), Middleton's (2001) statement is quite important: 'In the twenty-first century cities and towns are the magnets for modern stay and day visit tourism'. Large cities are generators for attractions (seaside resorts, theme parks and other) within accessible distance, but at the same time several of them attract tourists for their heritage. Prague, St Petersburg, Paris, Barcelona and many others attract millions of visitors each year.

There are also several socio-cultural attitudes that affect tourism. People from northern climates believe that lying on beaches has a therapeutic value, but more and more people are concerned about depletion of the global ozone layer and the toxic effects of too much exposure to unfiltered sunlight. This might change the holiday pattern of many people, or at least the holiday behaviour of tourists at sun-belt destinations. So far 'sun and beach' holidays are still very attractive.

In many Western countries there is a common belief that holidays are 'rights' and 'necessities for relieving stress', and paid holidays have become an institution.

Government regulations may have a much greater impact on tourism than generally believed. We see government interventions with respect to tourism in several fields:

- Guaranteeing fair competition between suppliers
- Consumer protection
- The timing of school holidays
- Frontier formalities for international travellers, e.g. the Schengen agreement and visa regulations (Li and Song, 2015; Liu and McKercher, 2016)
- Environment and sustainable development
- Regulations in the field of transport, tour operating, time-sharing, and compulsory environmental impact assessments.

The role of mass media communications is considerable. As Middleton and Clarke (2001) put it, 'the cumulative effect of television over the years in shaping travel and tourism expectations in the major demand-generating countries cannot be overestimated'. Television has a major influence on tourism demand; it is not only a medium for advertising but also, and above all, it brings destinations, attractions, people and events into millions of households worldwide on a daily basis. The impact of regular television holiday programmes is widespread on all social classes. The ability of television to draw attention to things that go wrong for tourists also has an effect on demand. Besides television we should pay particular attention to the internet, especially as a relatively new information medium, distribution channel and booking instrument, and even as a provider of virtual enterprises. Over the last two decades, the internet has achieved high market penetration, with more than a billion users worldwide. Tourism is a key area for the application of the internet in all major markets. The major growth markets for international tourism will predominantly be online. In the 21st century social media channels of all sorts have also become strong communication instruments in the tourism sector.

Finally, it is important not to forget the exposure of prospective holidaymakers to newspapers, magazines, radio, movies, etc., which also contribute to creating awareness and attitudes.

Tourism is confronted with a number of constraints, too. The carrying capacity of most places is not unlimited. More and more destinations are limiting further quantitative growth (e.g. Bermuda, the Seychelles) and/or introducing a visitor management system (Amsterdam, Bruges, Salzburg, Venice, etc.).

The growth of crime in tourism destinations – or at least the perception of escalating crime – is a further handicap for international tourism. Terrorism is a special form of crime. Terrorism is a recent constraint of the last decades. More and more, tourists have become target groups for terrorist movements to exert political pressure. Unfortunately, the list of examples is long – Egypt, Indonesia, Kenya (Buigut and Amendah, 2016), Peru, Colombia, Spain, Italy, Sri Lanka, etc. The terrorist attacks in the USA on 11 September 2001, although not directed towards tourism, discouraged many international tourists from visiting the USA.

The terrorist attacks in Paris and Brussels in 2016 also had a very important impact on international arrivals, especially long-haul travellers. The consequences were not only felt in Paris and Brussels, but on all tourism regions in France and Belgium. The fall in arrivals was much bigger in long-distance markets than in the neighbouring countries. This proves how important perception is. It took more than nine months to return to a more or less normal hotel occupation rate in the Belgian cities of Brussels and Bruges. The recovery period from a terrorism attack varies from a few months up to several years. In the case of a terrorist attack in Europe, a Japanese or American tourist often cannot easily distinguish France from Italy or Belgium from Spain. The impact of terrorism on tourism is very important. Baker (2014) put it as follows:

> The impact of terrorism on the travel and tourism industry can be enormous. It can lead to unemployment, homelessness, deflation, and many other social and economic ills. The contribution of tourism for many countries is so great that any downturn in the industry is a cause of major concern for many governments. The repercussions are felt in many other industries associated with tourism like airlines, hotels, restaurants and shops that cater to the tourists and allied services. Terrorism is an enigmatic and compelling phenomenon, and its relationship with tourism is complex and multifaceted.
>
> (See also Thompson and Thompson, 2010)

With respect to the impact of terrorism on tourism demand, the results from the German 'Reiseanalyse 2017' (travel analysis) are very interesting (Lohmann, 2017). A first conclusion is that the German market did not change in volume between 2015 and 2016. We refer to the net and gross holiday participation. This was the same in 2016 as in 2015. A second conclusion is that there are winner and loser destinations. The market share of some destinations went down, especially for Turkey with a decline of some 27 per cent (from 5.0 million or 6.4 per cent of all holiday trips in 2015 to 3.9 million or 4.7 per cent in 2016). Spain and Greece together received 1.1 million German holiday trips more in 2016 compared to 2015. These destinations are real competitors to Turkey. Thirdly, the 22 million Germans who reported that they had been influenced by terrorism expressed the following holiday intentions for 2017:

- I'm worried: 50 per cent
- No Islamic country as destination: 41 per cent (but the majority of these did not travel to an Islamic destination in 2016)
- Cautious as regards choice of destination: 27 per cent
- Will not visit an originally preferred destination: 18 per cent
- No air travel: 10 per cent (but 90 per cent of these did not take a flight holiday in 2016)
- Book later: 10 per cent.

Of further significance is Lohmann's statement (2017): 'Communication is very important. Terror and political instability at a destination only seem to play a role for holiday planning when constantly communicated in the media with special attention'.

Visa regulations are to a certain extent related to terrorism. A visa requirement is in many countries used to prevent terrorism. Research into the impacts of visa liberalization indicates that the volume of arrivals increases substantially. Liu and McKercher (2016) posit:

> Unlike distance, market access is a relative term that reflects the impact of cost, effort, time, and other variables on demand. It can be manipulated to enhance or diminish the relative competitiveness of destinations. Easing or eliminating visa requirements represents one such tool that can be used to increase market access. Limited research has been conducted on the impacts of such actions, though, other than some studies that

show a direct relationship between volume of arrivals and severity of visa restrictions. This study builds on that knowledge base by evaluating the impact of visa liberalization policies on the profile and resultant behaviors of the outbound China market that visits Hong Kong.

In another piece of research Li and Song (2015) suggest that the Beijing Olympic Games generated losses and they attribute this unexpected negative economic impact of the Beijing Olympics to visa restrictions.

The ageing population has made the over-60s an increasingly important group and has had an impact on holiday choice. Countries without a developed healthcare service have become less and less attractive for older travellers.

Most of these determinants are changing over time. In the 2007 publication *A Practical Guide to Tourism Destination Management* (UNWTO), examples of macro-environment changes are summarized (see Table 3.3). Some of them – trends within tourism – are dealt with in more detail in the next section.

The destination management, the management of hotels, tour operators and other entrepreneurs in the tourism sector should follow up the changes of the macro-environment with special attention. The changes may create new opportunities or threats. They can lead to another or adapted strategy and policy for the destination.

Trends in tourism demand

This section discusses a number of trends within tourism demand (Buhalis and Costa, 2006). There is no doubt that these trends are partly related to the socio-economic determinants discussed above.

Globalization of tourism demand

Globalization is a generic term comprising three basic elements. The first is the geographic element, which covers intra-regional and inter-regional travel. In French, we speak of the '*mondialisation*' of tourism, or its expansion to a global scale. Others see globalization in terms of convergence in world tastes, product preferences and lifestyles, which leads to the second element: growing standardization and market homogenization. There is a trend towards similar customer preferences worldwide. The third element is the existence of internationally similar practices, such as distribution systems, marketing, product development, etc. All three features are present in modern tourism development. The first and second characteristics are more demand-oriented; the third is supply-oriented.

On a world scale, long-haul travel and inter-regional flows are already important and are predicted to increase their market share from 18 per cent in 1995 to 22 per cent in 2030 (UNWTO, 2011). The latter percentage is lower than the forecast for 2020 made towards the end of the last century, which was 24 per cent (WTO, 1998). The main reason is transportation costs. The WTO report *Tourism Towards 2030: Global Overview* (2011) is clear:

> The total weighted cost of transport is assumed to grow at an average annual rate of 1.4% per year from 2010 to 2030. The steady decline in the cost of travelling by air in real terms over the past half century is unlikely to continue in the coming decades. Fuel costs are set to rise, as a result of expected increases in both the price of oil (as it becomes a scarcer resource) and taxation on aviation fuel. Technology innovation and a further increase of fuel efficiency of the fleet by some 1% per year – compared to 1.5% per year over the past 20 years – can only partly offset this. The rate at which air transport has become cheaper has already slowed in recent years; it is assumed that the factors

Table 3.3 Examples of macro-environment changes

Source: UNWTO (2007)

Economic	Socio-demographic	Political	Technological	Ecological
Exchange rates	Demographic trends	Global/regional conflicts	Global distribution systems	Environmental strain on popular destinations
Interest rates	Health threats	Regional relations		Market concern for responsible travel (triple bottom line)
Economic stability	Lifestyle and value	Changes in power structures	Internet and CD rom marketing	
Inflation	Trends	Occurrence of extreme events	Transport	Species awareness
Fuel prices	New tastes and social trends	Legal restrictions	Innovations	Increased focus on values, sustainability and ethics
Aviation costs	Leisure orientation	Positive political developments	Virtual reality	
Privatization	Sport, health and fitness		Video and teleconferencing	
Currency re-evaluations				
	Global village			
	Impact of the media			

mentioned above will combine to push the cost of air travel up from around 2012 onwards.

Real cost increases are assumed to be relatively gradual to 2020 (no more than 1% real growth per year on average), before increasing more quickly between 2020 and 2030. This reflects the likelihood of more stringent policies towards the use of fossil fuels with a resulting increase in the average real cost of travelling by air of between 1.5% and 2% each year.

Nevertheless, travel between regions will continue to grow slightly faster than travel within the same region. The expected evolution of the intra-regional/long-haul split of international tourist arrivals is very unequal per receiving region. Table 3.4 gives the share of long-haul arrivals per receiving region in 2010 and 2030.

By and large, it is expected that more originating and receiving countries will become involved in the process of globalization. Table 3.5 illustrates this phenomenon. In 1950 the top 15 destinations accounted for 97 per cent of the international arrivals. This share is reduced to 49 per cent in 2015. In other words, the non-top destinations increased their share from 3 per cent in 1950 to 32 per cent in 1990 and 51 per cent in 2015.

Globalization of tourism over the last two or three decades cannot be explained in terms of demand factors only. However, these are important when considering Baum's (1995) key factors in explaining the growth of international tourism. It would be unwise to overlook the great influence of technology. Technology has affected two different aspects of travel – transportation and communication. Without changes in aviation (air fares included), the globalization of tourism would have been impossible. The same probably applies to the changes in information technology.

Nonetheless, demand and technology together still provide an insufficient explanation. Supply factors, such as international hotel chains and the increasing number of cruise carriers, are important, and the role of the destination countries is very often underestimated. Many developing countries consider tourism to be a main source of wealth, and the benefits can be great (Vanhove, 1997). The incentive to encourage tourism is often related to demand as well; the broadening of tourist interest not only leads to a greater diversification of tourism development in established destinations but also to more destinations entering the tourism market.

According to Fletcher and Westlake (2006) the key drivers for globalization are: technological progress (specialization in production and communications technology), economic changes (liberalization of capital transactions), cultural and demographic trends (migrations and demonstration effects) and political stability (more international cooperation).

Table 3.4 Share of long-haul arrivals per receiving region in 2010 and 2030
Source: WTO

	2010	2030
Africa	55	49
Americas	25	25
East Asia and Pacific	22	17
Europe	13	13
Middle East	54	59
World	21	22

> **Table 3.5** World's top destinations by share of international arrivals, 1950–2015
>
> Source: based on UNWTO data

Ranking country destinations	World share in %				
	1950	*1970*	*1990*	*2000*	*2015*
Top 5 destinations	71	43	39	36	28
Rank 6–10	17	22	19	15	12
Rank 11–15	9	10	10	10	9
Other destinations	3	25	32	38	51
Total million arrivals	3	166	466	686	1189

   Globalization and internationalization are very close in meaning. They tend to be used interchangeably. Internationalization is used to refer to the increasing geographical spread of economic activities across national boundaries. We can illustrate this with a few examples from the hotel business. InterContinental Hotels Group was, in 2008, operational in 100 different countries. Starwood Hotels, Accor and Hilton Hotels Corporation operated respectively in 97, 95 and 78 countries (www.hotelsmag.com).

Declining growth rates and declining income-elasticity

The declining growth rate of international arrivals is another important trend. The figures in Table 3.6 speak for themselves. In the 1970s, 1980s and 1990s a 4 to 5 per cent annual increase was taken for granted. Since the turn of the century, and more precisely after the economic and financial crisis in 2008, we notice a changing trend. The average annual growth decreased to a little over 3 per cent. However, there are differences between the regions (see Table 3.11 and Table 3.12). But almost all regions show a declining growth rate. This trend can be explained by the world economic environment and the evolution of fuel prices (see Figure 3.2).

> **Table 3.6** Growth rate of international tourist arrivals worldwide, 1950–2030

Period	Percentage
1950–1960	10.6
1960–1970	9.1
1970–1980	5.3
1980–1990	4.7
1990–2000	4.5
2000–2010	3.4
2010–2030	3.3*

* WTO Forecast

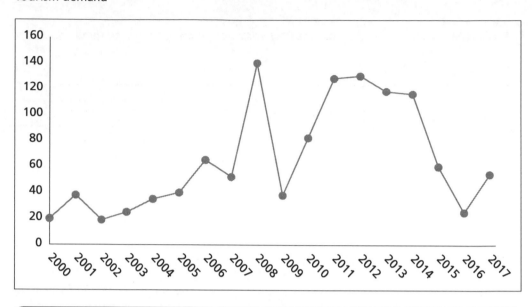

Figure 3.2 Price crude oil brent, 2000–2017 (US$ per barrel)

Source: US Department of Energy, Energy information Administration

There is not only a declining growth rate in international arrivals but also declining income elasticities. Gunter and Smeral (2016) did some very original research on this topic. Based on panel data analysis for 32 countries (the individual countries are grouped into six regions, see Table 3.7), they used the following tourism export demand equation (for quarterly tourism exports):

$$\ln XR_{it} = \alpha + \beta_1 \ln XP_{it} + \beta_2 \ln Y_t + u_i + e_{it} \tag{3.4}$$

where

XR_{it} = real tourism exports of country i at constant US dollar prices (i = 1, . . ., n) at time point t (t = 1, . . ., t)

XP_{it} = tourism export prices of country i relative to the global tourism export price

Y = income variable Y denotes a proxy for the real global GDP at constant US dollar prices. The latter variable is the same for all countries at a given point in time, thereby controlling for the development of the world economy by which all countries in the sample are equally affected at a given time point t.

α = represents the intercept

β_1 and β_2 = regression coefficients (elasticities)

The calculated income elasticities for three different time periods are given in Table 3.7. For all 32 countries together the income-elasticity goes from 2.22 in the first period to 0.34 in period 3. The econometric estimation using the information for the whole period 1977–2013 shows an income-elasticity of about 1.70. For 1994–2003 and 2004–2013, the income elasticities decreased from period to period. For the last decade, the values of the income elasticities were lower than 1. What are the underlying factors behind such drastic movements? The authors give three reasons. Firstly, there is a certain saturation process. The evolution of the net and gross holiday participation confirms a certain degree of saturation in many developed countries. It is an illustration of Engels's Law. Secondly, one cannot deny the slowing down of economic growth,

Table 3.7 Income elasticities of real tourism exports per period and region, 1977–2013

Source: Gunter and Smeral (2016)

Region	Period 1 1977–1992	Period 2 1994–2003	Period 3 2004–2013
Total (32 countries)	2.22	1.26	0.34
Northern Europe	1.77	1.04	0.56
Central and Western Europe	1.10	0.81	0.23
Southern Europe	4.54	1.26	0.20
The Americas	1.35	1.31	0.29
Asia	1.82	1.98	0.99
S-E Asia and Oceania	2.73	1.56	0.31

resulting in a change in consumer behavior. Thirdly, the dramatic deterioration in the economic environment explains the decline in income elasticities from the second to the third period. As a fourth factor one should add the spectacular increase in fuel prices (see Figure 3.2). Such an environment leads to higher uncertainty about the future and precautionary savings increases. Culiuc (2014) also found a decline in the income elasticities of international tourism demand. Gunter and Netto (2016) came to a similar conclusion for international travel to and from Brazil.

The income elasticities for the third period are abnormal for an abnormal economic environment. Most probably in the medium and longer term the income elasticities will come to a more normal level. There are signs that the world economy is recovering. This will lead to higher income elasticities but most probably lower than before the turn of the century.

Income elasticities also depend on the business cycle. Smeral (2012) revealed the existence of asymmetric income and price effects on tourism demand across business cycles. He posited:

> Based on the available data set there is empirical evidence, at least for EU15 and Japan, that elasticities of tourism import demand with respect to GDP differ depending on the phase of the business cycle. In the case of the EU15 it is shown that income elasticity during the slow-growth periods is smaller than in times of fast economic growth, whereas the opposite is true for the Japanese source market.

Smeral attributes the asymmetric income effects to two reasons: liquidity constraints and precautionary savings.

> Consumers postpone major increases of their consumption plans from the recovery to the expansion period and bring forward major negative adjustments in their consumption levels from the recession to the slowdown period. As a result, relative adjustments of the consumption and travel plans are stronger in the fast-growth period than in the slow-growth period, so that income elasticities vary.

There is evidence of cyclicality of the tourism demand for Spain, being one of the most significant tourism destinations worldwide (López Morales and Such Devesa, 2017).

Fragmentation of annual holidays

For several years there has been an increase in the number of holidaymakers taking more than one holiday per year (see Table 3.16). More free time, higher personal income and double-income families have led to the phenomenon of fragmentation. The main holiday has become shorter, but people are taking two or more additional (short) holidays a year. However, we are also confronted with time-efficient development. In a period of greater leisure time, an increasing proportion of the population finds less time to travel and is in a 'time poor–money rich' situation. Concepts of time-rich, time-poor, and money-rich will become more important in segmentation and the way in which markets purchase products (UNWTO, 2007). The outcome of this trend is an increasing number of products that offer the tourist the maximum excitement in a minimum of time.

Environmental awareness and the growing importance of eco-tourism

The environment is becoming one of the main concerns of our society, and everyone is aware of this. Tourist resorts are sometimes much less worried about it, but holidaymakers do not want to see dirty beaches and neither do they want to harm the environment. Climate change and increasing environmental and social responsibility are key trends (Taylor and Ortiz, 2009).

The landscape in all its diversity is the basic element, the main ingredient, the raw material of tourism. It is the very essence of tourism, and constitutes its driving force. From the tourist's point of view, the attraction of the landscape owes much to its diversity and the contrast it offers with his or her daily environment. It is the degree of this contrast that will determine the attraction for tourists. There is therefore a search for the real and authentic, and European travellers increasingly want nature to be more prominent in their vacations (Poon, 1993; Imm *et al.*, 2017).

A direct consequence of this movement is the boost in eco-tourism and nature-based vacations in Europe and the USA. Eco-tourism (a new buzzword) can mean a number of things, and is often old wine in a new barrel, but it is generally used to describe tourism activities which are conducted in harmony with nature, as opposed to more traditional mass tourism activities. According to Hawkins (1994), eco-tourism offers opportunities for many developing countries.

Other consequences are increasing costs of maintaining natural resorts, changes in tourism flows and seasonality, and increased environmental related legislation and costs (UNWTO, 2007). Certain resorts or regions are running the risk of, or have already fallen victim to, over-development and subsequent rejection by tourists. This is a consequence of this movement.

The link between environmental factors and repeat visitors is very close. Environmental factors do have a great impact on trip satisfaction. In a case study on the Great Barrier Reef in Australia, Jarvis *et al.* (2016) highlight that tourist satisfaction impacts the likelihood of returning and related revenues.

Changed values

In today's society there are several indications of changed values, such as a growing consciousness of nature and a search for the real and authentic. However, there is much more to the changes than this. Individualization is gaining in importance in our society, and for the tourism sector this implies that 'a' consumer no longer exists, but rather 'this' consumer. The consequence is evident – the tourist product has to be adapted to 'this' consumer. We can refer to a set of building blocks where the parts are assembled differently according to the personality of the consumer. However, time-poor markets are more likely to be seeking 'bundled products' purchased in one transaction (UNWTO, 2007).

Poon (1993) indicated as early as the beginning of the 1990s two other changed values. She was convinced that there were growing signs that the fashion for sun was beginning to fade, and sunshine was no longer sufficient to build a viable and sustainable tourism industry: 'Destinations have to begin to offer 'sun-plus' holidays, such as sun plus spas, plus nature, plus fishing'. The second changed value is the search for the different: 'The new traveller wants to experience the inexperienced, see the unexpected, gain impressions of new cultures and a new horizon'.

Changing lifestyles

Krippendorf (1987) argues that society has moved through three phases since the industrial era. In the industrial era, tourists were drawn from a population that 'lived to work', but over the past two decades people have begun to 'work to live'. Travel motivations have changed from 'to recover, to rest, to have no problems' to 'to experience something different, to have fun, to have a change, to be active'. Today there is a third phase, which has been described as the desire to experience 'the new unity of everyday life'. In this phase, the polarity of work and leisure has been reduced.

The vacation motivations of this group include:

- To broaden their horizon
- To learn something new
- To encourage introspection and communication with other people
- To discover the simpler things in life and nature
- To foster creativity and open-mindedness
- To experiment and take personal risks.

Some speak of a 'global lifestyle', which is a consequence of improved educational levels and the revolution in communication technology. The world is becoming increasingly cosmopolitan, with all its people influencing each other. This globalization process has many impacts on, and implications for, tourism. The most fundamental of these is the fact that increased travel is both a reason for, and the result of, the global lifestyle (WTO, 1999).

Tourism demand modifies quickly, and is no longer always coherent. The rapid modifications are revealed in the Mediterranean region, where the market share of the Mediterranean countries in the European market varies from year to year. The volatility of exchange rates, unequal evolution of salary costs and political factors influenced those shifts in the 1980s and 1990s. Since the millennium, terrorism and fear for personal safety dominate the movements.

Demand is not always coherent either. We may expect that a chairman of a large company will take his or her holiday in a five-star hotel, in an exotic destination – but is that really so? Not any more. That same chairman may also ask for a cycling holiday, which will allow travel from one place to another. This proves that we are no longer dealing with 'the' consumer but 'this' consumer, and provides a clear illustration of the so-called 'hybrid consumer'.

A 'healthy lifestyle' is another trend: 'The practice of healthy living reflects itself in holiday and tourism lifestyles and is responsible for the proliferation of health spas, saunas, fitness centres, "fat farms", gyms, massage . . . and other such additions to many hotels and resorts' (Poon, 1993). Müller (2001) speaks of 'wellness tourism'. The sedentary lifestyles of many people have led to an increased focus on health and well-being as a leisure activity (De Voldere, 2009).

The UNWTO *Practical Guide to Tourism Destination Management* (2007), emphasizes that people are becoming increasingly motivated by internal factors such as self-development and creative expression. People are seeking genuine experiences rather than staged ones.

More independent tourists as opposed to mass tourism

Fordian tourism was for a long time the prevailing paradigm, with mass tourism based on economies of scale and standardization (see, for example, hotel trademarks, franchise systems and tour operator vacations). In the 1980s we witnessed a great change in the operational paradigm of the tourism industry (Fayos-Solá, 1996; Cuvelier, 2000), which responded to the profound changes that Poon grouped under the headings: (a) new consumers; (b) new technologies; (c) new forms of production; (d) new management styles and (e) new prevailing circumstances. Fayos-Solá calls this phenomenon the 'New Age of Tourism' (NAT). He compares the Fordian paradigm and the NAT paradigm with respect to demand, inputs, management and environment. With respect to demand, the differences are very clear (see Table 3.8).

The new age of tourism is characterized primarily by a much greater segmentation of demand, the need for flexibility of supply and distribution, and achieving profitability through diagonal integration (economies of scope, system gains and synergies) instead of economies of scale (see Chapter 5). Segmentation of demand requires a good knowledge of the market in order to identify groups of customer traits and needs (see Cockerell, 1997; Smith, 1997). For Fayos-Solá, flexibility is important in several areas: in the organization, production and distribution of tourism products; in reservation, purchasing and payment systems; and in ways in which the tourism product is consumed (Fayos-Solá, 1996).

We find similar observations in Shaw and Williams (2004) where they give the characteristics of post-Fordian tourism consumption:

- Rejection of certain forms of mass tourism (holiday camps and cheaper packaged holidays)
- Fewer repeat visits and the proliferation of alternative sights and attractions
- Multiplication of types of holiday and visitor attraction, based on lifestyle search
- Much more information provided about alternative holidays
- Rapid turnover of tourist sites and experiences, because of rapid changes of fashion
- Growth of 'green tourism' and accommodation individually tailored to the consumer
- 'De-differentiation' of tourism from leisure, culture, retailing, education, sport and hobbies.

Fordism should not be confused with 'McDonaldization' (Shaw and Williams, 2004). McDonaldization of tourism consumption is a form of mass customization, presenting to tourists flexible products, based on efficient, calculable and predictable holidays.

There is evidence of this change of paradigm in the British tour operating market in the late 1980s. Indeed, Middleton (1991) posed the question, 'Whither the package tour?', demonstrating that the UK outbound market for traditional forms of air-inclusive package holidays reached maturity in the mid-1980s and declined in the latter half of the decade. The evidence also shows that profitable future growth for both tour operators and resorts lies in developing new forms of IT products. Mature tourists look for the core advantages of packages (price, reliability, etc.) without the traditional requirement and stigma of travelling and staying together in highly visible groups on chartered flights and in hotels. The following statement by Middleton is very important: 'So far as possible, customers should not be aware of being labelled and identified as tour groups. They will, of course, continue to be bound by the

Table 3.8 Comparison of the Fordian and NAT paradigms with respect to demand

Fordian age	New Age of Tourism (NAT)
Sun	Complex motivations
'Massification'	Individualism
Lack of tourist's own criteria	High expectations
Non-differentiated markets	Complex segmentation

specific times and product options which are the basis on which bulk purchase prices can be obtained from suppliers'.

Poon (1993) holds similar ideas. For her, new tourism exists if and where the following six conditions hold:

1 The holiday is flexible and can be purchased at prices that are competitive with mass-produced holidays (cruises v. land-based holidays).
2 Production of travel and tourism-related services is not dominated by scale economies alone; tailor-made services will be produced while still taking advantages of scale economies where they apply (yield management).
3 Production is increasingly driven by the requirements of consumers.
4 The holiday is marketed to *individuals* with different needs, incomes, time constraints and travel interests; mass marketing is no longer the dominant paradigm.
5 The holiday is consumed on a large scale by tourists who are more experienced travellers, more educated, more destination-oriented, more independent, more flexible and more environmentally conscious.
6 Consumers consider the environment and culture of the destinations they visit to be a key part of the holiday experience.

New types of holidays and tourism experience

It is not surprising to learn that, in the light of changing values and lifestyles, new types of holidays and recreation have arisen under the slogan: 'to experience something during the holiday'. Holidaymakers want to enjoy their holidays thoroughly, and this has resulted in an increasing interest in holidays devoted to sports or other hobbies; urban tourism; natural, health, wellness, culture, adventure and language holidays; second homes, etc. (see Mihalic, 2006). We speak of 'targeted product market development' (especially theme-based) oriented towards one or more of the three Es: entertainment, excitement and education.

There is a net polarization of tourist tastes: the comfort-based and the adventure-oriented. With respect to the latter, there is a trend to travel to high places (mountains), under water (tourist submarines) and the ends of the earth (e.g. the Antarctic Peninsula).

Creating the tourist experience is also a new form of tourism. Pine and Gilmore (1999) argue that there is a move from a service economy to an experience-based one, where goods and services in themselves are no longer sufficient. They are valued insofar as they are enhanced by the experience offered (Shaw and Williams, 2004). Companies and destinations stage an experience when they engage tourists in a memorable way. In this way one creates economic value (see Figure 3.3 borrowed from Pine and Gilmore). Personal moments of intense living and keen sensations are key attributes of experience tourism. There are two conceptual dimensions of experience (Haahti and Komppula, 2006). The first is the extent of participation of the tourist – either active or passive. Here we refer to holiday clubs such as Club Med, where tourists actively participate in and co-organize sports, shows, etc. The second conceptual dimension is the emotional mode and the extent of involvement in the experience. A good example is whale-watching, a growing activity worldwide (Cooper *et al.*, 2006). Müller and Scheurer (2005) applied the theory of Pine and Gilmore to tourism destinations. They developed a procedure for deliberate experience-staging in tourism destinations. We find a Finnish example of designing stages of experience in Haahti and Komppula (2006).

Three other research papers make the link between experiences and travel behaviour. Chen and Petrick (2016) demonstrate how experiential benefits (e.g. to do exciting things or to experience new cultures) influence the travel behaviour of Americans. Bajs (2015) illustrates the relationship between tourist behaviour and perceived value based on the Croatian example of Dubrovnik. Sarra *et al.* (2015) evaluated the tourism experience according to the satisfaction of tourists in Lisbon.

Tourism demand

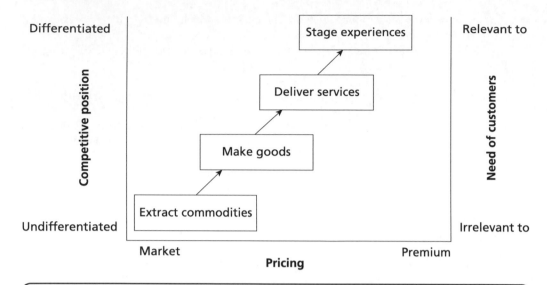

Figure 3.3 Economic differentiation and tourism value creation
Source: Pine and Gilmore, 1999

As well as the desire to experience something, there is also an increasing demand for animation and activity. Many tourists need to be encouraged to discover their own capacities and to develop them within the framework of holidays with a real content. That is why tourist 'animation' is very important. This can take different forms – movement, social life, creative activities, education and discovery, self-discovery, quietness, and adventure.

Increased quality-consciousness

Another trend can be summarized as the search for 'greater quality'. This fits in with the trend towards new forms of holidays. Increased quality does not mean more luxury, but what the Germans call *Erlebnistiefe* – holidays with meaning. Martin and Mason (1987) clearly emphasize this:

> Different types of people will make new and varied demands on the tourism products. For example: older people will look for better quality, and more secure surroundings while single people seek more social contact through tourism. In addition, there will be accompanying shifts in what people want out of their lives, which will affect their choices as tourists. Likely changes in attitude are:

● the development of greater awareness of the range of tourism choices available and demands for a higher standard of service and value for money from tourism operators and,
● growing concern about the quality of the tourism experience in all senses, including the nature of the facilities used, the state of the environment visited, and the health-enhancing (or detrimental) features of the activities undertaken.

The attraction of the countryside, quiet holidays with a content, holidays with attention to the environment and health, and visits to cultural cities are predominant trends. In the UK, the term 'green tourism' is a perfectly integrated concept that goes beyond 'rural tourism' (Green, 1990).

More experienced and educated holidaymakers

The holiday participation rates speak for themselves. One holiday per year has for a long time been a must for most people from developed countries. 'More experienced' does not only mean 'more quality-conscious', but also:

● An increased requirement for variety
● A greater desire for communication and personal attention on holiday
● The need for greater variety and choice
● More activity and adventure.

As well as having more experience, tourists are very often better educated than they were in the past.

Emerging tourism markets

The BRIC countries (Brazil, Russia, India and China) are emerging markets with a big potential demand. These markets can be seen in many destinations across the world. Cefalu (2006) speaks of 'Le fabuleux destin du marché émetteur Chinois' and Cooper *et al.* (2006) headline 'The Chinese tourism boom'. In 2005 more than 31 million Chinese travelled abroad (many to Hong Kong). It is interesting to note the following comment of Cooper *et al.*:

> Of a population of 1.3 billion, the number of Chinese with sufficient disposable income to engage in international tourism is estimated at some 50 million, mostly originating from the developed urban centres of Beijing, Shanghai and Guangzhou. A small increase of the share taking part in international tourism produces a very large increase in numbers.

There are also other new tourism-generating countries such as Indonesia, Malaysia, Mexico, Thailand, many former East-European countries and several countries from the Arabic world. Too many destinations underestimate the impact of the emerging markets on tourism demand. The best illustration can be found in Table 3.5. The market share of the top 15 destinations fell from 68 per cent in 1990 to 49 per cent in 2015 (see also UNWTO, 2011).

Monitoring source markets for destinations

The emerging markets make it even more difficult for any destination to make a choice among all the potential markets. For many reasons a destination cannot be operational in all these markets. All destination management organizations run short of marketing funds. Therefore a selection is forced. Choice of markets is also one of the most important features of a strategic marketing plan for a destination. Dwif-Consulting (Berlin), an organization with a long tradition in tourism research, developed a monitoring system for international markets (tourism destination index; DESTIX). They adapted and applied it for Berlin. This system is interesting because it is composed of four different types of indicators: (a) socio-economic indicators; (b) tourist indicators – Berlin; (c) tourist indicators – Germany; (d) dynamic indicators (see Table 3.9).

Such a system allows a destination management organization to rank the generating markets in different groups: A, B, C or D markets. A comparison of the results for Berlin between 2007 and 2010 shows significant movements between the distinguished groups. According to the destination the indicators can be changed and/or weighted in a different way. Certainly, one of them should be the seasonality of the tourism demand of the origin markets.

Table 3.9 Indicator and weighting system Berlin, 2010

Source: Feige (2010)

Socio-economic indicators	Weight (70 points)	Tourist indicators – Germany	Weight (70 points)
● Population	5	● Travel intensity of trips abroad	15
● GDP per capita	5	● Market share: trips to Germany/all trips abroad	20
● Discretionary income per capita	15	● Market share city trips	20
● Expenditure of private households for leisure, travel and culture	15	● Average expenditure per capita and day	15
● Human development index	5	**Dynamic indicators**	**Weight (70 points)**
● Media access (internet access)	10	● Population forecast 2015	5
● Unemployment rate	10	● Growth of GDP 2004–08	5
● Inflation	5	● Growth discretionary income 2004–08	5
		● Development of employment 2003–07	5
Tourist indicators – Berlin	**Weight (70 points)**	● Development of overnight stays in Berlin 2004–08 (%)	10
● Overnight stays from source market	30	● Development of overnight stays in Berlin 2004–08 (absolute numbers)	10
● Average length of stay	10	● Development of accessibility: non-stop air connections	10
● Distance	10	● Market estimation by German NTB	5
● Accessibility/non-stop air connections	10	● Market estimation by German Berlin TB	10
● Estimation of accessibility by experts	10		

Tourism demand worldwide

In 2015, according to WTO estimates, international tourist arrivals increased to 1,189 million whilst international tourism receipts reached €1,260 billion. An uninterrupted growth in international tourist arrivals has been witnessed during the second half of the 20th century, although the growth rate is declining (see Table 3.10).

The year 2001 was the first to show real stagnation (i.e. little decline) in international arrivals and receipts (expressed in €). In 2009 the impact of the financial and economic crisis is evident. The growth rate of about 4 per cent over the last decade (ignoring the year 2009) is still a good performance in comparison to most other sectors.

Over several decades, growth rates have proved to be resilient – at least on a global scale – to factors such as economic recession, variable exchange rates, terrorist activities and political unrest in many parts of the world (see Table 3.10, Figure 3.4). Of course, there has been a levelling off of movements due to specific circumstances, and the steady growth has slowed down or even declined on several occasions (1967–1968, 1973–1974, early 1980s, early 1990s and 2000s). The year 2009 was the first serious decline over more than five decades.

Looking now at tourism receipts, during the 1990s these grew in current US dollar terms at an average annual rate of 6.4 per cent. It is also important to emphasize that international tourism receipts at a global level have increased faster than other important export sectors. According to WTO–GATT–UNCTAD sources, the average annual percentage growth in current terms of tourism during the 1980s and 1990s was 9.6 per cent for tourism, 7.5 per cent for commercial services and 5.5 per cent for merchandise exports. During the period 2000–2008 tourism receipts grew worldwide by 9.1 per cent.

The financial crisis provoked a net decline in receipts of more than 8 per cent in 2009. Afterwards, receipts from international tourism recovered and grew up to 2014. The receipts were growing faster than the arrivals (see Figure 3.4), except for 2015. In the period 2005–2015 international tourism receipts grew by 6 per cent or 1 per cent more than the total export of goods and services.

Growth rates are very unequal across regions. For the period 2003–2009, the East Asia/Pacific region shows an annual growth rate of 10.0 per cent as opposed to 4.3 per cent for the Americas and 2.5 per cent for Europe. A logical consequence is a changed market share of the regions mentioned in Table 3.11; Europe and the Americas have been the losers and the East Asia/Pacific region is the great winner.

However, we must not wrongly interpret the evolution of market share. International tourism on a large scale started in the less developed world much later than in North America and Europe. All this is related to the later economic take-off in many developing countries. The result is a decrease in the market share of the Americas and Europe.

The very high market share of Europe can to a certain extent be attributed to the welfare level in Europe and the richness of tourist attractions. However, it is also important to take into account the fact that Europe is composed of a large number of small countries, which makes it favourable to international tourism. A trip of 300 km in several European countries is quite often a trans-border trip.

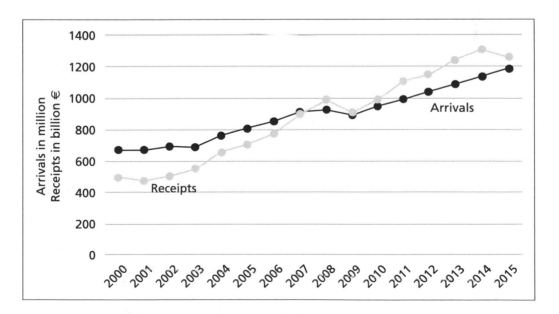

Figure 3.4 International tourist arrivals and receipts, 2000–2015

Table 3.10 Tourist arrivals and receipts from international tourism, 2000–2015

Source: UNWTO

Year	Arrivals (millions)	Receipts (billions of $)*
2000	674	495
2001	675	475
2002	696	504
2003	692	553
2004	764	657
2005	809	708
2006	855	777
2007	911	899
2008	928	989
2009	892	907
2010	951	989
2011	995	1,107
2012	1,042	1,149
2013	1,090	1,240
2014	1,137	1,309
2015	1,189	1,260

*Receipts can be strongly influenced by exchange rate fluctuations.

The WTO data in Table 3.12 is based on the UNWTO publication *Tourism Towards 2030: Global Overview* (2011). A distinction has been made between inter-regional (long-haul) and intra-regional travel. Although there are problems with forecasts for such a long period, four points should be noted:

1 The expected growth rate for the next two decades is much lower than the annual increase over the preceding two decades.
2 Europe registers a falling growth rate from about 4 to 2.3 per cent; the regions with a relatively strong growth rate are situated in Asia, Africa and the Middle East.
3 The market share of Europe in total inbound tourism is predicted to fall from 60 per cent to about 41 per cent.
4 Long-haul trips will represent about one-fifth of all international tourism in 2030. Over the period 2010–2030 long-haul travel worldwide will grow slightly faster, at 3.5 per cent per year, than the intra-regional travel (at 3.3 per cent). UNWTO forecasts 20 years ago revealed a much greater divergence in growth rate between long-haul and intra-regional travel. Consequently, the ratio between intra-regional and long-haul travel will shift from around 82:18 in 1995 to 79:21. In the WTO study *Tourism: 2020 Vision* the ratio for 2020 was still 76:24.

In future, arrivals will be more evenly spread over destinations. The difference in growth rates between sub-regions will produce a significant shift in their shares in the total of international

Table 3.11 International arrivals by region (millions), 1980–2015

Source: UNWTO

Region	1980	2000	2015	Annual growth rate 2010–2015* (%)	Market share	
					1980	2015
World	286	674	1,189	3.9	100.0	100.0
Africa	7	26	54	5.0	2.6	4.5
Americas	61	128	193	2.8	22.5	16.2
Asia/Pacific	23	110	279	6.4	8.2	23.5
Europe	186	387	607	3.0	64.1	51.1
Middle East	7	22	56	5.6	2.6	4.7

*Based on $(1 + (r)/100)^n$ or compound annual growth rate.

Table 3.12 Forecast inbound tourism by region, 1995–2030 (million arrivals)

Source: UNWTO database

Receiving region	Forecasts			Growth rate 2010–2030	Market share	
	1995	2010	2030		1995	2030
World	528	940	1809	3.3	100.0	100.0
Africa	19	50	134	5.0	3.6	7.4
Americas	109	150	248	2.6	20.7	13.7
Asia/Pacific	82	204	535	4.9	15.5	29.6
Europe	304	475	744	2.3	57.8	41.1
Middle East	14	61	149	4.6	2.6	8.2
Intra-regional	429	738	1403	3.3	82	79
Long-haul	99	202	405	3.5	18	21

tourist arrivals. As more and more destinations have been investing in tourism development, the traditional concentration of international tourist arrivals in a relatively few destinations will be further reduced. Almost all of the less visited sub-regions are gaining share at the expense of the most visited ones. By 2030, North East Asia will be the most visited sub-region, representing 16 per cent of total arrivals (up from 12 per cent in 2010), taking over from Southern and Mediterranean Europe, with a share of 18 per cent in 2010 (down to 15 per cent in 2030).

Holiday participation and holiday frequency

The net and gross holiday participation, also called net and gross travel propensity, are important indicators for tourism demand.

Net holiday participation

In Europe, several countries make a distinction between net holiday participation (four nights or more) and net short holiday participation (one to three nights – see Table 3.13). The net holiday participation refers to the percentage of the population who take at least one holiday (a tourism trip of four nights or more) in a period of one year, and is a measure of the penetration of holiday-taking among individuals in a population. In richer countries, the net holiday propensity varies between 60 and 80 per cent (see Table 3.13). The many travel constraints ensure that the net travel propensity never approaches 100 per cent; 80 per cent seems to be a ceiling. A comparison between national holiday surveys is not always possible. The applied definitions are very often unequal – are we talking of the total population, or only adults? In Norway, only the population in the age group 16–79 years is considered. What is the treatment of non-commercial holidays, such as visits to friends and relatives (VFR) and a (short) holiday in a second residence? How are business trips dealt with? The data in Tables 3.13 to 3.18 are based on the holiday surveys mentioned in Chapter 2. Annexe 3.1 shows the net participation rate of all EU countries (Eurostat, 2016). However, Eurostat applies another definition of net participation rate: the number of tourists, aged 15 or over, having made at least one holiday as a share of the total population. This definition is very unusual.

With respect to the data in Table 3.14, there is one feature that is notable. The net holiday propensity of the population of most countries listed has not increased over the past decade. In many European countries, net holiday participation is very stable and seems to have reached a ceiling.

Table 3.13 Net and gross (short) holiday participation in a number of European countries and USA, 2014* or 2015 (%)

Source: national holiday surveys; * = D.K. Shifflet, Travel performance/Monitor

Country	Net holiday participation	Gross holiday participation	Net short holiday participation	Gross short holiday participation[a]
Austria[c]	58.8	119.4	57.4	125.8
Belgium*	60.4	95.7	31.7[b]	50.4[b]
France[c]	66.3	192.3	52.4	204.3
Germany	77.1	100.0	56.6[f]	138.0
Netherlands[d]	73.0	140.2	41.0	80.5
Norway[e]	n.a.	208.1	n.a.	247.4
UK	n.a.	139.0	n.a.	n.a.
USA*	n.a.	142.0[g]	n.a.	390.6

[a] Should be handled with care
[b] Non-commercial short holidays excluded
[c] Population 15+ and year 2013
[d] Domestic VFR excluded
[e] Population aged 16–79
[f] 14–70 years
[g] Population 18+ ; concerns persons-stays and not holidays
*= 2014

Table 3.14 Net holiday propensity per country, 1990–2015

Source: national holiday surveys

	Austria	Belgium	France[a]	Germany[b]	Netherlands	Norway[c]	UK[d]
1990	45			69	70		
1991		61		67	71		60
1992				71	70		59
1993	45			75	71		61
1994		63		78	73		60
1995			68	78	72		61
1996	48	61	68	72	72		58
1997			66	74	72		57
1998		63	66	76	74		59
1999	50		66	75	74	76	55
2000	56	63	64	76	74	75	59
2001	54		64	76	74	76	60
2002	48[g]	59	66	75	74[e]	75	59
2003				77[f]	75	78	57
2004		60		74	75	77	60
2005	55		73	74	75	77	63
2006	63[e]	63	71	75	74	81	61
2007	59		69	75	74	78	n.a
2008	61	61	68	76	75	n.a	n.a
2009	59		68	76	75	n.a	n.a
2010	59	60	66	76	75	n.a	n.a
2011	60		66	76	76	n.a	n.a
2012	60	61	66	76	74	n.a	n.a
2013	59		66	78	74	n.a	n.a
2014	59	58		77	72	n.a	n.a
2015	59			77	73	n.a	n.a
2016	60			77			

[a] trips; population 15+
[b] 14 years and more
[c] 16–79 year-olds
[d] 16 years and older
[e] Not fully comparable with former years
[f] Increase due to methodological improvements
[g] From 2003, 15 years and older

Gross holiday participation

Gross holiday propensity (gross trip propensity) expresses the total number of holidays taken during a period of a year as a percentage of the total population. This is a measure of penetration of holidays, and not individual holidaymakers.

In several developed countries the gross propensity exceeds 100 per cent, and often approaches 130 and even 180. In other words, several people are taking two, three or more holidays a year.

Table 3.15 shows the gross holiday propensity for a number of European countries. Once again, the variability between European countries is great. The evolution, over the last decade, of gross travel propensity in Europe is very similar to that of the net propensity: stagnation for a number of years and a slow decrease for some countries in the recent past.

The same trend does not apply to the USA. The gross holiday propensity of Americans increased by 21 per cent in the last ten years. The gross holiday propensity for the USA is based on Shifflet data and is not comparable with European countries. Shifflet does not publish person-trip data. They publish person-days and person-stays data. The latter is a count of the number of stays Americans report. Each stay is a place where a travel party spent one or more nights. A person-trip might produce one stay of one or more nights or several stays if the visitors moved around. So the focus is on places visited rather than trips taken.

It might be questioned whether this stagnation or decline of holiday participation is compensated for by short holiday participation. Using available data, the answer to this question was affirmative until the beginning of this century. Later on there is no evidence (data for short holidays are in general less reliable than those for long holidays).

Simply dividing gross by net holiday propensity gives holiday frequency (travel frequency) – in other words, the average number of trips taken by those participating in tourism during the period in question. The European countries in Table 3.16 show great differences in holiday frequency, with a range of 1.3–2.9 holidays per year.

This travel frequency has been relatively stable over the last decade, with only Austria and the UK being slight exceptions. We have no explanation for the low holiday frequency for the German population.

The foregoing indicators all neglect the duration of a holiday. If this is taken into account, 'night participation', or the number of nights (short and long holidays) spent on holiday during one year per 100 inhabitants, makes sense. Applying this to Belgium, France, the Netherlands and the USA shows different trends per country and over time. The absolute number of nights for the four countries cannot be compared; for Belgium, non-commercial, second and short holidays are not taken into account. In Belgium, there is a slight shift from commercial to non-commercial nights.

In Europe there is a strong tendency towards shorter holidays (short holidays have a very stable duration), and there is evidence for this phenomenon in precise data for Belgium, France, Germany and the Netherlands (see Table 3.18). The US average duration time (average per stay; one leisure trip might include multiple stays) is not comparable with the data for the European countries. We notice a rather low average duration time for American holidays. This might be compensated for by a high short holiday propensity. Indeed, the number of person-stays increased from 866 million in 2006 to 1,251 million in 2015. There is a stable average duration of holidays during the recent past in the USA.

Seasonality

Seasonality patterns

Within most patterns of demand in tourism, there are regular fluctuations due solely to the time of the year. This is traditionally called 'seasonality'. In Chapter 1 we noted that seasonality is a typical economic characteristic of tourism, and the reasons for these annual fluctuations

Table 3.15 Gross holiday propensity per country, 1990–2015

Source: national holiday surveys; * = D.K. Shifflet, Travel performance/Monitor

Year	Austria	Belgium	France[a]	Germany	Netherlands	Norway[c]	UK[d]	USA*
1990	67			87[b]	117			
1991		97		84	120		118	
1992				92	117		118	
1993	70			101	123		122	
1994		100		107	126		127	
1995			171	103	124		129	
1996	74	96	172	97	128		117	
1997			158	98	124		123	
1998		96	158	100	129		121	
1999	79		151	98	130	159	116	
2000	86	99	155	98	126	152	126	
2001	82		154	99	131	150	128	
2002	76	95	159	98	147[e]	160	125	
2003	120[g]			103[f]	144	166	123	
2004	117	95		101	148	177	109	
2005	110		190	99	144	177	110	
2006	127	99	186	99	145	179	102	117[h]
2007	125		185	97	144	166	119	120
2008	123	102	177	99	146	202	116	117
2009	132		176	100	146	191	n.a	112
2010	129	96	172	99	148	209	n.a	121
2011	124		179	99	142	203	n.a	130
2012	132	99	186	99	140	206	n.a	136
2013	129		192	101	143	226	n.a	140
2014	122	95	n.a	100	139	224	n.a	144
2015	119		n.a	100	140	208	n.a	142
2016	130	n.a	n.a	99	n.a	n.a	n.a	n.a

[a] Personal trips; population 15 +
[b] 14 years and more
[c] 16–79 year-olds
[d] 16 years and older
[e] Not fully comparable with former years
[f] Increase due to methodological improvements
[g] Before 2003 total population; from 2003, 15 years and older and other survey method
[h] Population 18 years and older

Table 3.16 Holiday frequency in some European countries, 1990–2014
Source: national holiday surveys

	1990	2002	2008	2014
Austria	1.5	1.6	2.0	2.0
Belgium	1.6	1.6	1.7	1.6
France	2.5*	2.3	2.6	2.9**
Germany	1.3	1.3	1.3	1.3
Netherlands	1.7	2.0	2.0	1.9
UK (2006)	1.9	2.2	1.7	n.a

* = 1995
** = 2013

Table 3.17 'Night participation' in some countries, 1990–2015
Source: national holiday surveys; * = D.K. Shifflet, Travel performance/Monitor

Year	Belgium	France	The Netherlands	USA*
1990	13.0	n.a.	15.0	n.a.
1996	12.2	16.9	15.5	n.a.
2000	12.5	15.6	16.0	13.2
2002	11.9	15.9	17.0	13.0
2008	12.2	19.5	16.9	13.7
2010	11.5	17.3	16.4	14.1
2012	11.5	17.5	16.4	15.9
2014	11.4	17.9[a]	16.6	16.7
2015			17.0	17.0

[a]= 2013

were indicated – climate; institutional factors that are culturally specific such as the organization of school holidays in the generating markets, Christmas holidays and the 'Golden Week' in China and Japan; organization of annual paid leave and psychological pressure. Chapter 1 also revealed the impact of seasonality for tourists, tourism supply and public authorities.

The Gini coefficient (GC) is considered to be the best statistical instrument to measure seasonality. It measures the degree of inequality in the number of holidays across the months of the year. It is derived from the Lorenz curve, which displays the cumulative frequency of ranked observations starting from the lowest number. The GC is equal to the area between the Lorenz curve and the 45-degree line divided by the whole area below the line (Koenig and Bischoff, 2003). The GC is sensitive to the changes that take place in the months with demand close to the average (Duro, 2016). The GC is calculated with the following formula:

$$GC = 1 + \left[\frac{1}{n}\right] - \left[\frac{2}{n^2 \cdot \hat{x}}\right] \cdot (x_1 + 2x_2 + 3x_3 + \cdots + nx_n) \tag{3.5}$$

Table 3.18 Average duration of holidays (4+ nights)

Source: national holiday surveys; * = D.K. Shifflet, Travel performance/Monitor

Average duration of holidays (nights)	Belgium	Germany	The Netherlands	France	USA*
1982	15.5				
1988	14.1	16.0	12.2		
1990	13.0	15.8	11.8		
1996	11.5	13.8	11.3	10.3	
2002	11.3	13.5	11.0	9.7	
2008	11.1	12.5	10.7	9.2	
2010	10.9	12.2	n.a	8.2	6.2
2012	10.5	12.6	n.a	7.5	6.2
2014	10.9	12.5	n.a	7.5[a]	6.1
2016		12.6	n.a	n.a	6.3[b]

[a] = 2013; [b] = 2015

where

n = number of observations (12 in case of monthly data)
$\hat{x}$ = the mean of observations (average number of holidays)
$x_1, x_2, \dots \dots x_n$ are individual observations in decreasing order

GC can take values between 0 and 1; the lower the number the less seasonality.

The decomposition of the Gini index eases the identification of segments with similar characteristics from the point of view of their effects on seasonal concentration. This is sometimes helpful in marketing efforts (Fernández-Morales *et al.*, 2016; Duro, 2016).

The GC is not the only seasonality measure in tourism. Other statistical tools to measure the concentration of tourism demand are:

- Theil index (this is more sensitive to changes in the months with lower demand)
- Coefficient variation
- Seasonal ratio (max_t / min_t)
- Seasonal range ($max_t - min_t$)
- Coefficient variation
- Concentration index.

The seasonality pattern is highly influenced by the method of measurement:

- The measurement unit – holidays (arrivals) or nights
- Whether it includes just holidays (i.e. of four nights or more) or all holidays including short holidays
- To what extent business travel is taken into account
- Whether the pattern is based on the month of departure or the month of return
- Whether it is from the origin point of view (e.g. the British holidaymakers) or destination point of view (e.g. holidays in Wales). Taking the origin point of view (see holiday surveys), the ideal method consists of attributing the holiday nights to the month in which they take

place. In measuring the seasonality of the population of a particular country, this supposes knowledge of the date of departure and date of return of each individual holidaymaker of that country.

Seasonality of the taken holidays varies greatly from country to country (see Table 3.19). The share of the high season months is a good indicator. Besides the factors mentioned in Chapter 1, national traditions are responsible for a local pattern. Italian holidaymakers show an extremely high concentration in the month of August. On the other hand, British and German holidays are far less concentrated in the summer months. From that point of view, British and German tourists form an interesting customer group in terms of staggering of holidays.

Figures 3.5 and 3.6 show the staggering of holidays and short holidays in Belgium. Belgium provides comparable data for a long period. The difference between the figures is as expected, but in both types of holiday the summer period is dominant – albeit more markedly so for holidays than for short trips. The most striking point, however, is the growing trend towards increased staggering of holidays as well as of short breaks. Although the share of the July–August period is decreasing for both holidays and short trips, the 'winner' periods are slightly different for both types. This evolution for Belgium (which applies to other countries as well) is mainly due to a greater fragmentation of holidays. The spectacular growth of short breaks has been a further stimulus for greater staggering of the total holiday pattern. Besides these elements, changes in the regulation of school holidays and the growing influence of early retirement have encouraged a wider spread of tourism demand.

Belgium is an example where greater staggering would be welcome. Many other countries show an even greater concentration of tourism demand, and this implies that further staggering is necessary. Several countries are making great efforts to stimulate this, and solutions should tackle the causes of concentration.

Table 3.19 Share of the high season months July–August in total tourism nights, 2014

Source: Eurostat

Country*	Share of the months July–August in total tourism nights (%)
Belgium	41.3
Czech Republic	38.0
Denmark	35.5
Germany	26.6
Spain	37.6
France	37.1
Italy	50.5
Netherlands	32.9
Austria	33.8
Poland	40.8
Finland	23.9
Sweden	25.7
United Kingdom	26.2
Switzerland **	28.6

*EU countries with more than 100 million nights
** EFTA/EEA country

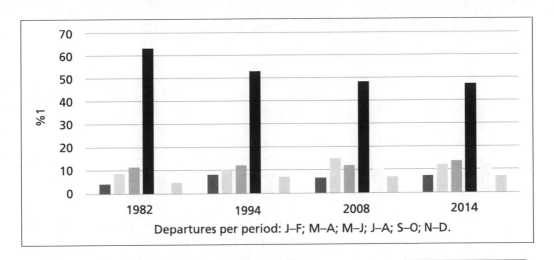

Figure 3.5 Staggering of holidays among the Belgian population based on month of departure, 1982–2014

Source: WES

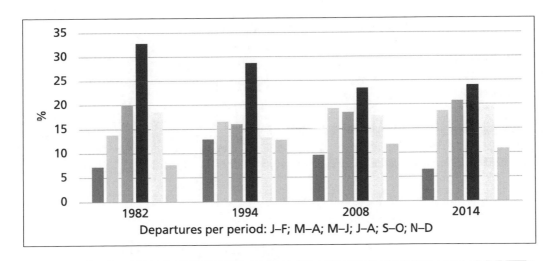

Figure 3.6 Staggering of short holidays among the Belgian population based on month of departure, 1982–2014

Source: WES

Improving holiday staggering: possible instruments and policy recommendations

Climate will not change in the short run, although some tourism firms have been successful with their indoor recreation facilities or 'all weather leisure centres' (e.g. Center Parcs in several European destinations, The Sandcastle Centre in Blackpool, the Cascades in Portsmouth, Butlin's Worlds' covered pool complexes) in attracting people in off-season periods.

The reorganization of school holidays is a possible policy instrument. The best-known example is the German case. Based on long-term planning, the country is divided into zones (each of one *Land* or a combination of *Länder*) with different dates for the beginning and end of the summer (and other) holiday periods. Between the zones there exists a rotation system (*das rollierende System der Ferienregelung*). Although less obvious, there are similar initiatives in France and the Netherlands. This instrument is the most effective stimulus for increasing staggering. By defining the zones, it is possible for all members of the same family to take a holiday at the same time. There are no global solutions; each country should take initiatives in the direction of better staggering.

Improving staggering of holidays requires a two-pronged approach related to 'can' (or ability) and 'want' (or willingness) – see the 'Noordwijk' conference organized by the Dutch government in 1991 (Ministerie van Economische Zaken, 1991). 'Can' includes people who can take a holiday at whatever time they like. They are not prevented from going on holiday by poor health or disability, and are not restricted for financial reasons or by school or work regulations. Whether people *want* to go on holiday outside the peak season depends on a number of factors:

- Whether the type of holiday product they want is available (e.g. snow).
- Whether the holiday facilities are available at an affordable price.
- Whether the potential holidaymaker is aware of the opportunities.
- Whether holidaymakers believe they will meet other people on holiday at the same time (a deserted resort is not very attractive).

From the destination point of view three different types of strategies can be applied to stagger holidays in the destination countries. All three strategies can and should be combined. The first strategy is supply-oriented and can take several different forms:

- Creation of the right vacation atmosphere in the off-peak periods. Local authorities and the tourism sector can do a lot to create the conditions that allow for better seasonal spread.
- Improvement of product supply (creating off-season products) in off-peak periods, and year-round attractions.
- Organization of events at a high level.
- Greater animation in off-peak periods.
- Creation of all-weather facilities.
- Obligation of air carriers, especially tour-operator carriers and low-budget carriers, to organize a minimum of flights in the off-peak season (e.g. Malta regulation) at risk of losing slots in high season.
- Introduction of the 'summer time' period (as in European countries). Extra daylight in the mornings is of less use to tourists than longer evenings.
- Stimulation of timesharing. Destinations with a good timesharing have a longer tourism season.

The second strategic line focusses on the demand side:

- The choice of origin markets with better staggering of holidays is very important (see Table 3.19). All things being equal, some origin markets are much more attractive in terms of the staggering of holidays than others.
- Many destinations concentrate on a small number of market segments. To reduce seasonality there is a need to change the customer mix by attracting new market segments (Andriotis, 2005).
- Promotion of off-peak periods.
- Attention paid to new market segments (MICE, special-interest tourists, incentive travellers).
- Special activities with the travel trade – tour operators and travel agencies.
- Promotional activities for families with children.
- Promotional activities for those aged 60+.

A specific price policy is a third possible strategy:

- Application of marginal pricing in the off-peak periods (see Chapter 5). A minimum requirement in the off-peak season is to cover the variable costs.
- Price differentiation, or lower prices in shoulder and off-peak periods.
- Discounts for young families with children and special offers for those aged 60+.

A combination of the quoted strategies and measures should lead to:

- Better use of accommodation.
- Less traffic congestion and fewer traffic accidents.
- Reduced overcrowding, leading to greater enjoyment.
- Higher standards of service.
- Price moderation during high season.
- Less damage to the environment.
- More interesting jobs in the tourism sector.
- Less over booking.

The population of tourism destinations – employers and employees –should be aware that five months of hard work is no longer the right attitude. The present situation is in some destinations stimulated by the social security system and/or the insufficient difference between income from work and the benefits paid to unemployed people. In some countries people work in tourism during the tourism season and in agriculture (or other seasonal activities) in the off-season.

With the expected further growth of tourism demand, increased staggering of holidays is the greatest challenge for demand management in the tourism sector in general in the next decade.

References and further reading

Akay, G., Cifter, A., and Teke, O. (2017). Turkish tourism, exchange rates and income. *Tourism Economics, 23 (1)*.

Andriotis, K. (2005). Seasonality in Crete: problem or the way of life? *Tourism Economics, 2.*

Bajs, I. (2015). Tourist perceived value, relationship to satisfaction, and behavioral intentions: the example of the Croatian tourist destination Dubrovnik. *Journal of Travel Research, 54 (1)*.

Baker, D.M. (2014). The effects of terrorism on travel and tourism industry. *International Journal of Religious Tourism and Pilgrimage, 2.*

Baum, T. (1995). Trends in international tourism. *Insights*, March.

Becken, S., and Lennox, J. (2012). Implications of a long-term increase in oil prices for tourism. *Tourism Management, 33.*

Buhalis, D., and Costa, C. (eds) (2006). *Tourism Business Frontiers*. London: Elsevier.

Buhalis, D., and Costa, C. (eds) (2006). *Tourism Management Dynamics*. London: Elsevier.

Buigut, S., and Amendah, D. (2016). Effect of terrorism on demand for tourism in Kenya. *Tourism Economics, 22 (2).*

Burkart, A.J., and Medlik, S. (1981). *Tourism: Past, Present and Future*, 2nd edn. Oxford: Heinemann.

CBS (2016). *Trendrapport toerisme, recreatie en vrije tijd*. Den Haag: NRIT Media.

Cefalu, F. (2006). Le fabuleux destin du marché émetteur Chinois. *Espaces, 237.*

Chen, C., and Petrick, J. (2016). the roles of perceived travel benefits, importance, and constraints in predicting travel behaviour. *Journal of Travel Research, 55 (4).*

Cheng, K., Kim, H., and Thompson, H. (2013). The exchange rate and US tourism trade, 1973–2007. *Tourism Economics, 19 (4).*

Chi, J. (2015). Dynamic impacts of income and the exchange rate on US tourism, 1960–2011. *Tourism Economics, 21 (5).*

Clark, C. (2000). Changes in leisure time: the impact on tourism. *Insights*, January.

Cleverdon, R. (1990). *Tourism in the Year 2000: Qualitative Aspects Affecting Global Growth*. Discussion paper. Madrid: WTO.

Cockerell, N. (1997). Urban tourism in Europe. *Travel & Tourism Analyst, 6.*

Cooper, C., Fletcher, J., Gilbert, D., and Wanhill, S. (1993). *Tourism Principles and Practice*. London: Pitman Publishing.

Cooper, C., Scott, N., and Kester, J. (2006). New and emerging markets. In D. Buhalis and C. Costa (eds), *Tourism Business Frontiers*. London: Elsevier.

Crouch, G. (1992). Effect of income and price on international tourism. *Annals of Tourism Research, 19.*

Crouch, G. (1993). Currency exchange rates and the demand for international tourism. *Journal of Tourism Studies, 2.*

Crouch, G., Oppewal, H., Huybers, T., Dolnicar, S., Louviere, J., and Devinney, T. (2007). Discretionary Expenditure and tourism consumption: insights from a choice experiment. *Journal of Travel Research, 45.*

Culiuc, A. (2014). Determinants of international tourism. International Monetary Fund (IMF) *Working Paper, No WP/14/82*, Washington, DC: International Monetary Fund.

Cuvelier, P. (2000). La fin du tourisme fordiste. *Espaces*, Décembre.

De Cantis, S., and Ferrante, M. (2011). Measuring Seasonality: Performance of Accommodation Establishments in Sicily Through the Analysis of Occupancy Rates. In A. Matias, P. Nijkamp and M. Sarmento (eds), *Tourism Economics. Impact Analysis*. Heidelberg: Physica-Verlag.

De Voldere, I. (2009). *Study on the Competitiveness of the EU tourism industry*. Rotterdam: ECORYS.

Duro, J. (2016). Seasonality of hotel demand in the main Spanish provinces: Measurements and decomposition exercises. *Tourism Management, 52.*

Dwyer, L., Forsyth, P., and Rao, P. (2000). The price competitiveness of travel and tourism: a comparison of 19 destinations. *Tourism Management, 21.*

Economist Intelligence Unit (1995). Real exchange rates and international demand. *Travel & Tourism Analyst, Occasional Studies, 4.*

Fayed, H., and Fletcher, J. (2002). Globalisation of economic activity: issues for tourism. *Tourism Economics, 2.*

Fayos-Solá, E. (1996). Tourism policy: a midsummer night's dream? *Tourism Management, 6.*

Feige, M. (2010). *Long-term International Monitoring in Tourism*. Vienna: TRC meeting, DWIF-Consulting.

Fernández-Morales, A., Cisneros-Martinez, J., and McCabe, S. (2016). Seasonal concentration of tourism demand: decomposition analysis and marketing implications. *Tourism Management*, 56.

Fletcher, J., and Westlake, J. (2006). Globalisation. In L. Dwyer and P. Forsyth (eds), *International Handbook on the Economics of Tourism*. Cheltenham: Edward Elgar.

Frechtling, D. (2001). World population and standard of living: implications for international tourism. In A. Lockwood and S. Medlik (eds), *Tourism and Hospitality in the 21st Century*. Oxford: Butterworth-Heinemann.

Goeldner, C., and Ritchie, B. (2003). *Tourism Principles, Practice, Philosphies*, 9th edn. New York: John Wiley.

Green, S. (1990). The future of green tourism. *Insights*, September.

Gunter, U., and Netto, A. (2016). International travel to and from Brazil – overseas tourism as a luxury good and a status symbol. *Tourism Economics*, 22 (5).

Gunter, U., and Smeral, E. (2016). The decline of tourism income elasticities in a global context. *Tourism Economics*, 22 (3).

Gunter, U., and Smeral, E. (2017). European outbound tourism in times of economic stagnation. *International Journal of Tourism Research*, 1.

Haahti, A., and Komppula, R. (2006). Experience design in tourism. In D. Buhalis and C. Costa (eds), *Tourism Business Frontiers*. London: Elsevier.

Hawkins, R.E. (1994). Ecotourism: opportunities for developing countries. In W. Theobald (ed.), *Global Tourism. The Next Decade*. London: Butterworth-Heinemann.

Holloway, J.C. (1992). *The Business of Tourism*, 3rd edn. London: Pitman.

Imm, S., Chia, K., Ho, J., and Ramachandran, S. (2017). Seeking tourism sustainability – A case of Tioman Island. *Tourism Management*, 58.

Jarvis, D., Stoeckl, N., and Liu, H. (2016). The impact of economic, social and environmental factors on trip satisfaction and the likelihood of visitors returning. *Tourism Management*, 52.

Koenig, N., and Bischoff, E. (2003). Seasonality of tourism in Wales: a comparative analysis. *Tourism Economics*, 3.

Krippendorf, J. (1987). *The Holidaymakers: Understanding the Impact of Leisure and Travel*. London: Butterworth-Heinemann.

Li, S., and Song, H. (2015). Economic impacts of visa restrictions on tourism: a case of two events in China. *Annals of Tourism Research*, 43.

Liu, A., and McKercher, B. (2016). The impact of visa liberalization on tourist behaviors – the case of China outbound market visiting Hong Kong. *Journal of Travel Research*, 55 (5).

Lockwood, A., and Medlik, S. (2001). *Tourism and Hospitality in the 21st Century*. Oxford: Butterworth-Heinemann.

Lohmann, M. (2017). Worried respondents and cool tourists: reported impacts of terror threats and factual destinations choice patterns. *Paper presented at the 52nd TRC Meeting*. Lisbon.

López Morales, J., and Such Devesa, M. (2017). Business cycle and external dependence on tourism: evidence for Spain. *Tourism Economics*, 23 (1).

Martin, W.H., and Mason, S. (1987). Social trends and tourism futures. *Tourism Management*, June.

Martins, L., Gan, Y., and Ferreira-Lopes, A. (2017). An empirical analysis of the influence of macroeconomic determinants on World tourism demand. *Tourism Management*, 61.

Middleton, V.T.C. (1991). Whither the package tour? *Tourism Management*, September.

Middleton, V.T.C., with Clarke, J. (2001). *Marketing in Travel and Tourism*, 3rd edn. Oxford: Butterworth-Heinemann.

Middleton, V.T.C., Fyall, A., Morgan, M., and Ranchhod, A. (2009) *Marketing in Travel and Tourism*, 4th edn. Oxford: Butterworth-Heinemann.

Mihalic, T. (2006). Nature-based products, ecotourism and adventure tourism. In D. Buhalis and C. Costa (eds), *Tourism Business Frontiers*. London: Elsevier.

Ministerie van Economische Zaken. (1991). *Improving Seasonal Spread of Tourism*. Noordwijk.

Morlotti, C., Cattaneo, M., Malighetti, P., and Redondi, R. (2017). Multi-dimensional price elasticity for leisure and business destinations in the low-cost air transport market: evidence from EasyJet. *Tourism Management, 61*.

Moscardo, G. (2006). Third-age tourism. In D. Buhalis and C. Costa (eds), *Tourism Business Frontiers*. London: Elsevier.

Müller, H. (2001). Tourism and hospitality into the 21st century. In A. Lockwood and S. Medlik (eds), *Tourism and Hospitality in the 21st Century*. Oxford: Butterworth-Heinemann.

Müller, H., and Scheurer, R. (2005). *Tourismus Destinationen als Erlebniswelt – Ein Leitfaden zur Angebots-Inszenierung*. Bern: FIF-Verlag.

NRIT (2003). *Trendrapport toerisme, recreatie en vrije tijd, 2002–2003*. Breda: NRIT.

Pham, T., Jago, L., Spurr, R., and Marshall, J. (2015). The Dutch Disease effects on tourism – The case of Australia. *Tourism Management, 46*.

Pine, B., and Gilmore, J. (1999). *The Experience Economy*. Boston: Harvard Business School Press.

Poon, A. (1993). *Tourism, Technology and Competitive Strategies*. Wallingford: C.A.B International.

Santana-Gellego, M., Ledesma-Rodriguez, F., and Pérez-Rodriguez, J. (2010). Echange rate regimes and tourism. *Tourism Economics, 16 (1)*.

Sarra, A., Zio, S., and Cappucci, M. (2015). A quantitative valuation of tourist experience in Lisbon. *Annals of Tourism Research, 53*.

Seetaram, N., Forsyth, P., and Dwyer, L. (2016). Measuring price elasticities of demand for outbound tourism using competitiveness indices. *Annals of Tourism Research, 56*.

Shaw, G., and Williams, A. (2004). *Tourism and Tourism Spaces*. London: Sage.

Smeral, E. (2012). International tourism demand and the business cycle. *Annals of Tourism Research, 39 (1)*.

Smith, S. (1997). *Tourism Analysis: A Handbook*, 2nd edn. Edinburgh: Longman.

Song, H., and Lin, S. (2009). Impacts of the financial and economic crisis on tourism in Asia. *Journal of Travel Research*, December.

Stäblein, F. (1994). School holidays. Presentation of an experience: rolling system of school holidays. *Conference on Staggering of Holidays*, Düsseldorf (unpublished Conference document).

Taylor, T., and Ortiz, R. (2009). Impacts of climate change on domestic tourism in the UK. *Tourism Economics, 4*.

Thompson, A., and Thompson, H. (2010) The exchange rate, euro switch and tourism revenue in Greece. *Tourism Economics, 16 (3)*.

Todd, G. (2001). World travel and tourism today. In A. Lockwood and S. Medlik (eds), *Tourism and Hospitality in the 21st Century*. Oxford: Butterworth-Heinemann.

Vanhove, N. (1997). Mass tourism – benefits and costs. In J. Pigram and S. Wahab (eds), *Tourism Sustainability and Growth*. London: Routledge.

Vanhove, N. (2001). Globalisation of tourism demand, global distribution systems and marketing. In S. Wahab and C. Cooper (eds), *Tourism in the Age of Globalisation*. London: Routledge.

Viner, D., and Nicholls, S. (2006). Climate change and its implications for internationl tourism. In D. Buhalis and C. Costa (eds), *Tourism Management Dynamics*. London: Elsevier.

WTO (1998). *Tourism: 2020 Vision*. Madrid: WTO.

WTO (1999). *Changes in Leisure Time: The Impact on Tourism*. Madrid: WTO.

UNWTO (2007). *A Practical Guide to Tourism Destination Management*. Madrid: UNWTO.

UNWTO (2011). *Tourism Towards 2030: Global Overview*. Madrid: UNWTO.

UNWTO (2017). *World Tourism Barometer*. Madrid: UNWTO.

Appendix 3.1

> **Table 3.20** Net holiday participation and net short holiday participation in EU countries, 2015
> Source: Eurostat

Country	Net short holiday participation*	Net holiday participation**
EU	40***	48***
Belgium	32	51
Bulgaria	16	22
Czech Republic	68	61
Denmark	43	73
Germany	68	63
Estonia	52	41
Ireland	47	55
Greece	12	30
Spain	45	47
France	49***	63***
Cyprus	34	53
Latvia	47	29
Lithuania	30	28
Luxembourg	58	75
Hungary	40	36
Malta	22	38
Netherlands	53	71
Austria	57	58
Poland	38	36
Portugal	28***	26***
Romania	15***	10***
Slovenia	31	52
Finland	83	69
Sweden	40***	49***
United Kingdom	n.a.	n.a.
Norway	72***	n.a.

*Number of tourists, aged 15 or over, having made at least one short holiday/ as share of total population
** Number of tourists, aged 15 or over, having made at least one holiday/ as share of total population
*** 2014

Chapter 4

Tourism supply

Tourism supply in the tourism system

The 'tourism system' is an expression often used but seldom precisely defined. The reason is quite evident. Tourism is a complex phenomenon: there are many different actors, and demand and supply are geographically separated whereas production and consumption take place on the same spot. A tourism system can be defined as a framework that shows the interaction between tourism supply at the destination, the bridging elements between supply and demand, and tourism demand (see Figure 4.1). The relationship between demand and supply, via the bridging elements, is a two-way link. In the tourism system, the supply at the destination is the key element.

Suppliers provide the basic elements that together form the overall visitor experience (Ritchie and Crouch, 2003). However, according to these authors there are many resources or factors that are required by tourism and hospitality enterprises – far more than the elements cited in Figure 4.1. For them, labour is a key factor. Other supply factors include food and beverage producers, local crafts, and manufacturers of equipment (such as amusement park rides, camping equipment, etc.).

Suppliers are connected to tourists through tourism marketing channels consisting mainly of intermediaries (tour operators, retail trade, meeting and convention planners, etc.) and facilitators, who assist in the efficient functioning of the tourism system (e.g. flow of information, marketing, money, knowledge). Other bridging elements include the different transportation modes.

The third component of the tourism system is the customer. There is competition to serve customer needs, and it is that competition that governs the actions of the travel trade. As discussed previously, tourists are not a homogeneous group of individual travellers. There is a great variety of tourism motivations, and the range of tourism segments has exploded over the last two decades.

Supply components

First, let us consider some supply elements in more detail. Without *attractions* there is no tourism. They are the key element of the tourism system, with the ability to draw people to destinations. The attractions can be of a very varied nature and are classified into three major groups:

1 Primary natural attractions
2 Primary man-made attractions
3 Purpose-built attractions.

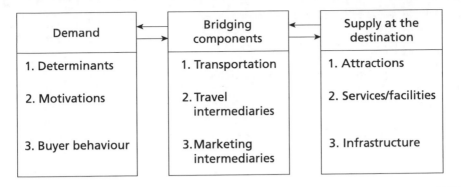

Figure 4.1 Components of the tourism system

Natural attractions include:

- Climate
- Beaches
- Landscape
- Fauna and flora
- Waterfalls
- Lakes
- Mountains.

Primary man-made attractions were not built or conceived for tourism purposes, but they have the capability to attract travellers. They can be subdivided into three groups:

1 Built attractions

- architecture (historic and modern buildings)
- cathedrals, churches, mosques
- abbeys
- monuments
- castles
- promenades
- archaeological sites
- natural parks
- indoor resorts
- gardens and parks
- leisure centres
- shopping malls
- sports stadia.

2 Cultural attractions

- museums
- theatres and sports
- art and crafts
- religion
- history
- folklore

- carnivals and other entertainment
- festivals.

3 Social attractions

- way of life of the destination's population
- ethnic groups
- language.

Purpose-built attractions were constructed or conceived especially for tourism purposes, and include:

- Theme parks
- Ski tracks
- Marinas
- Festivals
- Events
- Spas.

According to the scope, a distinction is made between three main groups. The first group consists of the 'longer-stay focussed attractions', which have the ability to attract people to a destination for several days or more; beach destinations are a typical example. These attractions should have sufficient appeal or variety of attractive components to satisfy tourists for some time. The second group consists of the 'touring circuit attractions', consisting of a combination of several attractions – not necessarily of the same kind – in different locations. Typical examples include Classical Greece, historical Egypt, Italian art cities, the cherry-blossom tour in Japan, the Canadian Rockies, cruise tours and many others. The third group consists of stopover destinations, which are interesting places to visit on the way to primary destinations. A typical example is a visit to Beaune on the way to destinations in the south of France.

The next component of tourism supply is the *tourism services/facilities*, also referred to as the 'superstructure' (Goeldner *et al.*, 2000). While attractions draw visitors away from home, facilities are a *sine qua non* to serve these visitors away from home. They support the tourism development rather than induce it. '*L'hôtel ne fait pas le tourisme*' (meaning 'tourism cannot be based on hotel facilities alone') is a well-known expression of K. Krapf, one of the pioneers of tourism research, and indeed good accommodation and/or restaurant services are not a guarantee of successful tourism. However, a lack of facilities will make it impossible to harvest the benefits of tourism development.

The main component of tourism facilities is the accommodation sector. For successful tourism, accommodations must be available in sufficient quantity and quality to match the demand of travellers who arrive at the destination. Given access, accommodations should precede any other type of development. Accommodations can be subdivided into commercial (hotels, motels, hostels, boarding houses, bed-and-breakfasts, cruise ships, shelters, lodges, farm-based facilities, and self-catering facilities such as camping, rented apartments/cottages/houses, Airbnb and holiday villages) and non-commercial services (second residences, mobile homes, visits to relatives and friends, and house exchange schemes). Many of these accommodation types can be further subdivided into classes based on the quality, facilities and the available services. Most countries support a hotel classification system, although there is still no worldwide accepted system; there is not even a system at regional levels (although the Benelux system is an exception). In some countries, efforts have been made to classify camping and rented apartments or villas.

Beside accommodations, there is a need in any destination for food and beverage services (restaurants, cafés, bars, etc.). Together with accommodation, these represent an important share – quite often more than 40 per cent – of tourism expenditure.

Many further services are required by the traveller. There is a wide variety of other facilities, including shops, health services, pharmacies, banks, hairdressers, theatres, casinos, cinemas, garages, sport and leisure services, etc., that serve the tourist as well as the resident population (see the TSA in Chapter 2).

Infrastructure is the third pillar of tourism supply. Traditionally, a distinction is made between transport infrastructure at the destination, and public utilities. The major elements of the first group are roads, railways, transport services for sightseeing tours, airports, cruise terminals, harbours, local transport networks, taxis and parking facilities. It is also impossible for a destination to function without the necessary public utilities – electricity, water supply, health care, communication networks, sewage, waste disposal, water treatment, etc. Although we tend to view these utilities as evident necessities, unfortunately not all destinations have them, and both the local population and tourists have to share the same lack of services.

In contrast to the two other supply components, the infrastructure does not provide receipts but costs. As Chapter 12 will demonstrate, these costs must be measured against the benefits of tourism development. Of course, infrastructure facilities are seldom developed for tourists alone; the local population also needs a water supply, electricity, telecommunications, etc.

There is another description of the supply components in the UNWTO (2007) *A Practical Guide to Tourism Destination Management*. This publication distinguishes six basic elements of a tourist destination:

- Attractions
- Public and private amenities
- Accessibility
- Human resources
- Image and character
- Price.

Three of these elements differ from the classical approach: human resources, image and character, and price. From a destination point of view they are important. A unique character or image is crucial in attracting visitors to the destination. It is not sufficient to have a good range of attractions and amenities if potential visitors are not aware of this. The image of the destination includes uniqueness, sights, scenes, environmental quality, safety, service levels, and the friendliness of people. Price is another supply component. That is the reason why pricing is dealt with in the supply chapter. Pricing is an important aspect of the destination's competition with other destinations. Price factors relate to the cost of transport to and from the destination as well as the cost on the ground of accommodation, attractions, food and tour services. Last but not least, human resources are important. Tourism is labour intensive and interaction with local communities is an important aspect of the tourism experience. A well-trained tourism workforce and citizens who are equipped and aware of the benefits and responsibilities associated with tourism growth are indispensable elements of tourism destination delivery. Accessibility is part of the bridging components.

Bridging components

The bridging elements of the tourism system are very often considered as an extension of tourism supply. This is quite evident for the transport infrastructure, such as highways, roads, railways, air and sea connections, and marketing intermediaries. It is less obvious for the travel trade. Tour operators and travel agencies are based in the generating markets (although this is of course not the case for incoming tour operators), and provide an essential link between supply and demand. All tour operators, however, make agreements with supply firms at the destination, and most either have many staff working in the receiving destinations or make use of the services of an incoming tour operator to support their customers at the destination.

Visa requirements are also a part of the accessibility element. They are a real constraint for tourism development in countries which require a visa as an entry condition.

Tourism supply, the tourist product and its lifecycle

In Chapter 1, the tourism product was considered as an amalgam of different components. From the point of view of consumers, the tourism product is the total experience from the moment they leave home until they return. The consumer makes use of many of the components mentioned in the above section. However, there are very many attractions and different types of accommodations, and this leads to thousands of possible combinations of these elements. In other words, the tourism product is not homogeneous. Even combining the same type of attraction and the same type of accommodation does not deliver the same product, so many intangible elements should be taken into account (see below).

The combination of the basic travel components – attractions, accommodation, facilities and transportation – is often the work of a tour operator or a travel agent. They produce 'tour packages' and 'incentive travel packages'. However, due to the internet, many travellers now create the tourism product for themselves.

In more general terms, a consumer visits a destination that is composed of attractions, facilities, infrastructure, transportation and hospitality (Mill and Morrison, 1992). Attractions draw tourists to the destination. Facilities (e.g. hotels, entertainment) serve the needs of the traveller while away from home. Transportation and infrastructure are necessary to help ensure accessibility of the destination to the tourist. Hospitality is concerned with the way in which tourist services are delivered to the tourist consumer.

So far, we have considered the consumer viewpoint. The producer at the destination has a very different view of the tourist product. The hotelier sells rooms, the restaurateur supplies food, the air carrier offers seats, and so on. They all supply different elements, and are more concerned about their own product and the similar products delivered by their competitors than about products supplied by the complementary firms. That is the reason why destination management is so important – to assure a horizontal integration of the different supply components (see Chapter 6). The market structure itself is mainly determined by the suppliers of the individual components.

The above might give the impression that tourist products are composed solely of tangible elements, but the reality is very different. A tourist product is rich in intangible elements. The most important intangible elements are image, hospitality, friendliness, courtesy, ambiance, security and understanding.

Each tourist product, from the viewpoint of both the producer and the consumer, has its own lifecycle composed of five stages:

1 Introduction or launch
2 Growth or development
3 Maturity
4 Saturation
5 Decline.

For Buhalis (2000), this lifecycle also applies to a tourism destination. Some writers use the term 'tourist area lifecycle', or TALC (Butler, 1980; Cooper *et al.*, 1993; Cole, 2012). The characteristics of supply and demand for each stage in the destination lifecycle are shown in Table 4.1.

Buhalis produced an interesting impact analysis for each stage of the lifecycle from the viewpoint of the destination characteristics (e.g. growth rate, price, visitor type), marketing response (e.g. product, price, distribution, communication), economic impact (e.g. revenue,

Table 4.1 Characteristics of the tourist destination lifecycle

Source: adapted from Buhalis (2000)

Stage	Supply	Demand
Introduction/launch/exploration	Begin	New trendy destination
Growth/development	Investment in accommodation and facilities	More people interested
Maturity	Increasing investment	Maximum visitors
Saturation/stagnation	Oversupply	Original demand changes
Decline and possibly rejuvenation	Special offer to boost visitation	Decline of demand

employment), social impact (e.g. crime at the destination, relationships between locals and tourists) and finally environmental impacts (e.g. water pollution, erosion, congestion). Lifecycles of destinations are not always the same; far from that. The Cole model (2009) sheds light on why resort lifecycles exhibit a great variation across destinations and their sensitivity to change. Intense marketing and public involvement can have a real influence on the lifecycle.

Product lifecycles can be extended in different manners (UNWTO, 2007):

- Promoting more frequent use of tourism offerings in the destination among current tourists.
- Developing and promoting more varied uses of products among current markets by packaging existing products more effectively (e.g. new experiences).
- Creating new uses and experiences by developing new attractions or redeveloping existing experiences.

TALC is, from the theoretical point of view, an appealing concept, but is of limited practical value. It is very difficult to identify the different stages and turning points, especially when there is a lack of an extended sequence of tourist arrival data from which to assemble the curve (Cooper *et al.*, 1993). Furthermore, a destination is an aggregation of many products and different market segments, each with their own evolution. Last but not least, nothing is known about the length of the TALC. The cycle is very variable. The lifecycle of a destination is to a large extent dependent on new impulses, either by chance or intent. In any case, from time to time each destination needs to undergo radical innovations in attractions, accommodations and facilities to cope with changing demand trends and competition from newcomers. There was a radical innovation project for Playa de Palma in Mallorca. This project involved a serious upgrading of the destination. The idea was to replace 'sun and beach' tourism by wellness and sports. This was a real challenge. Unfortunately, a change of the local government was also the end of the project.

Nevertheless, the tourist lifecycle provides a framework for understanding how products, destinations and their markets evolve (UNWTO, 2007; Komppula *et al.*, 2010). At the same time, it is a signal that tourism product development is very important.

Tourism product development

Product development is a key element of destination management. That is the reason why UNWTO and the European Travel Commission (ETC) published a handbook on product development (2011). This publication underlines that tourism product development (TPD) should start from two basic principles. Firstly, TPD is an integral part of overall tourism development strategic planning. Secondly, TPD should follow the key principles of sustainable development. These key principles are:

- Being authentic (reflecting the unique attributes of the destination)
- Having the support of the host community
- Respecting the natural and socio-cultural environments
- Being differentiated from competitors (avoiding 'me too/copy cat' developments)
- Being of a sufficient scale to make a significant economic contribution.

Nulty and Cleverdon (2011), the authors of the UNWTO–ETC handbook on tourism product development, give the necessary steps in the process of TPD. The steps in the process are:

1 Analysing the present situation
2 Identifying the opportunities
3 Prioritising the destination's own tourism sector's objectives.

The first step is analysing the present situation. There are five analytical tools that can help a destination understand where it is, what options it has in respect of the development of the tourism sector and how best to focus its product development and marketing strategies. These tools are:

- PEST analysis
- SWOT analysis
- TALC analysis
- Ansoff matrix
- BCG matrix.

It is very important that a destination understands where it fits and how it is perceived in the international marketplace.

The PEST analysis is very helpful in identifying where a destination is in terms of its political and socio-economic development. PEST analysis focusses on political, economic, socio-cultural and technological aspects. Understanding the macro-environment in which a destination operates is very important. Let us illustrate this with two items for each of the four components of PEST analysis. For each of the four pillars many more items should be considered:

1 Political

a Stability of the political environment;
b What is the economic development policy of the government and what is the position of tourism in it.

2 Economic

a Exchange rate;
b Energy availability.

3 Socio-cultural

a Demographic structure and trends in population, by age, education and income;
b Language knowledge.

4 Technological

    a   Use of technology in the development of innovative products;

    b   Use of technology to communicate directly with existing and prospective customers.

The SWOT analysis is a strategic planning method used to evaluate Strengths, Weaknesses, Opportunities and Threats of a project in a destination. The point is to detect the internal and external factors that are favourable and unfavourable to the achievement of the project. External factors can create opportunities and threats as well.

The third tool is Tourism Area Life Cycle (TALC) analysis. Various strategies can be used by destinations once a stagnation point has been reached, going from consolidation to rejuvenation. Possible actions that can lead to a rejuvenation phase are new product developments targeted at different segments, infrastructure improvements leading to increased carrying capacity or opening up of other areas in the destination to take pressure off saturated parts. The strategic tourism plan of Bruges is a good example of the latter. The idea is to bring visitors to other places in the inner city away from the concentration points.

The options for strategic growth are incorporated in a four-box model devised by Ansoff (1987). Profitable product market portfolios can expect to be continuously under competitive pressure. It may be necessary to update and augment products to match changing customer needs and changing market conditions. Ansoff devised a matrix for this (see Figure 4.2).

In many sun and beach destinations, holidaymakers have become more demanding. Product development can be to offer sun and beach plus. An example is Waccamaw Grand Strand Region plan in South Carolina.

Penetration was used by many destinations in Mediterranean and Caribbean countries in the past. Many beach resort areas were unsatisfied with their market share vis-à-vis their main competitors. They undertook an aggressive marketing campaign targeted at existing markets and segments to increase market share.

A good example of market development is the Caribbean Islands. They broadened their market from North America to Europe, recognizing that European demand is less seasonal and has a longer length of stay.

A fifth tool is the Boston Consulting Group (BCG) matrix (Kerin et al. 1990). The BCG model is in the first place a marketing planning tool. A destination can have several tourism

		MARKET	
		New	Existing
P R O D U C T	New	*Diversification* New product to new market	*Product development* New product to present market
	Existing	*Market development* Reposition present product to new markets	*Penetration* Modification and intensive promotion of existing products to present market

Figure 4.2 Ansoff product-market matrix

MARKET SHARE		
	High	Low
PRODUCT-MARKET GROWTH (%) — High	*Star*	*Question mark*
PRODUCT-MARKET GROWTH (%) — Low	*Cash cow*	*Dog*

Figure 4.3 Boston Consulting Group matrix

products, each with a different market share and different growth rate. One of the best-known product portfolio evaluation models is the BCG model. The BCG plots the tourism products of a destination in a matrix. The vertical axis shows the growth rate of the market while the horizontal one represents the market share of the product compared with its major competitors.

Having plotted its various products in the growth-share matrix, the destination then determines whether its product portfolio is healthy. An underbalanced portfolio would have too many dogs or question marks. In normal business, question marks are not a top priority. It quite often requires a lot of money to increase market share. In tourism one can be more tolerant towards question marks if the capital investment is relatively low with a good profit margin.

The marketing strategic response is to increase marketing support for stars and question marks in order to gain a higher share of an attractive market and diverting funds from cash cows, where the low market growth makes it unattractive for competitors to target, and ignoring or terminating dogs.

The BCG matrix also indicates where product development attention should be focussed. Product development in the stars and question marks will strengthen the destination's supply and enable it to maintain and grow market share.

The second step in the TPD process is the identification of tourism product or opportunities. The above-mentioned tools are very helpful for a destination to determine not only its current position and performance but to define the strategic directions in terms of product and market development in which it could be heading (see also Benur and Bramwell, 2015). Of course, these tools do not provide all the information required. Examination of market potential, profile and characteristics will be needed to establish the exact nature of the product that should be developed and how it should be presented and marketed.

The third step is prioritizing the objectives of the destination's own tourism sector. After ascertaining the range of product development opportunities, the next phase is to assess how approaches to realizing these opportunities are compatible with the destination's policy and tourism strategic objectives. A destination can set criteria for deciding if and how to support tourism product development. The criteria can be presented in three broad groups: economic, socio-economic, and management and coordination. In the above-mentioned handbook 20 criteria are suggested to determine a destination's approach to 'tourism product development' Here is a selection of some of the criteria in each group:

1 Economic:

   a To assist product innovation
   b To adjust the seasonal pattern

   c   To boost the development of small and medium enterprises in the hope of retaining a
       higher proportion of economic benefits through the reduction of leakage and more
       backward linkages.

2 Socio-economic:

   a   To assist the development of responsible tourism products (e.g. pro poor)
   b   To support community-based tourism projects.

3 Management and coordination:

   a   To ensure the development of sustainable tourism
   b   To enhance the quality of the product offering
   c   To build a strong positive image of the destination, by endorsing products of prestige
       and quality.

Tourism supply and market structures

In the first section of this chapter different types of activities could be distinguished, all of
which are operated by enterprises. Each of these firms supplies its own product. The market
structures within which these firms operate vary from pure competition to monopoly. To a
certain extent destinations at the local level can also be seen in the context of a particular
market structure. Looking at the variety of supply – attractions, accommodation firms, food
and drink, air carriers, travel trade, cruise companies and others – four market structures can
be detected in the tourism sector:

1 Perfect competition
2 Monopoly
3 Monopolistic competition
4 Oligopoly.

Sinclair and Stabler (1998) add a fifth market structure, 'contestable markets', but this is
similar to perfect competition and therefore no further distinction is made here.

   The need for giving special attention to market structures in tourism is evident from their
direct impact on pricing, price policy and the strategy of the firm. In the following sections, a
number of pricing systems applied in the tourism sector will be discussed.

Perfect competition

Bull (1995) defines perfect competition (or pure competition) from the seller's point of view –
as the situation where the seller is faced with a market-set price level but can sell all of his or
her output at that price. The firm cannot sell at a higher price than the market-set price, since
buyers would immediately move to other perfect substitutes. In such a market structure it is
assumed that there is a large number of firms and consumers, so that neither producers nor
consumers can affect the price. It is also assumed that the product or service is undifferentiated,
and that there is free entry and exit (Sinclair and Stabler, 1998). The optimal point of production
from the supplier's viewpoint occurs where the marginal cost is equal to the marginal revenue
or the market-set price. The many small producers are 'price takers'.

   It is difficult to find instances of perfect competition in the tourism sector. Small hotels,
cafés, and taxi-drivers in major cities are examples that are close to pure competition.
Minor differences in location or service lead to comparative advantage resulting from product
differentiation.

Monopoly

The opposite extreme is the monopoly or quasi-monopoly situation. A monopoly signifies a single seller, and monopoly power is maintained by barriers to entry into the industry (Tribe, 2005). The monopolist is in a position to be a price-maker. Are there examples in tourism of monopolies or near-monopolies? Yes – this can be the case with unique tourist attractions (e.g. some well-known museums). Tribe refers to car ferry services to the Isle of Wight in the UK. Other examples include national railway companies and domestic air carriers.

Can a monopolist impose any price? Of course not; the monopolist will try to discover the optimum price or the price that maximizes total revenue, as indicated in Figure 4.4.

The upper graph in Figure 4.4 shows the demand curve AB, and the lower graph shows the corresponding revenue curve DE. At the price of €100 there is no demand, and of course no revenue. At zero price there is a demand of 1 million units, but no revenue. Between these two extremes is a price that maximizes the total revenue, and this is €50. This price creates a demand of 500,000 units and a total revenue of 25 million euros. All other price levels lead to less total revenue. This implies that the demand curve AB is composed of two parts. In the range AC the demand curve is elastic; any decrease in the price results in an increase in demand and in revenue. In the range CB any decrease in price results in an increase of demand but a decrease of revenue: the demand is inelastic. Revenue maximization occurs where demand-elasticity equals −1.

Profits are maximized at a level of output where the marginal cost equals marginal revenue and the marginal cost is rising.

Monopolistic competition

Monopolistic competition is a type of market structure between perfect competition and monopoly. The characteristics of monopolistic competition are:

- Large number of suppliers and no substantial degree of concentration
- Very limited entry and exit constraints
- Limited economies of scale (unlike the cases of monopoly and oligopoly)
- Suppliers with some control over the price at which they sell their product.

Suppliers attempt to create market imperfections in order to have more control over pricing and market share. The hotel sector and retailing can in many cases be considered as typical examples of this market structure.

According to Sinclair and Stabler (1998), in the short run suppliers within a monopolistic competition can charge a price that provides them with a supernormal profit. In the long run, however, the higher profits combined with the low entry barriers will attract new competitors and, as a consequence, a fall in the demand for the original suppliers.

In this market structure, suppliers will attempt to minimize competition (Tribe, 2005) by:

- Product differentiation (brand loyalty via advertising, improvement to the tourism product, or adding value to tourism products along the value added chain such as seat size or frequent flyer awards in case of an air carrier)
- Acquisitions and mergers
- Cost and price leadership.

The latter two strategies cannot be applied to all situations of imperfect competition. Here we come close to an oligopoly situation.

Oligopoly

The essential characteristic of oligopoly is that a small number of producers dominate the industry. One can make a distinction between three types of oligopoly. In the case of two

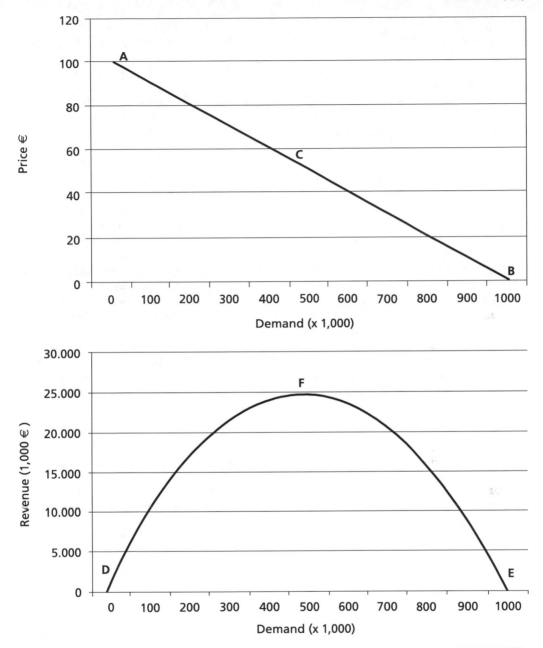

Figure 4.4 Demand, price and revenue maximization in a monopoly situation

Source: adapted from Tribe (2005)

suppliers, we speak of duopoly. In most cases there are several suppliers. They can supply either identical products (homogeneous oligopoly), or they can supply products which are not perfect substitutes (heterogeneous oligopoly). In the latter case suppliers differentiate themselves from competitors. Furthermore, there are some barriers to entry and to exit, and each actor has some control over price and output. There is a great interdependence between the producers, with each firm's price and output decisions depending, in part, on those of its competitors. The actions of firm X may cause reaction by firms Y and Z, which incites firm X to reassess its price. This leads to a chain of action and reaction (Tribe, 2005). This is the reason why producers operating in an oligopoly market often face the well-known 'kinked demand curve' (see Figure 4.5).

In Figure 4.5, ACB is the demand curve and P_0 is the prevailing price. The demand curve is elastic in the range AC, and inelastic in the range BC. If a producer decides to increase the price to the level P_1, the competitors will not follow and he or she will lose turnover and market share; the demand falls from Q_0 to Q_1. If the producer decreases the price to the level P_2 – all things being equal – he or she knows that competitors will follow. There is only a small increase in demand from Q_0 to Q_2, and the total revenue is less than before the price reduction. Indeed, the demand curve is kinked at point C, and beyond that point the demand curve is inelastic. In other words, in the case of oligopoly the producer has no reason either to increase or to cut prices – the prevailing market price is the profit-maximum price for the producer.

'Price wars' occasionally break out if a producer believes that he or she can effectively undercut the competitors. Bull (1995) claims that in order to avoid a 'price war', oligopolists may agree not to compete on price and perhaps to restrict competition by making special arrangements. This can lead to a cartel, which is classed as illegal by most national governments and by the European Union competition regulations because a cartel is considered to restrict free trade. According to Bull, in the 1980s and beginning of the 1990s agreement of this kind was still frequently found in the tourism sector. It should be recognized that the fare-fixing cartel of the IATA (International Air Transport Association) has disappeared in the last two decades due to deregulation of air transport, new air carriers and stronger competition legislation. Nowadays, competition between air carriers (at least on certain routes) is fierce. Agreements in the tour operator business are also unlikely; non-specialized tour operators

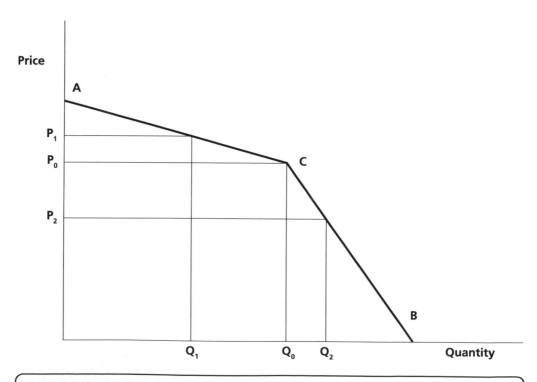

Figure 4.5 The kinked demand curve

battle for market share, and consequently profit margins are very low (Aguiló *et al.*, 2003). In general, oligopolists can alter their output and/or prices and take account of their competitors' possible reactions. The possible strategies and responses can be examined by means of game theory (Sinclair and Stabler, 1998).

Competition under oligopoly conditions is quite often based on advertising, quality, informal price agreements and follow-the-leader pricing (Tribe, 2005). Price wars are not excluded if one firm believes it is able to undercut competitors.

In tourism, there are many examples of oligopolistic competition. This is quite often the case with air carriers, air charters, cruise companies, tour operators, larger travel agencies (as in the UK), car rental companies, computer reservation systems, car ferry lines, holiday villages and, to a certain extent, large hotels. Destinations can also be confronted with oligopoly. It is well known that in the Mediterranean region each country keeps a close eye on the others' tourism products. The same applies to seaside destinations within the same country.

As a general conclusion, the relationship between market structures and pricing can be summarized as follows:

- Firms operating in a perfect competition (i.e. there are many buyers and sellers of homogeneous products with total freedom of entry and exit) are price-takers; they cannot influence the price.
- Firms in monopolistic competition (there are still many sellers but there is also the chance for product differentiation) or in an oligopoly (few sellers) are price-shapers; in other words, they can influence the price to a certain extent.
- Finally, a monopolist (only one seller) is a price-maker; he or she can set the desired price.

Key criteria in inter-firm competition

Based on theoretical models, and analysis of different tourism sectors, Sinclair and Stabler (1998) identified a number of key factors in inter-firm competition.

The first is the number and the size of firms. Where many small firms operate, the market is competitive. A small number of firms indicates an oligopolistic structure, and possibly a monopoly. Once a few large firms represent a large market share, oligopoly situations are not far away. This brings us to the second factor, the degree of concentration.

High concentration is suggestive of oligopoly or monopoly. Concentration is possible with a large number of firms – an example is the travel agency structure in the UK. A good indicator of concentration in a sector is the Gini coefficient (see Chapter 3), where a zero denotes that all firms are of the same size and a high value, approaching unity, indicates a highly concentrated market and (probably) high profits. The extent to which high concentration leads to higher profits is determined in part by ease of entry into and exit from the sector. The level of sunk costs involved in operating the firm is also important.

A third factor concerns the economies and dis-economies of scale. In the case of economies of scale, costs per unit of production decline as inputs and output increase. As long as average costs are falling, a firm will be stimulated to grow. The point at which the average costs start to rise again is where dis-economies set in. In tourism, there are several sectors where economies of scale can be realized. This is certainly the case in air travel, the cruise business, the car-ferry market and the accommodation sector. Sinclair and Stabler (1998) explain why economies of scale can be achieved, and why these economies can indicate market structure. Economies of scope, where additional products or services share common inputs, can lead to a similar situation. The authors state an important thesis:

> Evidence of unexploited economies of scale or scope, or potential for them to occur in the future through technical change, would indicate the likelihood of increased firm size and greater market power, so rendering the market less competitive. Conversely,

diseconomies of scale, or supply where widely differing input proportions are possible, would enhance the long-term viability of smaller firms and create a structure which is more competitive.

All this does not preclude many small firms from being successful in the same market. They focus on particular segments or niches.

The fourth factor consists of the capital indivisibilities, fixed capacity and associated fixed costs of operations. Some sectors in tourism are confronted with high fixed costs. This is certainly the case in the transport business and, to a lesser degree, in the accommodation sector. However, tour operators who operate their own hotels and aircraft also show relatively high fixed costs. With low occupancy rates, revenues are insufficient to cover fixed and variable costs. Reduction of capacity is, in the short run, rather difficult. In such situations, firms attempt to capture trade from competitors. Price policy becomes a key element, and firms can continue to function so long as they cover their variable costs. In the long run, a firm has more alternatives. Alternative strategies include altering the product, the choice of markets and the segments served.

A fifth factor concerns price discrimination and product differentiation. The price policy practised by tourism firms provides some indication of the market structure. In the case of a large number of firms and homogeneous products or services, the prevailing price should be respected – this situation can be approximated to perfect competition. Pricing and output strategies can be applied in imperfectly competitive situations. Oligopolists should take into account the possible reaction of the competitors. Firms operating under monopolistic competition endeavour to differentiate their product from that of rival firms. It is important to note that all firms operating under imperfect competition can benefit from price discrimination. For many products and services the willingness to pay is very different from segment to segment, and price discrimination can be applied where different consumers have distinct price-elasticities of demand. A higher price can be charged for those consumers with an inelastic demand, while lower prices are charged for consumers whose demand is more elastic. Discriminatory pricing in tourism is the rule in the air business, ferry travel, rail transport and the accommodation sector. Larger hotels offer tempting discounts at weekends, but charge business people with inelastic demand higher prices during the working week. We will return to this topic in the next section.

Product differentiation is also a common practice under imperfect competition. Product differentiation can take two forms: vertical and horizontal. The first case can be based on different quality products. Horizontal product differentiation can be realized via the supply of a range of product types (e.g. for young people, special interest groups, mass tourism).

A final factor concerns pricing policies and market-share strategies. Over the past two decades, price-cutting has been the rule in tourism in many sectors working in an oligopoly situation. In the air business there has been a combination of product differentiation and price cuts. Many remember the Laker Air story, where Laker offered low prices and a low product profile. Laker went bankrupt, but its price strategy was followed by many low-cost carriers (e.g. Air Berlin (up to 2017), Blue Air, Condor, Easyjet, Ryanair, Spanair and Ted in Europe, Frontier, Jet Blue, Song and Southwest in the USA) (see also Gross and Lück, 2014). These price cuts can have positive side effects for the destinations. Eugenio-Martin and Inchausti-Sintes (2016) proved the hypothesis that 'low-cost travel savings from tourists' place of origin are transferred, at least partially, to higher tourism expenditures at the destination' holds for most tourist profiles in the case of Canary Islands.

Price-cutting does not only occur among airlines; there are similar situations in other transport sectors. Where the entry of new companies is more difficult or uncommon, collusion may occur. This was the case prior to deregulation in the air business, when air fares were controlled by the IATA.

A typical example of oligopoly is the tour-operator market. In this sector, price leadership, price wars and attempts to increase market share are common practices in many European countries. Larger market share strategy leads to mergers and take-overs (for example, the Thomas Cook group and the TUI group). Integration is related to information advantages, cost savings and the possibility of increased market power.

Supply trends

'Supply trends' could well be the title of another book; it covers a variety of items. This section is limited to a number of major trends with a great or a particular economic impact:

● More destinations
● Concentration movement in the tourism sector
● Movements in the hotel sector
● Branding
● Technological evolution affecting tourism
● New types of accommodation and attractions – timesharing, cruises, the inclusive holiday villages explosion, Airbnb in the sharing economy, and theme parks.

More destinations

Every year, new regions are developed as destinations. The world is becoming increasingly explored, and adventure tourism is in the picture (mountains, tourist submarines, ends of the earth, etc.). There are not only more destinations, but also the product variety in the destinations is increasing year after year (see the demand trends described in Chapter 3).

Concentration movement in the tourism sector

Concentration is probably the major trend in the tourism industry. The concentration movement started many years ago, and has accelerated in the last decade. This process is manifestly present in several sectors of the tourism industry, including air transport, hotel groups, tour operators, travel agents, theme parks, computer reservations systems (CRSs) and car rental firms – considering diagonal integration.

The buying out of KLM by Air France – French interests own 81 per cent of the shares and KLM 19 per cent – although not totally unexpected, shocked Europe (*Le Monde*, 2003). Air France–KLM became the largest air carrier in Europe (see Table 4.2). In 2009 this group took a minority participation in Alitalia. Another shock was the fusion of Delta and Northwest Airlines in 2008. International Consolidated Airlines Group, S.A., often shortened to IAG, is a British–Spanish multinational airline holding company. It was formed in January 2011 by the merger of British Airways and Iberia, the flag carrier airlines of the United Kingdom and Spain respectively, with British Airways holding 55 per cent of the newly formed company. They would continue to operate under the present names BA and Iberia. In 2010 Shanghai Airlines merged with China Eastern Airlines and two years later Continental Airlines merged with United Airlines. The same happened with TAM Airways and Lan Airways in 2014. In the same year US Airways became an affiliate member of American Airlines.

A special form of concentration in the aviation sector is an airline alliance. An airline alliance is an aviation industry arrangement between two or more airlines agreeing to cooperate on a substantial level. Alliances may provide marketing branding to facilitate travellers making inter-airline codeshare connections within countries.

By the end of the last century, four alliances dominated the world air market (WTO, 1998): the American–British Airways alliance, the Star Alliance, the Delta–Swissair Group and the Northern-Continental Group. The WTO stated in 1998: 'While their ambitions may be thwarted by regularity intervention or corporate incompatibility, if the major airlines achieve

Table 4.2 World's largest airline companies, 2015

Source: annual reports

Airline	Turnover ($billion)	Aircraft in fleet	Passengers (million)	Staff (1,000)
American Airlines Group	40.9	1,789	146	118
Delta Airlines	40.5	1,330	139	83
United Continental Holdings	37.5	1,229	95	84
Lufthansa Group	35.5	600	108	120
Air France–KLM	28.9	534	90	96
International Airlines Group (BA + Iberia)	25.3	464	88	60
Southwest Airlines	20.2	720	144	50
China Southern Airlines	17.7	515	109	87

their objectives, most passenger flights will take place on one of just three airline groups before 2010'. Five years later the world map had changed completely.

This was not the end. In 2015 there are still three big alliances but with more members and changed partners. In 2015, Star Alliance was the largest with 23 per cent of total scheduled traffic, followed by SkyTeam with 20.4 per cent and Oneworld with 17.8 per cent, leaving 38.8 per cent for others. In 2015 the three alliances together carried 1,863 million passengers and represented 52% of the industry (see Table 4.3).

The first large alliance began in 1989, when Northwest Airlines and KLM agreed to large-scale codesharing. In 1992, the Netherlands signed the first open skies agreement with the United States, in spite of objections from the European Union, which gave both countries unrestricted landing rights on the other's soil. Normally landing rights are granted for a fixed number of flights per week to a fixed destination. Each adjustment requires negotiations, often between governments rather than between the companies involved. In return, the United States granted antitrust immunity to the alliance between Northwest Airlines and KLM. Other alliances would struggle for years to overcome the transnational barriers and lack of antitrust immunity, and still do so.

Table 4.3 The top three air alliances, 2015

Source: websites of the top three air alliances

	Star Alliance	Sky Team	Oneworld
Members	27	20	14
Employees (1,000)	433	482	383
Turnover (billion $)	179	141	131
Fleet	4,657	3,937	3,560
Daily departures	18,500	17,343	13,814
Passengers (million/year)	641	665	557
Number of destinations	1,330	1,062	1,016

The Star Alliance was founded in 1997, which led competing airlines to form Oneworld in 1999 and SkyTeam in 2000. Recently, low-cost carriers created their own alliances. In 2016, the first alliance of low-cost carriers was formed: U-FLY Alliance. In the same year Value Alliance, the world's largest alliance of low-cost carriers was formed.

This is a very clear example of an oligopoly situation. Dimanche and Jolly (2006) call it a 'fringed oligopoly'. It is a new cooperation model. We have a limited number of coalitions of world scope, centred around a number of powerful companies working together with a large number of smaller independent companies. The danger for travellers is if the groups unofficially divide up the world between them, creating such strong spheres of influence that competitors dare not challenge them, and thus cause possible fare rises. A distinction should be made between complementary alliances (i.e. between carriers who have separate, non-overlapping route networks which they link through an airport, coordinating flights and connections and feeding traffic to each other) and parallel alliances (i.e. between airlines who were, prior to the alliance, competitors on important routes). In the first case, alliances have little impact on competition but do improve the airlines' economics. The situation is different for parallel alliances. These tend to impact negatively on competition, and a likely outcome is fewer flights (for example, Lufthansa has withdrawn from Australia), reduced service levels and less traffic (Morley, 2003).

However, international airline alliances also have the effect of improving the efficiency and services of airlines. The activities can be broken down into five groups (Dimanche and Jolly, 2006):

- Joint procurement (e.g. fuel, catering, acquisition of planes)
- Joint operations (e.g. maintenance and repair)
- Joint back office (e.g. coordination of flight schedules, joint reservation systems)
- Co-marketing (e.g. code sharing of international flights)
- Co-services (e.g. joint ticketing).

These activities are already an indication of possible reductions of the airlines' costs. The cost-reduction opportunities can be broken down into four types (OECD, 2000; Morley, 2003):

- Finance and utilization (cost reductions due to greater asset utilization – aircraft, lounges, inventory, IT, etc.)
- Airline operation (such as staff and agency arrangements, sharing the expenses of marketing and promotion, flight and route efficiencies – all garnered through code-sharing services)
- External (payments to suppliers such as airports, aircraft manufacturers, catering, maintenance, handling)
- Risk-sharing (booking of block space on each other's flights and code-sharing).

Consumers also benefit from an air alliance (Middleton *et al.*, 2009):

- Consumers tend to prefer airlines serving a large number of cities that facilitate 'seamless' travel
- An alliance can offer far more variety of itinerary and routing choices
- Frequency, schedule convenience and convenience of connecting are major features of quality
- Consumers benefit indirectly from lower fares.

Other possible benefits are:

- More departure times to choose from on a given route
- Shorter travel times as a result of optimized transfers

- A wider range of airport lounges shared with alliance members
- Faster mileage rewards by earning miles for a single account on several different carriers
- Round-the-world tickets, enabling travellers to fly around the world for a relatively low price.

Tourism is likely to feel positive effects (particularly from complementary alliances) through tourists experiencing key service improvements, decreases in fares and total travel time, and easier connections. However, airline alliances may also create disadvantages for the traveller, such as higher prices when competition is erased on certain routes. The accommodation sector is following the same trend, with the consolidation of hotel groups. The effects are not always spectacular, but are nevertheless multiple.

The European tour-operating sector is also experiencing a centralization of power. Since the beginning of this century, the European tour-operating map has been redesigned. Preussag, formerly an industrial group, entered the tourism business in 1997, and is taking control of TUI, Germany's largest tour operator. In 1998, Preussag took over Thomas Cook and Carlson UK. Two years later the largest British tour operator, Thomson Travel, belonged to the Preussag group. The European Union agreed with this integration provided Preussag resold Thomas Cook. In 2000, the German group acquired GTT, the leading Austrian tour operator, and took a share of 10 per cent in the largest Italian tour operator, Alpitour. In the same year, Preussag began to take control of Nouvelles Frontières, completing the process in 2002. In 2001, Preussag formed an association with the Maritz Travel Company (United States), Internet Travel Group (Australia), Protravel (France) and Britannic (UK) to establish a global network for business travel called TQ3 Travel Solutions (de Boiville, 2003). Also in 2001, Preussag decided to regroup all its tourism activities in 15 countries under the name 'World of TUI'.

At the end of the 1990s, the second largest German tour operator, C&N (from the merger in 1998 of Neckerman and Condor, an affiliate of Lufthansa, formerly NUR Touristic and successor of Neckerman), began a series of take-overs. In 1999, the group acquired the French companies Aquatour, Albatros and Havas Voyages Loisirs. A year later, C&N bought Thomas Cook (which Preussag had been obliged to cede). In 2002, the group C&N Touristik changed its name to Thomas Cook. Meanwhile, Thomas Cook is also operational in Spain due to an agreement with Iberostar. The British tour operator MyTravel (formerly Airtours), the biggest British tour operator at that moment, joined Thomas Cook in 2007. The latter hoped to realize a cost-reducing effect of about £75 million. In the same year there was a merging of TUI and First Choice with a turnover similar to that of MyTravel (about €4bln). The German group Rewe was also active in acquiring other tour-operating companies. In 2017 Rewe came to an agreement with the Kuoni group to buy the European tour operator division.

This short and incomplete history of take-overs in the tour operator world illustrates a remarkable concentration movement in Europe. A major barrier for further concentration is created by the national monopoly authorities and the competition legislation of the EU (see the Thomas Cook story and Airtours' failed bid for First Choice in Needham, 2000).

Why is there such a concentration movement in the tour operator world? The reason can be found in an interview with J. Maillot, former president of Nouvelles Frontières, when he answered the question, 'What is the interest of the British and the German tour operators in investing in France?' His reply was very clear: 'They are not so much interested in investing in France but in having a European dimension. When a company is present in several countries of the EU, it makes economies of scale.' These economies of scale are in different fields: purchase of petrol, management of the fleet, currency management, etc. (de Boiville, 2003). Another phenomenon is that big integrated travel groups seek to cover all segments of the market (Needham, 2000).

This concentration movement does not exclude successful small tour operators. Not all tourism products can be 'industrialized' (e.g. Spain, the Dominican Republic, Tunisia), and many others cannot be standardized. Big tour operators concentrate on selling budget or mainstream package holidays.

Tour operators are more and more confronted with digital newcomers such as Booking. com, Expedia, direct booking and Airbnb. Therefore, some tour operators have changed their strategy. TUI is a good example. In the recent past the TUI group invested heavily in air carriers, hotels (365 days sunshine destinations), cruise ships and the running of resorts. In an interview (*De Tijd* 2.9.2017) F. Joussen, CEO TUI group, declared that TUI counts six air carriers, 16 cruise ships and more than 300 hotels. In 2017, more than 50 per cent of the TUI turnover will be realized in the non-traditional packaging business.

In addition to horizontal and vertical integration, many travel and tourism companies are utilizing a diagonal integration strategy whereby they establish operations to offer products or services that tourists commonly purchase but which are not directly part of the tourism product (Poon, 1993; WTO, 1998; Cunill, 2006) – i.e. they are diversifying. For example, airline companies are now offering insurance etc. (see Chapter 6).

The conclusion of this subsection is clear. The concentration of airlines, hotel groups (see below), tour operators and car rental firms will lead to economies of scale and to economies of scope, which will in turn lead to lower prices. However, it also presents a danger in that large groups might gain too powerful a hold on the markets.

Movements in the hotel sector

Worldwide, the hotel sector is the backbone of the accommodation industry. In many destinations it is the dominant accommodation type. The amount of accommodation is still growing. According to Marvel (2004), the number of rooms in hotels and similar establishments (inns, boarding houses and/or guesthouses) increased from 14.7 million rooms in 1997 to 17.3 million in 2002 (these figures are only indicative). There are several indicators that the number of hotels further increased in the last two decades.

The hotel sector is also the most labour-intensive sector of tourism. with the highest value added per man/night. An employment rate of 1.5–2 persons per hotel room is not exceptional in developing countries, although the rate is much lower in developed countries, varying from nearly zero in a 'Formule 1' hotel to 0.6 in a four-star hotel (Horwath International).

Table 4.4 The top ten hotel groups worldwide, 2015
Source: www.hotelsmag.com

	Number of rooms (1000)	Number of hotels
Marriott International	759	4,424
Hilton Worldwide	754	4,556
IHG (InterContinental Hotels Group)	744	5,052
Wyndham Hotel Group (Cendant)	678	7,812
Shanghai Jin Jiang hotel group	565	5,408
AccorHotels	512	3,873
Choice Hotels International	507	6,473
Starwood Hotels & Resorts	370	1,297
Best Western Hotels & Resorts	294	3,745
China Lodging Group	279	2,763

> **Table 4.5** The room supply of the top ten hotel companies in the world, 1970–2015
>
> Source: Peters and Frehse (2005) and www.hotelsmag.com

Year	Number of hotels	Number of rooms (1,000)
1970	4,987	503
1987	6,888	1,230
1996	20,048	2,403
2003	29,638	3,522
2008	33,811	4,127
2015	46,293	5,347

The hotel sector is characterized by a growing concentration movement. Nevertheless, there is a dominance of SMEs. According to Benhamou (2000), of the 350,000 'classified' hotels in the world, about 30,000 are commercialized under the name of the 50 largest groups. Their share in terms of rooms is much higher. Table 4.4 illustrates the top ten in 2015 with regard to room numbers.

All but four of these hotel groups are American companies; in the top 20 there are 13 American and only 3 European companies. Four Chinese groups have entered the top 20 and that is a new but not unexpected phenomenon. Most of the hotels belonging to the bigger hotel groups are not affiliated via ownership, but via franchise and management contracts.

The hotel sector is characterized by increasing chain penetration (see Table 4.5) and a growing number of franchise hotels. The largest hotel group (with regard to the number of hotels), Wyndham Hotel Group (formerly Cendant), neither owns nor runs a single hotel. Franchising can be described as a contractual bond of interest in which the franchiser, which has developed a pattern or formula for the manufacture and/or sale of goods/services, extends to the franchisee the right to carry on the business subject to a number of restrictions, controls and considerations (Hudson and Webster, 1994). In other words, it is a licence for a specific period of time to trade in a defined geographic area under the franchiser's name, and to use an associated mark or logo. The franchisee – or a third party – is expected to make the initial investment and to pay a royalty to the franchiser. For the franchisee there are several advantages:

- Less risk
- Easier access to loans
- Technical assistance
- Marketing support (connected to a booking system)
- Training of staff
- Internationally recognized brand identity
- Use of (not always) a free reservation phone
- Help in the operational procedure.

In return, the franchisee has to pay a royalty and meet the standards of the chain and the operational-quality standards. The main group of franchisees consists of individuals seeking to own and operate a hotel and who can see benefits from paying franchise fees to gain access to higher levels of demand and lower costs than they could otherwise achieve. There are also advantages for the franchiser (Cunill, 2006):

- Earns a fixed amount of earnings
- Can expand and internationalize the hotel group

● Operation cost of a computerized system can be shared by a large number of hotels.

Typical franchisers are Wyndham (with the brands Day's Inn, Horward Johnson, Knight Inn, Ramada, Super 8, Travelodge, etc.) and Choice Hotels (with the brands Comfort Inn, Comfort Suites, Clarion, Sleep Inn, Quality, EconoLodge, etc.). Both groups are purely franchising companies. But all international hotel groups have franchised hotels in their portofolios.

Another form of affiliation with growing importance is the management contract, which originated in the USA. For various reasons (to depreciate freehold property assets and tax treatment), insurance companies, savings and loan institutions, banks and consortia of private investors became willing owners of hotel property although they had no experience or interest in hotel management (Slatterly and Johnson, 1993). In the 1980s there was, in the USA, a trend towards explicit separation of ownership of hotels from their management. The function of hotel brands in this context is to ease expansion and provide assurance to hotel investors of the strength of the management of any hotel. The most important hotel management companies are Marriott International, China Lodging group, and AccorHotels. The main advantages for the management company are limited initial capital, reduced risk (e.g. building costs) and high ROIs.

A very special type of affiliation is 'hotel commercialization', or 'consortia'. It concerns companies specializing in commercialization (reservation systems) of independent hotels without a brand (or a franchised brand). Three well-known hotel reservation systems are REZsolutions Inc (Utell + Anasazi), Logis de France and Lexington Services Corporation.

Another trend in the hotel sector over the last three decades has been the explosion in branded budget hotel capacity. In the UK, the number of rooms in budget hotels increased from 18,155 in 1996 to 57,300 in 2002. A similar phenomenon is seen in France; in 2004 zero-star hotels represented 16 per cent and one-star hotels 12 per cent of French chain hotel rooms (Marvel, 2004).

On the edge of the scale are the 'boutique hotels' (Horner and Swarbrooke, 2004). These represent a focussed lifestyle product with a relatively limited number of rooms with specifically targeted niche markets, each with its own personality and identity. Mailliez and Siery (2009) use the term 'hôtel lifestyle' to define a boutique hotel. It responds to the expectations of demanding customers who look for a high personality offer with particular attention to design, new technologies, originality and 'convivialité'. It is true that boutique hotels are a marginal part of the hotel supply but they create a very high value added per room.

MICE tourism

Several destinations, very often cities, are very active in the MICE market (Meetings, Incentives, Conventions and Exhibitions). We find many convention and exhibition centres or international trade and exhibition centres in each continent of the world (WTO, 2004). There is a supply in developed and less developed countries. This is an interesting segment of the hotel business. According to the Dutch Office for Tourism and Congresses in 2007, one-fifth of all international business tourists in the Netherlands belonged to the MICE market (Destinatie Holland 2020, 2008). International association meetings are particularly important because they represent a high-yield market, with customers spending on average 2–3 times more than leisure visitors. Success in the MICE market depends on many factors. International associations favour capital cities and attractive destinations that offer what Lee *et al.* speak of as the seven As for convention destination competitiveness (UNWTO, 2007; Lee *et al.*, 2016):

1 Accessibility: airline service as well as the time and effort to travel to the destination.
2 Availability of facilities: covering not only the availability of a range of hotels and serviced accommodation and meeting space, but also facilities for conventions, such as audiovisual equipment, simultaneous translation and interpretation, and video-link teleconferencing.

3 Affordability: related to monetary costs.
4 Appropriate service.
5 Agreeable environment: climate, social and political stability, safety and security.
6 Attractions: tourism features such as shopping, entertainment and cultural and historical uniqueness.
7 Appealing image: tourism appeal, existing image and promotional appeal.

In addition, one could add 'professional conference organizers and support services in the destination'. Most destinations active on the MICE market run a 'Convention Bureau'.

The MICE market is not the exclusive domain of convention centres. Many hotels can be a meeting place for congresses, seminars and business activities provided they offer specific facilities and services. The attitude of hotel management and staff towards MICE customers is a further key factor for success in that business.

Branding

Positioning and branding are strongly interrelated. Positioning seeks to define how a tourism firm or destination is viewed by the tourism market in terms of the benefits it is likely to provide vis-à-vis the many competitive firms or destinations from which the tourist may choose (Ritchie and Crouch, 2003). On the basis of the positioning chosen, the firm (e.g. a hotel) or destination seeks to project this position to the marketplace through the development of a distinctive and strong brand (for example, the 'design' of Philippe Stark for Paramount Hotel and the 'location' for Park Lane Hotel, both in New York). It is a name, symbol, logo or other graphic that both identifies and differentiates. Branding is an identifying mark for consumers who cannot see the wood for the trees. Branding is becoming increasingly important for the large tourism groups and for destinations to distinguish themselves from competitors and competing products. In the online economy, we can expect a battle of brands (Nederlands Bureau voor Toerisme, 1998). According to Pike (2004), one important impact of branding for commercial organizations has been the increasing awareness of the balance sheet value of brands, referred to as brand equity. The brand can be an asset to the firm and as such it can affect the valuation of the firm. But for destinations, too, a brand can have great value (Kim et al., 2009). A country's image as a desirable tourist destination is an important factor in the development of potential visits. Another advantage is put forward by Middleton et al. (2009). These authors suggest that branding helps destinations to reduce medium- and long-term vulnerability to unforeseen external events. Recovery time after a crisis may also be shorter.

Okoroafo (1995) emphasizes the many benefits of strong branding (identification of the product or destination, assurance of product quality, limited ability for customers to make price comparisons, social visibility and product prestige), and concludes that the development of a brand name over time can offer the firm a competitive edge.

The strategies of travel groups vary from the single-brand philosophy (e.g. Club Med, Thomas Cook and the World of TUI) to a range of brands for specific markets. Thus, Accor uses the brands Ibis, Formule 1, Etap, Motel 6 and Red Roof Inn for the economically priced segment, Novotel and Mercure for the mid-price segment and Sofitel for the top-rank segment. Any pan-European or global brands should take very careful account of national and local market characteristics, traditions and sensitivities (Needham, 2000). Table 4.6 gives the ten biggest hotel brands in 2015.

For destinations, branding takes the form of a 'corporate identity'. It is a positioning in the form of the essential (e.g. attraction, quality). The basic elements are isotype, logotype and baseline. The corporate identity of Spain is well known, with the sun of Miro as the isotype, Espāna as the logotype and 'Spain marks' as the baseline (formerly 'Spain everything under the sun' and 'passion for life'). The Canary Islands use the baseline 'Canarias: warm nature'

Table 4.6 The ten biggest hotel brands, 2015 (1,000 rooms)

Source: www.hotelsmag.com

Brand	1,000 rooms
Best Western	294
Home Inn	257
Holiday Inn Express	236
Holiday Inn Hotels & Resorts	228
Marriott Hotels	221
Ibis	217
Hampton Inn	210
Hilton	206
HanTing Hotel	206
7 Days Inn	198

and St. Moritz in Switzerland 'St. Moritz: The Top of the World'. The benefits of effective destination branding are numerous (UNWTO, 2007):

- Destination awareness and demand creation. Consumers add the destination to their shopping list.
- Customer loyalty. To establish loyal relations with customers is a key objective of branding.
- Commercial value.
- A base from which to coordinate private sector efforts. A good brand can become a vehicle for coordination of public and private stakeholders.
- Leverage effect for other products of the destination.

A successful destination brand represents a major asset to any destination. However, success depends on:

- Brand credibility. The experience must live up to the expectations created.
- Deliverability. Do not over-promise and under-deliver.
- Differentiation. This is similar to 'good positioning'.
- Conveying powerful ideas. The destination brand must convey concepts, values and destination personality traits.
- Enthusiasm on the part of trade partners. The brand should be endorsed and used by the private sector in a destination.
- Finally, the brand should resonate with the consumer. The brand should encourage the consumer to visit the destination.

In Chapter 6 it will become clear that positioning and branding are key factors of a competitive destination.

Technological evolution affecting tourism

Technology has two different aspects: transportation and information technology. Transport technology will lead either to further decreases in transport costs or to shorter travel times. Larger (although this is not the policy of Boeing Company) and faster aircraft are being developed, newer and faster high-speed trains are forecast (such as the 500 km/h levitational train between Hamburg and Berlin), and ever-larger cruise ships are under construction.

Air transport and air fares are (and will be) influenced by several other trends, including:

- Air deregulation and an influx of low-cost airlines (Horner and Swarbrooke, 2004; Gil-Moltó and Piga, 2008).
- Further privatization of the world's national airlines, where major carriers take share holdings or acquire privatizing airlines. 'Privatization can be seen to be fuelling the spread of globalization' (Horner and Swarbrooke, 2004).
- Aircraft yield management (having the right type of aircraft for given routes).

Information technology is changing at an incredible pace. 'Information is the lifeblood of the travel industry' (Sheldon, 2006) – it connects tourists, tour operators, travel agents and tourism industry suppliers. For Poon (1993), information is the cement that holds together the different producers within the tourism sector – namely cruise lines, airlines, hotels, tour operators, travel agents, car rental firms and many other suppliers. It is essential to keep in mind that the links between tourism producers are provided not by goods, but by a flow of information. These information flows consist of data, services and payments. In the case of consumers, information is received in the form of advertising, promotions, counselling, bookings (e.g. airline tickets) and a matching information transaction flows from consumers to suppliers (e.g. payment).

Information technology is essential for the efficient and timely processing and distribution of all necessary information. Information technology is a generic term; in fact there are systems of information technologies. The largest and most important information systems in the tourism sector are the computer reservation systems (CRSs). The US Department of Transportation defines a CRS as 'a periodically updated central database that is accessed by subscribers through computer terminals'. CRSs have emerged as the dominant technology.

Computer reservation systems were developed by the airlines. They are primarily tools used by airlines to maintain inventory control of their seat offerings, and have played a significant role in facilitating increasing volumes of travel over the last three decades. A significant shift is now occurring towards global travel distribution systems and increased competition amongst airline groups seeking to broaden and strengthen their product distribution through developing regional global CRSs. A Global Distribution System (GDS) takes the inventory from a CRS (or from many of them) and distributes it via travel agents and other distribution outlets. A GDS has no specific airline inventory control functions other than to 'report back' (French, 1998). Since the early 1990s their function has expanded to include many other travel products (e.g. accommodation, rent-a-car, etc.) and embrace alternative means of distribution to travel agents, such as the internet (see Figure 4.6). The leading GDSs are Sabre, Galileo, Amadeus and Worldspan.

The consequence of these supply trends is an increasing requirement for CRSs to offer more travel information, faster processing time, and more comprehensive booking and reservation functions, as well as providing enhanced management accounting information (see yield management).

During the early days of computerized reservations systems, a flight ticket reservation was not possible without GDSs. As time progressed, many airline vendors (including budget and mainstream operators) have now adopted a strategy of 'direct selling' to their wholesale and retail customers (passengers). They invested heavily in their own reservations and direct-distribution channels and partner systems. This helps to minimize direct dependency on GDSs to meet sales and revenue targets and allows for a more dynamic response to market needs. These technology advancements in this space facilitate an easier way to cross-sell to partner airlines and via travel agents, eliminating the dependency on a dedicated global GDS federating between systems. Also, multiple price comparison websites eliminate the need for dedicated GDSs to provide point-in-time prices and inventory for both travel agents and end-customers. Hence some experts argue that these changes in business models may lead to complete phasing out of GDSs in the airline space. Lufthansa Group announced in June 2015 that it was imposing an additional charge when booking through an external Global Distribution System

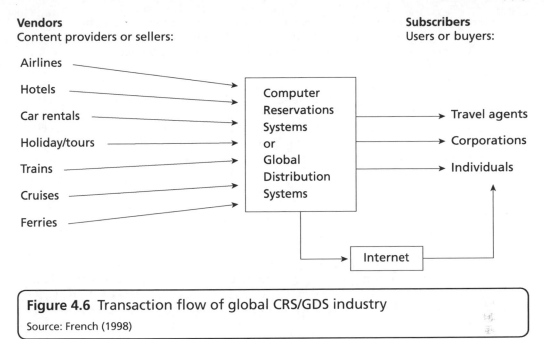

Figure 4.6 Transaction flow of global CRS/GDS industry
Source: French (1998)

rather than their own systems (Jainchill, 2015),. They stated that their choice was based upon the fact that the cost of using external systems was several times higher than their own. Several other airlines including Air France–KLM and Emirates also stated that they are following the development.

However, hotels and the car rental industry continue to benefit from GDS, especially last-minute inventory disposal using GDS to bring additional operational revenue. GDS here is useful to facilitate global reach using existing networks and has low marginal costs when compared to online air travel bookings.

CRSs are not the only form of information technology commonly used. Furthermore, CRSs are more popular with business-oriented travel agencies than with those specializing in leisure products. Nevertheless, there is a high penetration rate in all travel agencies in the largest European markets.

Other reservation systems include:

- Hotel reservation systems
- Reservation systems owned by independent companies (e.g. UTELL)
- Videotext (e.g. Prestel in the UK and Minitel in France)
- Product reservation systems owned by tour operators
- Car rental reservation systems
- National distribution systems (several of them are integrated into a GDS).

A particular form of information technology that has evolved spectacularly is the internet. The internet is in fact a network of networks. Two of its most used functions are electronic mail and the World Wide Web. Currently, the number of internet users is already very high. However, the number of users will grow further. We are not too far from the point where every home in the developed world will have a personal computer and possibly a modem or a wireless router. Each person will be able to access many information systems all over the world. UNWTO (2007) underlines the importance of the internet in the following terms:

Over the past ten years, the internet has achieved huge market penetration, with more than a billion users worldwide. Travel and tourism are key areas for the application of the internet in all major markets. The major growth markets for international travel will consist predominantly of internet users.

The internet is the primary medium for accessing travel information for planning in all major markets. This requires a complete transformation in the way in which tourism destinations and suppliers do their business.

The importance of the internet will continue to grow in all major markets, especially in Asia Pacific, with a further billion users worldwide anticipated by 2011. Increasingly access will be wireless. The growth of wireless internet access, particularly mobile access, has major relevance for travel and tourism in terms of increased use of the internet by visitors travelling to and within their destination(s). Many destinations and travel media companies such as Fodors are offering downloadable city guides and mapping tools; and Google has positioned itself as a provider of invaluable tools for travellers with its mapping and local geographical search tools.

There is no doubt that this evolution is affecting travel agencies and even tour operators, and will increasingly do so. In many developed countries one-third or more of all hotel and flight bookings go through the internet. The online travel agencies such as Booking.com, Orbitz, Expedia and Travelocity are commonplace. They get a dominant position on the market with all the possible dangers for the consumer. They are also a danger for many tour operators. But E-marketing can be an opportunity for travel agents. Middleton *et al.* (2009) refer to dynamic packaging.

Dynamic packaging is a travel industry term for a more flexible way of booking a holiday. Instead of offering customers a set package off the page of a tour operator's brochure, travel agents assemble the elements of the holiday to meet the customer's requirements. By using 'bed-banks' – companies that offer a database of hotel rooms at a discounting rate – the agents can match the prices of traditional tour operators while achieving better profit margins for themselves.

E-business is beginning to realize the ever-expanding opportunities of electronic connectivity both externally, through the internet, and internally, through intranets. It involves use of a variety of tools to obtain, manage, search, analyse, publish and communicate the various types of information (UNWTO, 2007; Sheldon, 2006).

The external dimension is about transformation of the value chain, linking the tourism supplier (or service provider) to the customer, and of the supply chain, linking the tourism supplier with its own suppliers. This brings in e-marketing, e-commerce and e-procurement. E-marketing exploits the internet and other forms of electronic communication to communicate in the most cost-effective ways with target markets and to enable joint working with partner organizations, with whom there is a common interest. E-commerce is the sales activity undertaken through electronic distribution channels. E-procurement streamlines the purchasing process by allowing a business to tie its inventory and procurement systems into the despatch and billing systems of its suppliers, or *vice versa*. Not only does this reduce costs through automation, it also facilitates identification of best value sources of supply.

The huge increase in available bandwidth, particularly wireless broadband (along with parallel enhancements in processing power and memory capacity), is facilitating access to the internet via a variety of media devices. This opens up a 'new frontier' for large-scale electronic distribution – to visitors travelling to and within destinations. Given that the internet and interactivity is permeating the traditional methods of communicating with customers (see the popularity of blogs, Facebook, Twitter, marketing through Web 2.0, etc.) the challenge for destination management organizations (DMOs) is to develop the infrastructure, the skill sets and the content to exploit the new opportunities through multiple channels. One of the conclusions of Pan *et al.* (2007) is that information technology advances and increasingly large numbers of travel blogs facilitate travel blog monitoring as a cost-effective method for destination marketers to assess their service quality and improve travellers' overall experiences (see also Middleton *et al.*, 2009).

New types of accommodation and attractions

Timesharing

Timesharing is a global industry, with more than 5,000 resorts and 4 million owners spanning all continents in the year 2000 (Hitchcock, 2001). It originated in Europe during the 1960s, but the real development of timesharing as a new sector took place in the USA. At the beginning of this century, the USA accounted for about one-third of all timeshare resorts and nearly 50 per cent of all timeshare owners. Within Europe, Spain has by far the largest number of timeshare resorts.

There is a good definition of timesharing in Goodall and Stabler (1990):

> Timeshare, sometimes referred to as interval ownership, is a form of multi-ownership of property of which examples can be found in the business sector, as well as in the leisure sector. It is a periodic right of use or occupation where property is divided on a temporal rather than physical basis. It confers on a number of purchasers the right to the exclusive and full use of property and facilities for predetermined periods of year. In principle this right is recognized as transferable.

There are two forms of timeshare. In the first there is a real property right (e.g. weekly blocks) lasting from up to 20 years to perpetuity. However, there is a net trend for shortening timeshare validity periods. The second form concerns a contractual right (e.g. corporate share, leasehold, holiday credits or points).

Timesharing is a relatively new trend in the accommodation sector, and it only represents a marginal share of the total accommodation capacity. However, there are several destinations (e.g. resorts in the Canary Islands) where timeshare is the backbone of the accommodation supply. Furthermore, this sector shows a very high growth rate. In the 1990s, the growth rate was still 7–8 per cent (Hitchcock, 2001). The timeshare market is now sweeping the Asia/Pacific region (Dean, 1997).

In the beginning, the developers of timeshare were small, independent and very often newly formed companies. Increasingly, the developers have become the construction industry and, since the mid-1980s, corporate interests from the hotel trade (e.g. Holiday Inn, Marriott or Marriott Ownership Resorts Inc., Sheraton, Hilton resorts) and even from the Walt Disney Company. Tour operators are also involved in timesharing by the acquisition of timeshare resorts or renting unsold timeshares. Club Mediterranée (buying out the French timeshare developer Club Hotel) and Tjaereborg (taking over the Club La Santa timeshare in Lanzarote, Canary Islands) have been involved in timeshare from very early on. In this way, tour operators are integrating vertically backwards into accommodation supply.

What, in fact, are the economic benefits of timesharing for a destination? Research from Joachimsthaler and Ragatz Associates (1995) highlights the economic benefits of a timeshare resort to a local community compared with conventional package holiday tourism. Case studies presented on Gran Canaria on the occasion of the AIEST Congress (AIEST, 1995) confirmed these benefits. The advantages for the destination are several, and include:

- Relatively high expenditure per man/day. Timeshare holders are considered to be high-quality customers (Hitchcock, 2001). As property owners, time-share holders also have the illusion of buying a cheap holiday. Sometimes they benefit from seat-only charters.

- Less pressure from the tour-operator business.
- The improvement of holiday accommodation (very often with recreational facilities).
- Higher occupancy rates.
- More responsible tourists.
- An extended season in the destinations.
- A stable level of employment owing to more repeat visitors and reduced seasonality.

Consumers also benefit from good accommodation and recreational facilities. They are, however, confronted with operational costs that are often much higher than they expected at the time of purchase. To be linked to a single destination is a second disadvantage, and to cope with this, exchange companies have been established which provided a mechanism for timeshare owners to swap their week(s) in one resort with week(s) in another, so enabling them to take a holiday in a different place at a different time of the year. These exchanges have been a real stimulus to growth. The market leader of exchange companies is Resort Condominiums International (RCI). Other timeshare developments worldwide are affiliated to Interval International (II). These exchange companies act as tour operators for timeshare owners. Greater flexibility is also the result of the Holiday Club concept (Haylock, 1995). In this case, instead of laying out a capital sum to buy a period of timeshare in a resort, the buyer acquires a number of holiday credits which can be used to take a holiday of his or her choice from within the Holiday Club's owned inventory. The Swiss-based company Hapimag was using this formula 40 years ago.

There are also variations within the timeshare industry. For example, three common forms of timeshares are:

- 'Fixed Timeshares' – the classical timeshare system in which the timeshare owner controls the 'property' for a specific week during the year as defined by a contract.
- Rotating weeks – a system in which the owner's week may rotate throughout a season or a year.
- Floating weeks – timeshare owners 'compete' for times each year. In this system the time-share owner has a greater potential to change his/her vacation time on a yearly basis.

Timesharing has sometimes had a bad press owing to hard-sell practices and/or non-bona fide developers. This is the origin of the EU directive of 1994 to govern certain aspects of the sale of timeshares. This directive seeks to mitigate the worst excesses of hard sell by giving the potential buyer the right to change his or her decision and cancel the contract without financial penalty within a certain period of time ('the cooling off period'). This directive has, together with the entry of powerful brands, improved the image and credibility of timesharing. Recently, timesharing has been extended to embrace products such as cruise ships, skiing or golf holidays, villas and even caravans, rather than being restricted to the traditional beach or mountain products (Hitchcock, 2001).

Cruises

For two decades cruise tourism has been the fastest growing segment of the tourism sector. Many factors contributed to the growth. Vogel (2011) refers to demand and supply factors. On the demand side we have the influence of:

- Ageing of the population
- Rising number of 'double income, no kids' couples
- Social trends like experience orientation and hedonism
- The high repeater rate.

On the supply side four other factors are very important:

- The ability of the cruise industry to make cruises affordable (economies of scale)
- Innovative and eye-catching ship design
- The development of new destinations
- Powerful branding.

Total worldwide cruise capacity by the end of 2015 will be 486,000 passengers and 298 ships (see Table 4.7). There is also large concentration in the cruise business. The Carnival group (with the brands P&O Cruises, Cunard, Princess Cruises, Ocean Village, Seabourn Cruise Line, Holland America Line, Carnival cruises, AIDA and Costa) represents 48.5 per cent of the total capacity. The second largest group, Royal Caribbean, has a market share of 21.6 per cent. The cruise industry is a typical example of an oligopolistic market structure which is rooted in the very high fixed costs required and the high entry barrier. Chang *et al.* (2017) posit that it is not easy for newcomers to establish a passenger base due to brand-awareness and reputation effects. Indeed, cruise passengers tend to prefer well-established companies to reduce their risk of high expenditure.

Annualized total passengers carried worldwide were 22.9 million in 2016, of which 13.2 million were from North America and 5.9 million from Europe. The cruise sector is showing a spectacular growth rate, and is expected to expand further in the coming decade. Worldwide, the cruise industry has an annual passenger compound annual growth rate of 6.5 per cent from 1990 to 2016. Growth strategies have been driven by larger capacity new builds and ship diversification, more local ports, more destinations and new on-board/on-shore activities that match demands of consumers. The market perspectives and the good financial performance of the cruise sector stimulate further investment. In 2014 the three major cruise lines showed a high net income/revenue ratio: Carnival 8 per cent, Royal Caribbean 9 per cent and Norwegian 11.0 per cent. However, it should be noted that the latter two companies showed very low profit ratios during several years in the recent past (Chang *et al.*, 2017).

Cruise ships are also becoming larger; several ships on order have a tonnage of over 100,000 (Peisley, 2000). Many of the new cruise ships becoming operational in the next three years have a capacity of 2,000 to 5,400 passengers. *Freedom of the Seas* was in 2009 the largest luxury cruise ship in the world, owned by Royal Caribbean. It has a tonnage of 160,000 tons and it has 15 passenger decks, holding 3,634 guests double-occupancy. In 2016, the largest cruise ship was the *Harmony of the Seas*, belonging to Royal Caribbean, with a capacity of 2,700 cabins, 6,410 passengers and 2,400 crew and 18 passenger decks.

Table 4.7 Cruise capacity, 2010–2015

Source: www.cruisemarketwatch.com/blog1

Cruise company	2010		2015	
	Capacity (1,000)	Ships	Capacity (1,000)	Ships
Carnival group	206	100	236	106
Royal Caribbean	99	42	105	42
Norwegian Cruise	33	17	44	22
MSC cruises	26	11	30	12
Other	53	84	71	116
Total	417	254	486	298

Cruise line efficiency can also be measured in operational efficiency (Lee and Brezina, 2016). Full occupancy in the cruise line industry is 'two passengers sailing inside each available guest stateroom or cabin'. It can be expressed mathematically as:

$$\text{Cruise ship occupancy rate} = \frac{\text{number of guests}}{(\text{number of cabins} \times 2)}$$

However, it is common for many families that cruise together to book a cabin for three or four passengers. Therefore, passengers per stateroom is a second efficiency indicator. Lee and Brezina use passengers per 1,000 gross registered tons as a third measure of efficiency. The results in Table 4.8 show that some cruise lines are more efficient than others.

The rapid development of cruising has also had an impact on a number of destinations. Several destinations in the Caribbean are complaining of the fall in use of traditional overnight accommodation. Furthermore, several destinations are becoming the playthings of the powerful cruise companies.

All-inclusive resorts

Poon (1993) defines the all-inclusive concept as:

> Holidays where virtually everything is included in one pre-paid price from airport transfers, baggage handling, government taxes, rooms, all meals, snacks, drinks and cigarettes to the use of all facilities and equipment, coaches and instructors. Even gratuities (tips and service charges) are included in this pre-paid price.

The all-inclusive concept originated in the French-based Club Méditerranée. The Club Med resorts were founded by the Belgian Gérard Blitz. The first village opened on Mallorca in 1950. Club Med dominates this accommodation type, with more than 100 resorts. During the last decades several reorganizations took place. In the beginning of the 1990s a new strategy was announced, returning to a focus on holiday villages and for upmarket vacationers. Major competitors include SuperClubs, Carnival corporation, Sol Meliá and Sandals. Other major all-inclusive chains are: Allegro Resorts, Robinson Clubs, Club Valtur, Clubs International, Club Aldiana. In the last two decades several other companies started with new inclusive resorts in many different countries (e.g. Cuba, Indonesia, Malaysia, Turkey and many others).

Table 4.8 Efficiency of cruise lines, 2011–2013

Source: Lee and Brezina (2016)

Cruise line	Occupancy rate	Passengers per 1,000 gross registered tons	Passengers per stateroom
Carnival Cruise line	1.16	32.2	2.31
Celebrity Cruise line	1.05	23.9	2.09
Disney Cruise line	1.48	30.8	2.96
Holland America Cruise	1.03	23.6	2.06
Norwegian Cruise	1.11	28.9	2.22
Princess Cruise	1.02	24.6	2.04
Royal Caribbean Cruise	1.09	28.0	2.17
Combined total	1.10	28.0	2.20

In the 1990s, all-inclusive resorts in Jamaica performed better than non-all-inclusive hotels. The success was attributed to aggressive marketing, good contacts with the travel trade, psychographic market segmentation strategies (couples only, families only, health, sport, etc.) and visitor satisfaction (Poon, 1998). 'All in' is further booming and gaining market share.

The Kuoni group sees a real future for the all-inclusive resorts (Bosshart and Frick, 2006).

> Tomorrow's mass tourism will take place in hyper holiday hubs. Gigantic holiday resorts will be built on the Mediterranean, in the United Arab Emirates, Qatar, China and Brazil. These hyper-modern recuperation centres will offer the entire spectrum of what the heart desires: warmth in all variations from direct sunshine to carefully measured thermo treatments, physical recuperation from cheap face lifting to individual organic anti-aging treatments. With everything – including the airport – conveniently located in the same place.

A frequent critique of all-inclusive resorts is that they do not support the local economy. Most resorts are located in remote areas away from major population centres. It is hard for the vacationers staying there to see any local sights or frequent local businesses. Due to this formula there is little incentive to eat or drink elsewhere.

Airbnb in the sharing economy

The sharing economy is rapidly deploying social technologies that are radically disrupting how people experience products and services. Empowered with the ability to create, broadcast and exchange their own products and services via online marketplace platforms, consumers are sharing nearly everything, including their homes (Richard and Cleveland, 2016). Travellers who want to take part in the sharing economy have no shortage of choices when it comes to marketplace platforms that connect individuals seeking to share their accommodations (see Airbnb, HomeAway, Flipkep, Housetrip, Homestay, Wimdu or villas.com). The growing supply of marketplace platforms has been fuelled by a strong demand for P2P rentals from consumers. Richard and Cleveland posit:

> Over the past few years the sharing economy has grown tremendously, disrupting the traditional tourism industry via the mass deployment of exponentially increasing capacity. In this new economy, ownership and access are shared by individuals creating, broadcasting and exchanging their own products and services.

Indeed, the accommodation sector is being confronted by peer-to-peer networks, with Airbnb. com as a pioneer. There are not many reliable data available to get an insight into the size of this new accommodation form. Furthermore, it is not always clear if bed and breakfast accommodation is included or not. There is some indication of the size of Airbnb in a number of European cities (*De Tijd*, 4th August, 2017). In 2017, the ratio of Airbnbs to hotel rooms amounted to 1 in 6 in Brussels, 1 in 3 in Paris and Amsterdam, and 1 in 8 in Berlin. But there is even less knowledge about the occupation rate of Airbnbs (for Belgium the average occupation is 30 nights a year).

According to Karlsson *et al.* (2017), Airbnb started in 2009 and was catering for 17 million guests in 2015. In the same year, Airbnb was valued at $25.5 billion, double the worth of Expedia and more than Marriot Hotels. But let us be careful with comparisons. This amount seems spectacular. However, it is not more than 2 per cent of the value of tourism expenditure of international tourists (see Chapter 3). Peer-to-peer (P2P) bookings are expected to grow to as much as 10 per cent of the market by 2025, thanks to a glut of underutilized assets (spare rooms) in the market, a favorable perception of price value and travellers' preferences for genuine local experiences (Richard and Cleveland, 2016).

Tourists can live with locals or in the houses of locals instead of staying in hotels or other accommodation. Airbnb's success is due to attractive prices and connecting with local people (Karlsson and Dolnicar, 2016).

To gain insight into what drives the supply side of P2P accommodation networks, an online survey among existing hosts was conducted by Karlsson and Dolnicar in Australia. The question used was: 'Please tell us your main reasons for renting out your property.' Three categories of answers emerged: income (82 per cent; for money, to afford luxury and to pay the bills), social interaction (31 per cent; in particular to meet people) and sharing (14 per cent; unused space and share my house). The answers are only indicative given the lack of sampling frame.

Richard and Cleveland give five drivers for growth within the lodging and travel segment of the sharing economy:

- Increasing supply.
- Price value. The sharing economy has the ability to compete on price due to the lower capital costs of noncommercial asset owners and the lack of management costs associated with a noncommercial asset.
- Genuine experiences. Beyond mere cost savings, some travellers prefer the experiential benefits of staying in a residence that these new platforms provide. (Opportunity to reside in a 'non-touristy' area, the feeling of being in a home, the advice that owners can provide about local experiences.)
- The perception of safety on the part of the guest.
- Seeking out quality and consistency. (One can raise questions about this last driver.)

According to Richard and Cleveland the rapid growth of P2P rental marketplaces represents a potential threat to established firms. They refer to a study of Zervas *et al.* (2015). Their advice to hotel chains is remarkable:

> Given the rapid growth of the shared economy within the lodging industry in terms of both available room nights and market valuation, traditional hotel chains would be wise to consider strategies that avoid direct competition with online marketplace platforms. Rather than risk cannibalization of existing brands or facing established competitors, offering a differentiated product within the sharing economy represents an opportunity for traditional hotel chains to significantly expand their market share. Since the sharing economy is comprised of underutilized existing assets, hotel chains can bypass the lengthy process of partnering with property ownership and the wait times required to build new properties. Hiltonbnb is a first example.

Despite the advantages of growth, price and unique experiences, P2P rentals via marketplace platforms have several weaknesses relative to their more traditional competitors. Airbnb has faced challenges that are indicative of those within the industry as a whole: encouraging illegal rentals, dodging accommodation taxes, and offering unsafe rentals.

Theme parks

Although there is no single agreed definition of a theme park, it is generally agreed that all theme parks are concerned with entertainment and physical experiences provided by a backbone of varied rides and attractions. Theme parks are distinguishable from amusement or other similar leisure parks by an overall themed experience which runs through all (or most) of the attractions (McEniff, 1993). The main characteristics of theme parks are as follows:

- They involve outdoor recreation
- They are visitor destinations in their own right
- They are based on rides, attractions and shows
- They are constructed around the needs of visitors, rather than relying on natural features
- They are focussed on entertainment but are increasingly paying attention to education.

Theme parks began very early in Europe. Tivoli Gardens in Copenhagen opened in 1843 and still operates today. According to Reece (2010) one of the most important events in the development of US theme parks was the opening of Disneyland in Anaheim, California, in 1955. Theme parks are becoming ever more attractive to excursionists and tourists interested in a short break. The bigger theme parks offer a real condensed holiday product. In 2014, 27 theme parks were each visited by more than 4 million visitors (see Table 4.9). The top 25 amusement/theme parks worldwide had in total 223 million visitors (see TEA Attraction Attendance Report 2014).

Two characteristics dominate the last decade. Firstly, the theme park sector faces a rather low growth rate. A comparison of the visitors of the parks retained in Table 4.9 shows

Table 4.9 Theme parks with more than 4 million visitors, 2008 and 2014

Source: TEA, Attraction Attendance Report 2015

Theme park	2008	2014
Magic Kingdom, Florida	17.1	19.3
Disneyland Anaheim, California	14.7	16.8
Disneyland Tokyo	14.3	17.3
Disneyland Paris	10.7	9.9
Disney Sea Tokyo	12.4	14.1
Epcot Center, Walt Disney World	10.9	11.4
Disney-Hollywood Studios, Walt Disney World	9.6	10.3
Disney's Animal Kingdom	9.5	10.4
Universal Studios JP	8.3	8.2
Everland (SK)	6.6	7.4
Universal Studios, Orlando	6.2	8.3
Seaworld Florida	5.9	4.7
Disney's California Adventure	5.5	8.8
Islands of Adventure at Universal Orlando	5.3	8.1
Ocean Park HK	5.0	7.8
Universal Studios Hollywood	4.6	6.8
Yokohama Hakkeijima Sea Paradise	4.6	n.a.
Songcheng Park		5.8
Nagashima Spa Land		5.6
Chimelong Ocean Kingdom		5.5
Hong Kong Disneyland HK	4.5	7.5
Busch Gardens Tampa Bay	4.4	4.1
Lotte World, Seoul	4.2	7.6
Seaworld California	4.1	4.7
Europa-Park, Rust. Germany	4.1	5.0
Tivoli Gardens	4.0	4.5
De Efteling		4.4
Walt Disney Studios Park at Disneyland Paris		4.3

a growth rate of not more than 2.8 per cent over the period 2008–2014. Theme parks were adversely impacted by the bad economic environment worldwide. Secondly, Asian countries are becoming more and more important on the theme park map. In 2008, 13 out of the 25 top parks were located in the USA and five in Asia. In 2014, Asia had ten parks in the top 25 – as many as the USA. There is still a strong focus on Asia from an investment standpoint, in all sectors of the attraction business. The continent is generally under-served in terms of attractions, and has a growing middle class increasingly meeting the income threshold necessary for themed entertainment to be viable.

The theme park world is dominated by three theme park groups: Walt Disney Attractions (134 million visitors in 2014), Merlin Entertainment Group (63 million visitors) and Universal Parks and Resorts (40 million visitors). All over the world Disneyland has had a tremendous impact on local theme parks. In Japan, Disneyland Tokyo spurred the growth of the Japanese theme park industry, as did Disneyland Paris in Europe (Camp, 1997). The Disney Company also has interests in Hong Kong Disneyland.

The penetration of theme parks based on the number of visits per capita is very unequal in the developed countries. The USA and Japan show the highest penetration; Europe is far behind, and within Europe the visits per capita vary from country to country (Camp, 1997). However, care must be taken in interpreting the penetration. Generally speaking, European tourists have a wider choice of tourism attractions.

The composition of receipts is also very different. In the USA, related parks' admission fees count for 40–45 per cent of income while more than 50 per cent comes from merchandise, food, drinks and other. In Europe, admission fees represent on average 55–60 per cent of total receipts, with a correspondingly lower share for merchandising. The composition of the revenues in Disneyland Paris, park division, is illustrative. In 2012, admission fees represented 57 per cent, merchandising 21 per cent, food 21 per cent and other 2 per cent.

There is also an evolution within the sector. New types of theme park are being developed away from the conventional Disneyland type of attraction. Many of the new parks focus on a particular theme (e.g. crocodiles – Jungle Crocs of the World, in Florida). There is also a trend in the existing and new parks to offer hotel and other accommodation, shopping facilities, shows and even educational activities.

Related to the theme parks are the integrated leisure complexes. These centres combine retail, leisure, entertainment, catering and accommodation into integrated complexes. Examples are Edmonton Mall in Canada and Bluewater Park and Trafford Park in the United Kingdom. Allied with this concept, albeit on a larger scale, is the emergence of what Benckendorff (2006) calls 'Fantasy Cities' or Urban Entertainment Destinations (e.g. Las Vegas and Times Square in the USA and Darling Harbour in Sydney). They have six common features (Benckendorff, 2006):

- They are developed around themes (e.g. sport, history).
- They are usually aggressively marketed.
- They operate day and night.
- They offer an array of standard entertainment 'modules' such as high tech amusements, themed restaurants and cinemas.
- They are socially and economically isolated from the local urban environment.
- They offer a modern environment constructed around technologies of simulation, virtual reality and the thrill of the spectacle.

These integrated leisure complexes are a real competitor to traditional attractions.

References and further reading

Aguiló, E., Alegre, J., and Sard, M. (2003). Examining the market structure of the German and UK tour operating industries through an analysis of package holiday prices. *Tourism Economics, 3.*

AIEST (1995). *Real Estate Business and Tourism Development.* St-Gall: Editions AIEST.

Ansoff, I.H. (1987). *Corporate Strategy.* New York: Penguin.

Arbel, A., and Woods, R. (1991). Inflation and hotels: the cost of following a faulty routine. *The Cornell H.R.A. Quarterly,* February.

Benckendorff, P. (2006). Attractions megatrends. In D. Buhalis and C. Costa (eds), *Tourism Business Frontiers.* London: Elsevier.

Benhamou, F. (2000). Mondialisation de l'hôtellerie. *Espaces,* February.

Benur, A., and Bramwell, B. (2015). Tourism product development and product diversification in Destinations. *Tourism Management, 50.*

Bosselman, F., Peterson, C. and McCarthy, Cl. (2000). *Managing Tourism Growth.* Washington, DC: Island Press.

Bosshart, D., and Frick, K. (2006). *The Future of Leisure Travel: Trend Study.* Kuoni.

Buhalis, D. (2000). Marketing the competitive destination of the future. *Tourism Management, 21.*

Buhalis, D. (2006). The impact of information technology on tourism competition. In A. Papatheodorou (ed), *Corporate Rivalry and Market Power-Competition Issues in the Tourism Industry.* London: I.B. Tauris & Co. Ltd.

Buhalis, D., and Costa, C. (eds) (2006). *Tourism Business Frontiers.* London: Elsevier.

Bull, A. (1995). *The Economics of Travel and Tourism.* Sydney: Longman.

Butler, R.W. (1980). The concept of a tourist area cycle of evolution. *Canadian Geographer, 24.*

Camp, D. (1997). Theme parks in Europe. *Travel & Tourism Analyst, 5.*

Cavlek, N. (2006). Travel and tourism intermediaries. In L. Dwyer and P. Forsyth (eds), *International Handbook on the Economics of Tourism.* Cheltenham: Edward Elgar.

Chang, Y., Lee, S., and Park, H. (2017). Efficiency analysis of major cruise lines. *Tourism Management, 58.*

Cole, S. (2009). A logistic tourism model. Resort cycles, globalisation, and chaos. *Annals of Tourism Research, 4.*

Cole, S. (2012). Synergy and congestion in the tourist destination life cycle. *Tourism Management, 23.*

Cooper, C., Fletcher, J., Gilbert, D., and Wanhill, S. (1993). *Tourism: Principles & Practice.* London: Pitman Publishing.

Cunill, O. (2006). *The Growth Strategies of Hotel Chains.* New York: Haworth Hospitality Press.

Daudel, S. (1991). Le yield management. *Les Cahiers d' Espaces, 24.*

Dean, P. (1997). The timeshare industry in the Asia-Pacific region. *Travel & Tourism Analyst, 4.*

de Boiville, G. (2003). Tour-operating Européen. Les grandes manœuvres. *Espaces,* January.

Dimanche, F., and Jolly, D. (2006). The evolution of alliances in the airline industry. In L. Dwyer and P. Forsyth (eds), *International Handbook on the Economics of Tourism.* Cheltenham: Edward Elgar.

Eugenio-Martin, J., and Inchausti-Sintes, F. (2016). Low-cost travel and tourism expenditures. *Annals of Tourism Research, 57.*

Fayad, H., and Westlake, J. (2002). Globalisation of air transport: the challenges of the GATS. *Tourism Economics, 4.*

French, T. (1998). The future of global distribution systems. *Travel and Tourism Analyst, 3.*

Gil-Moltó, M., and Piga, C. (2008). Entry and exit by European low-cost and traditional carriers. *Tourism Economics, 3.*

Goeldner, C., Ritchie, J.R.B., and McIntosh, R. (2000). *Tourism: Principles, Practices Philosophies*, 8th edn. New York: John Wiley.

Goodall, B., and Stabler, M. (1990). Timeshare: the policy issues considered. *Tourism Research into the 1990s*, Conference Proceedings of a Conference held at University College, Durham, 10–12 December 1990.

Gross, S., and Lück, M. (eds) (2014). *The Low Cost Carrier Worldwide*. Farnham: Ashgate.

Haylock, R. (1994). The European timeshare market. *Tourism Management, 5*.

Haylock, R. (1995). Developments in the global timeshare market. *Travel & Tourism Analyst, 4*.

Hitchcock, N. (2001). The future of timesharing. In A. Lockwood and S. Medlik (eds), *Tourism and Hospitality in the 21st Century*. Oxford: Butterworth-Heinemann.

Horner, S., and Swarbrooke, J. (2004). *International Cases in Tourism Management*. Oxford: Elsevier.

Hudson, T., and Webster, B. (1994). Franchising. In S. Witt and L. Mouthinho (eds), *Tourism Marketing and Management Handbook*. London: Prentice Hall.

Jainchill, J. (2015). Lufthansa to add surcharge for GDS bookings. *Travel Weekly,* June.

Karlsson, L., and Dolnicar, S. (2016). Someone's been sleeping in my bed. *Annals of Tourism Research, 58*.

Karlsson, L., Kemperman, A., and Dolnicar, S. (2017). May I sleep in your bed? Getting permission to book. *Annals of Tourism Research, 62*.

Kerin, R., Mahajan, V., and Rajan, P. (1990). *Contemporary Perspectives on Strategic Planning*. Boston, MA: Allyn and Bacon.

Kim, S., Han, H., Holland, S., and Byon, K. (2009). Structural relationships among involvement, destination brand equity, satisfaction and destination visit intensions: the case of Japanese outbound travellers. *Journal of Vacation Management, 4*.

Komppula, R., Hakulinen, S., and Saraniemi. S. (2010). The life cycle of a specific tourist product – Christmas in Lapland. In P. Keller and T. Bieger (eds), *Managing Change in Tourism*. Berlin: Erich Schmidt Verlag.

Koutoulas, D. (2006). The market influence of tour operators on the hospitality industry. In A. Papatheodorou (ed), *Corporate Rivalry and Market Power-Competition Issues in the Tourism Industry*. London: I.B. Tauris & Co. Ltd.

Lee, J., Choi, Y., and Breiter, D. (2016). An exploratory study of convention destination competitiveness from the attendees' perspective: importance-performance analysis and repeated measures of MANOVA. *Journal of Hospitality & Tourism Research, 40 (5)*.

Lee, S., and Brezina, S. (2016). Cruise line efficiency: an analysis of seven cruise lines' operational efficiency. *Tourism Economics, 22 (5)*.

Le Monde (2003). Air France-KLM: la difficile naissance du leader européen, *Le Monde*, 1 October.

Lockwood, A., and Medlik, S. (eds) (2001). *Tourism and Hospitality in the 21st Century*. Oxford: Butterworth-Heinemann.

Mailliez, T., and Siery L. (2009). Du 'boutique hotel' à l'hôtel 'lifestyle'. *Espaces*, November.

Marvel, M. (2004). European hotel chain expansion. *Travel & Tourism Analyst*, Mintel, May.

McEniff, J. (1993). Theme parks in Europe. *Travel & Tourism Analyst, 5*.

Middleton, V.T.C., Fyall, A., Morgan, M., and Ranchhod, A. (2009). *Marketing in Travel and Tourism*, 4th edn. Oxford: Butterworth-Heinemann.

Mill, R.C., and Morrison, A.M. (1992). *The Tourism System*, 2nd edn. London: Prentice-Hall.

Morley, C. (2003). Impacts of international airline alliances on tourism. *Tourism Economics, 1*.

Morrison, A.M. (1989). *Hospitality and Travel Marketing*. New York: Delmar Publishers Inc.

Nederlands Bureau voor Toerisme (1998). *Digitale Revolutie in de Toeristenbranche*. The Hague: NBT.

Nederlands Bureau voor Toerisme & Congressen (2008). *Destinatie Holland 2020*. The Hague: NBTC.

Needham, P. (2000). Trends and issues in the European travel industry. *Travel & Tourism Analyst*, 6.

Nulty, P., and Cleverdon, R. (2011). *Handbook on Tourism Product Development*. Madrid: UNWTO-ETC.

OECD (2000). *Airline Mergers and Alliances*. Paris: OECD.

Okoroafo, S. (1995). Branding. In S. Witt and L. Mouthinho (eds), *Tourism Marketing and Management Handbook*. London: Prentice Hall.

O'Toole, K., and Walker, K. (2000). Alliance survey. *Airline Business*, July.

Page, S., Brunt, P., Busby, G., and Connell, J. (2002). *Tourism: A Modern Synthesis*. New York: Thomson.

Pan, B., MacLaurin, T., and Crotts, J. (2007). Travel blogs and the implications for destination marketing. *Journal of Travel Research*, August.

Papatheodorou, A. (ed) (2006). *Corporate Rivalry and Market Power-Competition Issues in the Tourism Industry*. London: I.B. Tauris & Co. Ltd.

Peisley, T. (2000). Cruising in crises. *Travel & Tourism Analyst*, 5.

Peters, M., and Frehse, J. (2005). The internationalization of the European hotel industry in the light of competition theories. *Tourism, 1*.

Pike, S. (2004). *Destination marketing organizations*. Amsterdam: Elsevier.

Poon, A. (1993). *Tourism, Technology and Competitive Strategies*. Wallingford: C.A.B International.

Poon, A. (1998). All-inclusive resorts. *Travel & Tourism Analyst*, 6.

Ragatz Associates (1995). *The World Wide Resort Timeshare Industry*. American Resort Development Agency. Washington, DC: Ragatz Associates.

Reece, W. (2010) *The Economics of Tourism*. Upper Saddle River, NJ: Prentice Hall.

Richard, B., and Cleveland, S. (2016). The future of hotel chains: branded marketplaces driven by the sharing economy. *Journal of Vacation Marketing, 22 (3)*.

Ritchie, J.R.B., and Crouch, G. (2003). *The Competitive Destination*. Wallingford: CABI Publishing.

Sheldon, P. J. (2006). Tourism information technology. In L. Dwyer and P. Forsyth (eds), *International Handbook on the Economics of Tourism*. Cheltenham: Edward Elgar.

Sinclair, T., and Stabler, M. (1998). *The Economics of Tourism*. London: Routledge.

Slatterly, P., and Johnson, S. (1993). Hotel chains in Europe. *Travel and Tourism Analyst, 1*.

TEA (2010). *Attraction Attendance Report 2008*, www.parkworld-online.com.

Tisdell, C. (ed.) (2000). *The Economics of Tourism*. Cheltenham: Edward Elgar.

Tribe, J. (2005). *The economics of recreation leisure & tourism*, 3rd edn. Oxford: Butterworth-Heinemann.

UNWTO (2007). *A Practical Guide to Tourism Destination Management*. Madrid: UNWTO.

Vogel, M. (2011) Monopolies at Sea: The role of onboard sales for the cruise industry's growth and profitability. In A. Matias, P. Nijkamp and M. Sarmento (eds), *Tourism Economics: Impact Analysis*. Heidelberg: Physica-Verlag.

Vogeler, C. (1995). Timesharing: a tourism and/or real estate product. *Real Estate Business and Tourism Development*, 45th AIEST Congress, Gran Canaria. AIEST.

Wanhill, S. (2006). Competition in visitor attractions. In A. Papatheodorou (ed), *Corporate Rivalry and Market Power-Competition Issues in the Tourism Industry*. London: I.B. Tauris & Co. Ltd.

WTO (1998). *Tourism: 2020 Vision*. Madrid: WTO.

WTO (2004). *World Overview & Tourism Topics*. Madrid: WTO.

Zervas, G., Proserpio, D., and Byers, J.W. (2015). *The Rise of the Sharing Economy: Estimating the Impact of Airbnb on the Hotel Industry*. Boston: School of Management.

Chapter 5

Pricing and taxation

The preceding chapters were dealing with demand and supply in the tourism sector. The combination of demand and supply leads us to the important 'price' notion. From the preceding chapters it must be clear that price is a key element in inter-firm competition. That is the reason why we pay special attention to pricing in tourism. What are the objectives? What are the pricing methods or pricing approaches?

One component of the price consists of taxes and subsidies. They can be important in the tourism sector. Many EU countries apply a VAT rate with respect to tourism products which varies between 15 and 21 per cent or even more. In Chapter 2 we made the distinction between producer's price and purchaser's price. They are related to indirect taxes and subsidies. Therefore it seems advisable to combine pricing and taxation in one chapter. However, VAT is not the only tax in the tourism sector. In the last two decades there has been a proliferation of taxes levied on tourism (room tax, air ticket tax, departure tax, foreign travel tax, visa tax, restaurant tax, toll charges, eco-tourism tax, carbon tax, betting tax, etc.).

Pricing in tourism

Pricing objectives

Pricing objectives can be divided into three categories. The first consists of profit-oriented pricing objectives. Prices are established either to achieve a certain targeted profit or to generate the maximum profit. In the former, target profits are expressed as a percentage return on investments or sales. The Hubbart formula, which is applied in the hotel business (see page 138), is a typical method. In the case of profit maximization, the firm sets the price that will give the greatest profit. Yield management responds to this objective.

The second category consists of sales-oriented pricing objectives, focussing on sales volumes and/or larger market share and not so much on profits. Needless to say, this is not without danger. Sales-oriented pricing can fit into the competitive strategy of a firm. An example is low-cost carriers.

Last but not least is status quo-oriented pricing, where the position relative to the competitors is the main target. This can be called competitive pricing. A firm tries to match its competitors' prices closely (e.g. in the rent-a-car market, Budget and National follow Hertz). This is the 'follow-the-leader' approach.

Pricing approaches

Of pricing methods or pricing approaches, four methods deserve special attention: the Hubbart formula, the break-even analysis, yield management and peak load pricing. Before dealing with each of these four methods in turn, let us start with the distinction made by Morrison (1989) between unsophisticated, sophisticated and multistage approaches. We limit ourselves to a general overview.

Unsophisticated approaches are based not so much on research or costs but more on the intuition of the entrepreneur. Morrison mentions four such approaches:

1   The competitive approach, where firms set prices based on their competitors' prices.
2   The 'follow-the-leader' approach, which is very similar to the competitive approach and is often applied by smaller market-share companies (e.g. Burger King may follow McDonald's price changes).
3   The intuitive approach, which is based on the entrepreneur's intuition.
4   The rule-of-thumb or traditional approach. There are two well-known rule-of-thumb approaches. The first concerns the hotel sector, where it is believed that €1 should be charged per €1,000 investment costs – in other words, a hotel investment of €100,000 per room should have a room rate of €100. The second concerns the restaurant sector, where multiplying the food cost of a particular dish by a factor of 2.5 is still common practice. Tax inspectors might sometimes apply this rule.

All these approaches are based on few objective factors or at most one factor and do not consider the cost/profit structure of the firm and neglect the customers' expectations.

Sophisticated approaches take more factors into account. Morrison (1989) refers to the following methods:

- Target-pricing, where the target is usually set in terms of a specific return on investment (see the Hubbart formula).
- Price discounting and price discrimination, where discounting means offering rates below the rack rate or those advertised, and discriminatory pricing means selling services to some customer groups at higher or lower prices. Discounting and discriminatory pricing can be based on criteria such as market choice, form of service provided, and place and time.
- Peak load pricing or the practice of charging different prices for the same services demanded at different points in time (Loomis and Lindberg, 2006).
- Promotional pricing.
- Cost-plus pricing, where an amount or percentage is added to the estimated cost of a product or service.
- New-product pricing, which involves setting a different price for a new product. There are different strategies for introducing a new product; the two best known are price-skimming (an artificially high price for a new product) and penetration pricing (introducing a new product at a very low price).
- Price lining, where the firm pre-establishes prices that it feels confident will attract customers.
- Psychological pricing, where slightly lower prices are used to give customers the impression that they are receiving something extra.
- Leader pricing, where a firm offers a product for a short time at a price below its actual costs, or offers something special with the purchase of a product (e.g. a beer with the purchase of spaghetti).

In the *multistage approach*, nine factors should be taken into consideration when pricing (Morrison, 1989):

1   Competitors
2   Customer characteristics
3   Customer demand volumes

4   Costs
5   Channels
6   Corporate objectives
7   Corporate image and positioning
8   Complementary services and facilities
9   Consistency with marketing-mix elements and strategy.

For effective pricing, a multistage approach based on those factors is required. This will help a firm in deciding which is the best price approach and the most appropriate price level.

The Hubbart formula for determining room rates

The Hubbart formula is a typical method of determining target price in the hotel sector. This method is interesting and effective because it considers several of the factors of pricing mentioned above.

The rack rate is the result of different steps. The calculated price should be considered as an orientation rate – indeed, the Hubbart formula is cost-oriented. The method ignores the demand side and some critical supply-side variables, such as the competitive position of the company (Arbel and Woods, 1991), but the calculated price can always be adjusted to take into account the hotel positioning and the pricing policy of competitors (see Table 5.1).

Break-even analysis

Break-even analysis shows the relationship between costs (fixed and variable costs), demand volume and profits. The formula to calculate the break-even point is:

$$\text{Break-even point} = \frac{\text{(total fixed costs)}}{\text{(contribution margin)}} \qquad (5.1)$$

The contribution margin is defined as the difference between the selling price per unit and the variable cost per unit. This formula can also be used in target pricing. In this case, the formula becomes:

$$\text{Break-even point} = \frac{\text{(total fixed costs + target profit)}}{\text{(selling price per unit − variable cost per unit)}} \qquad (5.2)$$

Table 5.1 The Hubbart formula method

Starting point (step 1)	Desired return on investment after tax
Plus (2)	Undistributed expenses (e.g. interest, property tax, depreciation, energy costs, property maintenance)
Less (3)	Net revenues other departments
Equals (4)	Room profit
Plus (5)	Room expenses
Equals (6)	Required room revenues
Projection (7)	Projection of the number of rooms the firm expects to sell (projected occupancy rate)
Average room rate (8)	(6)/(7), or average rate per occupied room after discounts and commissions

For example, if

total fixed costs = €500,000
selling price per unit = €125
variable cost per unit sold = €40
target profit = €160,000

then the break-even point equals $(500,000 + 160,000)/(125 - 40)$ or 7,764 units.
In other words, 7,764 units should be sold to achieve a target profit of €161,000.

Break-even analysis is very often used in discount pricing. For example, if the firm were to give a discount of €15 per unit, what would be the necessary sales volume to achieve the target profit? The application of the formula $(500,000 + 160,000)/(110 - 40)$ indicates that the break-even volume increases to 9,429 units. The firm can then decide whether such an increase in volume is feasible in terms of capacity, additional costs and demand.

As with any method, the break-even analysis has a number of limitations. First, constant variable costs irrespective of the sales volume are assumed. Secondly, fixed costs are also supposed to be constant, which is not so evident; some fixed-cost items might increase at a certain level of turnover. Thirdly, the demand is not too sensitive to the prevailing price.

Yield management

Yield management, a method for managing capacity profitably, has its origins in the airline sector. Since then it has also gained widespread application in the hotel business and other tourism sectors. It can be defined as selling the right inventory unit to the right type of customer, at the right time and for the right price (Kimes, 1999). Yield management guides the decision of how to allocate undifferentiated units of capacity to available demand in order to maximize profit or revenue. The problem is to determine how much to sell at what price and to which segment. In short, yield management can be defined as the optimization of revenue through the differentiation of prices (Cavlek, 2006).

As such, yield management is a method that responds to profit-oriented pricing objectives, and in particular to profit or revenue maximization. At the same time, it is an application of discriminatory pricing (see Figure 5.1).

Let us first define the term 'yield'. In the hotel business, 'yield' is equal to the occupancy rate multiplied by the average room rate:

$$\text{Yield} = \frac{\text{room nights sold}}{\text{room available}} \times \frac{\text{actual average rate}}{\text{room rate potential}} \tag{5.3}$$

Yield management concerns the first and second terms of the above-mentioned formula. This method is by no means restricted to hotels.

Yield management should not be confused with pure price discrimination. The latter can be considered as a first step in the direction of yield management, but for Kimes (1999), yield management is essentially a form of price discrimination.

Figure 5.1 relates to price discrimination. The aim is revenue maximization. The total revenue with a single price P equals OPBQ. If the total demand is divided into three segments, each with its own price, the total revenue becomes $OP_1AQ_1 + Q_1EBQ + QDCQ_2$ – i.e. the total revenue with price discrimination is greater than the total revenue with a single price P_0 (OQ_1 units are sold at price P_1; Q_1Q_0 units at P_0 and O_0Q_2 units at P_2).

Tribe (2005) mentions three conditions that are necessary for price discrimination to take place. The first is that the product cannot be resold – in other words, consumer A (who is buying at a low price) cannot sell the product to customer B (at a higher price). Very often the

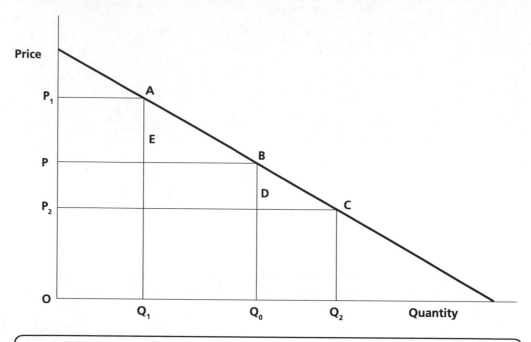

Figure 5.1 Total revenue with single pricing and price discrimination

products are not 100 per cent identical – for example, a full-fare air ticket is refundable and can be changed at no cost, unlike less expensive tickets. Tourism products as service products provide good conditions for price discrimination. The second is that the supplier should be able to identify different segments. Finally, there must be market imperfections.

According to Kimes, early yield management approaches used threshold curve methods in which a firm (for example, a hotel) closed rates when demand was above a certain level and opened rates when demand was below a certain point (see Figure 5.2). By the mid-1990s, many of the major hotel chains had adopted more sophisticated mathematical programming-based methods (see Yeoman and Ingold, 1999).

Figure 5.2 shows a typical booking curve AE for a tourist product – say a hotel room. Based on historical data, the booking curve normally moves in a band between the two dotted lines. This is the expected demand pattern, and depicts the 'threshold values' (Relihan, 1989). Three months before the consumption date (say 100 days), the bookings are rather low. At point B the booking curve is outside the threshold band, and prices should be adjusted upwards or discounts eliminated. At point C the actual bookings fall below the threshold, and this indicates that the management should open discount rates to encourage more reservations.

Lieberman (1993) warns of the myth that yield management is price discounting. Lieberman states:

> Raising and lowering prices dynamically for a given date, depending on demand, is a business decision . . . but it is not a yield-management decision. Yield management focuses on how much of a product to sell at established prices. It does not tell a hotel what prices to charge or whether to change prices. But it does indicate when to open and close rate classes.

Indeed, yield management focusses on two basic elements: allocation of capacity to the right type of customer, and demand at the right price in order to maximize revenue or yield. Applied to air transport, where should the separation be made between business and economy in an

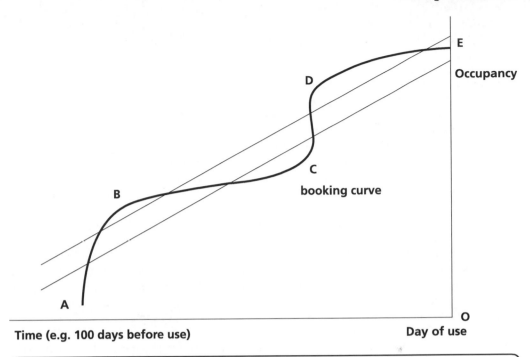

E

Occupancy

D

C

booking curve

B

A

Time (e.g. 100 days before use)

Day of use

O

Figure 5.2 Yield management and sales booking curve

aircraft on a particular scheduled flight? What is the allotment for inclusive tours? An air carrier has a lot of flexibility.

A successful yield management (system) should respond to a number of basic conditions (Kimes, 1999; Raeside, 1999). The first necessary condition is the possibility of segmenting the demand and the ability to segment by willingness to pay. This implies that the segments show different demand-elasticity (e.g. different time of use, type of traveller, early bookings with no refund restrictions). The second condition relates to a similarity of inventory units (e.g. rooms, seats). This pricing system also requires that the product can be sold well in advance, and that historical demand and booking patterns and a good information system are available.

Further conditions include:

- Fixed capacity. Many sectors in tourism are confronted with capacity constraints – once an airplane has been purchased, a cruise ship constructed or a hotel built, it is expensive and difficult to enhance its capacity.
- High fixed cost. This is related to fixed capacity; enhancing capacity is difficult in the short term.
- Low variable costs. Incremental costs to a hotel or airline are very low – in other words, an additional customer is inexpensive.
- Perishable inventory. This is a characteristic of all tourist products.
- Pricing knowledge. Most firms practising yield management rely on competitive pricing methods. By offering multiple rates, firms hope to increase their revenue.
- An overbooking policy. Firms protect themselves against the possibility of no-shows. An overbooking policy cannot be developed without historical data of no-shows.

The conclusions of Vila and Córcoles (2011) are interesting with respect to the application of yield management by Low Cost Carriers (LCCs) and Flag Companies (FCs). They tested two hypotheses. H1: Price variation over time will be higher for LCCs than for FCs. H2: Low-cost companies do not differ from each other with regard to the prices set as the date of departure gets closer. All of them adopt dynamic pricing strategies. The authors conclude:

> Empirical analysis has provided support for the aforementioned hypotheses. The results suggest that the methods used to set prices for the two strategic groups (LCCs and FCs) are different, thus our first hypothesis is supported. In this regard, there are two strategic groups with different pricing competitive strategies that do not interfere with one another. That is to say, the FC price setting method does not affect that of the LCCs, or vice versa. In the case of LCCs, we must accept the second hypothesis, which refers to the existence of intra-group similarities with respect to price strategies. In fact, there are no significant differences in pricing by LCC airlines, at least when there is a considerable time period between ticket purchase and the flight. (See also Salanti *et al.*, 2012.)

Airline pricing is sometimes apparently irrational. Why is it possible that a round-trip flight from Rome to Atlanta costs much more than a round-trip flight from Atlanta to Rome, even though both flights involve the same travel? Yield management is partly responsible. Reece (2010) gives a good explanation. Firstly, each airline must set its prices on its own. A price coordination between two or more carriers could violate the competition law. Each company does its own yield management system based on its own demand and supply. Secondly, the airlines' yield management systems determine prices separately for each origin and destination combination in function of demand and seat availabilities. The reality can be even more complex due to different fare classes, codesharing and possible promotional discount fares from one airline on a specific route.

To conclude this section, a few points should be noted:

1 The application is much more complex than the text above might suggest. Air carriers and hotel chains make use of mathematical models (Raeside, 1999).
2 Consistent pricing should take into account regular customers. Even when demand is unusually heavy for an upcoming date, it would be unwise to refuse a loyal customer's request for a normally available discount rate (Lieberman, 1993).
3 The difference between working days and weekends makes the application more difficult. In case of multiple-night stays during low- and high-demand days, trade-offs need to be addressed by the yield management system.
4 Hotel managers should be aware that rooms are not the only service sold in a hotel. The restaurant, conference space and parking facilities all contribute to a hotel's profitability (Kimes, 1989).
5 Yield management can be very important at the local level when several hotels are located in the neighbourhood. Hotels within a limited vicinity are substitutes for each other, and the price at which hotel rooms are offered affects the demand for the rooms (Relihan, 1989).
6 Price-inelastic (high rate-paying) demand occurs just before arrival (e.g. business travel), and price-elastic demand occurs well in advance.

Yield management (price discrimination) is nowadays a common practice in many sectors of the tourism industry. The application is complex, and requires a lot of data and advanced computer models. Based on contacts with yield managers in the tourism industry, revenue increases of 6–7 per cent are not unusual. However, yield management is open to all competitors. In some cases, avoiding the loss of market share is already a positive contribution.

Peak load pricing

Peak load pricing refers to the practice of charging different prices for the same product at different points in time. It is a special case of marginal cost pricing (Loomis and Lindberg, 2006).

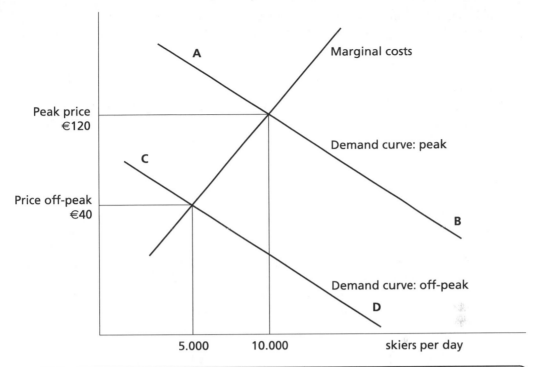

Figure 5.3 Peak load pricing

Source: Loomis and Lindberg (2006)

The demand for many tourist products is much higher during some periods of the year than other periods. The capacity of the facilities should to a certain degree respond to the demand of peak periods. This implies an excess capacity in off-peak periods. The costs of this capacity can be covered by adopting a marginal cost pricing policy. In that case peak customers pay more than off-peak customers.

Let us suppose during peak periods an excess demand for ski holiday services over the available supply. In Figure 5.3 curve AB represents the average demand at peak times and curve CD the average demand off-peak. The quantity demanded on peak days is double that on off-peak days. During the off-peak period, low user prices are set at €40 where supply is equal to the marginal benefit of off-peak users. During the peak period user price is much higher (€120) where marginal cost is equal to marginal benefit of peak users. We suppose that there are twice as many off-peak days as peak days (weekends, breaks and holidays).

The difference between peak and off-peak price represents two types of costs. Firstly, in peak periods there are the higher operating costs to provide services to a large number of visitors. Secondly, a capital charge equal to the annualized value of capital increase at the ski resort to accommodate peak periods, divided by the number of users in the peak period.

What are the advantages of peak load pricing? Loomis and Lindberg (2006) indicate four advantages:

1   Multiplying peak usage by the capital charge per customer equals total revenue remaining after payment of operation costs. If the remaining revenue exceeds the annual capital costs of the investment, then expansion of the capacity is rational. This implies that capacity extension can be justified until the number of consumers in the peak period multiplied by the daily capacity charge, equals the annual capital costs associated with the capacity

increase. In other words the value of the capacity charge required to clear the market during the peak period indicates whether increase of facilities is justified from an economic viewpoint.

2   This price approach stimulates consumers to use the facilities during off-peak periods. They can profit from an economic benefit. At the same time they contribute to a reduction in seasonal variation.

3   The peak price is situated on the demand curve AB which express the willingness to pay.

4   Peak load pricing reduces equity problems since some low-income users (e.g. retired people) can use the services during off-peak periods when prices are less.

Pricing and elasticity of demand

At the end of this section we should underline the significance of price-elasticity in the pricing process (see Chapter 2). If a tourism activity or destination is price-elastic and the price is increased, the total revenue will decrease. On the other hand when the price-elasticity is less than 1, a price increase will result in a revenue increase. As a result, for a unique tourist destination where price is inelastic, prices increases can be justified. It is important to know whether the current and proposed prices are in the inelastic part of the demand curve. Indeed we have seen in Chapter 3 that a linear demand curve has an elastic and an inelastic part. A nonlinear demand curve may have a constant price elasticity.

Tourism and taxation

To avoid any misunderstanding this section is dedicated exclusively to indirect taxes and subsidies (also called negative indirect taxes). Some authors (Forsyth and Dwyer, 2002; Gago *et al.*, 2009) make a distinction between general taxes (sales taxation and VAT) and differential tourism taxes (tourism can face higher rates of a general tax or they may be specific levies such as accommodation taxes). Tax receipts generated by tourism come both from general indirect taxation and from specific tourism taxes. For a typology of tourism taxes we refer to Gooroochurn and Sinclair (2005). UNWTO has identified more than 40 different types of taxes applied to the tourism industry in both developed and undeveloped countries. Income and company taxes are here not under discussion. In this section we pay attention to three topics:

● Why a tourism tax?
● Who pays the tax?
● Optimal taxation is not evident.

A tourism tax: why?

Many destinations have created a tourism or tourist tax. One speaks of 'tourist tax' or 'tourism tax' when taxes fall largely on tourists or tourist firms (airport tax, tourist tax in a hotel, carbon tax). They are a type of indirect tax such as VAT or sales tax. The question arises as to why destinations tax tourism. Mak (2006) gives four reasons why destinations tax tourism:

1   To diversify the tax base or to build greater revenue elasticity into their own fiscal system

2   To export taxes to non-resident tourists (see Forsyth *et al.*, 2014)

3   To tax away excess profits or economic rents from tourism to benefit residents

4   To correct for market failure (e.g. monopoly power, public goods and externalities).

Successful tax exporting depends on two conditions. Firstly, the tax must be passed to the consumer. Secondly, the tourists should not be residents in the jurisdiction that levies the tax.

Governments are not always aware that high taxes increase the cost of tourist products and can discourage people from travelling. A good example was the imposition in the Balearic Islands of a daily 'eco-tax' on tourists in 2002. In this respect price-elasticity is very important (see page 149). It is possible that the local tourism sector pays the tourism tax and not the foreign visitor (see below; see also Forsyth and Dwyer, 2002).

In Chapter 10 we shall see that one of the advantages of developing tourism in some countries is the availability of free natural resources which are inexhaustible such as beaches, sun, mountains, etc. The question is how to internalize these benefits. Good destination management can produce economic rents and high profits to tourism business. But how can the local population benefit? Taxing economic rents is in many cases a solution. Overstay taxes (room tax) and entry tax can have this objective. Here we refer to Mak (2006):

> Tourism's economic rents are returns that are in excess of the marginal social cost of providing services to tourism. Tourism suppliers obviously will try to capture these rents by charging higher prices where and when they can. On the other hand, destination lawmakers may wish to extract as much of the rents as possible to increase tourism's benefits to residents. Taxation is one way to extract economic rents from tourism.

An example of correction of market failure is the imposition of a CO_2 tax or noise tax on flights. The EU recommendation to impose a 'green tax' on all air tickets goes in the same direction. Forsyth and Dwyer (2002) speak of earmarking of special tourism taxes. The most well-known example is tourism promotion by the public sector. Tourism taxes are also levied to finance the external costs that tourists provoke (Gooroochurn and Sinclair, 2005).

Taxes can also be used as an instrument to compete with other destinations. In the EU there is a great difference in VAT rates applied in the hotel sector; they vary from 3 per cent in Luxemburg to 25 per cent in Denmark. Lowering VAT rates for hotels and restaurants is a hot topic in the EU (Gago *et al.*, 2009; Manente and Zanette, 2010). The financial crisis is for the tourism sector an opportunity to put governments under pressure to reduce VAT rates for hotels and restaurants.

Who pays the tourism tax bill: the tourist or the producer?

Those who impose a tourism tax are not always aware of the incidence of the tax. Somebody is paying the tax, but who? Is it the consumer or the producer (Forsyth and Dwyer, 2002)?

We should make a distinction between consumer price (p^C) and producer price (p^P). The consumer price is the price the buyer pays. This is not the amount the producer receives. The producer has to transfer taxes (t) to the government (Berlage and Decoster, 2005).

$$p^P = p - t \quad \text{(t is a lump sum)} \tag{5.4}$$

$$p^C = p \tag{5.5}$$

In the case of a tax on the consumer, the price the consumer pays is higher than the price the producer receives. We get:

$$p^C = p + t \tag{5.6}$$

$$p^P = p \tag{5.7}$$

Equations (5.4) and (5.6) are identical when one substitutes (5.5) into (5.4) and (5.7) into (5.6)

$$p^C = p^P + t \tag{5.8}$$

Pricing and taxation

The difference between a tax on the producer and on the consumer only leads to a different interpretation of the market price p. In the case of a value tax (e.g. VAT) the more the value the more the wedge between producer price and consumer price. Equation (5.6) becomes:

$$p^C = p + r.p \quad \text{(r stands for the tax rate)}$$

$$p^C = (1 + r)\, p \tag{5.9}$$

Figure 5.4 proves the equivalency of a tourism tax on consumer and producer. It does not make a difference if we impose the tourism tax on the tourist or on the tourism firm.

In Figure 5.4 one notices that a tax on the demand (e.g. admissions to beaches) shifts the demand curve to the left. In the case of a tax on the producer the supply curve shifts to the left.

An important question is 'who pays the tourism tax?' The answer to this question depends on the elasticity of demand and supply. We illustrate this with a graph (see Figure 5.5). What is the effect of a tax of €5 per unit tourism service on the demand and supply of that service? We take two different demand elasticities: a low elasticity (left-hand part of Figure 5.5) and a high elasticity (right-hand part of Figure 5.5). Due to the tax, the supply curve has shifted to the left. In the first case (low demand elasticity) the price paid by the tourist is no longer the equilibrium price E_0 or €20 . He pays €24, but this is not the price received by the supplier (€19). The tax also influences the volume of sales. The volume Q reduces from 4,000 to 3,500 units.

The same tax in a situation of a high elasticity is quite different. Starting from the same equilibrium price E_0, the consumer pays €22 and the producer receives €17. The produced volume Q falls from 4,000 units to 3,000.

The conclusion is clear: the less elastic the demand, the more the consumer is vulnerable to a shift of the tax onto the producer via an increase of the consumer price. It is not difficult to prove that the breakdown of the tax burden on the producer also depends on the inclination of the supply curve. Also, in the case of the shift of the tax onto the consumer, the consumer price increases the more elastic the supply curve is.

A good example of how the effect of a tax or a tax reduction is divided between consumer and producer can be found in the study of Manente and Zanette (2010). At the same time it illustrates that a tax reduction can be used as a competition instrument. Manente and Zanette

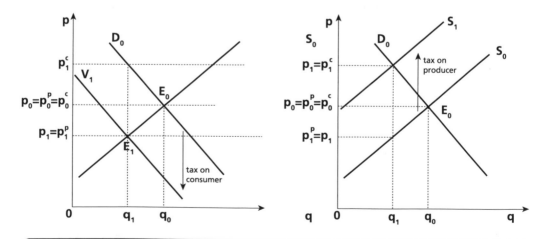

Figure 5.4 Equivalency of a tax on consumer or on a producer
Source: Berlage and Decoster (2005)

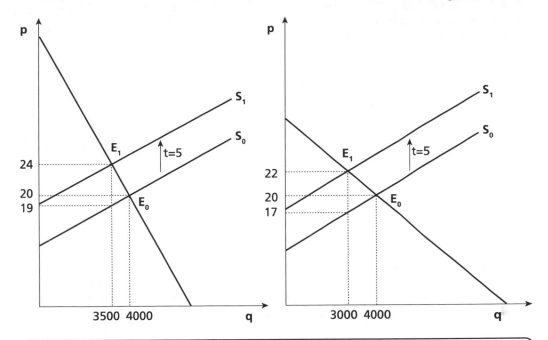

Figure 5.5 Effect of a fixed producer tax with a low and a high demand elasticity

calculated the macro-economic effects for Italy of a VAT reduction in the hotel and restaurant industry from 10 to 5 per cent (r = 0.1 and r = 0.05). Their working hypotheses were:

- the demand for hotel and restaurant products in Italy in 2007
- a situation of perfect competition
- the above-mentioned equation (5.9), $p^C = (1 + r) p$
- a supply elasticity of $\varepsilon^s = 1.5$ or $\varepsilon^s = 2.0$
- a demand elasticity of $\varepsilon^d = -1.06$, being the average of demand elasticities for domestic and foreign demand.

They found the following results:

- variation of $p^C = -2.7$ to -3.0 per cent
- variation of $p^P = +1.6$ to $+1.9$ per cent
- growth of tourism nights = $+2.8$ to $+3.2$ per cent.

In other words the VAT reduction results in lower prices for the tourist services, an increase of the producer price and an increase of tourism nights. The authors also calculated the impact of a rising demand on investment in tourism and other sectors. They used the following relation with the OLS method (for the technical aspects see Chapter 8):

$$\text{Log } I_t = \alpha + b_1 \log TN_t + b_2 \log r_t + \varepsilon_t \qquad (5.10)$$

where

I = investments in hotel and restaurant industry
t = 1997 to 2007

TN = tourist nights and expected tourist nights
r = real interest rate

The overall impact in terms of VAT is an estimated loss of − €616 million compared to an initial VAT receipt of €4.9 billion. In a period of economic crisis that amount of losses in VAT should be compared with the corresponding employment creation due to more tourism consumption and more investments (minus employment lost due to less public consumption). The job creation is estimated at 2.7 million full-time jobs or a job effect of + 3.8 per cent for the Italian economy. If the market works efficiently and the suppliers are correct, the VAT reduction makes sense.

The best and most comprehensive method of measuring the impact of a tax on the tourism sector is to make use of a dynamic Computable General Equilibrium (CGE) analysis (see Chapter 10) (Gooroochurn and Sinclair, 2005; Dwyer *et al.*, 2012; Dwyer *et al.*, 2013).

Dwyer *et al.* (2012) assess the potential economic effects on the Australian tourism industry of the introduction of a carbon tax. Their conclusion is quite clear.

> The tax is projected to lead to changes in key macroeconomic variables, reducing growth in real GDP, real consumption, and employment. Most tourism industries in Australia will experience a small but significant contraction in output relative to projected baseline values over the period to 2020 in line with a reduction in growth for the economy as a whole. A slightly larger reduction in tourism employment, relative to that of other Australian industries, is projected for the period. The largest falls occur in the accommodation; air and water transport; and the cafes, restaurants and food outlets industries. Since direction of impacts on the tourism industry can be expected to be similar for any pricing scheme to reduce carbon emissions, the analysis has implications for tourism policy globally.

Forsyth *et al.* (2014) use the same method to measure the impacts of Australia's departure tax. The study estimates the expenditure effects of the increase in Australia's Passenger Movement Charge (PMC) as well as the economic impacts on the Australian economy and the tourism industry. A CGE model is used to estimate the economic impacts of the increased charge on the inbound, outbound and domestic market. The authors come to interesting conclusions:

> While there are several effects which work in conflicting directions, by far the largest effect is in the inbound tax effect. In retrospect, this is not surprising since a country gains from getting its visitors to pay its taxes. It should be noted that while an individual country will gain, the imposition of a tax by a country may, and probably will, be negative for global welfare. Additionally, the impact of a switch from outbound travel expenditure to domestic spending will be positive, regardless of whether it is to domestic travel or to increased expenditure on other goods and services. On balance, a tourism industry can gain or lose from a passenger tax increase, depending on the price elasticity of the demands for inbound and outbound travel, the balance of inbound and outbound travel, and on the extent to which domestic tourism is a substitute for outbound tourism.

Tax receipts not always what is expected

Optimal tourism taxation is not obvious. Many factors should be taken into account (Mak, 2008). Taxation should comply with the principles of equity, efficiency, stability, simplicity and cost effectiveness (Gooroochurn and Sinclair, 2005). Equity depends on the impact of a tax on the domestic population with lower incomes. The higher the proportion of domestic demand in total demand (local people and inbound tourism), the higher will be the equity effects.

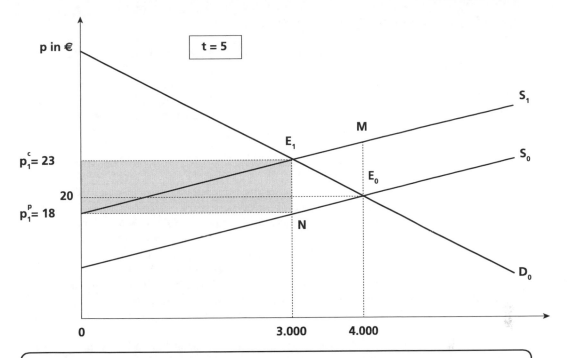

Figure 5.6 Tourism tax and government receipts

Of utmost importance is the efficiency of a tourism tax. A government of a destination does not always receive the tourism taxes they expect. Let us illustrate this with a theoretical example. We suppose a government introduces a tourism tax of €5 per day tripper. Before they imposed the tax the destination counted 4,000 excursionists per day. The local authority hoped to collect €20,000 per day. With a demand and supply curve as in Figure 5.6, the introduction of the tourism tax reduces the demand from 4,000 to 3,000 visitors per day. The local government does not collect €20,000 but only €15,000. The consumer does not pay €25 but €23 (€3 above the original equilibrium price). And the producer is contributing €2 per day tripper in the tourism tax.

In the case of a more elastic demand curve, the local government would receive even less and the local producer would contribute more than €2 per excursionist.

A practical example was the introduction of an air ticket tax or eco-tax (€11) in the Netherlands in 2008. This led to a large number of Dutch tourists departing from Belgian and German airports instead. Some airports used the absence of the air ticket tax in their country as a promotion argument. A year later the Dutch air ticket tax was removed.

Here one of the conclusions of Gooroochurn and Sinclair (2005) is relevant:

> It is clear that proposed policies for taxing tourism should be subject to considerable scrutiny before being approved or implemented. Different types of policies have different effects on international tourists, domestic residents, and sectors within the economy. Although the imposition of relatively heavy taxes on the tourism sector appears appealing in terms of income generation, it may also be contractionary in terms of lowering GDP and the number of arrivals. Competitiveness in the international arena is reduced by higher taxes, which may prejudice the ongoing development and growth of tourism industry.

We were confronted with such a situation in Barbados in the early 1990's (see Chapter 6).

References and further reading

Arbel, A., and Woods, R. (1991). Inflation and hotels: the cost of following a faulty routine. *The Cornell H.R.A. Quarterly,* December.

Berlage, L., and Decoster, A. (2005). *Inleiding tot de Economie.* Leuven: Universitaiere Pers.

Cavlek, N. (2006). Travel and tourism intermediaries. In L. Dwyer and P. Forsyth (eds), *International Handbook on the Economics of Tourism.* Cheltenham: Edward Elgar.

Daudel, S., Vialle, G., and Humphreys, B. (1994). *Yield Management.* Paris: Institute of Air Transport.

Dwyer, L., Forsyth, P., and Spurr, R. (2012). Whither Australian tourism? Implications of the carbon tax. *Tourism Management, 19.*

Dwyer, L., Forsyth, P., Spurr, R., and Hogue, S. (2013). Economic impacts of a carbon tax on the Australian tourism industry. *Journal of Travel Research, 52 (2).*

Forsyth, P., and Dwyer, L. (2002). Market power and the taxation of domestic and international tourism. *Tourism Economics, 4.*

Forsyth, P., Dwyer, L., Spurr, R., and Pham, T. (2014). The impacts of Australia's departure tax: tourism versus the economy. *Tourism Management, 40.*

Gago, A., Labandeira, X., Picos, F., and Rodriguez, M. (2009). Specific and general taxation of tourism activities. Evidence from Spain. *Tourism Management, 30.*

Gooroochurn, N., and Sinclair, M. (2005). Economics of taxation. Evidence from Mauritius. *Annals of Tourism Research, 2.*

Ingold, A., and Huyton, J. (1999). Yield management and the airline industry. In I. Yeoman and A. Ingold (eds), *Yield Management: Strategies for the Service Industries.* London: Cassell.

Kimes, S. (1989). The basis of yield management. *The Cornell H.R.A. Quarterly,* November.

Kimes, S. (1999). Yield management: an overview. In I. Yeoman and A. Ingold (eds), *Yield Management: Strategies for the Service Industries.* London: Cassell.

Kimes, S., Chase, R., Choi, S., Lee, P., and Ngonzi, E. (1998). Restaurant revenue management. Applying yield management to the restaurant industry. *The Cornell H.R.A. Quarterly,* June.

Lieberman, W. (1993). Debunking the myths of yield management. *The Cornell H.R.A. Quarterly,* February.

Loomis, J., and Lindberg, K. (2006). Pricing principles for natural and cultural attractions in tourism. In L. Dwyer and P. Forsyth (eds), *International Handbook on the Economics of Tourism.* Cheltenham: Edward Elgar.

Mak, J. (2006). Taxation of travel and tourism. In L. Dwyer and P. Forsyth (eds), *International Handbook on the Economics of Tourism.* Cheltenham: Edward Elgar.

Mak, J. (2008). Taxing cruise tourism: Alaska's tax on cruise ship passengers. *Tourism Economics, 3.*

Manente, M., and Zanette, M. (2010). Macroeconomic effects of a VAT reduction in the Italian hotel and restaurants industry. *Economic Systems Research, 22.*

Morrison, A. (1989). *Hospitality and Travel Marketing.* New York: Delmar Publishers.

Müller, H., and Heller, A. (2007). *Evaluation einer Tourismusförderungsabgabe (TFA) in der Stadt Bern.* Bern: FIF.

Origet du Cluzeau, Cl. (1996). Le yield mangement comme stade paroxystique de la loi du marché. *Revue d'Espaces, 139.*

Raeside, R. (1999). Quantitative methods. In I. Yeoman and A. Ingold (eds), *Yield Management. Strategies for the Service Industries.* London: Cassell.

Reece, W. (2010). *The Economics of Tourism.* New Jersey: Prentice Hall.

Relihan, W. (1989). The yield management approach to hotel room pricing. *Cornell H.R.A. Quarterly, 30 (1).*

Salanti, A., Malighetti, P., and Redondi, R. (2012). Low-cost pricing strategies in leisure markets. *Tourism Management, 33.*

Sawhney, S., and Lewis, R. (1992). Hotel yield management in practice: a case analysis. *Journal of Hospitality and Leisure Marketing*, 2.

Sheldon, P.J. (1995). Information technology and computer reservation systems. In S. Witt and L. Mouthinho (eds), *Tourism Marketing and Management Handbook*. London: Prentice Hall.

Tribe, J. (2005). *The economics of recreation, leisure & tourism, third edition*. London: Elsevier.

Vila, N., and Córcoles, M. (2011). Yield management and airline strategic groups. *Tourism Economics, 17 (2)*.

Yeoman, I., and Ingold, A. (1999). *Yield Management*. London: Cassell.

Chapter 6

Competition and the tourism destination

Introduction

During the last decades there has been a growing interest in tourism literature in the notion of the 'competitive destination'. In the preceding decades competition in tourism was very often identified with the price component and was frequently restricted to the micro-level (see Chapter 5). It cannot be denied that for a destination as well as for an enterprise et al., price is a vital element of competitiveness (see Chapters 1 and 3; Dwyer *et al.*, 2000; Baldassin *et al.*, 2017). However, since the beginning of the 1990s (see AIEST, 1993; Poon, 1993; Goeldner *et al.*, 2000) the tourism sector and tourism scientists have been aware that besides comparative advantages and price, many other variables determine the competitiveness of a tourism enterprise or destination. More and more authors and practitioners are focussing on the competitive destination. A well-known generic definition of competitiveness is given by the OECD (1997): 'The degree to which a country can, under free and fair market conditions, produce goods and services which meet the tests of international markets while simultaneously maintaining and expanding the real incomes over the longer term.'

The idea of the competitive destination contains two elements: destination and competitiveness. A tourism destination is a well-defined geographical area within which the tourist enjoys various types of tourism experiences. Ritchie and Crouch (2003) distinguish several levels of tourism destinations:

- A country
- A macro-region consisting of several countries (e.g. Africa)
- A province or another administrative entity
- A localized region (e.g. Flanders, Normandy)
- A city or town
- A unique locale with great drawing power (e.g. a national park, Iguaçu Falls, Disney World in Orlando, the Notre Dame in Paris).

In relative terms, very few tourists visit a macro-region or country such as Spain, the USA, etc. Tourists are interested in regions and towns, such as Andalucia in Spain, the Algarve in Portugal, New York in the USA, and the Flemish art cities. These are 'tourism clusters'. Porter (1998) defines clusters as: 'geographic concentrations of interconnected companies and institutions in a particular field. Clusters encompass an array of linked industries and other entities important to tourism'. He refers to the California wine cluster as a good example. This includes hundreds of commercial wineries, thousands of independent wine-grape growers, an extensive complement of industries supporting both wine-making and grape-growing (suppliers of grape stock, irrigation and harvesting equipment, barrels, labels), advertising firms, local institutions involved with wine, and the enology program at the University of California at Davis. Applied to tourism, we can define a cluster as a group of tourism attractions, enterprises and institutions directly or indirectly related to tourism and concentrated in a specific geographical area. Competition in tourism is mainly between clusters and not so much between countries (Bordas, 1994).

According to Ritchie and Crouch (2000), 'The fundamental product in tourism is the destination experience. Competition, therefore, centres on the destination.' For most tourists, this experience takes place in a rather small geographical area such as a town or a region. This is an entity which, from the tourism management point of view, is managerial. Competitiveness is a complex notion. The definitions offered in the literature have either a macro or a micro connotation (Dwyer and Kim, 2004). From the macro perspective competitiveness concerns the improvement of real income of the community. It encompasses all social, cultural and economic variables affecting the performance of a destination in international markets. In the micro perspective, in order to be competitive, any organization (e.g. a hotel, a carrier), must offer products and services for which the customers are willing to pay and receive value for money. Dwyer and Kim underline that competitiveness is a relative concept (one always compares) and is multi-dimensional (there are salient attributes).

In the literature others make a distinction between comparative and competitive advantage. For a tourism destination comparative advantage relates to factor endowments such as climate, nature, scenery, culture, fauna and flora. Competitive advantage relates to how well the destination utilizes the available resources to add value to available resources. It is a question of deployment of resources. Later on we shall see that those notions are vague and not workable.

Some authors define 'destination competitiveness'. Let us consider some of them. They are far from unequivocal. Dwyer *et al.* (2000) state: 'Tourism competitiveness is a general concept that encompasses price differentials coupled with exchange rate movements, productivity levels of various components of the tourist industry and qualitative factors affecting the attractiveness or otherwise of a destination'. We will come back to that definition when we deal with the price competitive model. Dwyer and Kim (2004) define destination competitiveness as: 'The ability of a destination to deliver goods and services that perform better than other destinations on those aspects of tourism experience considered to be important by tourists'. Others refer to the maintenance and /or improvement of market share (d'Harteserre, 2000). For Hassan (2000), competiveness is the destination's ability to create and integrate value added products that sustain its resources while maintaining market position relative to competitors. This definition brings us close to Ritchie and Crouch (2003):

> 'Competitiveness in tourism' can be described as the elements that make a destination competitive: . . . its ability to increase tourism expenditure, to increasingly attract visitors while providing them with satisfying, memorable experiences and to do so in a profitable way, while enhancing the well-being of destination residents and preserving the natural capital of the destination for future generations.

We find the same elements in the Poon (1993) and WES (1994) approaches. From this we can conclude that competitiveness in tourism has several dimensions: economic, socio-cultural and environmental. Cvelbar *et al.* (2016) posit that, 'there is consensus in the literature that we need to address competitiveness in a broader sense, not only as economic output per unit of input, but also to acknowledge social distribution and environmental protection of resources'. However, not all the competition models dealt with in this chapter show an awareness of these ideas.

Competitiveness has become a central platform of tourism policy. As competition increases and tourism activity intensifies, tourism policy focusses on improving competitiveness by creating a statutory framework to monitor, control and enhance quality and efficiency in the industry, and to protect resources (Goeldner *et al.*, 2000). It is evident that the decisive competitive factors are influenced by the type of destination. A distinction can and should be made between different types of destination such as:

- Sun and beach
- City
- Cultural
- Winter sport
- Nature
- Luxury
- Other (MICE, sport, etc.).

While there is some agreement about the content, the conceptual models developed to enhance competitiveness are very different. The following models will show the differences:

- The competitive forces and generic strategies of M. Porter
- The 'Porter diamond', or the determinants of competitive advantage
- The Poon concept
- The WES approach
- The Bordas demand model
- The conceptual model of destination competitiveness of Ritchie and Crouch
- The price-competitiveness approach of Dwyer, Forsyth and Rao
- The Dwyer–Kim model.

These models are neither predictive nor causal. Ritchie and Crouch (2002) are right when they state that 'models should not be used to make a decision; they assist in decision making but should be no substitute for the role of the decision maker'.

Six of the above-mentioned models focus exclusively on 'destination' competitiveness. Poon makes a distinction between industry players and destinations. Porter's first model – competitive forces – primarily concerns industry players, although there are applications at the destination level (see Bordas, 1994).

In the following sections of this chapter, special attention will be given to the key elements of each of these concepts. Based on the models and long personal experience in tourism, I have dared to formulate ten key factors for a competitive destination. The last section will provide a synthesis of two benchmarking models. The first and most well-known is the Travel and Tourism Competitiveness Index (TTCI) of the World Economic Forum. A comparison of this index with my ten key factors is made. The second benchmarking model is the partial model of competitiveness of Modul University (Önder *et al.*, 2017).

The competitive forces of M. Porter

In contrast to the other concepts listed above, Porter's theories about competitive forces and about determinants of competitive advantages do not originate in the tourism sector. It was only later that tourism scientists applied the theory to the tourism industry. According to Porter, the essence of formulating a competitive strategy is relating a company to its environment. In his book *The Competitive Strategy* (1980), Porter proposes the model of the 'five forces' for investigating the competitive environment (see Figure 6.1):

1   The threat of entrants
2   The power of suppliers

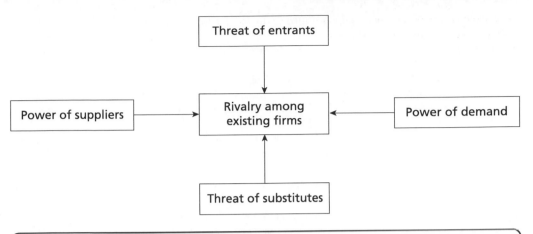

Figure 6.1 The five competitive forces of Porter

3 The power of buyers
4 The threat of substitutes
5 Competitive rivalry.

The state of competition in a tourism industry, as in any other industry, depends on these five competitive forces. The strength of these forces determines the profit potential of each sub-industry (e.g. tour operator, air carrier, theme park), where profit potential is measured in terms of long-run return on invested capital. Not all tourism sub-industries have the same potential, as the total profit potential is for all industries in general.

The first competitive force is the threat of *new entrants*, which can be controlled by barriers to entry such as:

- Economies of scale
- Capital requirements
- Product differentiation
- Switching costs
- Access to distribution channels
- Lack of experience (Tribe, 1999)
- Advertising barriers
- Government policies
- Expected retaliation
- Exit costs.

New entrants may stimulate more price competition, or more attention may be paid to product differentiation as they attempt to win market share. In tourism, the threat of new entrants is quite high in most sectors, and even the threat of new destinations is very realistic. Every year, more air carriers, more hotels, new accommodation, more theme parks, more events and new tourism destinations appear on the global tourism map.

The *threat of substitutes* can take very different forms. Self-catering is an alternative to hotel accommodation; high-speed trains can substitute for short distance air carriers; direct sales can, to a certain extent, replace CRS; and the internet is a threat to the traditional travel agent selling classical uncomplicated products. Substitutes limit the potential returns of an industry by placing a ceiling on the prices firms in the industry can profitably charge. However, there are further threats. Domestic tourism can be an excellent alternative to outbound tourism, and pure leisure activities may keep potential tourists at home. On the whole, the threat of substitutes is a reality in tourism.

The buyers' *power of demand* is great under the following circumstances:

- If a buyer group purchases large volumes relative to seller sales. The power of UK tour-operator business in Benidorm and other resorts in Spain relative to the local hotel sector is a typical example. Shaw and Williams (2004) give another example about the strategy of tour operators in the Aegean. They point out that due to asymmetrical power relationships between tour operators and local resort hotels, the latter have to accept low prices; the tour operators use their cancellation rights and may delay payment. All that has very negative effects on the destination.
- If the products a buyer group purchases from a sector are standard or undifferentiated (e.g. hotel rooms).
- If the products a buyer group purchases from the sector represent a significant proportion of the buyer's cost or purchases (as is the case for hotel accommodation as part of a package tour).
- If a buyer group earns low profits (see low profit margins of many tour operators).

Very often a buyer can exert considerable power over the selling sector. The bargaining power of buyers is also influenced by the level of buyer knowledge (Tribe, 1999). It is well known that a hotel sector (which is very fragmented and atomized) that is highly dependent on tour operators has limited bargaining power. Prices are under pressure and profit margins are reduced to nil or even below zero. Such a situation leads to lower maintenance standards and absence of modernization, and the vicious circle of deterioration can and will start.

The *bargaining power of suppliers* should also be considered (Porter, 1980). A supplier group is powerful if:

- It is dominated by a few companies (there is a degree of monopoly or oligopoly) and is more concentrated than the industry it sells to (e.g. air charter companies relative to tour operators).
- The industry is not an important customer of the supplying group.
- The group's product is differentiated, or it has built up switching costs.
- The group's product is an important input to the buyer's business (e.g. flight costs for a tour operator).
- The group poses a credible threat of forward integration (e.g. an air carrier starts a tour-operator's business).
- There are high costs of switching suppliers.

In practice, this is the case for credit card companies (Visa, American Express) and CRSs such as Sabre and Galileo supplying a booking service for hotels, airlines and car hire companies. Backward vertical integration can be a possible solution to avoid supplier power by take-over of the supplying firm. Tribe (1999) refers to Thomson's ownership of its carrier Britannia.

Porter's last competitive force is the *rivalry among existing firms*. This rivalry can be great in a situation where:

- There is slow sector growth.
- There are high storage costs or perishability.
- There are high fixed costs.
- There is lack of differentiation.
- There is a high strategic stake (to be successful in one market).
- There are numerous or equally balanced competitors.
- There is over-capacity or big changes in capacity.
- There are high exit barriers.

Many sub-sectors in tourism are susceptible to one or more of these characteristics. This is the case for air carriers, hotels and car rental firms. Strong rivalry is the logical consequence, with either a price war or a marketing-led competitive strategy. There is a good practical application in Knowles (1994), where he relates the CRSs to the five basic competitive forces in order to determine the state of competition.

Is this theory of competitive forces applicable to tourism destinations? There can be no doubt of this if a destination is considered as a cluster at regional or local level. The cluster is in reality a big firm composed of hundreds of parts. There are some references to various destinations in the preceding paragraphs, but let us consider the practical example of the Caribbean area (see Table 6.1).

Another application of Porter's five forces model can be found with Moreno-Izquierdo *et al.* (2016) in the transport sector and is indirectly related to destinations. In recent decades, the air transport sector has experienced major changes, including the emergence of the low-cost airlines. The strategies adopted by these new companies have given rise to a revitalization of the sector, particularly in Europe and the USA. Moreno-Izquierdo *et al.* (2016) analyse the pricing strategy followed by the low-cost carriers based on Porter's analysis. The research is based on the study of a total of 90 traditional tourist routes between the UK and Spain. The authors observed that concentration (Porter's force: the threat of new entrants) and rivalry with other companies (a number of airlines operating a route) are the factors that most affect the final price. The advance purchase of flights is another element which highly influences the final price paid by the user, and could be related to the demand for seats at a given time.

The combined strength of these five forces determines the profit potential (in the case of tourism destinations, potential value added of the industry) and its marketing strategy. For each firm, and also for each destination, a specific competitive strategy can be developed that reflects the particular circumstances of a firm, industry or destination. For Porter, an effective competitive strategy takes offensive or defensive action in order to create a defendable position against the five competitive forces and thereby yield a superior return on investment for a firm – or in our case, value added for a destination. He formulates three potentially successful generic strategic approaches to outperforming other firms or destinations, and these are described below.

Table 6.1 The application of competitive forces to the Caribbean

Competitive forces	Application to the Caribbean
The threat of new entrants	New seaside resorts in Caribbean countries – Cuba is only one example
The power of suppliers	Air carriers from the USA with regular flights to the different countries in the Caribbean
The power of buyers	The bargaining power of cruise carriers for mooring in the individual countries
The threat of substitutes	The Caribbean destinations have many competitive destinations in Central America and the Canary Islands
Competitive rivalry	The competition between destinations is great, due to undifferentiated supply, overcapacity in several destinations and perishability of supplied products

Porter's generic competitive strategies

In addition to responding to and influencing tourism structure, firms and destinations must choose a position within the industry. At the heart of positioning is competitive advantage. Porter distinguishes two basic types of competitive advantage: lower costs, and differentiation (Porter, 1990). Here, the theory is adapted to the tourism sector. Lower cost is the ability of a firm or a destination to design, produce and market a comparable service more efficiently than its competitors. Differentiation is the ability to provide unique and superior value to the buyer in terms of product quality and special features. However, there are limits to both types of advantage. A low-cost producer must offer acceptable quality of service to avoid nullifying its cost advantage. On the other hand, a differentiator may not achieve a cost position far enough above that of the competitors to offset its price premium.

Competitive scope is a third important variable in positioning. Scope is important to tourism because the sector is segmented. A firm or destination can define this scope in different terms:

● The range of tourism products
● The distribution channel
● The type of buyers
● The geographic area.

The combination of the two basic advantages and the scope advantage gives three generic strategies, or three different approaches, to arrive at a better economic performance in terms of higher return on investment or higher value added. These are illustrated in Figure 6.2.

Overall cost leadership is the first generic strategy. Achieving a position of low overall cost is not so easy; it requires a high market share or other advantages, volume production, standardized tourism products, and a management team that pays attention to cost control. The firm should possess sufficient financial means to support an aggressive price policy and cope with start-up losses. Some big tour operators in European countries are (or were) in an overall cost leadership position. However, the profit margins are at present not very high, and far below the normal rate of 3 per cent.

Having a low-cost position defends the firm against competitive forces:

● Powerful buyers (its price is lower than the price level of its next most efficient competitor)
● Powerful suppliers (there is more flexibility to cope with increases of input prices)
● There are entry barriers in terms of economies of scale
● It is in a favourable position vis-à-vis substitutes.

		Competitive advantage	
		Lower cost	Differentiation
Competitive scope	Broad target	*Cost leadership*	*Differentiation*
	Narrow target	*Cost focus*	*Differentiation focus*

Figure 6.2 The generic strategies of Porter

At destination level, several Spanish destinations and the Dominican Republic provide examples of low-cost leadership, or are the victims of the bargaining power of strong buyers. They may be successful in the short and medium term, but will not be competitive in the long term. This is not a sustainable economic development.

Differentiation is the second generic strategy. With such a strategy, a firm or destination seeks to be unique in the sector regarding some dimensions that are widely valued by customers, such as brand image, customer service, dealer network, design, technology, language knowledge, security, safety, just-in-time, etc. In the hotel business, attributes such as functional utility (e.g. type of bathroom, size of beds), symbolic utility, or being associated with a certain group and experience utility (e.g. aesthetics, knowledge, friendliness) are very efficient differentiation strategies.

Differentiation provides a certain amount of protection against competitors because of firm or destination loyalty by customers and the resulting lower sensitivity to price. As a consequence, it creates a premium price. In many sectors of the tourism industry, differentiation is the rule. Hotel chains covering the broad scope but targeting different segments are well known. The French group Accor has a diversified brand portfolio consisting of Sofitel, Mercure, Novotel, Ibis, Formule I and Etap, ranging from five stars down to purely functional hotels. Accor has also announced the establishment of a backpacker chain, Base Backpackers, indicative of its intention to be a prominent operator across all market segments (McVey and King, 2003).

Focussed or niche strategy is the third generic strategy. Here, the firm or destination focusses on a particular buyer group, segment, market or product. In other words, the scope is narrow. In practice, there are two variants: differentiation focus and cost focus. With a niche strategy, a firm can be a big fish in a small pond. Most small tour operators apply this strategy. However, it is not without danger – for example, a tour operator specializing in the 'Egypt product' can be very successful, but a terrorist attack (as has happened in Egypt more than once) can finish the company. The demand for a specialized product can decrease, and the focus strategy can be imitated. This happens quite often in tourism.

The determinants of competitive advantage in tourism

In his book *The Competitive Advantage of Nations*, Porter (1990) developed a model that attracted much attention in the tourism sector. Taking into account the examples in his book and paraphrasing the title of his book, we can speak of 'the competitive advantage of regions'. In the context of this book, and referring to the introduction of the current chapter, a title 'The competitive advantage of tourism destinations' makes sense, especially as Porter, together with Bordas, applied his model to Barcelona – a city which is very successful in the short holiday and MICE market.

Porter claims that the success of a firm does not only depend on its strategy and positioning (see the five competitive forces of Porter) but also on its being embedded in the environment. Regions, destinations and clusters succeed in a particular industry or activity because their home environment is the most dynamic and the most challenging, and this stimulates firms to upgrade their advantage. This is his central thesis. In tourism there are many clusters – groups of companies directly and indirectly related to tourism and concentrated in a specific geographical area. The tourism product as a composite product – attractions, accommodation, transport and other facilities – stimulates the clustering process (see Michael *et al.*, 2006). Typical examples of tourism clusters are Bruges, Venice, Iguaçu and Ibiza.

The starting point for the development of strategies to improve the competitive position of a destination is identical to that for the determinants of competitiveness (Smeral, 1996). Based on the Porter model, competitive advantages of a destination emerge in a dynamic system consisting of four interdependent determinants, which together form a diamond – a

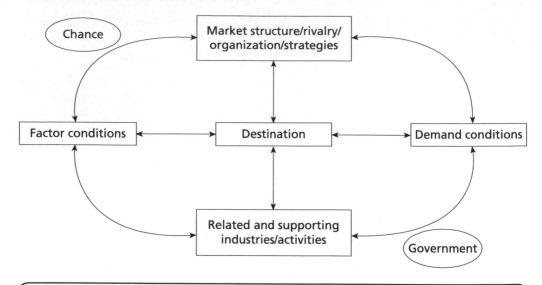

Figure 6.3 The determinants of competitive advantages of destinations

term Porter uses to refer to these determinants (Porter, 1990; see Figure 6.3). These determinants are:

1 Factor conditions, or the destination's position regarding factors of production necessary to compete in the tourism industry
2 Demand conditions, or the nature of (home) demand for tourism products and services
3 Related and supporting industries/activities – i.e. the presence or absence in the region of supplier industries and related industries
4 Market structure, rivalry, organization and strategies, or the conditions in the destination governing how companies are created, organized and managed, and the nature of (domestic) rivalry.

There are also two additional variables – chance and government – which can influence the system in important ways and are necessary to complete the theory. The 'diamond' is a mutually reinforcing system. The effect of one determinant depends on the state of the others. Favourable demand conditions, for example, will not lead to competitive advantage unless the state of rivalry is sufficient to cause firms (e.g. hotels) to respond to them. Advantages in one determinant can also create or upgrade advantages in another. What is the possible content of the determinants of a tourism cluster in general?

Factor conditions

The key elements of factor conditions are factor endowments and their permanent upgrading. Without factor endowments and attractions in particular – natural, cultural or man-made – there is no tourism activity. What do we understand by factor conditions? They include:

1 Factor endowments

- natural resources (beaches etc., but also population and geographical location)
- cultural and historical resources (monuments, cultural heritage, museums, art collections, customs, handicraft, canals, events, etc.)

- capital and infrastructure resources (accommodation, transport infrastructure, site development)
- human resources

2 Factor prices
3 Production efficiency.

Smeral (1996) underlines an important dimension with respect to factor conditions. The factors most important to the competitive advantage of a destination are not inherited but created. The stock of existing factors is less important than the rate at which they are created, upgraded and specialized.

Demand conditions

Demand conditions (as the second broad determinant of competitive advantage), when applied to a tourism cluster, are slightly different from the original formulation in the Porter model. We can distinguish the following elements:

- Size of the market
- Structure of the market (diversity in core markets, seasonality, degree of internationalization, share of long-haul travellers, etc.)
- Position in fast-growing markets
- A strengthening tourism culture of consumers and host societies (Cooper *et al.*, 2001)
- Protection of the consumer-tourist
- First-time visitors
- Sophisticated tourists (to recognize new trends).

The last aspect is of the utmost importance. We agree with Pechlaner and Smeral (2001) that 'Quality-conscious tourists exert constant quality control, pushing suppliers towards high-quality and attractively-priced market segments. Early market saturation forces suppliers to readjust quickly by instituting innovations and accessing international markets.'

Related and supporting industries/activities

The competitive position of a destination also depends on the diversity and the quality of supporting suppliers. In any destination, there is a need for many different types of suppliers to provide:

- Access to the destination (train, air, road, sea)
- Parking facilities
- Cultural, entertainment and sports facilities
- A souvenir industry
- Food and fashion (sophisticated consumer goods, high-quality food, restaurants)
- Shopping facilities
- High-quality services (e.g. taxi drivers, travel agents, tourism guides, banks, sport facilities, education, hairdressers, cleaners, ski schools, etc.)
- Competitive producers (e.g. construction industry, restoration work, etc.)
- Vocational training
- Policing
- Health care.

Market structure, rivalry, organization and strategy

The key element of this determinant is the availability of a tourism strategic plan supported by all parties involved, both public and private sector. However, this determinant involves many more aspects, including:

● A strategic tourism plan (including physical planning)
● The marketing of a destination
● An organizational structure
● A market structure with an impact on competition
● The firm size
● Cooperation among SMEs
● Public–private partnership
● Important coordinators (e.g. national air carriers such as KLM)
● Quality management (at the level of the destination as well as at the level of the individual firm)
● Destination management (e.g. information system, reservation centre)
● Image building
● Building strategic alliances.

Local government

In the prevailing economic system, tourism policy without the involvement of the public sector is not very realistic. Unfortunately, tourism policy is too often identified with public authorities. The definition of the determinants in a tourism cluster will have shown that a successful competitive policy depends on the involvement of both public and private sectors. Nevertheless, some specific public actions can stimulate or impede tourism development – for example, the hotel-stop regulation in Bruges, implementation of visitor management, traffic planning, taxation, etc.

The Porter model can be considered as an instrument to analyse the competitive situation of a destination. It has been applied successfully in Barcelona, Bruges, Ibiza and Madrid, and probably in several other destinations. Tables 6.2 and 6.3 illustrate such an application for Bruges (Vanhove, 2002).

We find another application of Porter's model in Ribes *et al*. (2011). Ribes *et al*. focus on an analysis of the tourism competitiveness of 173 residential tourism destinations on the Spanish coast and islands, applying Porter's competitive advantage theory. This analysis is conducted with a hypothesis test using a structural equation model based on Porter's competitive diamond.

Different variables were selected to measure the competitive success of the residential destination: (a) the production or income of the destination, measured in absolute or per capita terms; (b) the level of employment measured in terms of employment rates; (c) the proportion of residents from the main issuing markets; (d) the degree of ageing of the destination population; and (e) the percentage of housing in the destination that is not used for first residence purposes.

By analysing a range of variables, it is possible to develop attributes related to competitiveness which constitute Porter's diamond model. The application confirms that the theory is appropriate for explaining the tourism development processes in residential tourism destinations on the Spanish coast. However, not all the determinants of Porter's diamond have a positive effect on the competitiveness of tourism destinations in Spain. The supporting and related industries determinant is a cause for concern. This determinant has in this case a negative influence on competitiveness.

The Poon concept

Poon (1993) emphasizes the changes in tourism when she compares new tourism (flexible, segmented, diagonally integrated, environmentally conscious) with old tourism (mass, standardized and rigidly packaged) with respect to consumers, management, technology, production

Table 6.2 Strengths with respect to competitiveness: the case of Bruges, 2002

Determinant	Strengths
Factor conditions	• product policy
	• cultural patrimony
	• historic town centre recognized as UNESCO world heritage site
	• interesting museums
	• good hotel accommodation
	• price policy and price level
	• geographical location in Europe
	• language knowledge
	• small-scale atmosphere
	• professional reception infrastructure for tourists
	• security
Demand conditions	• market size and growth potential
	• many international visitors
	• no dominance of organized group travel
Related and supporting activities	• accessibility
	• parking facilities
	• shopping facilities
	• typical souvenirs
	• gastronomy and good food in general
	• two hotel schools
Market structure, rivalry, organization and strategy	• well-organized hotel sector, 'vzw hotels Brugge' alliance between art cities in Flanders
Local government	• Bruges: cultural capital of Europe in 2002

and frame conditions. For her, new tourism changes the rules of the game and calls for new strategies to ensure competitive success (Poon, 1993):

> The more rapid the changes in the firm's environment, the more important becomes strategy formulation and implementation. The travel and tourism industry is undergoing rapid and radical transformation. Therefore, competitive strategies are more important than ever for the survival and competitiveness of industry players.

Poon is rather critical with respect to Porter's generic competitive strategies. These generic strategies, although relevant, are, for her, inadequate tools to explore competitive success for tourism players. Porter's analysis is, according to Poon, more applicable to the manufacturing sector than to services. Furthermore, his strategies are more appropriate in a static environment and during the maturity stage of a product. Poon's central thesis is that 'Innovation – introduction of new products – is far more important than low cost, differentiation or focus'. We can understand this statement to a certain extent, but it is not true to say that Porter neglects the innovation factor. In his book *The Competitive Advantage of Nations* (1990),

> **Table 6.3** Weaknesses or points for improvement with respect to competitiveness: the case of Bruges, 2002

Determinant	Weaknesses or points for improvement
Factor conditions	• inadequate MICE infrastructure • international hotel chains (brands) • more active cultural experience required • evening activities and the hinterland as a support
Demand conditions	• attitude of local population (a minority) towards tourism
Related and supporting activities	• connection to Lille • lack of a national air carrier as coordinator risk of degrading quality level (prices) of services (e.g. some taxi drivers and restaurant keepers)
Market structure, rivalry, organization and strategy	• no strategic planning (one in preparation) • low communication budget • lack of a quality plan • no destination management information system • public–private partnership • insufficient joining with international hotel networks
Local government	• no extension of hotel capacity

and more particularly in the chapter about determinants of national competitive advantage, he makes a distinction (with respect to factor conditions) between generalized factors and advanced and specialized factors:

> The most significant and sustainable advantage results when a nation possesses factors needed for competing in a particular industry that are both advanced and specialized. The availability and quality of advanced and specialized factors determine the sophistication of competitive advantage that can potentially be achieved and its rate of upgrading. In contrast, competitive advantage based on basic/generalized factors is unsophisticated and often fleeting.

There are also well-known examples in tourism of successful applications of the generic strategies.

The Poon concept of competitive strategy has two dimensions: a micro- and a macro-level. She deals with 'competitive strategies for industry players' and 'strategies for tourism destinations'.

Competitive strategies for industry players

New tourism changes the rules of the game in the industry and calls for new strategies to ensure competitive success. Poon has identified four key principles of competitive success, and for each there are a number of strategies (see Table 6.4).

Table 6.4 Competitive strategies for industry players

Source: adapted from Poon (1993)

Principles	Strategies
Put consumer first	• link marketing with product development • satisfy the consumer • develop a holistic approach to the holiday experience
Be a leader in quality	• develop human resources • improve process continuously • use technology creatively
Develop radical innovations	• don't be afraid of new ideas • never stop learning • build a capacity for continuous innovation
Strengthen your strategic position	• seek an advantageous position in the value chain • integrate diagonally • influence the competitive environment

Some of these principles and associated strategies need further explanation, and there are five important topics. The first relates to the holistic approach. A holiday experience is much more than the bed-nights at a hotel or apartment. It begins on arrival. The actions of immigration officers or customs and the attitude of taxi-drivers are all part of the holiday experience. At the destination, other critical factors in the holiday experience include the food, the behaviour of the police, the beggars on city streets, dirty streets, harassment of tourists on the beach or in restaurants, and so many other factors. Poon states that the success of certain holiday providers – Disneyland, SuperClubs, Sandals, Center Parcs – is because they have taken a holistic approach to the holiday experience.

Secondly, Poon claims that 'quality' will be the most significant factor for competitive success among industry players. Tourists want quality, flexibility and value for money. Therefore, creative recruitment of personal, the empowering of the front line, investment in education and motivation are very important.

Thirdly, radical innovation is a little bit misleading. It is not possible to develop a new holiday concept each year, but it is possible, at regular intervals, to consider exploring new markets, providing new services, developing new processes, developing a culture for innovation and encouraging new ideas.

Fourthly, what does it mean to seek an advantageous position in the value chain? A value chain is an analytical tool developed for tracing the process of value creation in an industry (Porter, 1987). The value chain can be thought of as all the interconnecting operations that make up the whole consumer experience of a product. Poon applies it to the tourism industry to provide insights into how the industry creates value (see Chapter 8).

A topic of great importance, and directly related to the value chain, is diagonal integration. The objective of diagonal integration is to produce a range of services (e.g. transport, insurance, holiday and personal banking) and sell them to consumers. Firms become involved in closely related activities to reduce costs and to get nearer to their consumers. Ownership may not be necessary, unlike in horizontal or vertical integration.

Strategies for tourism destinations

The second dimension of Poon's concept of competitive strategy is at the macro- or destination level. The issue is not whether to develop tourism, but rather how to develop the sector in such a way that the destination benefits. Points related to this thesis include how to use tourism to generate other sectors, how to limit tourism's negative social and cultural impacts, and how to build a dynamic private sector. In a similar way to that outlined with regard to the competitive strategies for tourism players, Poon identifies four strategies that tourism destinations need in order to enhance the development of a new and sustainable tourism. The basic strategies with respect to destinations are shown in Table 6.5.

Let us focus on some of these strategies. First, so far not all countries and destinations have respected the principle of responsible tourism. Capacity control is still an exception (as, for example, in Bermuda and the Seychelles), and comprehensive planning is not yet the rule in tourism destinations (WTO, 1992; Bosselman *et al.*, 1999). Fortunately, there are more and more examples of visitor management.

Secondly, making tourism a leading sector deserves special attention. Indeed, tourism can activate a lot of services and activities, such as car rental, food, crafts, souvenirs, construction, incoming tour operating, etc. Special attention should be paid to avoid leakages. In many destinations, local vegetable production or fruit growing can replace imported products on condition that the local producers can assure a regular supply, with the necessary quality and without too many price variations. Local architecture and local products can enhance authenticity. The implementation of the Nusa Dua project in Bali (Indonesia) is a successful illustration of this. A good example of manufacturing as a function of tourism is the production of fashion clothing in Togo, where the local garments are not only sold to tourists but their design and quality is also adapted to the European market so that they are sold in Paris with great success. The stimulation of authentic souvenirs can be a source of income for hundreds of families and small enterprises. Good examples include Bali, with woodcarving, stone carving, paintings and jewellery; Bruges, with lace and chocolates; the 'santons' in Aix-en-Provence; and china-works in China.

Thirdly, the plea for a transformation of the role of National (Regional) Tourist Offices from promotion to product development deserves attention.

Fourthly, public–private partnership at destination level is a necessity if an effective tourism policy is to be achieved, to encourage all efforts in the same direction and gather together the necessary financial means to implement a strategic marketing plan.

Table 6.5 Strategies for tourism destinations

Source: adapted from Poon (1993)

Principles	*Strategies*
Put the environment first	● build responsible tourism ● foster a culture of conservation ● develop an environmental focus
Make tourism a lead sector	● develop tourism's 'axial' potential ● adapt strategies of development ● develop the service sector
Strengthen distribution channels in the marketplace	● ensure adequate air access ● transform the role of NTOs in the marketplace ● focus on product development at home
Build a dynamic private sector	● don't be afraid of new tourism ● let quality be the guide ● build public/private sector cooperation

Last but not least, and also at destination level, quality management is considered to be a basic strategy. Governments must take steps to establish and enforce standards and to stimulate quality planning at the destination level.

The WES approach

The WES (Westvlaams Economisch Studiebureau) approach originated from a demand by the Inter-American Development Bank for the analysis of the competitive positions of a number of countries in the Caribbean area. Special attention was given to explaining the differences in the competitive positions of these Caribbean destinations and to formulating how to improve these positions. Long-term competitiveness was the focus. 'Competitiveness' was defined as a destination's capacity to reach its objectives in the long run in a more efficient way than the international or regional average. This means that a competitive destination is able to realize a higher profitability than the average, with low social costs and without damaging the environment and available resources.

From the beginning, a clear distinction was made between indicators of competitive performance, and factors that contribute to competitiveness. The former are historic measures that describe how a destination has performed in the past (e.g. international arrivals, tourist nights, accommodation capacity and occupancy rates, tourism receipts). For most of these indicators, market shares can be derived. The latter are capabilities or conditions that it is believed will contribute to or detract from the ability of a destination to be competitive in the future. The WES approach reveals a number of decisive factors of competitiveness, and these are summarized in Table 6.6.

Typical of the WES approach is the attention paid to macro-economic factors. Application of multiple regression analysis shows the impact of the income factor on the generating markets and the real exchange rate. The purchasing power indicator of generating country X against receiving country Y is defined as:

$$\text{(Exchange rate currency X in currency units Y)}\left[\frac{\text{CPI country X}}{\text{CPI country Y}}\right] \tag{6.1}$$

where the first term is equal to the exchange rate of country X in terms of the currency of country Y. CPI stands for Consumer Price Index (see example in Chapter 3).

Countries like the Bahamas and Barbados were found to be too expensive due to an over-valued currency. Fiscal policies in a number of Caribbean destinations were tourism-unfriendly. Heavy taxes on raw materials necessary for tourism had a very detrimental effect. Countries that considered tourism as a money-making machine were working against their own interests.

A second relevant factor – for the Caribbean – related to industrial relations. In the more traditional tourism countries of the Caribbean area, these relations were not good and were responsible for low room occupancy rates in hotels.

Another relevant factor in the competitiveness of different countries was the presence or absence of a destination management or tourism policy in general. Based on extensive research with American and European tour operators, it became evident that not all destinations had the ability to or were prepared to respond to future growth products such as adventure tourism, eco-tourism and all-inclusive accommodation.

The price-competitiveness approach

The preceding sections may give the impression that price is an irrelevant factor with respect to competitiveness. Most models neglect or minimize factor price. In Chapter 1 we saw that price-elasticity cannot be overlooked. This is also the view of Dwyer *et al.* (2000) when they

Table 6.6 Factors affecting the competitive position, WES

Source: WES (1993)

Factors	Variables

Macro-economic factors	• Income-generating countries
	• Real exchange rate
	• Availability and cost of capital
	• Fiscal policy
	   – import taxes
	   – cost price increasing taxes
	   – taxes on profit
	   – tourism tax
	   – cruise tax

Supply factors	• Tourist product
	   – attractions
	   – accommodation
	   – price level
	• Labour
	   – availability
	   – cost
	   – quality and training
	• Infrastructure
	   – transport
	   – public utilities

Transport factors	• Availability of regular services • Availability of charter services • Availability of cruise services
Demand factors	• Market dependence • Penetration in distribution channels • Marketing efforts • Presence in future growth product markets
Tourism policy	• Institutional framework • Policy formulation • Planning capacity • Commercialization • Government budgetary support

state that 'changing costs in particular destinations relative to others, adjusted for exchange rate variations, are regarded as the most important economic influence on destination shares of total travel abroad'. Edwards (1995) also emphasizes the role of factor price when he maintains that a fall in relative cost is linked to a rise in market share. Dwyer *et al.* (2000) define destination competitiveness as: 'a general concept that encompasses price differentials coupled with exchange rate movements, productivity levels of various components of the tourist industry, and qualitative factors affecting the attractiveness or otherwise of destination'. Consequently, these authors consider two other groups of factors besides price:

1 Socio-economic and demographic factors
2 Qualitative factors.

The latter category comprises variables such as tourist appeal, image, quality of tourist services, destination marketing and promotion, cultural ties, etc. Price factors (which affect the cost of tourism to the visitor) include the cost of transport services to and from the destination and the cost of ground content. The price factor is calculated using a series of steps:

- Step 1: choose origin countries or generating markets.
- Step 2: choose destination markets or competitors.
- Step 3: assess expenditure pattern of tourists from different origin markets (only products and services consumed by tourists).
- Step 4: compile relevant price data (the authors made use of the World Bank's International Comparison Programme, ICP).
- Step 5: calculate purchasing power parities (PPP) for tourism expenditure (PPPs indicate the levels of expenditure required in different destinations to purchase the same basket of tourism goods and services). According to Forsyth and Dwyer (2009) the purchasing power parity (PPP) theory is based on the assumption that in efficient markets, identical goods should have only one price. In the absence of transportation and other transaction costs, competitive markets will equalize the price of an identical good in two countries when prices are expressed in the same currency.
- Step 6: adjust PPPs by exchange rates to derive price competitiveness indices (PII).

$$\text{Price competitive index} = \frac{\text{exchange rate}}{\text{PPP}} \times \frac{100}{1} \qquad (6.2)$$

Let us take a practical case to explain the price competitive index. A Japanese tourist considers Australia and France as possible destinations. A basket of goods and services consumed by a typical Japanese tourist in Australia would cost AU\$1,000, but the same would cost €840 in France. The exchange rate between AU\$ and € is AU\$1 = €0.60. In this case, the price competitive index equals (0.60/0.84)100 = 71.42 – thus France is about 28.5 per cent more expensive regarding the ground component than Australia for the Japanese tourist. However, for the travel component France is 4 per cent cheaper. A similar exercise for some other destinations is illustrated in Table 6.7, and this reveals very great differences between the price levels for the different destinations – for both ground and travel components. An index of less than 100 indicates that the particular destination is less competitive than Australia with respect to the Japanese market.

These are valuable indicators, but the PII cannot be taken as the only important competitiveness factor. A visit to Australia cannot be compared with one to Italy, which offers a completely different experience. As Dwyer *et al.* are aware; overall competitiveness is determined by both price and non-price factors. However, PIIs can be relevant in comparing identical products. They do have limitations, and the authors of the model cite several:

- Accuracy of data collection
- Comparison of airfares
- Differences of accommodation
- Prices can vary between regions in the same country
- One country can be expensive for one tourism product but far less expensive for another.

Table 6.7 Price competitive indices for various destinations, 1997 (Australia = 100; origin country Japan)

Source: adapted from Dwyer *et al.* (2000)

Country	Ground component	Travel component	Ground + travel component
New Zealand	95.6	83.1	88.5
USA	85.6	120.2	99.7
Italy	89.1	97.3	93.3
UK	73.6	102.2	86.2
Spain	100.7	75.3	84.4
Turkey	180.2	86.5	115.4
China	366.6	297.4	292.1
Thailand	385.6	229.5	325.6

The Bordas model

The Bordas model was originally presented at the AIEST Congress in Argentina in 1993, and was further developed at the Tourist Research Centre (TRC) meeting in Swansea in 1994. It is a typical demand (marketing) model, and does not fit into the general concept of competitiveness. Furthermore, this model was conceived for long-haul destinations, the central theme of the Bariloche AIEST Congress. It should be noted here that the model is not tested for any causal relationship, and several retained explanatory variables are difficult to express in quantitative units.

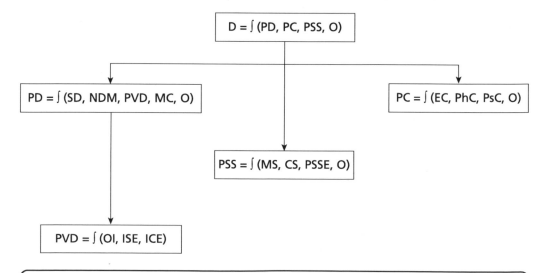

Figure 6.4 Basic relations in the Bordas model

The basic relationships retained in the model are illustrated in Figure 6.4, where:

D   = long haul demand from market n to destination i
PD   = primary demand or consumers from market n interested in and preference for
          destination i
PC   = perceived costs
PSS   = performance of sales system of destination i in market n
O   = other variables
SD   = secondary demand or consumers in market n with interest in destination i but without
          any preference
NDM   = consumer needs, desires and motivations (perception of benefits are very important)
PVD   = perception of destination i by the consumers (consumer should be able to perceive
          the benefits)
MC   = magnetism of competitors (capacity of competitors to transform SD into PD)
OI   = organic image or image of destination i among the consumers who make up the SD
          and based on received general (very often non-tourism) information from various
          sources (e.g. mass media)
ISE   = information from social environment (relatives and friends)
ICE   = information from the trade and communication network (e.g. ads, brochures)
EC   = economic/monetary cost (transportation, costs at the spot)
PhC   = physical cost (tiredness and stress)
PsC   = psychological cost (commercial and physical risk)
PuC   = purchasing costs or cost to get access to information and to the trade
MS   = magnetism of the sales system (capacity of the sales system to create interest in the
          destination and capability to attract customers)
CS   = conductivity of the system or the capacity to close a sale (which percentage of
          customers who were in contact with the sales system decided to buy the destination)
PSSE   = post-sale service efficiency (creating loyalty and recommendation).

In this marketing model for long-haul destinations there are two key elements. The first is the 'perceived value' of the destination, where image is the central point. The benefits of authenticity should be well known. Bordas distinguishes three types of benefits: functional, symbolic (very often associated with the need for self-esteem and belonging) and existential benefits (associated with the need for personal fulfilment, knowledge and belonging). Potential tourists have an image of the destination, and very often the image has been created independently of any tourism activity. If there is a bad image, it is difficult to change it. Tourism promotion will in most cases not be successful in changing an existing image. Only an improvement in the supply side and the creation of new and/or upgraded products can be helpful.

The second element is the 'perceived cost'. This has several facets: the economic costs, the physical effort, the psychological costs, and the difficulties in gaining access to information and what Bordas calls the sales system. The further the destination is from home, the greater the uncertainty about travel and living costs, the higher the physical cost of travel (waiting time in airports, stress, jet-lag, immobility in the aircraft, etc.), and the more significant the psychological cost (hygiene, health care and risks of all kinds). A lot can be done to reduce these costs and to enhance the competitiveness of the destination. There should be a combined effort by the tourist authority, immigration control, air carrier and others to reduce the perceived costs.

There are three important drawbacks to this model. First, it is a one-sided model – i.e. only demand-oriented. Secondly, the model is still a gross concept without any test. The use of 'other factors' in several components of the model illustrates the trial phase. Thirdly, some variables are difficult to measure. Nevertheless, the model emphasizes a number of factors neglected or underestimated in other approaches.

The Ritchie and Crouch conceptual model of destination competitiveness

The most comprehensive model is without doubt the Ritchie and Crouch model. The first test took place on the occasion of the AIEST Congress in Bariloche (AIEST, 1993), where Congress participants were members of a panel. Over the following ten years the concept was improved and elaborated, and led to the publication of an interesting handbook, *The Competitive Destination* (Ritchie and Crouch, 2003). The cornerstone of the publication is the conceptual model of destination competitiveness (see Figure 6.5). It is a device that provides a useful way of thinking about a complex issue. The authors envisage three main uses of the model:

1 As a communication tool – a lexicon for understanding, diagnosing and discussing a destination's competitiveness
2 As a framework for management in order to avoid overlooking potentially important factors
3 As an instrument for a destination audit.

Comparative and competitive advantage

The starting point of the model is the thesis that destination success is determined by two different kinds of advantages: *comparative* and *competitive*. Comparative advantages reflect the resource endowments of the destination, provided either by nature or by the overall society within which the destination resides (human, physical, historical and cultural resources; knowledge; capital; infrastructure; and tourism superstructure). Competitive advantages are those that have been established as a result of effective resource deployment (maintenance, growth and development, efficiency, effectiveness and audit) – in other words, how well the destination utilizes the available resources, or the destination's ability to add value to the available resources. According to Sánchez and López (2015) competitive advantages refer to a destination's skill in using resources in an effective way in the long run.

However, for Ritchie and Crouch comparative advantage and competitive advantage are generic concepts. Greater depth is necessary. What do these concepts mean in the context of a tourist destination? So that the model would be managerially useful, they further examined the categories or components that constitute resource endowments and resource deployments in order to understand how these constructs are best made operational to determine destination competitiveness.

The components of the model

The components of the model are:

● The global (macro-) environment
● The competitive (micro-) environment
● Core resources and attractors
● Supporting factors and resources
● Destination policy, planning and development
● Destination management
● Qualifying and amplifying determinants.

Destination policy, planning and development (DPPD) and destination management (DM) can be considered as the two core components, and these will be discussed separately.

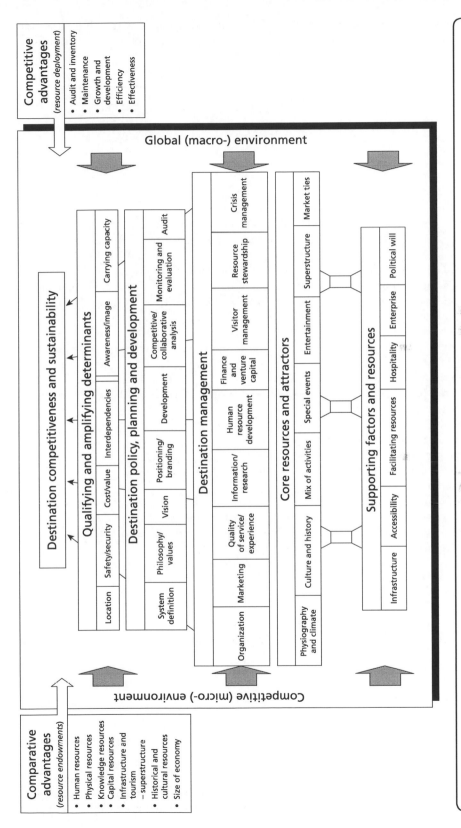

Figure 6.5 The Ritchie and Crouch conceptual model of destination competitiveness

Source: Ritchie and Crouch (2003), published by CABI Publishing and reproduced with kind permission

The global (macro-) environment recognizes that tourism is an open system. It is subject to many influences and pressures that arise outside the system itself. Some of them were discussed in Chapter 3. The eight global forces shaping world tourism are:

1 Economic
2 Climatic
3 Geographical
4 Environmental
5 Demographic
6 Social and cultural
7 Technological
8 Political.

All these forces create threats and opportunities. A destination manager should be aware of these challenges and opportunities and try, together with the sector, to formulate the right policy.

The competitive (micro-) environment is part of the tourism system; it concerns the actions and activities of entities in the tourism system that affect the goals of each member of the system (companies and organizations). How is destination competitiveness affected by the way in which the tourism system functions? The components are:

1 Suppliers (who supply the sector with basic factor inputs, e.g. labour, food and beverages, energy)
2 Tourism enterprises
3 Intermediaries (e.g. trade, trade shows) and facilitators (e.g. credit cards, market research consultants)
4 Customers
5 Competing destinations
6 Destination management organizations
7 Related and supporting industries (e.g. theatres, shopping facilities)
8 Other stakeholders.

An important conclusion is that there is an association between domestic rivalry among tourism enterprises (which produce the core commercial services) and the creation and persistence of competitive advantage (see also Porter, 1990).

Core resources and attractors describe the essence of the destination appeal, or the pulling force. It is these factors that are the key motivators to visiting a destination. Ritchie and Crouch distinguish seven categories:

1 Physiography and climate (e.g. scenery, wildlife, beach)
2 Culture and history (e.g. the cathedral of La Sagrada Familia in Barcelona, although it was built in another era and for religious reasons)
3 A broad range of activities
4 Special events
5 Types of entertainment (e.g. Broadway shows in New York)
6 Superstructure
7 Market ties (e.g. religion, ethnic roots).

Most of these attractors speak for themselves. Nevertheless, the local destination management organization can do a lot to enhance the attractiveness of each of these categories and so increase the competitiveness of the destination. Indeed, competitive advantage relates to a destination's ability to employ the attractions effectively over the long term. Russia has many attractions, but is not successful in developing tourism activities. Ritchie and Crouch make an important point with respect to the factor of activities:

> The real reason for visiting a destination is to do things – to actively participate in activities that stimulate for the moment, and then to leave as a participant who has vibrant memories of what he or she has done. In seeking to make a destination attractive and competitive, it is essential to ensure that it offers a broad range of activities, of memorable things to do.

Supporting factors and resources support or provide a foundation upon which a successful tourism industry can be established. This category contains elements that enhance the destination's appeal. Their absence or insufficiency will be a constraint for the destination to pull tourists. The model refers to six groups:

1 Infrastructure
2 Accessibility (e.g. visas, airline access)
3 Facilitating resources (human and financial resources)
4 Hospitality (e.g. resident attitudes)
5 Enterprise (tourism enterprise contributes to destination development)
6 Political will (allocation of scarce resources).

The qualifying and amplifying determinants are described as factors of competitiveness that either moderate, modify, mitigate and filter or strengthen, enhance and augment the impact of all other factors, DPPD and DM included. They are situational conditioners on which a destination has no or little influence. However, destinations with an eye on these conditioners will be more likely to behave proactively; they can foresee opportunities and threats. What are these qualifying and amplifying determinants for Ritchie and Crouch? They mention six situational conditioners:

1 Location
2 Destination safety
3 Destination cost level (a destination has not much influence on costs)
4 Destination interdependencies – synergistic or adversarial
5 Destination image (strong images are hard to develop and even harder to change, once formed)
6 Carrying capacity (the upper limit to the volume of demand a destination can handle).

Success factors: destination policy, planning and development, and destination management

Destination policy, planning and development (DPPD) and destination management (DM) are the other two categories of the model. In the framework of resource deployment and modern management of a region or destination, they might be considered as the key categories. What do the authors have in mind when they talk about DPPD and DM?

> DPPD is essentially an intellectual process that uses information, judgement and monitoring to make macro-level decisions regarding the kind of destination that is desirable, the degree to which ongoing performance and related changes in the nature of visitation and the physical character of the destination are contributing to the achievement of the kind of destination that stakeholders want ... DM is more a micro-level activity in which all the stakeholders carry out their individual and organizational responsibilities on a daily basis in efforts to realize the macro-level vision contained in policy, planning and development.

(Ritchie and Crouch, 2003)

A highly competitive destination does not exist by chance. It requires a well-planned environment within which the appropriate forms of tourism development are encouraged and facilitated. Tourism policy is the key to providing this environment – but what should be understood by tourism policy? According to Goeldner *et al.* (2000), it is 'A set of regulations, rules, guidelines, directives, and development/promotion objectives and strategies that provide a framework within which the collective and individual decisions directly affecting tourism development and the daily activities within a destination are taken'.

Contemporary tourism policy focusses on competitiveness and sustainability, which are also the major parameters of tourism destination management (TDM). Successful TDM involves economic/business management skills balanced with environmental management capabilities. Economic/business skills are those related to effective resource development and deployment. Goeldner *et al.* (2000) refer to:

- Strategic planning
- The marketing of the destination
- Financial management
- Operations management
- Human resources management
- Information management
- Organization management.

Environmental management capabilities are those that are critical to effective destination stewardship, and include:

- Water quality management
- Air quality management
- Wildlife management
- Forest/plant management
- Visitor management
- Resident/community management
- Commemorative integrity.

Strategic tourism planning is the cornerstone of DPPD. For destination purposes, strategic planning may be defined as the process whereby an organization analyses the strengths and weaknesses with respect to the supply development and demand development, decides the position it seeks to attain, and defines strategies and programmes of activity to achieve the aims (Morrison, 1989; Goeldner *et al.*, 2000). It describes the process of developing long-term plans for tourism development and marketing. It should provide a common structure and focus for all of the destination's management activities. In a strategic planning process, there are three basic questions (see Figure 6.6):

1 Where are we now?
2 Where do we want to be in 5–10 years' time?
3 How do we get there?

There are also three concepts:

1 Mission, goals and objectives
2 Strategies
3 Projects, plans and programmes.

This scheme and also the terminology used is different from the Ritchie–Crouch presentation. However, the basic philosophy is the same.

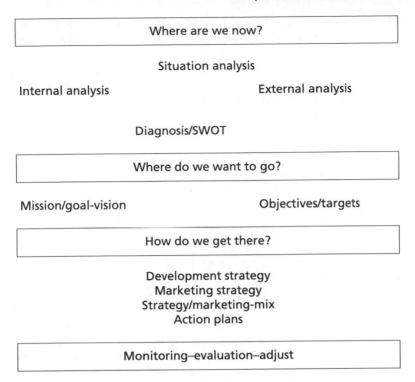

Figure 6.6 Basic questions and concepts of strategic planning

The starting point of the planning process is a situation analysis of the present supply and market/marketing. Within the situation analysis there are two components: internal and external analysis. The elements from the above-mentioned components, 'micro-environment' and 'global macro-environment', provide an excellent starting point. A careful assessment (or explanation of the present situation) of the internal and external analysis leads to a SWOT analysis (Strengths, Weaknesses, Opportunities and Threats).

The first basic concept is the mission or vision or goal (not everybody considers these terms to be synonyms). Young (1966) states that this 'is a value to be sought after, not an object to be achieved'. It is a guide for all parties as to what the purpose of the organization is. The mission statement acts as a confirmation of what business the destination is in, from both supplier and consumer viewpoints. The mission statement for Belgian macro-tourism products can serve as an illustration: 'To realize a contribution to the economic development of the destinations by a rational use of the tourist production factors, and satisfy the leisure needs of the tourists with respect to the environment and the well-being of the local population' (De Keyser and Van Impe, 1996).

Next we consider the 'objective' or 'vision' as a strategic goal. With respect to destinations, there are two types of objectives. The first is objectives for regional tourism development. These objectives can take different forms, such as employment creation, better use of present supply, extension of the supply, greater revenue creation through quality improvement of the supply, diversification of the local economy, protection of natural resources, etc. The second is marketing objectives. These could include more arrivals, longer stay-overs, higher expenditure per man-day, staggering of the demand, or diversification of markets. Targets are operational objectives, and are expressed in quantitative terms (e.g. an increase of value added of 20 per cent in the next five years).

Strategy is the next basic concept. Strategy can be considered as the road to be followed to fill the gap between where we are now, and where we want to go. With respect to regional development in general, there are several dimensions to enhancing development (Vanhove, 1999). Tourism as a sector is one of these dimensions; the application of the Porter model is another. Human resources development and the stimulation of entrepreneurship are two other roads that can be followed. Physical and financial resources policies are also part of tourism destination development strategies. Marketing strategy should in the first place be concentrated on seven core elements:

1   Tourism scope (e.g. holidaymakers or excursionists; winter and/or summer holidays)
2   Market choice based on objective criteria
3   Formulation of product–market combinations
4   Segmentation and the choice of target markets
5   Positioning and the development of a destination brand (Crouch and Ritchie, 2004)
6   Alliances with other organizations and/or competitors
7   Communication.

We also need a strategy with respect to policy instruments. Goeldner *et al.* (2000) refer in the first place to the secondary components of tourism demand policy, or what is traditionally called the marketing mix or operational marketing: product policy, price policy, distribution policy and promotion policy. However, there are more policy instruments, such as research, training, finance, and the macro-management organizational structure. Many of these elements belong to the action programmes. Strategies without action programmes and implementation plans lead to a dead end. What are the facilities required to realize the strategy? Which events could support the vision? Which programmes could be encouraged (e.g. entrepreneurship programme, cultural programme, winter destination programme, etc.)? The final stage of tourism strategic planning includes the monitoring, steering and evaluation of all the different phases of the strategic plan, and last but not least, the destination audit.

Destination management

The DPPD component creates the framework for a competitive destination. The destination management component of the Ritchie–Crouch model focusses on those activities that implement the tasks prescribed by the DPPD. As such, it seeks to enhance the appeal of the core resources, strengthen the quality and effectiveness of the supplying factors and resources, and adapt best to the constraints or opportunities imposed or presented by the qualifying and amplifying determinants. In the model, destination management consists of nine components, each of which consists of individual destination managerial tasks that must be carefully attended to by the destination manager. They are:

1   Organization (administrative and managerial tasks)
2   Marketing (traditional marketing tasks)
3   Quality of service experiences (the destination should provide a high-quality visitor experience)
4   Information/research
5   Human resource development
6   Finance and venture capital
7   Visitor management (e.g. visitor information centre, ability to deal with crowds)
8   Resource stewardship (taking care of the tourism resource base)
9   Crisis management.

These components are all highly interdependent, and it is not obvious which should be considered first. If there is one component that must be realized before the others, it is organization – in other words, the setting up of a destination management organization (DMO). In most countries there is the need for DMOs at national, regional and local levels. For the major components of organizational development and policy, we refer to Chapter 8 of Ritchie and Crouch (2003). Tourism policy broadly defines the roles of the DMO. The latter should be functional from both strategic and operational perspectives. Ritchie and Crouch emphasize leadership and coordination as essential features of a DMO. The other components of destination management speak for themselves. It is important to note that the DMO should not try to carry out all these management functions itself, but should keep an overall eye on the situation.

The Dwyer–Kim model

A few years ago, Dwyer and Kim (2004) developed a new model – the integrated model of destination competitiveness. The difference between the conceptual models (e.g. Crouch and Ritchie) and integrated models lies mainly in the addition of demand factors to the integrated models (Sánchez and López, 2015). We can also find the basic ideas of this model in Dwyer *et al.* (2004) with an application to Australia and Korea. The key elements of their model are:

- Core resources and supporting factors. Core resources are subdivided into two categories, endowed (e.g. cultural) and created (e.g. events, shopping). Supporting factors relate to general infrastructure, quality of service, accessibility, hospitality, etc.
- Situational conditions (economic, social, cultural, political, legal, etc.; these can be compared to the qualifying and amplifying determinants of Ritchie and Crouch).
- Destination management factors (public sector and private sector activities). This category includes: destination policy, planning and development, DMOs, human resource development and environmental management (which we also find with Ritchie and Crouch).
- Demand conditions; the three main elements being awareness, perception and preferences. A destination may be competitive for one group of visitors but not for another group, depending on the travel motives. It is difficult to convince a sun and beach holidaymaker to spend a holiday only in heritage destinations.

The arrows in Figure 6.7 have a special meaning. The single direction arrows from supporting factors to endowed resources and created resources indicate that a mere existence of these resources is insufficient. One always needs accommodation, transportation, restaurants, shopping, entertainment, etc. Otherwise there is no value added creation.

There is a two-way causal link between resources and supporting factors, on the one hand, and demand and destination management, on the other hand. The features of resources influence demand, whilst the nature of demand conditions influences the types of products developed within a destination. In the same vein the management of public and private organizations influences the types of products developed. But features of resources have an impact on destination management (e.g. how to achieve and maintain sustainability).

The box representing destination competitiveness is linked backwards to the determinants of competitiveness and forwards to the box representing destination or national prosperity – and ultimately the welfare and well-being of the population. In the Dwyer–Kim model destination competitiveness and destination/national prosperity each have a number of indicators. Possible indicators of destination competitiveness are subjective attributes such as 'destination appeal' and more objective attributes such as market share or foreign exchange earnings. Indicators of economic prosperity relate to macro-economic variables such as income per capita, employment levels, economic growth and added value.

The Dwyer–Kim model contains many of the variables identified by Ritchie and Crouch. But it differs from the Ritchie–Crouch model in two respects. Dwyer and Kim recognize 'demand conditions' as an important determinant of destination competitiveness. They also

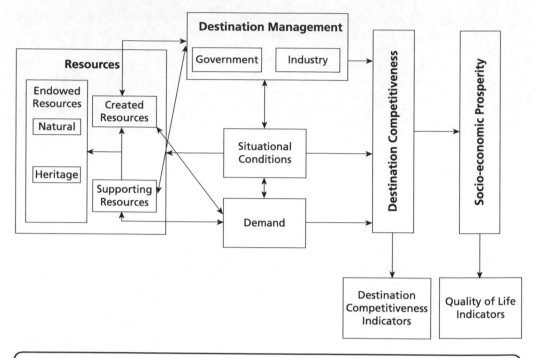

Figure 6.7 The Dwyer–Kim integrated model of destination competitiveness (Dwyer and Kim, 2004)

emphasize that socio-economic prosperity is the required outcome of destination competitiveness: 'destination competitiveness is not an end but a means to an end'. However, the latter is not completely absent in the Ritchie–Crouch model.

Synthesis of the models

Needless to say, the analysed competition models are all different. The starting point and/or the line of approach is not the same. However, each of them has the merit of emphasizing one or more particular aspects:

- The Porter (1980) model emphasizes the competitive forces of enterprises and (to a lesser extent) of destinations, and the related generic competitive strategies.
- The Porter (1990) model emphasizes the home environment and related determinants.
- The Poon concept emphasizes innovation, quality and making tourism a lead sector.
- The WES approach emphasizes macro-economic factors and tourism policy.
- The Dwyer *et al.* approach emphasizes the price component.
- The Bordas approach emphasizes marketing orientation, perceived value and perceived costs.
- The Ritchie and Crouch model emphasizes destination policy, planning and development, and destination management.
- The Dwyer–Kim model pays particular attention to demand conditions.

From these models we can draw three important conclusions and a number of key factors of destination competitiveness. The latter will be dealt with in the next section.

1 Competitiveness of a destination is not a matter of just one or two factors; tourism is a complex issue, and many factors are involved. This conclusion should not be considered as a criticism of the Dwyer *et al.* approach. These authors have tried to show the great price discrepancy between destinations and how to measure the differences in tourism purchasing power. They also recognize the role of productivity levels of various components of the tourism industry and qualitative factors affecting the attractiveness of a destination.

2 The Ritchie–Crouch concept is by far the most comprehensive model, but the Porter (1990), WES and Dwyer–Kim models also contain a great variety of components. Poon's concept is based on a large number of factors, but focusses more on typical factors such as innovation, quality and the role of tourism in the development of a destination, region or country.

3 The Ritchie–Crouch, Porter and WES models have one common denominator. All emphasize strategic planning (tourism policy), attractions, supply and demand factors, and accessibility.

Ten key factors for a competitive destination

Based on the models described, and long personal experience in the field, I have formulated my own list of ten key factors for a competitive destination. These are not presented in order of importance. The order depends on the geo-economic situation and on the local circumstances under which a destination is functioning. Furthermore, many of the factors are interrelated. Each of the factors will be explained in more detail.

1 Attractions
2 Macro-economic factors
3 Innovation
4 Strategic planning
5 Positioning and branding
6 Destination management
7 Strategic alliances
8 Make tourism a lead sector
9 Quality management
10 Accessibility

Attractions

Attractions – natural, cultural or man-made – are a basic requirement. There can be no tourism without attractions. 'Un hotel ne fait pas le tourisme' was a well-known statement of K. Krapf, one of the founding fathers of research in tourism. The attractions are the raw materials. With respect to the attractions three elements are crucial for competitiveness:

● Sustainable development (see also Hassan, 2000)
● Upgrading of attractions
● Staging offers (or to express it in Müller's terminology, 'Angebots-Inszenierung') (see Chapter 3).

There are hundreds of examples where local authorities have not respected sustainable development and a corresponding carrying capacity. Many tourism regions are now paying the bill for an uncontrolled growth. Hassan (2000) formulated ten agenda items for a sustainable development policy for the new millennium. They reveal that environmental commitment will be the foremost issue for the economic revitalization of the tourism industry. Hassan's following statement is important:

> The fact that sustainability is linked to being focused on people's needs and oriented to their demands seems to be consistent with sustaining the promise of need orientation for generations to come. This demand-oriented approach is going to be the guiding philosophy to develop responsible tourism that meets marketplace expectations.

But a tourism product or destination also has a product cycle. It is therefore necessary to upgrade the existing tourism products and/or their components from time to time. Product development is also necessary in the framework of growing segmented markets. It is important to anticipate problems before signs of decay and to take steps to ameliorate them. Hassan (2000) makes a distinction between stabilization strategies (strengthening of existing tourism products and market penetration targets) and a revitalization strategy (new products and/or new markets). In this respect the experience philosophy can be helpful. Nowadays a holiday is increasingly considered as an experience. In the framework of the experience economy, 'Angebots-Inszenierung' in tourism becomes very important. It contributes to the value added in the tourism destinations. Here we refer to the definition of competitiveness in the introduction of this chapter. Two other aspects of the 'attractions' factor are intangible elements: the quality of human resources and the hospitality of all stakeholders at the destination. Is 'Austrian charm' not a competitive advantage?

Macro-economic factors

Macro-economic factors are very important. It starts with the income level in the generating countries or markets. Even more attention should be given to the real exchange rate. The latter relates to relative price level and exchange rate. Many countries (destinations) are too expensive due to an 'over valued' currency. Before the introduction of the euro, in Italy and Spain, the exchange rate was the instrument par excellence to keep a competitive position in the Mediterranean area. The Bahamas and Barbados suffered for a long time from too strong a link of their national currency to the American dollar. The tourism relationship between America and Europe is dominated by the $/€ ratio.

Heavy taxes on the raw materials necessary for tourism also have a very detrimental effect. Countries which consider tourism as a cash cow, work against their own interest. Another relevant macro factor is the availability and cost of capital and labour. The tourism sector in many western European countries suffers from high labour costs. The tourism sector cannot cope with the higher productivity level in several industrial and service sectors. Switzerland is a typical example (see also Cvelbar *et al.*, 2016).

Innovation

Product development brings us to a third commandment: permanent attention to innovation in the destination. In her model, Poon is in favour of radical innovation. Radical innovation is a little bit misleading. It is not possible to develop a new holiday concept each year, but one can, at regular intervals, consider exploring new markets, providing new services, developing new processes, developing a culture for innovation and encouraging new ideas. In practice we should make a distinction between:

- Product innovation
- Process innovation (e.g. faster ski-lifts, use of information technology for checking in and checking out)
- Other elements typical of the tourism sector (e.g. new markets, new communication policy).

Strategic planning

'Il n'y a pas de vent favorable pour celui qui ne sait pas en quel port se rendre' (Montaigne, 16th century). I always consider a destination as a big enterprise with hundreds of business units. There is nowadays no big firm in the industrial or service sector without a strategic plan. The success of a destination in the middle and long term depends on a good strategic plan in which an answer is given to three basic questions:

● Where are we now? (situation and SWOT analysis)
● Where do we want to go? (mission, vision, objectives and targets)
● How do we get there? (marketing strategy, action plans)

In such a strategic tourism plan for a destination, it is recommended that a distinction be made between development and marketing objectives. Development objectives can be: tourism as a sector for development; better use of existing capacity; creation of jobs, etc. Marketing objectives can take different forms: more tourists, longer overstay, staggering of nights, etc. The choice of the objectives has a direct impact on development strategies (physical, human and information resources), marketing strategies and the tourism policy in general of the destination. Particularly important are the six basic marketing strategies (see above). One of the many benefits of a good strategic plan is to ensure that all the stakeholders are working with the same end in view.

Positioning and branding

A major characteristic of the tourism sector is the strong competition between the many destinations. The globalization trend and the growing influence of the internet gives to positioning and branding a very special meaning in the tourism sector. It is a battle for the consumer's mind. Paraphrasing the definition of Kotler *et al.* (1999), a position is the way the destination is defined on important attributes – the place the destination occupies in consumers' minds relative to competing destinations. Essential elements of good positioning are:

● Image creation
● Presentation of the benefit(s)
● Differentiation
● Delivering.

Examples of good positioning, among many others, are the Canary Isles, Bruges and St. Moritz. Positioning and branding are strongly interrelated. Branding is a central element in the strategic positioning of tourism products and destinations. Destination branding is growing rapidly as an approach to tourism destination promotion (Govers and Go, 2009). For destinations it takes the form of a 'corporate identity'. Due to the revolution in distribution channels as a consequence of the growing influence of the internet, branding is becoming increasingly important. A destination brand is, according to Ritchie and Crouch (2003):

> A name, symbol, logo, word mark or other graphic that both identifies and differentiates the destination; furthermore, it conveys the promise of a memorable travel experience that is uniquely associated with the destination; it also serves to consolidate and reinforce the recollection of pleasurable memories of the destination experience.

It is a huge task to bring this definition into practice. Promotion agencies very often underestimate the difficulty of developing a good brand. Symbols, logos and baselines should be understood by the potential consumer. An excellent example was the former corporate identity of Spain with the sun of Miro and the baseline 'Spain: everything under the sun'. Murphy *et al.* (2007) show that in a research project for Northern Australia, tourists were able to articulate different destination brand personalities for each region.

Destination management

As we have seen in one of the preceding factors, destination strategic planning is essentially an intellectual process that uses information, judgement and monitoring to make macro-level decisions regarding the kind of destination that is desirable, and the degree to which ongoing performance and related changes in the nature of visitation and the physical character of the destination are contributing to the achievement of the kind of destination that stakeholders want. Destination management is more of a micro-level activity in which all the stakeholders carry out their individual and organizational responsibilities on a daily basis in an effort to realize the macro-level vision contained in policy, planning and development (Ritchie and Crouch, 2003).

The manager of a destination can be compared with the CEO of a big firm. He or she is responsible for maintaining a sustainable competitive advantage to ensure its economic profitability and avoiding degradation of the factors that have created its competitive position. Crucial tasks are the functioning of the destination management organization, marketing, visitor management, resource stewardship and the introduction or follow up of a management information system (see also Cvelbar *et al.*, 2016).

Strategic alliances

Competition is not simply about how firms and destinations compete against one another, but also about how they cooperate with other firms or destinations in order to increase competition. Partners invest time, effort and resources while collaborating to achieve both individual and shared goals. Strategic alliances can enhance the productivity and competitiveness of the firms and organizations involved. Alliances can take place within the destination (e.g. Millstättersee in Austria), between the tourism sector and other sectors (e.g. the cooperation in St. Moritz between the local destination management and firms of luxury products) and between destinations (e.g. the art cities in Flanders and BOTA – Best of the Alps, twelve ski resorts in five different countries). Millstättersee is an example of how the performance of a destination can improve through operating cooperation, quality management and common sales and marketing.

Make 'tourism a lead sector'

Referring to the definition of a competitive destination in a preceding section, making tourism a lead sector deserves special attention (see Poon, 1993). Indeed, tourism can activate a lot of services and activities such as car rental, food, crafts, souvenirs, construction, incoming tour operating, etc. Special attention should be paid to avoid leakages. In many destinations, local vegetable production or fruit growing can replace imported products on condition that the local producers can assure a regular supply, of the necessary quality and without too many price variations. Local architecture and local products can enhance authenticity. Manufacturing for the tourism sector and the stimulation of the market for authentic souvenirs can be important sources of value added and employment.

Quality management

Many industrial firms are aware of the importance of quality. For Japanese firms it is a key element of competition. We notice that gradually more and more tourism firms are paying attention to quality (see AIEST congress in Cha-am, 1997). 'Service quality is defined in the tourism marketing literature as a subjective construct, whereby the customer (tourist) compares the obtained service quality with the expected service (quality)' (Weiermair, 1997). Not many destinations apply a quality policy. However, it is possible. It is said that: 'Quality is never an accident. It is always the result of intelligent effort.' This effort starts with a quality plan which is based on many pillars (e.g. tourism attractions, beach and promenade, accommodation, restaurants, bars, terraces, traffic and parking, etc.) Each of these pillars has several attributes which should be evaluated. The quality plan is the next step. That plan needs the support of all stakeholders in the destination. A successful implementation will depend to a large extent on the capacities of the quality manager, who has to work in cooperation with the local authorities and the tourism sector.

Accessibility

It is impossible for a destination to be competitive without being accessible. Accessibility is a question of price, time, safety and security. The Caribbean area is a typical example. In the 1990s, several Caribbean destinations suffered from the bankruptcy of two big American air carriers (Eastern Airlines and Pan AM). Several destinations in the region became far less accessible or needed more travel time. Many destinations try to attract low-cost carriers or lobby for a high-speed train stop. Safety is a third element of accessibility. In the more recent past dozens of destinations have registered a real fall in demand due to insufficient safety and security.

Importance-performance analysis (IPA)

One important remark should be made. There is a fundamental difference between factors of destination competitiveness and attribute determinance. Although an attribute may be considered to be important, it will not be a determinant of competitiveness if there is little difference among destinations on the attribute.

Determinant attributes must respond to two requirements that interact with each other: importance (high or low) and performance (good or poor) (Crouch, 2007). It can be useful to apply an 'Importance-performance analysis, or IPA' (see Figure 6.8; Enright and Newton, 2004). A standard approach adopted by IPA is to combine measures of importance and performance into a two-dimensional grid. This eases data interpretation and elicits suggestions for action. Quadrant I includes factors that are very important with good performance. In Figure 6.8 that is the case for factors or attributes c and d. The destination should strive to maintain these. Quadrant II includes factors of low importance but with a good performance. This is the quadrant of wasted efforts. Quadrant III identifies factors of low importance and poor performance and consequently low priority. Quadrant IV is the area with factors of high importance but poor performance. This is the critical area for improvement. Enright and Newton applied the IPA analysis to Hong Kong.

The Travel and Tourism Competitiveness Index (TTCI)

Besides the conceptual models of competitiveness dealt with in the preceding sections, there are a number of tourism benchmarking models:

● The Travel and Tourism Competitiveness Index – TTCI of the WEF
● The partial model of destination competitiveness of Modul University
● Sustainable tourism benchmarking tool – STBT (Cernat and Gourdon, 2007)
● European Tourism Indicator System – ETIS (Tourism Policy Unit, European Commission, 2015).

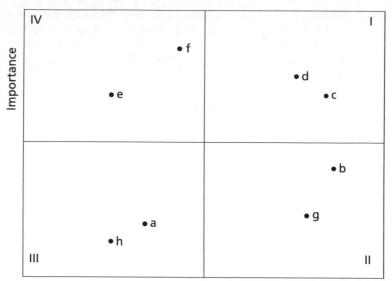

Figure 6.8 Importance and relative competitiveness of tourism attractors
● attractors a to h

In this section we give our attention to the first two models. The Travel and Tourism Competitiveness Index (TTCI) is the most well-known and the most universal. Early in 2007 the World Economic Forum (WEF) published the TTCI for the first time. This is in every respect an interesting study. In the preface of the report, Klaus Schwab, Executive Chairman, WEF, gives the background to the TTCI:

> The World Economic Forum has been actively engaged in studying issues related to national competitiveness for nearly three decades, motivated by a desire to better understand the drivers of growth and prosperity. Over the years, our goal has been to provide benchmarking tools that enable countries to identify key obstacles to competitiveness, and to provide a platform for dialogue among government, business, and civil society to discuss the best ways of removing them. In this light, given the importance of the Travel & Tourism (T&T) industry to the world economy, the fundamental objective of the Travel & Tourism Competitiveness Report (TTCR) is to explore the factors driving T&T competitiveness worldwide.

When it comes to comparing and contrasting the key competition factors with the TTCI, what are the similarities and what are the important points of divergence? To describe the Travel and Tourism Competitiveness Index (TTCI) we make use of the text of Blanke and Chiesa (2009). The TTCI has been developed within the context of the WEF's Industry Partnership Programme for the Aviation, Travel and Tourism sector.

> The TTCI aims to measure the factors and policies that make it attractive to develop the T&T sector in different countries. The Index was developed between September 2005 and October 2006 by the World Economic Forum (WEF) in close collaboration with their strategic design partner Booz Allen Hamilton, and their data partners the International Air Transport Association (IATA), the UNWTO, and the WTTC.

Although the Competitiveness Monitor (former TTCI) was well received by the international community, it remained according to Blanke and Chiesa somewhat limited in scope:

> In this context, the WTTC decided that joining efforts with the World Economic Forum and other industry organizations would provide access to a greater breadth of data and would better ensure the optimal use of the findings in promoting public-private dialogue with the goal of improving the T&T environments of countries. Thus, the TTCI should be seen as a natural extension of the work previously carried out within the context of the Monitor, enhanced by further economic data and input from a variety of industry experts.

To keep the TTCI methodology up to date and allow it to respond better to policy needs, the WEF and its data partners (Deloitte, IATA, IUCN, Strategy&, UNWTO and WTTC) have reviewed the Index a third time. The review highlighted a number of areas for improvement, which have been implemented in the new index structure. While some of the main drivers of T&T competitiveness remain unchanged, some other factors have become more relevant while measurements and data availability improve over time (Crotti and Misrahi, 2016).

In the revised the TTCI, the new methodology is organized into four sub-indexes and is based on 14 pillars. Each pillar counts a number of indicators. Overall, the new methodology uses more indicators (90 instead of 79). Two-thirds of the data set for the TTCI is statistical data from international organizations, with the remaining third based on survey data from the WEF's annual Executive Opinion Survey (see Table 6.8). The TTCI provides a platform and a strategic benchmarking tool for business and governments to develop the T&T sector.

Table 6.8 Structure of the TTCI, 2015

Source: WEF Travel and Tourism Competitiveness Report, 2015

Subindex	Pillars	Number of indicators
Enabling environment	1 Business environment	12
	2 Safety and security	5
	3 Health and hygiene	6
	4 Human resources and labour market	9
	5 ICT readiness	8
T&T policy and enabling conditions	6 Prioritization of travel and tourism	6
	7 International openness	3
	8 Price competitiveness	4
	9 Environmental sustainability	10
Infrastructure	10 Air transport infrastructure	6
	11 Ground and port infrastructure	7
	12 Tourist service infrastructure	4
Natural and cultural resources	13 Natural resources	5
	14 Cultural resources and business travel	5

By allowing cross-country comparison and benchmarking of countries' progress on the drivers of T&T competitiveness, it informs policies and investment decisions related to T&T development (see Table 6.9).

The standard formula for converting each hard data variable to the 1-to-7 scale is:

$$6 \times \left(\frac{\text{country value} - \text{sample minimum}}{\text{sample maximum} - \text{sample minimum}} \right) + 1$$

The sample minimum and sample maximum are the lowest and highest values of the overall sample, respectively. For some variables, a higher value indicates a worse outcome. In this case Blanke and Chiesa reverse the series by subtracting the newly created variable from 8. Each of the pillars has been calculated as an unweighted average of individual component variables. The sub-indexes are then calculated as unweighted averages of the included pillars. The overall TTCI is the unweighted average of the four sub-indexes.

Spain leads the 2015 TTCI ranking for the first time, and Europe – with a total of six countries in the top 10 – is confirmed as the region with the most T&T-competitive economies. A more detailed analysis raises a number of questions about the value of the ranking. It is difficult to understand and to accept the ranking for France and Thailand. With respect to Prioritization of Travel & Tourism they rank respectively 31 and 40. We are afraid that there is a loose relationship between the chosen indicators and the corresponding pillar. However, this not the only strange ranking. Many tourism experts will have problems with the ranking of Germany for the pillar 'cultural resources and business travel'. This country takes a top 5 position in the TTCI for this pillar and rank 18 for natural resources. Therefore, as far as the interpretation of the results is concerned, we sometimes have to proceed with caution. Can the number of large sports stadium be an indicator for cultural resources?

This brings us to five weak points of the TTCI. The four sub-indexes have the same weight and this is open for discussion. More important is the evaluation of some pillars based on the opinion of CEOs and top business leaders in all economies. We wonder if CEOs are always the right people to give a correct evaluation of some pillars. Tourism destinations may not be identified with countries. Even within one country there can be competitive and non-competitive destinations. Furthermore, each country has its own national evaluators (on a scale

Table 6.9 The top ten rankings of the TTCI, 2015
Source: WEF Travel and Tourism Competitiveness Report, 2015

Country	Overall index 2015	TTCI value
Spain	1	5.31
France	2	5.24
Germany	3	5.22
USA	4	5.12
United Kingdom	5	5.12
Switzerland	6	4.99
Australia	7	4.98
Italy	8	4.98
Japan	9	4.94
Canada	10	4.92

from 1 to 7). This can lead to surprising rankings. Lastly, not all variables are theoretically justified and relevant for tourism competitiveness (Crouch, 2007; Mazanec *et al.*, 2007; Mazanec, 2010). Mazanec *et al.* find that neither the tourism-related factors 'tourism price competitiveness' and 'tourism-related infrastructure', nor the more loosely associated dimensions of 'environmental preservation' and 'openness', were confirmed as factors contributing to overall destination competitiveness. Many indicators are totally irrelevant. These few remarks should not be considered as an underestimation of the value of the TTCI. My own ten key factors for a competitive destination based on competition models are not above criticism.

It will now be interesting to compare the ten key factors with the TTCI pillars. The above-formulated ten key factors for tourism competitiveness are in fact the tourism success factors. The 14 pillars of the TTCI are by definition growth factors. In principle there should be a great similarity. We find the factors of accessibility (safety and security included), marketing (branding included), attractions, and the macro-economic situation in both approaches. However, the exchange rate is considered in the pillar 'business environment'. Attractions are only partly considered in the TTCI. The latter focus on cultural heritage and this is in the real tourism world only a minor part of natural, cultural and man-made attractions. The TTCI does not refer to the success factors of innovation, strategic planning, destination management, strategic alliances, 'make tourism a lead sector' and quality management.

How can we explain the divergence between the tourism success factors and the pillars in the TTCI? Six considerations may be relevant. Firstly, tourism success factors are mainly based on a tourism-economic approach while the TTCI is more a business-economic-tourism approach. We agree it is a question of nuance. Secondly, the starting point in the competition models is 'the destination' and in most cases destinations do not cover the whole country. All components of the TTCI refer to national data or opinions which relate to the whole country. One can raise the question as to what extent it is relevant for the tourism sector to have access to drinking water or health facilities, a positive or negative attitude to tourism, etc. in non-tourism regions of the country. Thirdly, the concept of competitiveness is slightly different in both approaches. Value added creation is the key element behind the formulation of the ten key factors. The TTCI focusses on growth. Fourthly, the competition models are more dynamic. The emphasis is on strategic planning, destination management, innovation and quality management. The approach of the WEF seems to be more static. The index gives a picture of relevant factors. Fifthly, we have the impression that the TTCI is conceived more for developing than developed countries, although this was probably not the intention of the authors. In the TTCI, the WEF focus on factors of growth. This partly explains the choice of the pillars and corresponding components. Finally, success factors and components of a competitiveness index are not independent of the type of tourism product (cultural, beach, mountains, events).

The partial model of destination competitiveness of Modul University

A second tourism benchmarking tool is 'the partial model of destination competitiveness of Modul University' and focusses on city tourism in Europe (Önder *et al.*, 2017). In the abstract to their contribution they posit:

> The authors provide a synthesis of various frameworks for sustainable tourism indicators for subnational regions and cities, concluding that it is more feasible to analyse existing sustainable tourism indicators than to introduce new measures lacking in direct practical applicability for the organizations. The application of data envelopment analysis (DEA) for benchmarking urban tourism destinations is then demonstrated by assessing measures available in TourMIS. Findings include inefficiency scores that suggest both managerial and political implications. Furthermore, the concept of a virtual reference destination

assisting managers and politicians to analyse their destination's strengths and weaknesses is introduced.

Data envelopment analysis (DEA) is a nonparametric method that measures the relative efficiency of Decision Making Units (DMUs) which are assumed to have the same objectives (Wöber and Fesenmaier, 2004; Wöber, 2007). It is used to empirically measure productive efficiency of DMUs. Although DEA has a strong link to production theory in economics, the tool is also used for benchmarking in operations management, where a set of measures is selected to benchmark the performance of manufacturing and service operations. In the circumstance of benchmarking, the efficient DMUs, as defined by DEA, may not necessarily form a 'production frontier', but rather lead to a 'best-practice frontier'.

TourMIS (www.tourmis.info) is a marketing decision support system that supports the tourism industry by collecting, storing, processing, and disseminating tourism-related information. The system provides free access to a number of important tourism indicators such as bed nights, arrivals and accommodation capacities in tourism destinations (countries, regions, cities). Since 2000 this initiative has provided the tourism industry with predominantly free access to overall data and functions of TourMIS. The programme modules contained in the method-base are developed according to the specific requirements of tourism managers at the Department of Tourism and Hospitality Management at Modul University, Vienna.

The Modul competition model starts from the three pillars of sustainable tourism of the United Nations Environment Programme. In that programme sustainable tourism is defined as 'Tourism that takes full account of its current and future economic, social and environmental impacts, addressing the needs of visitors, the industry, the environment and host communities'. Sustainable tourism therefore considers not only environmental issues but also societal and economic issues related to the host regions. Effective management of this growing industry requires the impacts of tourism across these three dimensions to be determined and measured (see Figure 6.9).

Önder *et al.* (2017) give an overview of potential objectives for city tourism policy makers as well as indicators for their measurement. These objectives and indicators are categorized as

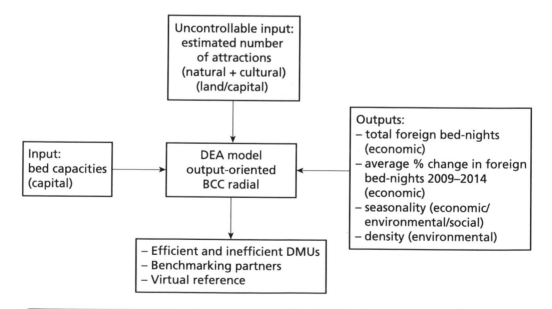

Figure 6.9 DEA (Data Envelopment Analysis) model

Source: borrowed from Önder *et al.*, 2017

economic, social and environmental. Let us illustrate this with an example of each component of sustainability:

Objectives	Indicator
● Economic: Seasonality	Distribution of demand
● Environmental: Energy use	Consumption of non-renewable energy per night
● Social: Satisfaction of residents with tourism	Overall survey

The resources which represent inputs into tourism products are categorized as capital, land and labour.

Input factors	Indicator
● Land: Climate	Number of sunny days
● Capital: Governance	Budget of local tourism organization
● Labour: Human resources	Professional experience in tourism

A major problem is the availability of the data of objectives-indicators and input-indicators in TourMIS. That is the reason why in practice only a limited number of indicators are retained. Hence the use of a 'partial' model of destination competitiveness. Specifically, six indicators were modelled in the DEA framework of the study of Önder *et al.*, as shown in Figure 6.9. Two input variables were used: bed-capacities (controllable variable) and estimated number of attractions (natural and cultural, uncontrollable variable). Input variables are classified as either controllable or uncontrollable depending on whether they are under the control of the decision-makers or not. In terms of type, both of these are capital indicators, while attractions can additionally be labelled as a land indicator, as the data include natural as well as cultural attractions. On the output side, four indicators were used: (1) total foreign bed-nights (economic); (2) average percentage change in total foreign bed-nights between 2009 and 2014 (economic); (3) seasonality based on total foreign and domestic bed-nights (economic/environmental/social) and lastly (4) density (environmental).

The final sample for the case study included 27 European cities, the selection of which was made solely on the data availability for all six indicators. Efficiency measurement system software version 3.1 was used for all DEA computations. The results show that ten cities were inefficient, while the remaining 17 were efficient based on the given input/output combination. This study shows that applying DEA to TourMIS data for calculating efficiency scores for cities yields valuable information for tourism decision-makers to enhance their destinations in various ways.

Benchmarking partners are provided by the data envelopment analysis and are the results of the linear programming exercise which is the core part of DEA. The virtual reference is the 'weighted composite' which is generated by combining similar, better performing business units (in this case 'destinations/cities'). It is a linear combination of two or several efficient business units. The better performing business units (= benchmarking partners) and weights are provided by the DEA. The virtual reference serves as a target ('possible goal') for the business unit under evaluation.

The weakness of this model is the limited number of variables. It is an attempt made to run DEA using indicators stemming from three dimensions of sustainability, using data from TourMIS. The model is also very volatile. If the sample is increased by one or more cities and/or one or more variables, the efficiency scores might change. Furthermore, it is not clear for what type of competitiveness the 'Partial model of destination competitiveness stands for'.

References and further reading

AIEST (1993). *Competitiveness of Long-haul Tourist Destinations*, 43rd AIEST Congress, Bariloche. St-Gall: AIEST.

Baldassin, L., Gallo, M., and Mattevi, E. (2017). Tourism in European cities: price competitiveness of hotels in towns of artistic interest. *Tourism Economics, 23 (1)*.

Blanke, J., and Chiesa, T. (2009). The Travel & Tourism Competitiveness Index 2009: Measuring Sectoral Drivers in a Downturn, *Travel and Tourism Competitiveness Report 2009*. Geneva: World Economic Forum.

Bordas, E. (1994). *Competitiveness of Tourist Destinations in Long-distance Markets*. Paper presented at TRC Meeting, Swansea, 1994 (unpublished).

Bosselman, F., Peterson, C., and McCarthy, Cl. (1999). *Managing Tourism Growth*. Washington, DC: Island Press.

Brackenbury, B. (1993). The competitiveness of long-haul destinations – the tour operator's point of view. *Competitiveness of Long-haul Tourist Destinations*, 43rd AIEST Congress, Bariloche. St-Gall: AIEST.

Buhalis, D. (2000). Marketing the competitive destination of the future. *Tourism Management, 21*.

Cernat, L., and Gourdon, J. (2007). *Developing The Sustainable Tourism Benchmarking Tool*. New York: United Nations.

Chan, E., and Wong, S. (2006). Hotel selection: when price is not the issue. *Journal of Vacation Marketing, 2*.

Cooper, C., Fayos-Solà, E., and Pedro, A. (2001). Globalisation, tourism policy and tourism education, *TedQual, 2*.

Crotti, R., and Misrahi, T. (2016). *The Travel & Tourism Competitiveness Index 2015: T&T as a Resilient Contribution to National Development*. Geneva: World Economic Forum.

Crouch, G. (2007). *Destination Competitiveness and Attribute Determinance*. Palma de Mallorca: IATE conference.

Crouch, G., and Ritchie, J.R.B. (2004). Application of the audit concept for destination diagnosis. In S. Weber and R. Tomljenovic (eds), *Reinventing a Tourism Destination*. Zagreb: Scientific Edition Institute for Tourism.

Cvelbar, L., Dwyer, L., Koman, M., and Mihalic, T. (2016). Drivers of destination competitiveness in tourism; a global investigation. *Journal of Travel Research, 55 (8)*.

Dale, C. (2000). The UK tour-operating industry: a competitive analysis. *Journal of Vacation Marketing, 4*.

De Keyser, R., and Van Impe, P. (1996). *Het internationaal toeristisch marketingplan voor België*. Brugge: WES.

De Pelsmacker, P., and Van Kenhove, P. (1994). *Marktonderzoek. Methoden en Toepassingen*. Leuven: Garant.

d'Harteserre, A. (2000). Lessons in Managerial Destination Competitiveness in the case of Faxwoods Casino Resort. *Tourism Management, 1*.

Dwyer, L., Forsyth, P., and Rao, P. (2000). The price competitiveness of travel and tourism: a comparison of 19 destinations. *Tourism Management, 21*.

Dwyer, L., Livaic, Z., and Mellor, R. (2003). Competitiveness of Australia as a tourist destination. *Journal of Hospitality and Tourism Management, 1*.

Dwyer, L., and Kim, C. (2004). Destination competitiveness: determinants and indicators. *Current Issues in Tourism, 5*.

Dwyer, L., Kim, C., Livaic, Z., and Mellor, R. (2004). Application of a model of destination competitiveness to Australia and Korea. In S. Weber and R. Tomljenovic (eds), *Reinventing a Tourism Destination*. Zagreb: Scientific Edition Institute for Tourism.

Edwards, A. (1995). *Asia-Pacific Travel Forecasts to 2005*. Research report. London: EIU.

Enright, M., and Newton, J. (2004). Tourism destination competitiveness: a quantitative approach. *Tourism Management, 25*.

European Commission (2015). *European Tourism Indicator System*. Brussels: European Commission.

Fayos-Solá, E. (1996). Tourism policy: a midsummer night's dream? *Tourism Management*, 6.

Forsyth, P., and Dwyer, L. (2009). *Measuring Destination Price Competitiveness*. Mallorca: IAST congress.

Go, F. (2000). Integrated quality management for tourist destinations: a European perspective on achieving competitiveness. *Tourism Management*, 21.

Goeldner, R., Ritchie, J., and McIntosh, R. (2000). *Tourism: Principles, Practices, Philosophies*, 8th edn. New York: John Wiley & Sons.

Gohr, C.L., Neto, L., and Santana, E. (2002). Competitive strategies: a study of the hotel sector of Itapema/Santa Catarina. *Turismo*, 10.

Gooroochurn, N., and Sugiyarto, G. (2005). Competitiveness indicators in the travel and tourism industry. *Tourism Economics*, 1.

Govers, R., and Go, F. (2009). *Place Branding: Glocal, Virtual and Physical Identities, Constructed, Imagined and Experienced*. Hampshire: Palgrave Macmillan.

Hassan, S. (2000). Determinants of market competitiveness in an environmentally sustainable tourism industry. *Journal of Travel Research*, 3.

Jacob, M., Tintoré, J., Aguil, E., Bravo, A., and Mulet, J. (2003). Innovation in the tourism sector: results from a pilot study in the Balearic Islands. *Tourism Economics*, 3.

Knowles, T. (1994). The strategic importance of CRSs in the airline industry. *Travel & Tourism Analyst*, 4.

Kotler, P., Bowen, J., and Makens, J. (1999). *Marketing for Hospitality and Tourism*. London: Prentice Hall International.

Mazanec, J. (2010). *Tourism Destination Competitiveness/ Second Thoughts on the World Economic Forum Reports 2008 and 2009*. Vienna: TRC meeting.

Mazanec, J., Wöber, K., and Zins, H. (2007). Tourism destination competitiveness: from definition to explanation. *Journal of Travel Research*, August.

McVey, M., and King, B. (2003). Hotels in Australia. *Travel & Tourism Analyst*, August.

Michael, E., Lynch, P., Hall, C., and Mitchell, R. (2006). *Micro-Clusters and Networks: The Growth of Tourism*. Oxford: Elsevier.

Middleton, V.T.C. (2001). *Marketing in Travel and Tourism*, 3rd edn. Oxford: Butterworth-Heinemann.

Moreno-Izquierdo, L., Ramón-Rodríguez, A., and Perles-Ribes, J. (2016). Pricing strategies of the European low-cost carriers explained using Porter's Five Forces Model. *Tourism Economics, 22 (2)*.

Morgan, M. (1996). *Marketing for Leisure and Tourism*. Hemel Hempstead: Prentice Hall.

Morrison, A.M. (1989). *Hospitality and Travel Marketing*. New York: Delmar Publishers Inc.

Müller, H.R. (2003). *Tourismus und Ökologie – Wechselwirkungen und Handlungsfelder*. München: Oldenburg-verlag.

Müller, H.R. (2004a). *Qualitätsorientiertes Tourismus-Management*. Bern: UTB/Paul Haupt-Verlag.

Müller, H.R. (2004b). *Tourismusdestination als Erlebniswelt – Ein Leitfaden zur Angebotsgestaltung*. Bern: FIFVerlag.

Murphy, L., Moscardo, G., and Benckendorff, P. (2007). Using brand personality to differentiate regional tourism destinations. *Journal of Travel Research*, August.

OECD (1997). *Industrial Competitiveness: Benchmarking Business Environments*. Paris: OECD.

Önder, I., Wöber, K., and Zekan, B. (2017). Towards a sustainable urban tourism development in Europe: the role of benchmarking and tourism management information systems – a partial model of competitiveness. *Tourism Economics, 23 (2)*.

Pearce, D. (1997). Competitive destination analysis in Southeast Asia. *Journal of Travel Research*, 4.

Pechlaner, H., and Smeral, E. (2001). *Customer Value Management as a Determinant of the Competitive Position of Tourism Destinations*. Paper presented at the 36th TRC Meeting, Interlaken, 2001.

Petrillo, C.L. (2002). Position and strategic choices of Italian tour operators in European competition. *Tourism, 1*.

Poon, A. (1993). *Tourism, Technology and Competitive Strategies*. Wallingford: C.A.B International.

Porter, M. (1980). *The Competitive Strategy: Techniques for Analysing Industries and Competitors*. New York: The Free Press.

Porter, M. (1985). *Competitive Advantage: Creating and Sustaining Superior Performance*. New York: The Free Press.

Porter, M. (1987). From competitive advantage to corporate strategy. *Harvard Business Review, 1*.

Porter, M. (1990). *The Competitive Advantage of Nations*. London: The Macmillan Press.

Porter, M. (1998). Clusters and the new economics of competition. *Harvard Business Review*, November/December.

Ribes, J., Rodríguez, A., and Jiménez, M. (2011). Determinants of the competitive advantage of residential tourism destinations in Spain. *Tourism Economics, 17 (2)*.

Ritchie, J.R.B., and Crouch, G. (2000). The competitive destination: a sustainability perspective. *Tourism Management, 21*.

Ritchie, J.R.B., and Crouch, G. (2002). Country and city state destinations. *TedQual, 1*.

Ritchie, J.R.B., and Crouch, G. (2003). *The Competitive Destination: A Sustainable Tourism Perspective*. Wallingford: CABI Publishing.

Sánchez, A., and López, D. (2015). Tourism competitiveness: the Spanish Mediterranean case. *Tourism Economics, 21 (6)*.

Shaw, G., and Williams, A. (2004). *Tourism and Tourism Spaces*. London: Sage.

Smeral, E. (1996). Globalisation and changes in the competitiveness of tourism destinations. *Globalisation and Tourism*, 46th AIEST Congress; Rotorua. St-Gall: AIEST.

Tribe, J. (1999). *The Economics of Leisure and Tourism*. Oxford: Butterworth-Heinemann.

Vanhove, N. (1999). *Regional Policy: A European Approach*, 3rd edn. Aldershot: Ashgate.

Vanhove, N. (2002). Tourism policy-between competitiveness and sustainability: the case of Bruges. *The Tourist Review, 3*.

Vanhove, N. (2005). Innovation: engine of growth in tourism. In P. Keller and T. Bieger (eds), *Innovation in Tourism: Creating Customer Value*. St-Gallen: AIEST.

Vanhove, N., and De Keyser, R. (1997). Quality management in a resort. A practical application. *The Tourist Review, 3*.

Weiermair, K. (1997). *On the concept and definition of quality in tourism*. St. Gallen: 47th AIEST congress.

WEF (2015). *Travel and Tourism Competitiveness Report*. Geneva: WEF.

WES (1994). *The Competitive Situation of Tourism in the Caribbean Area and its Importance for the Region's Development*. Washington/Brugge (unpublished report).

Wöber, K. (2007). Data envelopment analysis. *Journal of Travel and Tourism Marketing, 21 (4)*.

Wöber, K., and Fesenmaier, D. (2004). A Multi-Criteria Approach to Destination Benchmarking: A Case Study of State Tourism Advertising Programs in the United States. *Journal of Travel and Tourism Marketing, 18*.

WTO (1992). *An Integrated Approach to Resort Development*. Madrid: WTO.

Young, R. (1966). Goals and goalsetting. *Journal of the American Institute of Planners*, March.

Chapter 7

Forecasting tourism demand

Introduction

'Forecasting can be defined as the art of predicting the occurrence of events before they actually take place' (Archer, 1975). Forecasting is a subject that fascinates many people who are interested in the economics of tourism. Estimates of future demand at destination level are very important in managing and planning tourism development and the necessary investment. However, forecasting in the tourism sector is not an easy job. As explained in Chapter 3, many variables have an impact, and some of them are unpredictable.

Owing to the many explanatory factors, forecasting in tourism is different from forecasting in most other sectors. The aim cannot be to provide very precise predictions – for example, an increase of arrivals of, say, 5.3 per cent. Those who believe in precise estimations start with the wrong attitude. In tourism, forecasting means indicating the future direction of demand – or, in other words, getting an idea of the magnitude of the expected evolution. Knowledge of the extent of future demand should provide sufficient information for a destination management policy, allowing a limit to the range of uncertainty and thus a reduction in investment risks.

Forecasting in tourism focusses on the destination level and far less on individual enterprises. Large attractions (for example, theme parks) are an exception to the general rule, but very often these are in fact visitor destinations in their own right.

Tourism forecasting requires a particular philosophy. It is often said that 'forecasting in tourism is an art'. This should not be interpreted as an aversion to forecasting methods – on the contrary. However, according to Archer (1975), sound forecasting requires a sensible amalgam of rigorous scientific analysis and sound practical experience. A 'good feeling' can be helpful. Accurate information should be the starting point (see Chapter 2), and we can learn a lot from the past – although it is a mistake to depend too much on trends. It is also wise to start from several scenarios. Consulting people from the tourism industry is a valuable complement to any forecasting method. Finally, it is recommended that forecasts be revised from time to time.

What do we forecast in tourism? There is a great variety of forecasting aims, such as expenditure, arrivals at the destination, demand for accommodation and transport services, possible product trends, etc. This variety probably explains the great interest within the tourism sector in forecasting techniques.

Forecasting in tourism poses several particular problems:

1 The development of new destinations and new types of tourism, and the marketing changes of large groups, can influence existing trends.
2 The great variety of packages and independent travel leads to complex scenarios – most of which are competitive, although others are complementary.
3 In a destination, decisions are made by thousands of decision-makers in public organizations and enterprises.

4   Tourism suffers from a lack of sufficient reliable historic data in compatible series.
5   There is a full range of economic and other variables.
6   Tourism is very vulnerable to terrorism, diseases, natural disasters, political and economic changes.

It is noticeable that the forecasting literature of the last few decades is, more than for other economic subjects of tourism, to a large extent dominated by a relatively limited number of writers: Archer, Frechtling, Smeral, Song and Witt. However, this chapter will show that other authors have also contributed to a better knowledge of forecasting in tourism.

The chapter focusses on four main topics. The first section deals with the different concepts of demand measurement, while the second pays attention to a number of qualitative forecasting methods. The quantitative methods are discussed in the third section, and the final section is dedicated to a number of interesting applications of regression analysis.

Concepts of demand measurement

Market demand can have several meanings. The first point that should be clarified is the definition of the 'market level'. Demand can be measured for:

- Product level – total product, specific tourism forms or specific item
- Geographical level – world, country, county or destination
- Time level – present, or short, medium or long term.

Each type of demand measurement serves a specific purpose. A tour operator will apply short-term forecasting to determine the necessary seats and hotel rooms. A national tourist office needs more medium- and long-term forecasting to secure the necessary infra- and superstructure (accommodation) to cope with an increasing demand.

Besides the different 'market levels', a distinction should be made between total market, potential market, available market, served market and penetrated market (see Figure 7.1). A potential market is only a part of the total population. The potential market consists of those consumers that profess some interest in a defined product (e.g. a destination). In many surveys the customers are not only asked if there is an interest in the destination but also if they have the intention to visit the destination in the coming three or five years. However, customers may have an interest in visiting a destination but not have the financial means and/or access to that destination (for example, somebody may wish to visit Mombasa in Kenya, but be unable to stand the climate). The available market therefore consists of those consumers who have the interest and the necessary income to visit a destination, along with no access constraints.

The served market is a part of the available market. The destination management can decide to pursue only well-defined segments (e.g. middle and upper classes) of a limited number of countries.

The penetrated market consists of the set of consumers who actually purchase the tourist product. From Figure 7.1, it is clear that this is only a fraction of the total population.

Although assessment of each type of market is not an obvious measurement, it is an interesting idea and has a practical value in the framework of the marketing of a product or a destination. When the destination management is not satisfied with the present demand, a number of actions are possible: (a) a growth in the available market by lowering the price or improving access conditions; (b) extension of the served market; or (c) a promotion campaign within the potential market.

Market demand for a destination is the total volume that would be bought by a defined customer group in a defined geographical area in a defined time period in a defined marketing environment under a defined marketing programme. Several elements are relevant:

● Total volume (arrivals, nights or receipts)
● Customer group (whole market or segment)
● Time period (short, medium or long term)
● Marketing environment (e.g. business cycle, technological environment)
● Marketing programme (e.g. promotional budget).

It is important to realize that total market demand is not a fixed number but a function. For this reason it is also called the market demand function or market response function. In Figure 7.2, the horizontal axis shows increasing levels of marketing expenditure in a given period of time; the vertical axis indicates the corresponding demand level. The curve represents the estimated level of market demand as a function of varying levels of marketing effort. Some base sales would take place without any effort – the so-called market minimum. When marketing expenditure takes place the demand increases, but this is not infinite – beyond a certain level, increased marketing efforts do not yield further demand. This suggests an upper limit of market demand, called market potential. The distance between the market minimum and the market potential shows the marketing sensitivity of demand. In an expansible market the distance between Q_1 and Q_2 is relatively large (e.g. the long-haul market for Bali), whereas in a non-expansible market the distance between Q_1 and Q_2 is relatively small (e.g. the home market of a seaside destination). It is important to note that a market demand function is not a picture of market demand over time.

The market demand corresponding to a given effort is known as the market forecast in a given marketing environment. The latter is crucial for correct interpretation of the results. If the marketing environment changes, the curve will move either upwards or downwards

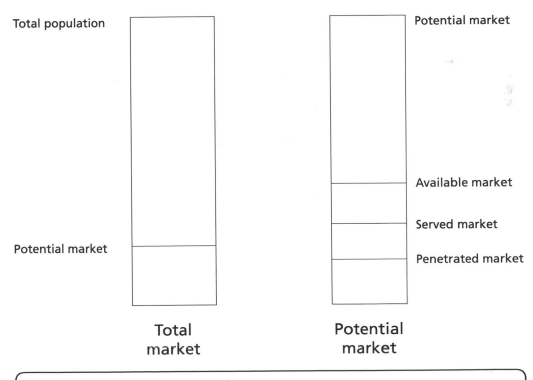

Figure 7.1 Levels of market definition
Source: Kotler (1984)

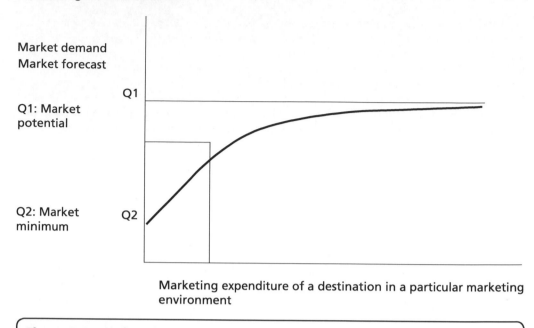

Market demand
Market forecast

Q1: Market
potential

Q2: Market
minimum

Marketing expenditure of a destination in a particular marketing environment

Figure 7.2 Market demand
Source: Kotler (1984)

accordingly. In the following sections, the marketing environment is not always the same. Assumptions are also introduced regarding the marketing environment.

Besides market demand, company demand can also be considered. A company can be a hotel, resort, or even a particular destination. Company demand is the company's share of total demand. Company demand is, like market demand, a function – the company demand function. It is subject to all the determinants of market demand plus all the other elements that influence company market share.

Qualitative methods

Quantitative methods (the subject of the next section) are based on existing (historical) data. This is less the case with qualitative methods. Qualitative approaches of assessing future demand are based on the pooled opinions of groups of experts, or simply the consumer. They can never lead to precise mathematical results, but indicate a possible range of future tourism demand. As we have seen, this is sufficient for decision-making with respect to investments, marketing and destination management. Although they have a value of their own, qualitative methods are a useful complement to more quantitative analysis. The qualitative methods can be divided into three main categories:

1 Traditional approaches
2 The Delphi method
3 Judgement-aided models.

Traditional approaches

There are in practice two traditional methods. The first is based on the holiday surveys dealt with in Chapter 2. A careful analysis of comparable surveys over a long period can provide data to distinguish emerging trends, and although this does not provide a prediction in the strict sense of the word, it can nevertheless give useful indications for certain destinations.

The second traditional method concerns surveys of travellers in the generating markets. This approach may offer useful insights about the potential markets, the attitude or the prevailing image of potential tourists towards a destination. The surveys very often include the opinion of tour operators and travel agencies. In contrast to the first traditional method, the survey approach is a type of primary market research. It can be conceived and implemented to achieve particular (forecasting) objectives. This method, which is expensive and time-consuming, can be a useful complement to demand forecasts solely based on trend extrapolation or projections starting from alternative growth rates. The survey method takes into account possible changes of causal factors, and the effects of individuals' subjective judgements about the future.

The Delphi model

The Delphi method was pioneered in the early 1960s by the Rand Corporation, and was originally used to provide long-range forecasts of technological developments. Later the application field was extended to include economics, politics, medical developments and tourism. Archer (1976) defines the Delphi model as:

> A systematic method of combining the knowledge and experience of experts in many disciplines to form a group consensus of opinion about the likely occurrence of specific future events. Usually the aim is to provide an indication of the degree of probability that these events will take place within specified time periods.

In essence, the Delphi technique is a special type of survey to forecast the occurrence of specified long- (or short-) term events and to generate estimates of the probability of specified conditions prevailing in the future. The technique is a means of reaching consensus among experts through administering a series of questionnaires, collating judgements and providing feedback from each series of questionnaires to all participants. The feedback is reviewed by each participant before he or she responds to a next round of the questionnaire. Comments and considerations from earlier rounds are taken into consideration, so that ultimately the most desirable solution emerges from the collective knowledge of the experts.

The Delphi method can be very helpful where data are insufficient, or where changes in a previous trend are expected or new elements might interfere, with the result that mathematical-type analysis may be inappropriate. Usually the aim is to provide an indication of the degree of probability that certain phenomena or events will take place within a specified time period. A good application is illustrated by the Alliance Internationale de Tourisme Delphi study on the future trends of tourism (Obermair, 1998). This gives the result of an international experts' survey about long-term global tourism trends. More than 200 selected international experts from over 60 countries contributed to this study, and agreed to give their personal view of the future of tourism for the next 5–15 years and to develop this vision further in a survey of three rounds.

The technique involves several steps:

1 *Problem definition.* What should be forecast, and what are the relevant factors?
2 *Selection of panel members.* This is based on the expertise required and on the experts' willingness to participate, and is a very important step in the Delphi method. If the make-up of the panel members is basically homogeneous, 10–15 individuals is appropriate; in other cases 20–30 members are necessary for appropriate results (Taylor and Judd, 1989). It is, however, difficult to formulate a general rule about the minimum number of panel members, as this will be influenced by the content of the research and the geographical area covered.

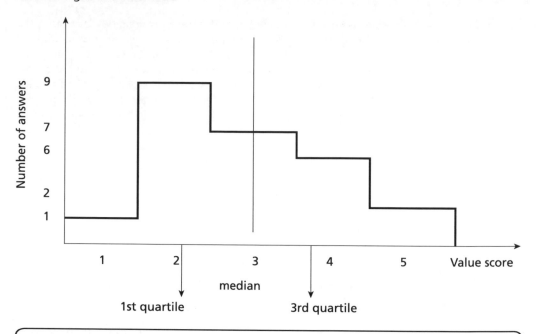

Figure 7.3 Responses categorized by the median and quartile values

The 'non-response' rate must also be taken into account. An important point is the anonymity within the group of panel members.

3   *Preparation and distribution of first questionnaire.* A series of questions is prepared and tested. The wording of the questions should avoid any influence on the answers. It is important to provide each panel member with a package of background information about the topic areas, and this package can include internal and external data.

4   *Analysis and summary of questionnaire responses.* The responses for each question are statistically categorized by the median and quartile values. Special attention might be given to relevant comments. Figure 7.3 helps to interpret the results. Value score 1 stands for very improbable, very low or very negative; a score of 5 represents very probable, very high or very positive. The median is the central value of the answers in a distribution in which all the responses are valued in an increasing or decreasing order. It is the middle observation – i.e. the value above which half of the responses lie and below which half lie. The first quartile is the value score at or below which one-quarter of the answers lie; the third quartile is that value score at or below which three-quarters of the answers lie. The inter-quartile range is the difference between the first and the third quartiles, and covers (by definition) 50 per cent of the observations. A high inter-quartile value is an indication of a wide range of opinions; a low value indicates convergence.

5   *Start of the second round.* The synthesis of the first round is sent to the panel members. Each member is positioned, for each question, with respect to the other panel members. Items for which there is consensus may possibly be dropped in the second round. The panel members are invited to re-examine and reconsider their original responses in the light of the distribution of answers of the other panel members. If a participant's answer still lies outside the main range, he or she might be invited to provide reasons for this point of view. It is the essence of the method that the range of responses by panel experts will decrease and converge toward the mid-range of the distribution.

6   *Analysis of the answers of the second round.* The replies to the second round are processed and summarized in a similar way to the reactions to the first round. A third or fourth round

may follow, but there are unlikely to be major changes in expert opinions after the second round. It is supposed that the median will move toward the 'true' answer with each succeeding round as a group consensus emerges.

7   *Development of a final report.*

Although the method takes time, there are several successful applications in the tourism sector (see Müller *et al.*, 1991; Moeller and Shafer, 1994; Frechtling, 1996; Obermair, 1998). The preparation of the questionnaire and the selection of the panel are of utmost importance to achieve a reliable result. This method makes use of the advantages of a group decision without the disadvantages. In a group decision, there is always the danger of one or two experts dominating the proceedings and of the tendency to a 'bandwagon effect'. On the other hand, this method does not allow exchange of ideas among the experts.

Delphi study results are very often expressed in the form of the probability that trends or events will occur during specific time periods. However, these results are not valid in a statistical sense (Archer, 1976). Although used for short-term forecasts, the most common application of the Delphi technique concerns long-term forecasting (Smith, 1997; Cunliffe, 2002). I am in agreement with Cunliffe that the Delphi method can provide information regarding the future.

The application of the Delphi technique is not only used for forecasting purposes. It is also a good technique to get a better insight into particular phenomena to guide correct policy decisions, as these three examples show:

1   Lee and King (2008) for the development of Taiwan's hot spring tourism sector
2   Lohmann and von Bergner (2012) to identify global challenges for tourism
3   Ballatyne *et al.* (2016) to identify managers' preferences for visitor interpretation at Canterbury Cathedral World Heritage Site.

Judgement-aided models

The most common qualitative approach is to bring together a panel of experts and ask them to achieve a consensus on a particular event or question. The aim is to generate as much debate and interchange of ideas as possible in order to reach an agreement upon a forecast. Seminars are very often used in tourism. This technique can be instructive. The major danger is the 'bandwagon' effect.

A second judgement-aided method is 'scenario-writing'. A scenario is an account of what could happen, given the known facts and trends. For example, in demand forecasting a hypothetical sequence of events is described showing how demand is likely to be affected by a particular causal process. In other words, this is a construction of a hypothetical sequence of circumstances in order to focus attention on the causal processes. Attention is focussed both on the variables and on the decision points that occur. The intent is to indicate what actions can be taken to influence the level of demand at each stage, and what the repercussions of such actions might be (Uysal and Crompton, 2000). Scenario-writing is not a real forecasting technique per se, but rather a method of clarifying the issues involved. The technique attempts to cast light on possible and plausible futures. For Archer (1975), it can form a valuable input to group forecasting such as the Delphi technique.

In the implementation of this technique there are three components:

1   A description of the current situation (baseline analysis)
2   At least one future image (a description of the potential situation in the future)
3   For each future image, at least one future path showing how the current situation could develop into the eventual future image.

Martin and Mason (1990) provide details of a good application of the scenario method. Their analysis highlights two prime areas of uncertainty about the direction of future change in the

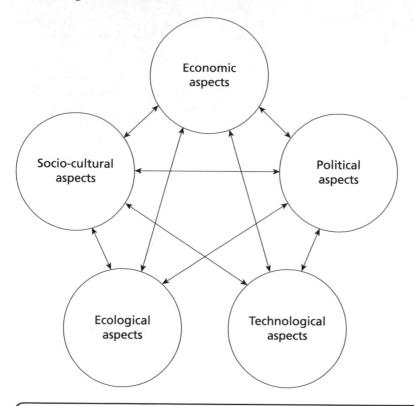

Figure 7.4 The interaction of relevant dimensions contributing to future trends in tourism
Source: Schwaninger, 1989

UK: the way attitudes and social values will develop, and the outlook of the economy and the future rate of growth. A particular application of scenario-writing in leisure and tourism is illustrated by Schwaninger (1989). Here, the writer analyses the interaction between economic, political, socio-cultural, ecological and technological aspects (see Figure 7.4).

A third judgement-aided method is 'morphological analysis', although there appear to be few applications of this method in the field of tourism. Here the aim is to structure existing information in an orderly manner and so identify the probable outcome of events. The method is carried out in a series of steps (Archer, 1994; Uysal and Crompton, 2000):

1 The most important variables are identified (intuitively or based on multivariate regression).
2 Each of the variables is considered in turn to assess its possible magnitude and effects.
3 Parameters are placed in a multidimensional matrix (called a morphological box) to assess their interaction on demand – this process provides an indication of various attainable levels of demand under varying assumptions about the performance of each variable.
4 An estimation is made of the most desirable level of demand in relation to the variables at work, followed by an assessment of how this level might be achieved.

Quantitative methods

This section deals with three different quantitative approaches: univariate time-series methods, regression analysis, and gravity and trip-generation models.

Univariate time-series methods

Univariate approaches are concerned solely with the statistical analysis of past data concerning the variable to be forecast. Univariate time-series methods start from the assumption that a variable may be forecast without reference to the factor(s) that determine the level of the variable. As such, they are non-causal techniques, or forecasting by extrapolation (Witt and Martin, 1991). Extrapolation presupposes that the factors that were the main cause of growth or decline in the past will continue to be the cause in the future. In a volatile sector such as tourism, with many influencing variables, extrapolation is a technique that should be applied with great care.

In the literature there are several univariate time-series models: moving average, exponential smoothing (single and adaptive smoothing), double exponential smoothing, trend curve analysis, decomposition methods and the Box–Jenkins approach (see also Frechtling, 1996). Most of these methods have little value for tourism.

The most widely used technique in tourism is *trend extrapolation* based on time series. A time series is a set of data collected regularly – daily, weekly, monthly, quarterly or yearly – over a period of time. Although trend curve analysis is rather simple and naïve, there are circumstances where it makes sense to make use of it. There are a number of conditions for its use:

- Time-series data must be available
- The future must be similar to the past
- It must be possible to detect trends
- It provides a short-term forecast
- It requires a stable environment.

The most common trends take a straight-line form:

$$Y = a + bT \qquad (7.1)$$

where

Y = the dependent variable or the forecast variable (e.g. number of visitors)
T = time period (t = 1 to n)
a = a constant to be estimated using regression analysis
b = regression coefficient or slope (changes of Y in function of T)

The factor T does not represent any particular independent or explanatory variable, although it is possible that the time factor T can represent one or more independent variable(s). This can be the case with 'fashion trends' in visiting a particular destination.

However, the nature of the trend is not always linear (see Figure 7.5); there are many different trend expressions. Besides the linear trend, the most common other expressions are:

● Exponential	$Y = ae^{bT}$ (e = 2,718) (b < 1 and b > 1)	(7.2)
● Semi-log	$Y = a + b \log T$	(7.3)
● Log-log or log linear	$Y = aT^b$	(7.4)
● Hyperbola	$Y = a + b/T$	(7.5)
● Modified exponential	$Y = ae^{b/T}$	(7.6)
● Quadratic	$Y = a + bT + cT^2$	(7.7)
● S-shaped curve	$Y = 1/(a + be^{-t})$	(7.8)

The exponential function can be converted into a linear equation by taking natural logarithms of both sides of the equation: $\log Y = \log a + bT$. According to Song and Turner (2006), tourism

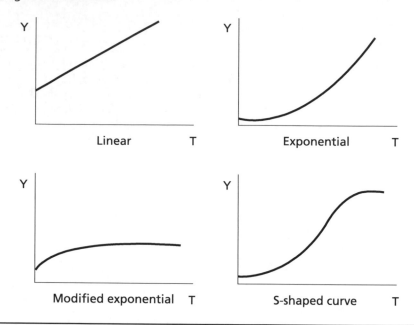

Figure 7.5 Some possible trends in tourism

is very often regarded as a luxury product, which often exhibits a nonlinear relationship between the demand for tourism and explanatory variables. Therefore many tourism forecasting studies use the double log linear functional form to linearize the relationship for ease of estimation.

The S-shaped curve or the logistic curve is appropriate when there is an introduction stage, a rapid growth stage and finally a maturity stage.

Many writers also refer to *the Box–Jenkins method*, developed by G. Box and G. Jenkins (Witt and Martin 1991; Witt *et al.*, 1994; Archer, 1994; Frechtling, 1996; Witt *et al.*, 2004). This approach became popular owing to its ability to handle any time series, its theoretical foundations and its operational success. It is a highly sophisticated technique. There are two types of the Box–Jenkins approach; in its simplest form it is univariate, while in the more complex application one or more independent variables are taken into account. It is normally used in its univariate form. This method is appropriate for forecasting horizons of 12–18 months, and when there are enough observations available. According to Frechtling, 50 observations are a minimum; for others, 60–100 monthly data are required. A good description of the method can be found in Frechtling (1996).

The Box–Jenkins approach (ARMA or ARIMA – Autoregressive Integrated Moving Average) searches for the combination of two forecasting methods (autoregression and moving average) and their parameters that minimizes the error in simulating the past series. If the combination passes the statistical checks for validity, it can be used in forecasting the series. Autoregression is a forecasting model that is based upon the strong relationship between the data for one time period and the corresponding data for the preceding time period. The moving average component implies that the forecast variable depends on previous values of the error term (the actual values minus the forecast values). The use of seasonal data and the resulting relatively large number of observations permits the use of ARIMA (Witt *et al.*, 1994, 2004; Chu, 2009). ARIMA models can only deal with time series that are stationary in their means and variances. If this is not the case, differencing is used to achieve stationarity. A first difference is computed by subtracting the first historical value from the second, the second from the third, etc.; the results are then tested for a stationary mean. If this does not appear, then the first differenced series is differenced again. The number of times a series must be differenced to achieve stationarity is indicated by its 'integration' index.

There are five phases in applying the Box–Jenkins approach (Frechtling, 1996):

1   The preparation phase, or achieving stationarity and removing seasonality from the time series.
2   The identification phase, or examining for autocorrelation and selection of model (the autoregressive method, the moving average method or the autoregressive moving average method).
3   The estimation phase (parameters are estimated in the tentative models).
4   The diagnostic checking phase (the parameters of the preceding phase are inspected for significance).
5   The forecasting phase, which implies the use of the model that produces significant parameters to forecast the transformed series. Residuals should be examined for stationarity of mean and variance, and for autocorrelation.

This is a very sophisticated method, and the forecaster should make use of the statistical packages. The Box–Jenkins method is quite often used in the airline business, and is thus sometimes called the 'airline model'.

Regression analysis or causal methods

In the preceding section there was no causal relationship between the forecast variable and an explanatory variable. Causal methods try to explain why the dependent variable or forecast variable changes as it does over time. These changes can be influenced by one or several variables. Tourism demand is so complex that in most cases several factors have an impact on the dependent variable at the same time.

There are many reasons to move to causal models. First, time-series analysis cannot predict turning points and consequently is unable to forecast accurately at the moment when an accurate forecast is most needed. Due to the introduction of one or more causal factors, a turning point can be detected and predicted. Secondly, there might be so much variation in the forecast variable that a trend cannot be detected. Thirdly, an understanding of causal relationships can be interesting and useful. Indeed, the objectives of regression models are threefold: (1) to forecast and (2) to identify explanatory factor(s), and (3) to test the efficiency of one or more variables (Crouch et al., 1992). Causal models are useful and add another dimension to forecasting. Knowledge of explanatory variables can be the basis for improving tourism policy or for formulating a strategy. A couple of the case studies in a further section of this chapter are illustrative.

In the literature, a distinction is made between two types of causal modelling in tourism (Frechtling, 1996). The first approach is the linear regression method, where the dependent variable is explained by one (single regression) or more (multiple regression) explanatory factors. The second type is the structural model (Turner and Witt, 2001a; Smeral, 2004). Here we are confronted with a set of regression equations linked together by certain variables that are both dependent and independent variables.

This section focusses on the first type. Let us start from the following relationship:

$$Y = f(X_1, X_2, X_3, \ldots X_n)$$
(7.9)

This can be written as:

$$Y = a + b_1 X_1 + b_2 X_2 + \ldots b_n X_n + e$$
(7.10)

where

Y = dependent variable, forecast variable or variable to explain (e.g. arrivals)
$X_1 \ldots X_n$ = independent or explanatory variables
a = the intercept constant
b = slope coefficients or regression coefficients to be calculated with regression analysis
n = number of independent variables
e = error term

Equation (7.9) can also be a multiplicative function of the type:

$$Y = aX_1^{b_1}X_2^{b_2}X_3^{b_3}\ldots X_n^{b_n} \tag{7.11}$$

which can be transformed in a log-linear function of the type:

$$\ln Y = \ln a + b_1 \ln X_1 + b_2 \ln X_2 + b_3 \ln X_3 + \ldots b_n \ln X_n \tag{7.12}$$

In the latter case, the regression coefficients b_1, b_2, etc. become elasticity coefficients.

In most cases the Y and X data are time series, but this is not always the case. Y can represent a series of observations within a particular time (e.g. a year) in a cross-section analysis.

The most commonly used measures of international tourism demand are tourist arrivals and tourist expenditure.

What are the possible independent variables? Many explanatory factors are discussed in Chapter 3. Frechtling (1996) makes a distinction between (a) push factors (also called emissive factors – or those characteristics in the generating market that encourage people to take holidays, e.g. income, leisure time, education level); (b) pull factors (those that attract tourists to a destination, e.g. visiting friends and relatives, commercial ties, cultural ties, special events); and (c) resistance factors such as war, prices, distance, travel time, safety, etc.

In any case, there should be a theoretical background or a justification of common sense to retain a possible explanatory factor. In practice, the most frequently used variables are (see also Smeral, 2003):

- Income generating country(ies)
- Commercial ties
- Price/relative price
- Price substitutes
- Access cost (transport price)
- Distance
- Travel time
- Exchange rate or real exchange rate (Kulendran, 1996)
- Promotion efforts or destination marketing programmes
- Population growth
- Supply capacities
- Competitive destinations
- Business cycle
- Trend factor
- Qualitative factors
- Dummy variable(s) (war, natural disaster, terrorism, etc.)
- Lagged independent variables.

In international demand equations, income, relative prices, transport costs, trend variables and exchange rate are the five most used independent variables (Smeral, 2003).

Dummy variables are specially constructed variables, and represent the presence or absence of certain effects that influence the dependent variable in the regression equation. They refer to one-off events such as a war. Dummy variables can only take two values: 1 when the event occurs, and 0 otherwise. They are quite often used in tourism forecasting, and are treated as any other exogenous variable. Their coefficients are estimated from the usual least-squares formula. Measurement of the impact of mega-events on tourism flowing through the use of dummy variables has been discussed by Witt and Martin (1991).

Lagged independent variables are very often used to take account of a time lag in the relationship between a dependent and an independent factor. For example, the income of year t – 1 influences the number of arrivals in year t. Sometimes a lagged dependent variable is included in tourism demand functions to allow for habit persistence and supply rigidities.

Smeral (2014) makes an important remark. He warns about asymmetric income effects on demand across business cycles:

> Expenditure for outbound travel (tourism imports) in five source markets are analysed using econometric models that can capture varying magnitudes of price and income effects depending on the phase of the business cycle. The main reasons why income elasticities may vary across the business cycles are loss aversion, liquidity constraints and precautionary saving, as well as the intensity and time structure of substitution effects between expenditures on tourism imports, domestic tourism and other goods and services.

In the literature there is much attention given to the determinants of tourism demand but little to the measurement of tourism demand. Song *et al.* (2010a) pay attention to the measurement of the endogenous variable. Tourist arrivals and tourist expenditure are both regarded as plausible measures but the fluctuations of both endogenous variables can be driven by different influencing factors. Empirical research with respect to Hong Kong tourism leads to the following conclusion:

> The empirical results show that the different patterns of TA (TA_P or tourist arrivals *per capita*) and TE/TE_P (tourist expenditure) fluctuation are likely to be driven by different influencing factors. Tourist arrivals (both TA and TA_P) are more likely to be affected by origin country income and 'word-of-mouth'/habit persistence effects, while tourist expenditure is driven mainly by destination prices relative to those in the origin country. The forecasting performance of the four models estimated using different dependent variables is also investigated and the results show that aggregate expenditure can be predicted most accurately, followed by total visits and per capita visits, while forecasts of the per capita expenditure are the poorest.
>
> (Song *et al.*, 2010a)

However, the authors make an important remark:

> It should be noted that the conclusions drawn from this study are based on a particular data set related to the demand for Hong Kong tourism. Therefore, any attempt to generalize the findings should be made with caution, although the methodology and procedure are readily applicable to the investigation of other destination–origin country/region pairs across different time horizons.

Test for significance

All explanatory variables should be tested for significance. In the first place, the signs of the regression coefficients should conform with expectations. Secondly, the regression coefficients must be significant. Therefore we should calculate the t-ratio:

$$t = \frac{b_i}{s_{b_i}} \tag{7.13}$$

where

t = t-ratio
b_i = regression coefficient factor b
s_{b_i} = standard error of the explanatory variable b_i

With a confidence interval of 95 per cent, a t-ratio of 2.0 or more indicates that the regression coefficient is significantly different from zero. The critical t-values are influenced by the number of observations and the number of parameters to be estimated; they can be found in most statistical handbooks.

If the calculated regression coefficients are not sufficiently significant, the corresponding independent variable should be excluded.

It is also very important to avoid a correlation among the independent factors, called multicollinearity. The latter is responsible for inaccurate estimation of the regression coefficients (small t-ratio). A symptom of multicollinearity is a large coefficient of determination accompanied by statistically insufficient estimates of the coefficients of the independent variables. There is a further assumption that the independent variables are not affected by the dependent variable – for example, expenditures abroad (Y) can influence the exchange rate (X value).

For an accurate forecasting equation, a number of additional tests are necessary. The first question that arises is, 'does the equation accurately simulate its time series?' Therefore we have to calculate the coefficient of determination R^2 or $\bar{R}^2$ (coefficient of determination adjusted for degrees of freedom) and the F-statistic.

The coefficient of determination (R^2) indicates the percentage of the variation of the forecast variable around its mean that is explained by the independent variables; this varies between 0 and 1. A value of 1, which is exceptional, means that the explanatory variables completely explain (100 per cent) the variation in the dependent variable. $\bar{R}^2$ (coefficient of determination adjusted for degrees of freedom) is calculated by using the following formula:

$$R^2 = \frac{\text{Total variance} - \text{Residual variance}}{\text{Total variance}} \text{ or } 1 - \frac{S^2_{y.x}}{S^2_y} \tag{7.14}$$

$$\bar{R}^2 = \left(1 - \frac{\sum(Y - \hat{Y})^2}{\sum(Y - \bar{Y}^2)}\right)\left(\frac{n}{n - m}\right) \tag{7.15}$$

where

$\bar{R}^2$ = coefficient of determination adjusted for degrees of freedom
$\hat{Y}$ = calculated dependent variable based on the regression equation
$\bar{Y}$ = the mean of the dependent variables
Y = dependent variable
n = number of observations in the dependent variable data series
m = number of parameters (explanatory variables plus one)

The F-test indicates whether the variance in the dependent variable explained by the independent variables is sufficiently larger than its unexplained variance. The formula is:

$$F = \frac{\bar{S}^2_{y.c}}{\bar{S}^2_{y.r}} \tag{7.16}$$

where

$\bar{S}^2_{y.c}$ = adjusted variance of the calculated values of Y

$\bar{S}^2_{y.r}$ = adjusted variance of the residuals

Statistical textbooks give the minimum value of F to determine whether it is significant or not according to a defined level of confidence. As a rule of thumb, with a number of degrees of freedom of six and more, an F-value of 5 is significant at the 0.05 level.

A last test that is recommended is the Durbin–Watson. This test should indicate whether any relevant explanatory variables have been omitted. The regression equation based on least squares analysis assumes that the residuals or error terms are independent of one another. If this is not the case, this should be an indication that at least one explanatory variable has been left out of the equation. In time series, such a pattern is an indication of 'serial correlation' or 'autocorrelation', the latter being a measure of the influence of one data point on the one close to it. It means that there is a cross-correlation of a signal with itself and that the observations are therefore not independent. The consequence is biased regression coefficients. However, serial correlation will also bias our equation's accuracy of fit, or the correlation coefficient and the F-value. Serial correlation can be tested with the Durbin–Watson test (Durbin–Watson d statistic):

$$d = \frac{\sum (e_{t+1} - e_t)^2}{\sum e_t^2} \qquad (7.17)$$

where

d or DW = Durbin–Watson statistic
e = residual
t = time period

The DW values can vary between 0 and 4; a DW value equal to 2 indicates total absence of serial correlation. Most statistical handbooks contain tables of the critical values. It is generally accepted that there is no serial correlation with DW values between 1.5 and 2.5. If the d value falls outside this range, the best remedy is to look for the missing variable(s).

A basic question is how to use the tested equations (7.10) or (7.12) to forecast. Only significant variables should be used as the starting point. It is supposed that there are indicators for the behaviour of these retained factors for the time horizon considered, although the latter is not always the case. Often independent variables must be forecast to obtain a projection of the dependent variable. In other cases some independent variables are projected, combined with constant values for the remaining explanatory factors.

It is also recommended that two or more scenarios – pessimistic and optimistic – be considered to take account of uncertainties about the future evolution of one or more independent variables.

A generic demand model

To model inbound and outbound tourism demand, Song and Lin (2009) start with a simple multiplicative equation. They refer to a publication of Song *et al.* (2003).

$$Q_{it} = AY_{it}^b \, P_{it}^c \, e_{it} \qquad (7.18)$$

where

Q_{it} = demand of tourists from tourists in a destination from a generating market i
Y_{it} = income in the generating country i at time t
P_{it} = tourism price in a destination relative to that in the generating market i
e = error term; it captures the influence of other factors not included in the model
b and c are parameters that need to be calculated

We consider this demand equation as a 'generic demand function' Why? It is a nonlinear demand function based on two very important determinants: income and price.

Equation (7.18) can be transformed to a linear model by taking the logarithm of the dependent and independent variables.

$$\ln Q_{it} = \ln A + b \ln Y_{it} + c \ln P_{it} + dummies + \ln e_{it} \tag{7.19}$$

where

b and c are income and price elasticities
Y_{it} = stands in most cases for real GDP per capita
P_{it} = is the relative price calculated from CPI_d / CPI_i
CPI_d = consumer price index destination
CPI_i = consumer price index of origin country i

Equation (7.19) is a static model and its dynamic form can be written in ADLM (autoregressive distributed log model) form as follows (Song and Lin, 2009):

$$\ln Q_{it} = \ln A + c \ln Q_{it-1} + b \ln Y_{it-1} + c \ln P_{it-1} + dummies + \ln e_{it} \tag{7.20}$$

Equation (7.20) indicates that the tourism demand is influenced by the current values of the independent variables and the lagged dependent and independent variables. According to Song and Lin this specification is more plausible than the static model, because it takes the time path of tourists' decision-making process into consideration.

Gravity and trip-generation models

Gravity models focus on the effect of distance or travel-time constraints on tourism demand, and are based on Newton's Law – i.e. two bodies attract each other in proportion to the product of their masses and inversely by the square of their distance apart. Gravity models pay a lot of attention to demographic and geographic factors, push and pull factors between the origin and receiving destinations (represented by populations), and restraining (e.g. distance) variables (Crouch *et al.*,1992; Smith, 1997).

Trip-generation models are sometimes derived from gravity models; in other cases they are merely refined forms of consumer-demand equations. They place more emphasis than do consumer models on the influence of distance as a travel constraint (Archer, 1975, 1976). Applied to tourism, the basic gravity model normally takes the form shown in the following equation:

$$I_{ij} = G\left(\frac{P_i P_j}{D_{ij}^b}\right) \tag{7.21}$$

where

I_{ij} = gravitational attraction between two bodies i and j (e.g. number of tourists travelling from destination i to destination j)
P_i = population country i (can be attractiveness or capacity of destination i)
P_j = population country j (e.g. wealth or propensity to travel at origin j)
D_{ij} = distance between i and j
b and G = parameters

This equation can be converted into:

$$I_{ij} = G P_i P_j D_{ij}^{-b} \tag{7.22}$$

In practice, gravity models are not used in this simplified form. Population and distance are often replaced by some more appropriate explanatory variables. Archer gives an example:

$$I_{ij} = G X_i^a A_j^c C_{ij}^{-b} \tag{7.23}$$

or, in logarithmic form:

$$\ln I_{ij} = \ln G + a \ln X_i + c \ln A_j - b \ln C_{ij} \tag{7.24}$$

where

I_{ij} = number of tourists travelling between country i and destination j
X_i = group of factors which generate travel in origin country i
A_j = the attractiveness of destination j
C_{ij} = the cost in terms of money and/or time in travelling from origin i to destination j

It is really not very different from any other causal model. Forecasting follows the same procedure as with multiple regression analysis. In fact, a gravity model contains three groups of variables:

1   Those characterizing the generating market. This is the push force for outbound tourists from the generating country i (see Morley *et al.*, 2014).
2   Those characterizing the receiving destination. This is a vector of pull variables for inbound tourists to country j.
3   Those that provide the constraints between generating and receiving countries or regions.

The problem with most gravity models is the absence of a sound theoretical background. Distance alone is not an accurate measure for travel constraints. Furthermore, there is a real danger of multicollinearity.

   Trip-generation models are even closer to traditional causal models. Examples of gravity and trip-generation models can be found in Labor (1969), Armstrong (1972), Crampon and Tan (1973) and Lesceux (1977). The Labor model is a typical trip-generation model, and interesting because of the independent variables used:

$$\log\left(\frac{I_{ij}}{P_i}\right) = \log G + a \log Y_i + b \log AN_i + c \log DU_i - d \log D_{ij} \tag{7.25}$$

where

I_{ij}/P_i = actual number of trips from country i to country j (per head)
Y_i = income per capita in country i
AN_i = an ancestry link; number of persons per 1,000 inhabitants in origin i who were born in country j
DU_i = a dummy variable to measure the effect on travel of the existence of a common border between countries i and j
D_{ij} = distance factor

Case studies of regression analysis

In the literature there are many interesting examples of the application of causal models to explain or to forecast tourism demand. This section deals with six illustrative cases:

- Case 1: The Greek model (Dritsakis–Athanasiadis)
- Case 2: The Australian model (Crouch–Schultz–Valerio)
- Case 3: Econometric explanation of EU tourism imports, 1978–2007 (Smeral)
- Case 4: Tourism demand models: Mainland US to Hawaii (Nelson, Dickey and Smith)
- Case 5: German tourism demand in South Tyrol (Brida and Risso)
- Case 6: The WTTOUR–Smeral model

The choice of these models is inspired by the application objective. One or two are not very up to date. Nevertheless they can from the pedagogical point of view be considered as illustrative.

CASE STUDY

Case 1: The Greek model (Dritsakis–Athanasiadis)

The first case is based on a study by Dritsakis and Athanasiadis (2000). This model is built up from several explanatory factors, but is not used for any forecasts. What are the characteristics of the Greek case?

The relationship between the model's variables takes a log-linear (double log) form. This has two advantages: first, it is practical to use logarithmic transformations for nonlinear functions in order to provide a linear fit so that the OLS (ordinary least squares) method can be employed; and secondly, the parameters (slope coefficients) measure the elasticity of the respective explanatory variables. The model takes the following form:

$$\ln \frac{AR_{jt}}{P_{jt}} = a_{1j} + a_{2j} \ln \frac{Yd_{jt}}{P_{jt}} + a_{3j} \ln C_{jt} + a_{4j} \ln CON_{jt}$$
$$+ a_{5j} \ln N_{jt} + a_{6j} \ln INV_{t-2} + a_{7j} \ln AD_{jt} + a_{8j} D_t + a_9 T + U_{jt} \qquad (7.26)$$

where

j	=	1, 2, . . . , 15 (country of origin)
t	=	1, 2, . . . , 34 (1 = 1960)
AR_{jt}	=	number of tourists in Greece from country j in year t
P_{jt}	=	population of country j in year t
Yd_{jt}	=	disposable national income (1980 prices) of country j in year t
C_{jt}	=	average total cost for a ten-day stay in Greece including travel expenses (1980 prices) from country of origin j in year t
CON_{jt}	=	average cost for a ten-day stay in other competitive Mediterranean countries including travel expenses (1980 prices) from country j in year t

N_{jt} = exchange rate of the currency (current prices) of the country of origin vis-à-vis the Greek drachma in year t

INV_{t-2} = gross investment (1980 prices) in fixed assets in Greece, with a 2-year time lag

AD_{jt} = advertising expenditures (1980 prices) in the country of origin in year t

D_t = a dummy variable that measures political stability in Greece (1 in years 1967, 1974, 1980, 1982, 1983, 1989; 0 otherwise)

T = time trend

U_{jt} = error term

$a_{1j}, a_{2j}, \ldots a_{,9j}$ = parameters to be estimated

The OLS method was used in order to estimate the separate demand functions for each country of origin. What follows are the results for the origin country Germany. The first figure shows the regression coefficient, and the figures in parentheses are t values.

Yd	0.942	(1.178)
C	−0.822	(−1.302)
CON	1.712	(4.041)
N	2.965	(7.431)
INV_{t-2}	0.671	(7.612)
AD	1.297	(2.107)
D	−0.516	(−2.728)
T	0.089	(1.967)
Const.	−11.761	(−2.781)
R^2	0.973	
F	47.50	
DW	1.679	

The sign of all regression coefficients corresponds to the expectations: positive for income, exchange rate, investment in fixed assets, cost in competitive destinations and advertising expenditures; negative for cost of stay and the dummy variable.

All but two variables are significant at the t = 5 per cent or 95 per cent confidence level; this confidence level is a little bit lower for disposable income and cost of stay. It may be owing to a certain degree of multicollinearity.

The R^2 (corrected for degrees of freedom), F and DW assume very acceptable values.

The income elasticity for German tourists travelling to Greece equals 0.94; this means that an increase of disposable income in Germany will bring a 0.94 per cent increase in tourist arrivals in Greece. Price-elasticity equals −0.82, which is quite logical. Notice the very high N value. This is an indication that German tourists were very sensitive to a devaluation of the drachma. Advertising expenditure in Germany seems to be effective; the corresponding elasticity is rather high. The significant T-value is an indication of a certain preference of Germans for Greece.

CASE STUDY

Case 2: The Australian model (Crouch–Schultz–Valerio)

The second case study concerns the marketing of international tourism to Australia (Crouch *et al.*, 1992). The demand model used in this study is based on conventional economic and marketing theory. The objective of the study was to measure the effect of marketing efforts on five Australian origin markets. It is an example of an efficiency test of marketing efforts. For the same reasons – better fit to the data and direct estimates of demand elasticities – as for the first case, the Australian writers use a log-linear function. It takes the following shape:

$$\ln Ta_{it} = b_0 + b_1 \ln Y_{it} + b_2 \ln RP_{it} + b_3 \ln AF_{it}$$
$$+ b_4 \ln ME_{it} + b_5 T_t + b_6 D_1 + b_m D_n + e \qquad (7.27)$$

where

Ta_{it} = number of arrivals in Australia from country i in year t
Y_{it} = real per capita disposal personal income in origin country i in year t
RP_{it} = relative price of tourism in Australia to tourism in the origin country i in year t
AF_{it} = airfare between country i and Australia in year t
ME_{it} = marketing expenditures by the ATC in origin country i in year t (TM = total expenditures and AD represents advertising expenditures)
T_t = time trend
$D_1 \ldots D_n$ = dummy variables for disturbances
e = random error
$b_1 \ldots b_m$ = regression coefficients

Some variables need further explanation. The dependent variable is defined as the number of arrivals divided by the population, to remove the effect of population increase on arrivals. The income factor is corrected for inflation and population effects. The definition of the factor 'relative price' is important. The relative price of tourism in Australia to foreign visitors is represented as the Australian consumer price index (CPI) multiplied by the origin country/Australia exchange rate and divided by the CPI of the origin country. The airfares are converted to 'real' figures by dividing the airfare by the CPI of the origin country. Marketing efforts are measured in two different ways: total marketing expenditures of the Australian Tourist Commission (ATC), and advertising-only expenditures. The trend factor represents the 'fashionableness' of Australia over time.

The study concerns five typical markets for Australia. The results suggest that the international marketing activities of the ATC have played a statistically significant role in influencing inbound tourism. The main study results for the US market can be summarized as follows (the figures in parenthesis are not t-ratios but significance levels):

Y	2.67	(0.0002)
RP	−0.92	(0.004)
TM (lagged by 1 year)	0.11	(0.05)
D_3	0.33	(0.05)
$\bar{R}^2$	0.92	
DW	1.75	

All other variables are not significant. The retained variables in the equation with the best fit show a high confidence level. Income-elasticity is reasonably high (2.67), price-elasticity is close to unity (−0.92), and the marketing expenditure shows an elasticity of 0.11.

CASE STUDY

Case 3: Econometric explanation of EU tourism imports (Smeral)

'The impact of the financial and economic crisis on European tourism' was a study conducted by Smeral (2009). In this study the author concentrates on analysing and forecasting demand for international travel of the EU15 countries in terms of tourism imports at constant prices and exchange rates. The model used is close to the generic demand model we have seen in a previous section. The demand for foreign travel in the EU15 can be explained on the basis of disposable income, relative prices, habits and dummy variables. In equation (7.28) travel habits are not retained.

$$\Delta \ln RTM_{EU15t} = \alpha + b \, \Delta \ln Y_t - c \, \Delta \ln \left[\frac{MP_{EU15}}{BIPD_{EU15}} \right]_t + d \, D_{80} + f \, D_{92} \qquad (7.28)$$

where

RTM_{EU15t} = real tourism imports of the EU15 (million $, at 2000 prices and exchange rates)
Y = real gross domestic product of the EU15 (million $; reference year: 2000)
MP_{EU15} = price index of real tourism imports of EU15 (dollar basis; 2000: 100; average price index for foreign stays)
$BIPD_{EU15}$ = GDP deflator of the EU15 (dollar basis; 2000: 100) or the overall price index to indicate the development of the price index for domestic tourism

D_{80} = dummy variable for the year 1980; takes the value 1 for 1980 (the dummies are used for data irregularities

D_{92} = dummy variable for the year 1992

The relationship is an OLS application, using the absolute differences of natural logarithms of annual values for the period 1978–2007. The estimate results below can be considered as very acceptable. The variance of the independent variables explains 79 per cent of the variance of the dependent variable. The regression coefficients are statistically significant. The income elasticity equals 2.2 and the price elasticity amounts to −1.1. These elasticities seem to be very plausible. Values in parentheses are t statistics.

α	−1.38	(−1.29)
Y	2.22	(5.32)
$(MP_{EU15.} / BIPD_{EU15})$	−1.12	(−4.74)
D_{80}	9.36	(3.86)
D_{92}	11.00	(4.52)
R^2	0.79	
DW	1.59	

In the same study Smeral tested a second equation with travel habits as an additional independent variable. Although this exogenous variable was also significant, the second model has not been included here.

Smeral also applied the equation (7.28) for a number of individual countries. The results are given below for Australia and the USA. For Australia, the elasticity of tourism imports with respect to changes in GDP amounts to 2.2; for the USA the same elasticity is much higher (3.4).

	Australia		USA	
α	−2.37	(−1.00	−6.21	(−2.95)
Y	2.19	(3.45)	3.36	(4.91)
(MP / BIPD)	−0.89	(−7.34)	−0.88	(−7.25)
D_{04}	16.64	(2.71)		
R^2	0.76		0.87	
DW	2.00		2.09	

Based on equation (7.28), forecasts for 2009 and 2010 were derived to show the impact of the financial crisis on European tourism.

CASE STUDY

Case 4: Tourism demand models: mainland US to Hawaii (Nelson, Dickey and Smith)

This case is a good example of the usefulness of regression analysis, not for forecasting but to detect the factors which influence tourism flows. The knowledge of these factors can be very helpful for the tourism management of a destination. This study was undertaken to determine the factors which effect the Hawaiian market from mainland US, and to develop strategies that might be used to counter the downward trend. Visitor data for the period 1993 through 2007 were utilized. The authors gave special attention to airfares. The latter was a growing concern of the travel industry in that period and Hawaii is at least 2,400 miles from any other US state.

An interesting characteristic of this case is the fact that two types of regression analysis are conducted: (a) time series mixed model which combines variables that explain variation over time and those that explain state to state variation (in total 735 observations); and (b) cross-section analysis to study exogenous variables explaining spatial variation in the number of visitors from the various mainland states (49 observations per year). Both studies were conducted using double log regression analysis

The time series model used was:

$$LHV = b_0 + b_1\,LCGSP + b_2\,LCA + b_3\,LP_1 + b_4\,LP_2 + b_5\,LP_3$$
$$+ b_6\,LDO + b_7\,COP + b_8\,CI + b_9\,CPI + Error\ term. \qquad (7.29)$$

where

LHV = log values Hawaii visitors from mainland US
CGSP = Chained Gross State Product
LCA = Chained Airfare
P_1, P_2 and P_3 = linear plateau vectors which accommodate the effect of two recessions and September 11, 2001
LDO = Distance from Orlando from the principal airport cities of the 49 mainland states as a competitive variable
COP = Crude oil price
CI = Cold index; this index stands for the influence of the cold winter weather in northwestern and north central regions to travel to Hawaii
CPI = Consumer price index

The parameter estimates of the fixed effects of the time series mixed model are:

Exogenous variable	Regression coefficient	t-value
Intercept	−1.385	−2.91
Chained GSP	0.996	18.32
Chained airfare	−0.211	−7.41
P_1	0.028	12.41
P_2	−0.048	−7.25
P_3	−0.030	−6.05
DO	0.687	5.53
COP	0.00157	8.42
CPI	−0.0049	−11.73
CI	0.130	1.83
R	0.18	

It is important to notice that all fixed effects except CI are significant at less than the .0001 level. For the cold index the t-value is still 1.83. The correlation coefficient is equal to 0.18 which is not very high but significant at the .0001 level. The most important effects are for CGSP and P_1. The airfare elasticity coefficient is very significant but rather low (−0.21).

The cross-section model takes the following form:

$$LHV = b_0 + b_1 LCGSP + b_2 LCA + b_3 LDO + b_4 CI + Error\ term \qquad (7.30)$$

Based on this model, cross-section regressions were conducted by year (1993 to 2007).

All factors show a t-value >2 for all years except the factor CI for a couple of years. The R^2 is very high and varies between 0.93 and 0.96. CGSP is the most important independent variable. The airfare elasticity is high for each of the years ranging from −1.30 to −2.36.

Airfare elasticities estimated from a time series mixed model and the cross-sectional regressions cannot be compared. There is a great discrepancy. The authors propose using the term 'temporal elasticity' for the elasticity from the time series estimation, and that estimated from cross-section analysis 'spatial elasticity'.

This case study proves that regression analysis can also be useful to improve a tourism policy. Based on the results of both regression analyses Nelson *et al.* formulate a number of suggestions for tourism management:

1   Airfare is for US mainland visitors a major factor geographically but not temporally to travel to Hawaii. Distances to Hawaii from the mainland are

Table 7.1 Estimation results for cross-section regressions by year

Source: Nelson *et al.* (2011)

year	$b_1 = LCGSP$	$b_2 = LCA$	$b_3 = LDO$	$b_4 = CI$	R^2
1993	1.089	−1.302	0.427	0.136	0.938
1994	1.065	−2.227	0.229	0.089	0.962
1995	1.048	−1.740	0.307	0.122	0.947
1996	1.076	−1.811	0.334	0.123	0.954
1997	1.131	−1.700	0.397	0.109	0.9430
1998	1.061	−1.705	0.317	0.135	0.949
1999	1.069	−1.823	0.337	0.124	0.949
2000	1.065	−1.865	0.358	0.148	0.951
2001	1.082	−2.194	0.341	0.122	0.946
2002	1.095	−1.700	0.402	0.179	0.936
2003	1.118	−2.270	0.373	0.156	0.941
2004	1.112	−2.114	0.417	0.168	0.934
2005	1.103	−2.117	0.396	0.148	0.935
2006	1.092	−2.227	0.363	0.165	0.942
2007	1.030	−2.363	0.313	0.117	0.941

   not going to get shorter and cheaper. The tourism policy of Hawaii should focus on the air connections. Direct flights from many eastern states would be helpful.

2   To break the trip to Hawaii into two parts with a stopover at Los Angeles or California (Disneyland), for example.

3   If distance is so important, the entire eastern US mainland needs more marketing efforts. The population lives predominantly in the east and in eastern USA there is competition from Caribbean destinations.

4   The significance of the CI regression coefficient in the cross-section regressions implies that more marketing of winter holidays to Hawaii in the northwestern and north central states could pay off in the long run.

CASE STUDY

Case 5: German tourism demand in South Tyrol (the Brida and Risso approach)

This is another case where the focus is not on forecasting but on finding the independent variables which explain the flows. Based on the knowledge of the exogenous factors, tourism policy can be adapted.

This study investigates the main determinants of the German demand for tourism in South Tyrol. The important share of Germans in the South Tyrolean market, with more than 80 per cent of the total of international tourism arrivals in the region, is the reason for studying this market.

Brida and Risso (2011) employ a panel data model to estimate short-run and long-run elasticities for tourists visiting the province of South Tyrol. Panel data permit the use of a complete database in order to explain the influence of several variables in decisions made by tourists. The possibility of using a large number of observations provides more degrees of freedom in the estimation process. Another advantage is that this approach also reduces the problem of multicollinearity.

The model utilized is the dynamic data panel model proposed by Arellano and Bond (1991). They apply it to a panel data set collected from 116 different tourism destinations of South Tyrol. The available data consists of the annual overnight stays of international tourists in the tourism destinations of South Tyrol from 1987 to 2007. This means there are 2,436 observations.

Dynamic panel methodology, based on both cross-section and time series data, has the advantage that it takes account of all of the information relating to the dataset under consideration. The authors consider the past consumption as an explanatory variable. This is justified, taking into account the large number of German repeat visitors in South Tyrol. From a theoretical point of view, the demand for tourism is a function of the quantity of German tourism demanded in the past, the relative cost of living between the Italian region and Germany, the income of the origin market, and travel cost.

The model specification takes a double form: linear and a dynamic model or the generalized method of moments (GMM) proposed by Arellano and Bond.

The linear model takes the form:

$$\ln Q_{i,t;} = \alpha + \beta_1 \ln Q_{i,t-1} + {}_{,}\beta_2 \ln PT_{i,;t} + \beta_3 \ln PCO_{i,;t} + \beta_4 \ln GDP_{i,;t} + \chi_t + \mu_i + \varepsilon_{i,t} \tag{7.31}$$

where

$Q_{i,t;}$ = foreign tourists in destination i during the year t (overnights stays of international visitors in hotels and apartments)
$Q_{i,t-1}$ = foreign tourists in destination i during the year t−1
$PT_{i,;t}$ = relative cost of living of a German tourist in Italy
PCO = price of crude oil
GDP = real per capita GDP in Germany
χ_t = a time specific effect
μ_i = a destination specific effect
$\varepsilon_{i,t}$ = error term

The dynamic model takes the following form.

$$\Delta \ln Q_{i,t;} = \beta_1 \Delta \ln Q_{i,t-1} + \beta_2 \Delta \ln PT_{i,;t} + \beta_3 \Delta \ln PCO_{i,;t}$$
$$+ \beta_4 \Delta \ln GDP_{i,;t} + \Delta \varepsilon_{i,t} \qquad (7.32)$$

Where all variables are in first differences; that means that $\Delta \ln Q_{i,t} = \ln Q_{i,t} - \ln Q_{i,t-1}$ and the same applies for all exogenous variables.

The application of the two models led to the estimations in Table 7.2.

Table 7.2 The estimation of the β coefficients for the linear and the dynamic model

Source: Brida and Risso (2011)

Variable	Linear model		Dynamic model	
	β-values	t-values	β-values	t-values
$Q_{i,t-1}$	0.9889	501.34	0.7588	34.74
$GDP_{i,;t}$	1.2855	6.31	0.4639	2.19
$PT_{i,;t}$	−0.0471	−5.14	−1.0529	−4.83
$PCO_{i,;t}$	−0.0483	−4.24	−0.0458	−3.54

The regression coefficients in Table 7.2 show a number of interesting results:

- All four variables are very significant.
- The β_1 value or the habit of persistence or tourism consumption in the previous year has a great impact on the holidays of the current year. Good service in the region is necessary to keep the high repeat visitors rate.
- The short-run income elasticity is rather low; the long-run income elasticity (by dividing the estimated regression coefficient by $(1 - \beta_1)$, under the assumption that in the long run $\ln Q_{i,t;} = \ln Q_{i,t-1}$) is very high and amounts to 1.92.
- The short-term and long-term price elasticities are quite high. Indeed, German tourists visiting South Tyrol have many alternatives for similar tourism products in Germany, Austria and Switzerland. This should be an indication for South Tyrol that price competitiveness is important.
- The elasticities for cost of living and travel cost are very low (short-run and long-run as well).

The next case is of a completely different nature and more complicated. It is based on a structural model.

> **CASE STUDY**

Case 6: The WTTOUR–Smeral model

The fourth case study considers the WTTOUR–Smeral model (WTTOUR stands for 'World Trade Tourism Model'). This model already has a long history, and was applied for the first time in 1992. Another application dates from 2003, and was presented at the TRC Meeting in Venice in the same year (Smeral, 2004). It can be considered as a typical example of a structural model. A structural model is a causal forecasting method in which linked multivariate equations are used to model the relationship between multiple dependent and independent variables simultaneously. The model is composed of two parts: a tourism import function and a tourism export function (all functions are in absolute values).

The tourism imports (outbound in monetary terms) of a country k are described by the following equation:

$$M_k = b_0 + b_1 GDP_k + b_2 RMP_k + b_3 DV_k + U_k \qquad (7.33)$$

Weighted import prices (RMP) are defined by:

$$RMP_k = \sum_{i=1}^{25} g_{ik} \frac{VPI_i}{VPI_k} \qquad (7.34)$$

where

M_k	=	imports country k (time series 1975–1999)
k	=	each country in the model is both a country of origin and a country of destination
GDP_k	=	real GDP at 1985 prices and exchange rates
RMP_k	=	weighted import prices
DV	=	dummy variable (specific structural variables, supply factors, marketing effects)
VPI	=	US\$ consumer price indices
GIM	=	imports weighted (or weighted outbound tourism in monetary terms) by country of origin
RXP	=	relative weighted export price indices
N	=	matrix of overnight stays
ROW	=	rest of the world
U_k	=	error term

$$g_{i,k} = \frac{n_{i,k}}{n_{T,k}}$$

$$g_{j,k} = \frac{n_{j,k}}{n_{T,k}}$$

$$g_{i,T} = \frac{n_{i,T}}{n_{T,T}}$$

Matrix N gives an overview of overnight stays by countries of origin and destination for 1998. Elements n_{ij}, with $(i, j = 1, \ldots, 25)$, denote the number of overnight stays by guests from country j in country i. The sums of columns and rows (n_{Tj} and n_{iT}) denote the total overnight stays in the destination countries, and the demand for overnight stays in the country of origin. The total number of overnights in 1998 is denoted as n_{TT}.

Real tourism exports (inbound tourism in monetary terms) of a country k are described by the equations:

$$X_k = c_0 + c_1 GIM_k + c_2 RXP_k + c_3 DV_k + U_k \tag{7.35}$$

$$GIM = \sum_{i=1}^{25} g_{k,i} M_i \tag{7.36}$$

$$RXP_k = VPI_k \Big/ \sum_{i=1}^{25} g_{I,T} * VPL_i \tag{7.37}$$

$$ROW = \Sigma\, X_i - \Sigma\, M_i \tag{7.38}$$

The explanatory demand variable for each country of destination is the weighted sum of imports (GIM), weighted by the country-specific guest structure by countries of origin for country k.

The relative weighted export price indices (RXP) are made up from the consumer price indices in destination k relative to price indices of competing countries (consumer price indices of destination countries, weighted by the overall demand structure).

This structural model provides a number of interesting results:

- Income elasticity of import functions per country
- Income-elasticity of export functions per country
- Price-elasticity of import functions per country
- Price-elasticity of export functions per country.

The unweighted average income-elasticity of import function equals 2.45, and the export functions show an average demand elasticity of 1.09. Smeral (2003) attributes this big difference to the structure of the model: export functions are estimated through imports, and structural effects play a major role both on the demand and the price sides. Tourism imports of a country depend on its income as generating country, whereas exports depend on the income of many different tourism importing countries.

The price-elasticity of import functions averages at –1.24, and the average price-elasticity of tourism exports equals –1.0.

Smeral uses the results of this model to forecast imports and exports up to the year 2020, and introduces assumptions concerning GDP growth and CPI variables drawn from several available sources. Furthermore, in Smeral's basic scenario EU enlargement (only four countries) is taken into account.

Table 7.3 Forecast of real tourism imports and exports at constant prices and exchange rates, 1985 (annual changes in per cent)

Source: adapted from Smeral (2004)

	Imports			Exports		
	1980–2001	2001–2010	2010–2020	1980–2001	2001–2010	2010–2020
Japan	7.7	3.2	2.4	3.9	3.6	2.5
USA	6.8	4.0	2.8	7.8	4.6	3.1
EU15	4.8	3.6	2.4	4.2	3.3	2.3
EU19	4.9	3.8	2.6	4.1	3.4	2.4
IC 25*	5.1	3.8	2.7	5.0	3.8	2.6

* 25 industrialized countries

Some important results are summarized in Table 7.3. One very significant conclusion that can be derived from the application of the WTTOUR model is a downward slide of annual growth rates in the industrialized countries. However, the long-term growth rates are still above the overall economic growth rates. Smeral states that 'Travel will gradually lose its character of luxury good and saturation trends will become apparent, at least in some sectors'. Smeral is aware that other explanatory factors will also play an important role. He refers to sociological and demographic factors, values, lifestyles, tastes, fashions, attractive supply, marketing communication and transport technology, political developments, etc.

Final remarks

This chapter concludes with some important comments.

All six case studies discussed in this chapter concern international tourism at the national level. This is also the case for the contributions referred to in the bibliography, and can be generalized to almost all quantitative forecasting applications in tourism. The explanation is quite logical: data are collected at national level. As a consequence, it is much more difficult to apply quantitative methods at a lower geographical level such as a region or a destination. For smaller areas it is recommended that quantitative methods be combined with market share analysis (Pelzer, 1977) – the position of a destination with respect to competitive power, tourism policy, supply, etc.

In the tourism literature, quantitative methods attract more attention than qualitative models. However, so far there is no evidence that quantitative methods are always superior. It is very difficult to capture such a complex phenomenon as tourism in a limited number of variables. Although a lot of progress has been made in tourism forecasting over the last two decades, (Chu, 2009; Gut and Jarrell, 2007; Han *et al.*, 2006; Kim and Moosa, 2005; Morley, 2009; Smeral, 2009; Song *et al.*, 2010b; Witt *et al.*, 2004) there are still many deficiencies (Prideaux *et al.*, 2003). Sociological and psychological factors are difficult to express quantitatively, and unexpected crises and disasters are impossible to forecast. Where possible, a combination of rigorous quantitative analysis with qualitative approaches or a consensus of expert opinion is recommendable. Chu (2009) stresses that the need and relevance of forecasting demand has become a much discussed issue in the recent past:

> This has led to the development of various new tools and methods for forecasting in the last two or three decades, ranging from very simple extrapolation methods to more complex time-series techniques, or even hybrid models that use a combination of these for purposes of prediction.

Most qualitative forecasting methods are better for medium- and long-term projections than quantitative models. They are more flexible and open to more explanatory factors. Multiple regression analysis in tourism is more successful in testing the significance and/or efficiency of independent factors (policy factors) than in its long-term forecasting function. The situation is different for short-term forecasts because in many cases there are reliable projections of the basic independent factors, and it can be hoped that the other explanatory variables will not change in the short run.

The preceding point should not be an argument for paying less attention to forecasting. It is worth returning to the statement at the beginning of this chapter: 'Those who believe in precise estimations start with the wrong attitude. In tourism, forecasting means indicating the future direction of demand – or, in other words, getting an idea of the magnitude of the expected evolution.' Knowledge of the direction of demand narrows the range of uncertainty, and this is vital for all investment and management decisions.

References and further reading

Archer, B.(1975). *Demand Forecasting Techniques*. Paper presented to a Seminar organized by the Organisation of American States, Mexico City (unpublished).

Archer, B. (1976). Forecasting tourism demand. In S. Wahab (ed.), *Managerial Aspects of Tourism*. Cairo: Salah Wahab.

Archer, B. (1994). Demand forecasting and estimation. In B. Ritchie and C. Goeldner (eds), *Travel, Tourism and Hospitality Research*. New York: John Wiley & Sons.

Arellano, M., and Bond, S. (1991). Some tests of specification for panel data: Monte Carlo evidence and an application to employment equations. *Review of Economic Studies*, 58.

Armstrong, C. (1972). International tourism: coming or going? The methodological problems of forecasting. *Futures*, June.

Arthus, J. (1972). An econometric analysis of international travel. *IMF-Staff Papers*, 19.

Ballatyne, R., Hughes, K., and Bond, N. (2016). Using a Delphi approach to identify managers' preferences for visitor interpretation at Canterbury Cathedral World Heritage Site. *Tourism Management, 54*.

Brida, J., and Risso, W. (2011). An econometric study of German tourism in South Tyrol. In A. Matias, P. Nijkamp and M. Sarmento (eds), *Tourism Economics*. Heidelberg: Physica-Verlag.

Chu, F. (2009). Forecasting tourism demand with ARMA-based methods. *Tourism Management, 30*.

Costa, P., Manente, M., Minghetti, V., and van der Borg, J. (1994). *Tourism Demand to and from Italy: The Forecasts to 1995 from the TRIP Models*. Venice: Ciset.

Crampon, L., and Tan, K. (1973). A model of tourism flow into the Pacific. *The Tourist Review*, 3.

Crouch, G., Schultz, L., and Valerio, P. (1992). Marketing international tourism to Australia. *Tourism Management*, June.

Cunliffe, S. (2002). Forecasting risks in the tourism industry using the Delphi technique. *Tourism*, 1.

Dritsakis, N., and Athanasiadis, S. (2000). An econometric model of tourist demand: the case of Greece. *Journal of Hospitality & Leisure Marketing, 2.*

Edwards, A. (1988). *International Tourism Forecasts to 1999*, EIU Special Report. London: EIU.

EIU (1992). *World Travel Forecasts, 1989–2005*, EIU Special Report. London: EIU.

EIU (1995). Real exchange rates and international tourism demand. *Travel & Tourism Analyst, 4.*

Frechtling, D. (1996). *Practical Tourism Forecasting*. Oxford: Butterworth-Heinemann.

Frechtling, D. (2001). *Forecasting Tourism Demand: Methods and Strategies*. Oxford: Butterworth-Heinemann.

Gut, P., and Jarrell, S. (2007). Silver lining on a dark cloud: the impact of 9/11 on a regional tourist destination. *Journal of Travel Research, 46.*

Han, Z., Durbarry, R., and Sinclair, T. (2006). Modelling US tourism demand for European destinations. *Tourism Management, 27.*

Huybers, T. (2003). Modelling short-break holiday destination choices. *Tourism Economics, 4.*

Kim, J., and Moosa, I. (2005). Forecasting international tourist flows to Australia: a comparison between the direct and indirect methods. *Tourism Management, 26.*

Kotler, P. (1984). *Marketing Management: Analysis Planning and Control*. London: Prentice-Hall International.

Kulendran, N. (1996). Modelling quarterly tourist flows to Australia using cointegration analysis. *Tourism Economics, 3.*

Labor, G. (1969). Determinants of international travel between Canada and the United States. *Geographical Analysis, I.*

Lee, C., and King, B. (2008). A determination of destination competitiveness for Taiwan's hot spring tourism sector using the Delphi technique. *Journal of Vacation Marketing, 15 (3).*

Lesceux, D. (1977). *La demande touristique en Méditerranée*. Aix-en-Provence: Centre d'Etudes du Tourisme.

Lim, C., and McAleer, M. (2002). Time series forecasts of international travel demand for Australia. *Tourism Management, 23.*

Lohmann, M., and von Bergner, N. (2012). *A qualitative approach to identify global challenges for tourism*. Paper presented at the 47th TRC meeting, Bern.

Martin, B., and Mason, S. (1990). Tourism futures. The use of scenarios analysis in forecasting. Paper presented to Conference on Tourism Research into the 1990s held at University College, Durham, 10–12 December 1990 (unpublished).

Moeller, G., and Shafer, E. (1994). The Delphi technique: a tool for long-range travel and tourism planning. In B. Ritchie and C. Goeldner (eds), *Travel, Tourism and Hospitality Research*. New York: John Wiley & Sons.

Morley, C. (2009). Dynamics in the specification of tourism demand models. *Tourism Economics, 1.*

Morley, C., Rosselló, J., and Santana-Gallego, M. (2014). Gravity models for tourism demand: theory and use. *Annals of Tourism Research, 48.*

Müller, H., Kaspar, Cl., and Schmidhauser, H. (1991). *Tourismus 2010. Delphi-Umfrage 1991 zur Zukunft Schweizer Tourismus*. Bern/St. Gallen, ITV-FIF.

Nelson, L., Dickey, D., and Smith, J. (2011). Estimating time series and cross section tourism demand models: Mainland United States to Hawaii data. *Tourism Management, 32.*

Obermair, K. (1998). *AIT Delphi Study. Future Trends in Tourism*. Vienna: Alliance Internationale de Tourisme.

Pelzer, J. (1977). *Développement dans les méthodes de prévision de la demande touristique, basé sur l' évolution des parts de marché*. Paris: OECD.

Prideaux, B., Laws, E., and Faulkner, B. (2003). Events in Indonesia: exploring the limits to formal tourism trends forecasting in complex crises situations. *Tourism Management, 24.*

Santos, G. (2007). *Estimating the Potential of Tourism Destinations and Generating Regions Using Gravity Models and the Origin-destination Matrix*. Palma: IATE conference.

Schwaninger, M. (1989). Trends in leisure and tourism for 2000–2010: scenario with consequences for planners. In S. Witt and L. Mouthinho (eds), *Tourism Marketing and Management Handbook*. Cambridge: Prentice Hall.

Smeral, E. (1994). *Tourismus 2005*. Vienna: Wifo.

Smeral, E. (2003). *Die Zukunft des internationalen Tourismus*. Vienna: Wifo.

Smeral, E. (2004). Long term forecasts for international tourism. *Tourism Economics, 2.*

Smeral, E. (2009). The impact of the financial and economic crisis on European tourism. *Journal of Travel Research, 1.*

Smeral, E. (2014). Forecasting international tourism with due regard to asymmetric income effects. *Tourism Economics, 20 (1).*

Smeral, E., and Weber, A. (2000). Forecasting international tourism: trends to 2010. *Annals of Tourism Research, 4.*

Smith, S. (1997). *Tourism Analysis: A Handbook*, 2nd edn. Edinburgh: Longman.

Song, H., and Lin, S. (2009). Impacts of the financial and economic crisis on tourism in Asia. *Journal of Travel Research,* December.

Song, H., and Turner, L. (2006). Tourism demand and forecasting. In L. Dwyer and P. Forsyth (eds), *International Handbook on the Economics of Tourism*. Cheltenham: Edward Elgar.

Song, H., and Witt, S. (2000). *Tourism Demand Modelling and Forecasting: Modern Econometric Approaches*. Oxford: Elsevier.

Song, H., Li, G., Witt, S., and Baogang, F. (2010a). Tourism demand modelling and forecasting: how should demand be measured. *Tourism Economics, 16 (1).*

Song, H., Witt, S., and Li, G. (2003). Modelling and forecasting the demand for Thai tourism. *Tourism Economics, 4.*

Song, H., Witt, S., Zhang, X., and Lin, S. (2010b). Impact of financial/economic crisis for hotel rooms in Hong Kong. *Tourism Management, 31.*

Song, H., Wong, K., and Chon, K. (2003). Modelling and forecasting the demand for Hong Kong tourism. *International Journal of Hospitality Management, 4.*

Taylor, R., and Judd, L. (1989). Delphi method applied to tourism. In S. Witt and L. Mouthinho (eds), *Tourism Marketing and Management Handbook*. Cambridge: Prentice Hall.

Taylor, T., and Ortiz, R. (2009). Impacts of climate change on domestic tourism in the UK: a panel data estimation. *Tourism Economics, 4.*

Turner, L., and Witt, S. (2001a). Forecasting tourism using univariate and multivariate structural time series models. *Tourism Economics, 2.*

Turner, L., and Witt, S. (2001b). Factors influencing demand for international tourism: tourism demand analysis using structural equation modelling, revisited. *Tourism Economics, 1.*

Uysal, M., and Crompton, J. (2000). An overview of approaches used to forecast tourism demand. In C. Tisdell (ed.), *The Economics of Tourism*. Cheltenham: Edward Elgar.

Witt, S. (1989). Forecasting international tourism demand: univariate time series methods. In S. Witt and L. Mouthinho (eds), *Tourism Marketing and Management Handbook*. London: Prentice Hall.

Witt, S., and Martin, C. (1991). Demand forecasting in tourism and recreation. In C. Cooper (ed.), *Progress in Tourism, Recreation and Hospitality Management*, Vol. 1. London: Belhaven Press.

Witt, S., and Moutinho, L. (1999). Demand modelling and forecasting. In L. Moutinho (ed.), *Strategic Management in Tourism*. Glasgow: C.A.B. International.

Witt, S., and Song, H. (2001). Forecasting future tourism flows. In A. Lockwood and S. Medlik (eds), *Tourism and Hospitality in the 21st Century*. Oxford: Butterworth-Heinemann.

Witt, S., Brooke, M., and Buckley, P. (1991). *The Management of International Tourism*. London: Unwin Hyman.

Witt, S., Song, H., and Wanhill, S. (2004). Forecasting tourism-generated employment: the case of Denmark. *Tourism Economics, 2.*

Witt, C., Witt, S., and Wilson, N. (1994). Forecasting international tourist flows. *Annals of Tourism Research, 21 (3).*

WTO-ETC (2008). *Handbook on Tourism Forecasting Methodologies*. Madrid: WTO-ETC.

Chapter 8

Tourism as a development strategy

Introduction

Most less developed countries and less developed regions are confronted with the basic questions, 'What are the strategic options for a durable development?' and, 'To what extent can tourism be a solution?' More and more authors and practitioners are focussing on the competitive regions and not the competitive countries. With respect to tourism, 'regions' is replaced by the term 'destinations' (Porter, 1998; Sharpley and Telfer, 2002; Ritchie and Crouch, 2003; Weber and Tomljenovic, 2004; Vanhove, 2011). Very few tourists visit countries such as Spain, the USA, etc. Tourists are interested in regions and towns, such as Seville and Andalucia in Spain, the Algarve in Portugal, New York in the USA. These destinations are 'tourism clusters'. Porter (1998) defines clusters as: 'geographic concentrations of interconnected companies and institutions in a particular field. Clusters encompasses an array of linked industries and other entities important to tourism.'

Applied to tourism, we can define a cluster as a group of tourist attractions, enterprises and institutions directly or indirectly related to tourism and concentrated in a specific geographical area. Competition in tourism is mainly between clusters and not so much between countries. Porter applied his theory to Barcelona as a tourist cluster.

One can consider a destination as a large enterprise with hundreds of components to which the value chain theory of Porter can be applied (Porter, 1985). There is also a close link between the above-mentioned clusters and a value chain. The value chain is a very important notion in regional development.

In this chapter the focus is on four interrelated topics. The starting point is the value chain. Talking about the value chain, the theory of technical polarization, well-known in regional economic science, is never far away. In a second section we deal with the possible options for a good strategy for regional development. Sustainable development is a crucial option with respect to tourism. This is the subject of the third section. A key point of this chapter is the question 'Can tourism be a strategic option for regional development: when and why?'

Tourism and the value chain

Poon (1993) describes a value chain as an analytical tool developed for tracing the process of value-creation in an industry:

> Understanding how an industry creates value is the key to understanding the role of each player in the industry. It is also key to understanding why and how each players'

position could change as the rules of the game change. The value chain was developed in the 1980s (Porter, 1985) and has been applied mainly to the manufacturing industry. It was applied to the tourism industry to provide insights into how the industry creates value.

(Poon, 1993; see also UNWTO, 2013)

Poon applies the concept of the value chain to the tourism industry to provide insights into how the industry creates value. A distinction is made between primary and support activities. The primary activities in tourism consist of (see 'direct level' in Figure 8.1):

- Transportation (e.g. baggage handling)
- Accommodation, restaurants
- On-site services (e.g. airport transfers, tours)
- Wholesale/packaging (tour operators)
- Marketing and sales
- Retail distribution
- Customer service (e.g. complaint management).

Support activities for the tourism industry are very similar to those in other industries (see 'indirect level' in Figure 8.1):

- Firm infrastructure (e.g. franchise and management contracts, finance, strategic alliances)
- Human-resource development (e.g. recruitment)
- Product and services development
- Technology and systems development (e.g. systems of payment, database development, access to CRSs)
- Procurement of goods and services.

The idea of the value chain is based on the process view of organizations, the idea of seeing a manufacturing or service (e.g. tourism) organization as a system, made up of subsystems each with inputs, transformation processes and outputs. Inputs, transformation processes, and outputs involve the acquisition and consumption of resources – money, labour, materials, equipment, buildings, land, administration and management. How value chain activities are carried out determines costs and affects profits. Most organizations (destinations) engage in hundreds, even thousands, of activities in the process of converting inputs to outputs. These activities can be classified generally as either primary or support activities that all businesses must undertake in some form (www.mindtools.com).

All this can be illustrated with examples from the tourism sector. At their destinations, tourists travel by local bus or taxi, taste the local gastronomy and buy local produce and handicrafts. When hotel properties are developed, their construction and operations imply the use of suppliers in diverse areas such as construction materials, food, furniture, electronic equipment and many others. These linkages are important for all economies, but more so for developing countries where tourism creates demand that otherwise might not have existed for specific products from agriculture, construction, industry or handicrafts. In some cases, such demand even translates into the recovery of lost activities and skills.

According to Poon, two basic principles are necessary in order to gain an advantageous position in the value chain. There is the need to influence the process of wealth creation, and also to build strategic alliances. The former requires control over two key agents: information (wealth is created through a number of information-driven activities) and consumers (getting close to the consumers and understanding them).

A topic of great importance, and directly related to the value chain, is diagonal integration. The objective of diagonal integration is to produce a range of services (e.g. transport, insurance, holiday and personal banking) and sell them to consumers. Firms become involved in closely related activities to reduce costs and to get nearer to their consumers. Ownership may not be necessary, unlike in horizontal or vertical integration.

One of the key attractions for firms in diagonally integrating is the lower costs of production. This becomes possible through economies of scope, synergies and system gains. Economies of scope refers to lower costs associated with the joint provision of more than one product or service, rather than producing each separately.

Economies of scope do not accrue from scale, but from variety. The joint provision of hotel rooms and car rentals is a good example. The cost for a hotelier of adding the provision of car rentals to hotel rooms will be cheaper than two companies producing car rental services and hotel rooms separately. Synergies are benefits that follow from the operation of inter-related activities, where each activity can generate benefits that reinforce other activities. As such, synergies can create scope economies. Thus it is possible for an air carrier to create synergy by linking its credit card to its frequent flyer programme, e.g. for every euro spent on its credit card, users can earn a free mile.

'Systems gains' refers to economies derived from creating and engineering linkages between different activities. Chains of activities are an example of these benefits, where each activity can share common databases.

When looking into the role of tourism in development, it is of particular importance to strengthen such linkages. This can be done through adequate legislation and regulation on investment – particularly foreign investment – by supporting the diverse sectors to connect to the tourism value chain and by providing them adequate financing and training, allowing them to produce in line with tourism demand. The UNWTO diagram in the publication *Sustainable Tourism for Development* (2013) illustrates the tourism value chain (see Figure 8.1, adapted from UNWTO, 2013) and the range of services and goods directly and indirectly related to tourism demand.

The value chain brings us to 'Value Chain Analysis (VCA)'. VCA analyses income flows in the tourism sector in a destination and assesses where and to what extent local people participate at each step. It focusses on the dynamics of inter-linkages within the productive sector. It identifies opportunities to enhance local economic input and uncovers areas along the tourism value chain where the local population could become more involved (UNWTO, 2013). An interesting VCA was made by Ashley (2006) for Luang Prabang town and surrounds in Laos. The following results are striking. The accommodation sector did not offer very large benefits to the local people. Only 6 per cent of the $8.7 million spent by tourists on accommodation reached the locals, due to low wages in the sector and the use of family labour. However, up to 50 per cent of the $7 million tourists spent on food and drink reached the locals, along with 40 per cent of the $4.4 million spent on crafts and curios (Scheyvens, 2013). A VCA was also undertaken in Cape Verde in 2008 as a part of a larger study examining many aspects of tourism to make recommendations on a programme of interventions to improve its development impact (UNWTO, 2013).

Possible options for a good strategy for regional development

The development of a region implies the outlining of a strategy. A good strategy implies knowing where we are, where we want to be in five or ten years and knowing how to get there. Choices always have to be made. This brings us to the dimensions of or options for a regional strategy, a central point of strategic thinking.

When analysing regional strategies we often have the impression that only a restricted number of dimensions are considered. Generally, the choice of the sector and the improvement of infrastructure are central. Sometimes, they are the only points of attention. A good strategy

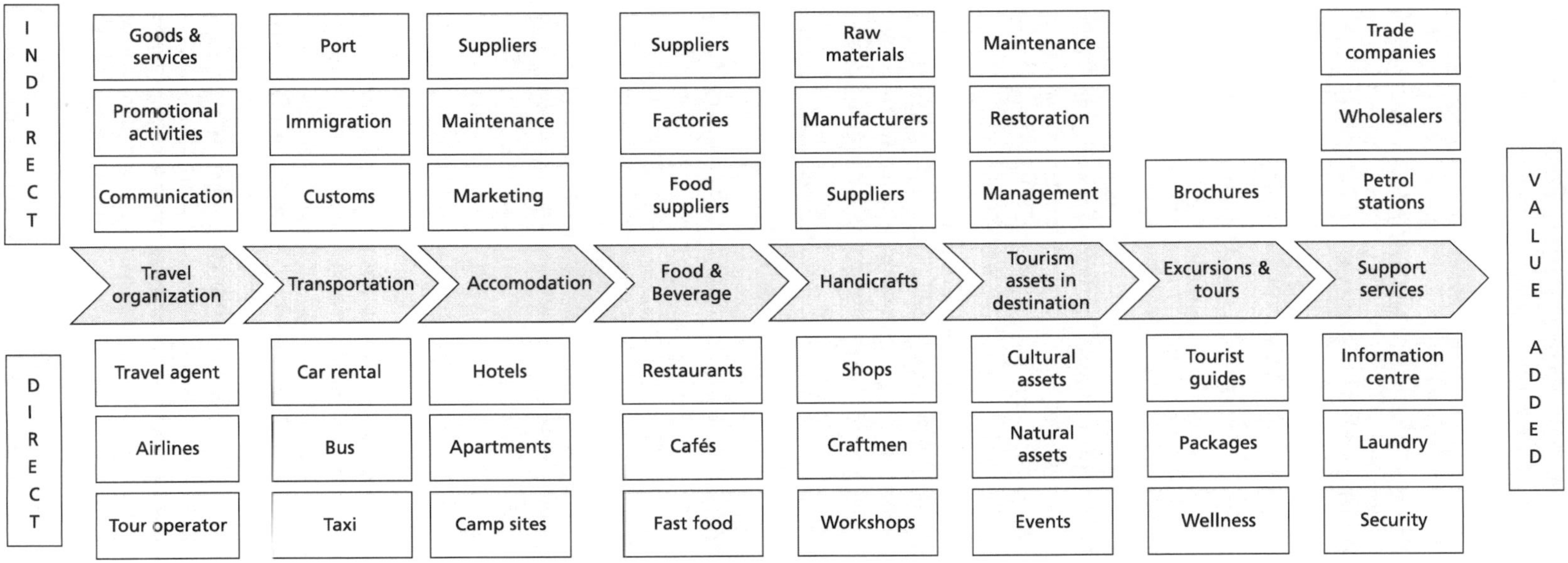

Figure 8.1 The tourism value chain

Source: UNWTO (2013). Adapted scheme

should take many more dimensions into account. A strategy for a region has a very large number of dimensions or options. In *Regional Policy: A European Approach*, 17 possible key dimensions of a regional strategy are described (Vanhove, 1999).

This does not mean that each of the 17 key dimensions is at stake in any strategic plan for a potential tourism region. Six of these dimensions can be of great importance in the case of a choice in favour of the tourism sector. The working hypothesis is of course that the region makes use of the necessary natural and or cultural attractions to attract international visitors in large numbers. As such, tourism is a basic sector. These six dimensions are:

- A sectoral choice in favour of tourism should be compared with a development in agriculture, different types of manufacturing, transport, international banking, etc. What are the opportunity costs of tourism development? One important remark should be made. A successful tourism sector also needs the development of many other sectors (e.g. agriculture). Here we refer to the value chain. In many regions the comparative advantages of tourism are important (see below).
- 'Work to the workers' or 'workers to the work' is a second possible strategic option. Overconcentration of population in big cities leads in most cases to extremely high economic and social costs. It might be of great importance to be successful with tourism development in regions far away from the big cities. With this in mind, the following consideration of Proença and Soukiazis (2008) is interesting:

  > From a regional perspective, tourism by its nature can act as a means of distributing development away from industrial centres towards less developed regions. As tourism can be developed in a short time span, and with only moderate levels of investment, it can have a rapid and even instantaneous impact on a regional economy.

  We also refer to Sahli and Nowak (2007): 'the government should implement policies (e.g. subsidization) to slow down migration from the rural region to the city in the case of tourism boom'.
- Geographical distribution or concentration of tourism activities. Depending on the kind of natural or cultural attractions available, tourism activities can be concentrated in a limited number of destinations or spread across many places. A good example of a voluntary geographical concentration is the tourism planning in Bali.
- Application of the Porter model with respect to tourism. The upgrading of the 'diamond' of the Porter model is very important (Briedenhann and Wickens, 2004).
- Reception infrastructure for the tourism sector. Which infrastructure do we need to support the development of the tourism sector? The infrastructure needs vary from destination to destination.
- Sustainable development. The latter is extremely important for the long-term development of the tourism sector and becomes clear in the next section.

Complementary to the aforementioned options, Bosselman *et al.* (1999) make a distinction between three possible growth management strategies. Firstly, some strategies focus on the quality of development, with the objective encouraging only development that meets certain standards. A good example is the conservation policy of Bruges. In many destinations architectural controls have been applied, particularly where the maintenance of a particular historic character was desired (see architecture in Nusa Dua in Bali and historic dances in Bali). Secondly, other strategies manage the quantity of development. Many countries throughout the world are desperate for almost any kind of development that will bring enough value added and jobs. Unfortunately, sustainable tourism development is not always respected and in the long term this will provoke serious growth problems. Thirdly, many strategies emphasize the location of development by expanding or contracting existing areas to attract growth. The concentration model of Bali is a good example. Very often location-oriented management techniques are used. They fall under the umbrella of land-use planning.

Sustainable tourism

In its publication *Sustainable Tourism for Development,* UNWTO (2013) underlines a fundamental requirement of the tourism sector. The tourism sector should embrace the principles of sustainable tourism and focus on the achievement of sustainable development goals: 'Sustainable tourism should not be regarded as a separate component of tourism, as a set of niche products, but rather as a condition of the tourism sector as a whole, which should work to become more sustainable'. UNWTO has defined sustainable tourism as 'tourism that takes full account of its current and future economic, social and environmental impacts, addressing the needs of visitors, the industry, the environment and host communities'. UNWTO formulates 12 aims for sustainable tourism (UNWTO, 2013):

- Economic viability: To ensure the viability and competitiveness of tourism destinations (and their enterprises), so that they are able to continue to prosper and deliver benefits in the long term.
- Local prosperity: To maximize the contribution of tourism to the prosperity of the host destination, including the proportion of visitor spending that is retained locally.
- Employment quality: To strengthen the number and quality of local jobs created and supported by tourism, including the level of pay, conditions of service and availability to all without discrimination by gender and race.
- Social equity: To seek a widespread distribution of economic and social benefits from tourism throughout the recipient community, including improving opportunities, income and services available to the poor.
- Visitor fulfilment: To provide a safe, satisfying and fulfilling experience for visitors.
- Local control: To engage and empower local communities in planning and decision-making about the management and future development of tourism in their area, in consultation with other stakeholders.
- Community well-being: To maintain and strengthen the quality of life in local communities, including social structures and access to resources, amenities and life support systems, avoiding any form of social degradation or exploitation.
- Cultural richness: To respect and enhance the historic heritage, authentic culture, traditions and distinctiveness of host communities.
- Physical integrity: To maintain and enhance the quality of landscapes, both urban and rural, and avoid the physical and visual degradation of the environment.
- Biological diversity: To support the conservation of natural areas, habitats and wildlife, and minimize damage to them.
- Resource efficiency: To minimize the use of scarce and non-renewable resources in the development and operation of tourism facilities and services.
- Environmental purity: To minimize the pollution of air, water and land and the generation of waste by tourism enterprises and visitors.

Tourism as a strategic option for regional development

Until relatively recently, tourism was not considered to be a vehicle for economic development. The first Lomé Conference for ACP countries, in 1975, rejected tourism as a sector to be supported in the developing process of less developed countries. At that time, the attitude towards tourism was rather negative in some publications (de Kadt, 1979) – tourism provoked leakages, lack of foreign exchange, inflation, etc. (see Scheyvens, 2013). Fifteen years later, on the occasion of the fourth Lomé Conference, the attitude had completely altered. Tourism had become a very important vehicle for development. Why the radical change? In the 1980s many publications proved the benefits of tourism, and gradually the attitude of international organizations changed. The second Lomé Conference paid little attention to this, but by the third Lomé Conference, in 1985, the difference in attitude was noticeable. Tourism at last received the interest it deserved.

Why was it so long before tourism was recognized as a valuable component of economic development? In the 1970s, many publications highlighted import leakages, income transfers, foreign ownership, tourism as a factor of inflation, destruction of culture, mono-industry and social impacts. It cannot be denied that all these negative factors exist to some degree in many destinations; however, from an economic point of view it is not realistic to deny the positive factors.

To define the role of tourism as a strategic dimension in regional and national development, and as a background for the tourism multiplier (see Chapter 10), some notions of regional (destination) economics are considered first.

Basic and non-basic activities

In regional development theory great emphasis is placed on the basic/non-basic approach, a distinction being made between basic and non-basic activities. A non-basic activity is defined as an activity that for economic reasons needs to be performed within the areas considered (e.g. shops, primary schools); a basic activity is one that, although performed within the boundaries of the area, need not to be located there (e.g. industrial plants, universities). It follows from this definition that non-basic activities are not exported to other areas; since the same holds for other areas, neither are there imports of those activities. By definition, therefore, there is no inter-regional trade of services or goods produced by non-basic industries. It should be emphasized that a basic industry is not necessarily an importing industry; it may export its products just as the area might import its products. In terms of a region's (nation's) balance of payments, a basic industry will reduce imports or contribute to exports (or both). It follows that basic activities generate initial income in the region. This income will be spent partly in the region, and the relationship to non-basic activities is quite evident.

However, the concept of non-basic activity is more complex than is generally presented. So far, we have linked non-basic activity to basic activities through the spending of consumers' income earned in basic activities, but there are also non-basic activities that originate in spending by the basic industries themselves. If basic industries purchase goods or services (e.g. transportation services), although part of these services may have to be performed within the area, they certainly are not non-basic in the sense used so far. These goods are produced, or these services are rendered, only because the basic industry is located in and producing within the region (Klaassen and Van Wickeren, 1975); their production is induced as a secondary production. Secondary effects can be called non-basic in so far as they must be produced within the region, and basic in so far as they need not. With the introduction of the secondary effects the distinction between basic and non-basic becomes vaguer, and a distinction between multipliers for different industries becomes necessary (see below).

Surprisingly, in regional economics, agriculture and industry are mostly classified in the group of basic activities, and tertiary activity is considered to be in the non-basic group. The very term 'basic industries' illustrates that general idea; however, it is, of course, too rough a classification. Not all agriculture and industrial activities are basic, and not all services rendered are non-basic. Tourism is an excellent example of the latter, all the services rendered by the tourism sector of a region being exports to other regions. Its contribution to the balance of payments of the region is by definition positive, and tourism generates initial income in the region. Tourism is also a good illustration of an activity that by its own spending supports other branches; when the tourist sector purchases goods (for instance, a hotel buying bread from the bakery) or services (e.g. transportation services) these may be produced in the region but cannot be compared with non-basic activities in the strict sense.

As a basic activity, tourism can be a development vehicle with comparative advantages for backward regions and developing countries. Therefore, the next section focusses on the comparative advantages of tourism.

Comparative advantages of tourism

The comparative advantages are directly related to natural attractions (e.g. sun, beaches, mountains, etc.) and many cultural attractions (e.g. churches, castles, abbeys, museums, etc.). These attractions are raw materials that can become beneficial as attractions at limited cost, and the danger of exhaustion is more or less non-existent. We find a similar line of thought from UNWTO. Several tourism studies posit that the availability of natural resources is the main source of comparative advantage (Croes and Rivera, 2016). Many regions or destinations in less developed countries have a comparative advantage in tourism over developed countries. They have assets of enormous value to the tourism industry – culture, art, music, natural landscapes, wildlife, climate, sun and beach, and world heritage sites (Scheyvens, 2013).

The same idea was expressed by Mossé (1973) some time ago:

> Besides, the host country may have been endowed by nature with an abundance of readily marketable assets for whose enjoyment tourists are willing to pay: sandy beaches, picturesque sites (mountains and forests), a sunny climate, and the remnants of ancient civilizations. Out of the 20 dollars, the tourist may well have gladly spent 5–6 dollars to enjoy these 'free utilities', as Bastiat would have called them, on whose supply the host country did not have to spend a penny, either in local or in foreign currency.

The question is how to internalize these benefits. The only channels are higher value added creation in the supplying enterprises, good destination management and the related taxes.

This first comparative advantage should be situated in a broader context of international trade theory. The theories of factor endowments (Heckscher–Ohlin theory) and absolute advantage (Vellas and Bécherel, 1995) can be applied. The first theory posits that the international tourism specialization of a country will be directly linked to an abundance of the resource necessary to develop the supply of tourism products for which there is a demand. Vellas and Bécherel make a distinction between three categories of factor endowments: (a) natural resources, culture and cultural heritage; (b) human resources and (c) capital and infrastructure resources.

The theory of absolute advantage (and technological advantage) is a development of Adam Smith's analysis of international trade. Absolute advantage plays a crucial role in international tourism. As Vellas and Bécherel (1995) put it:

> Certain countries have unique tourism resources which can be either exceptional natural sites, like the Grand Canyon, or, more usually, architectural or artistic resources known all over the world. These man-made resources motivate tourists to visit a country. Their importance in terms of international tourism factors is determined by their uniqueness which gives a country a monopoly or a near-monopoly.

This statement applies as well to natural attractions; the word 'countries' can be replaced by 'destinations'. Typical examples of such unique tourism resources are the Taj Mahal, the Borobodour Temple, the Angkor Wat, the Pyramids, the Acropolis, the Forbidden Palace, Bali, Machu Picchu, the Iguaçu Falls, the Norwegian Fjords, Paris, London, Venice, Bruges, Prague, Vienna and so many others.

The second comparative advantage concerns the import content. There are grounds to believe that tourism on average has a lower import content than other basic economic sectors. A number of publications support this thesis (UNCTAD, 1971; Theuns, 1975). The reason is evident: the tourists are buying services that the local population can provide to a large extent. Furthermore, it is not too difficult – at least in most regions – to develop the agricultural sector, in the long run, towards meeting the needs of the hospitality industry. Mossé supports this point of view: 'As a source of foreign exchange, tourism is on a par with other export industries, but with one difference: they {export industries} require costly inputs' (Mossé, 1973; Vanhove, 1977).

The third advantage is the high growth rate. This growth, together with the good prospects and high-income elasticity, makes tourism a preferential sector for economic development.

Fourthly, tourism has a stabilizing effect on exports. Export markets in raw materials are unstable, and therefore foreign earnings are uncertain. This is not the case with tourism products (either in terms of volume or price). The price obtained for raw materials is governed by the world market price, and is subject to terms-of-trade conditions. To avoid a deterioration of terms-of-trade, tourism development is often a solution. Mass tourism yields important amounts of foreign exchange, which allows the country to import manufactured goods. The counterpart is a limited quantity of resources.

A fifth comparative advantage is related to the labour-intensive nature of the sector. This high labour intensity is notable in the accommodation sector, the subcontracting sector, services, etc. This comparative advantage finds a lot of support in economic theory.

Other benefits of the tourism sector

Besides the comparative advantages mentioned above there are other benefits. Development of tourism on a large scale, based on mass tourism, creates external economies. Improvements in transportation networks, water quality and sanitation facilities may have been prompted by the tourist industry, but also benefit other sectors of the economy. An international airport – a *sine qua non* for tourism development – provides improved access to other regions for locally produced goods.

Another benefit is the generation of entrepreneurial activity. According to Mathieson and Wall (1982), the extent to which the tourism sector can establish links with local entrepreneurs depends on:

- The types of suppliers and producers with which the industry's demands are linked
- The ability of local suppliers to meet these demands
- The historical development of tourism in the destination area
- The type of tourist development.

In terms of technical polarization, tourism creates backward linkages. When a number of big hotels are located in a region, there is an immediate demand for large volumes of agricultural products and different kinds of services. Local suppliers are often unable to meet this demand in quantity and quality. After a number of years, however, the imported supplies might decrease and the local supplies increase, depending on the ability of local suppliers to meet the new demands. Entrepreneurial activity may be further stimulated by the external economies created (Mathieson and Wall, 1982; Krippendorf *et al.*, 1982; Vanhove, 1986; Frechtling, 1994). This brings us back to the value chain. Tourism is a more diverse industry than many others. Mshenga *et al.* (2010) provide a good illustration of tourism and economic linkages for Kenya. They show the contribution of tourism to micro and small enterprise growth.

The fact that tourism products are consumed at the point of production opens an opportunity for local business of all sorts. Local people can benefit through the informal economy by selling goods and services directly to tourists (Scheyvens, 2013).

Many benefits of tourism are mentioned in the literature. The subject is as chaotic and diverse as the Tower of Babel. Frequently mentioned variables include expenditure, income generation, employment creation, foreign exchange earnings, tax receipts, social benefits, the tourism multiplier, the transaction multiplier, and many more benefits or presumed benefits. Very often these variables are not put into their right context or relationships.

Economic disadvantages

Each coin has two sides. Tourism also has some social, ecological and economic disadvantages. This section is limited to the consideration of some negative economic impacts. There is no economic activity or project without costs. A distinction is made between private costs (e.g. a hotel) and external diseconomies. The costs the latter impose are called incidental costs. The sum of private costs and incidental costs is called the social costs of an activity. There is an extensive literature dealing with the benefits and costs of tourism. Some authors have emphasized the cost side (Krippendorf, 1975; de Kadt, 1979), others have stressed the benefits (Archer, 1991), and a third category pays attention to both sides of the coin (Mathieson and Wall, 1982; Bull, 1995; Frechtling, 1994).

It is often commented that few studies have attempted to pay attention to the economic costs of tourism in a systematic way. Mathieson and Wall assert that research has been limited largely to the measurement of the more obvious costs, such as investment in facilities, promotion and advertising, transportation and other infrastructure. Most studies have failed to address the indirect costs, such as the importation of goods for tourists, inflation, the transfer of the profits, economic dependence and opportunity costs (Mathieson and Wall, 1982). Nevertheless, a correct assessment of benefits takes into account a number of these elements.

Indeed, all transfers and imports should be eliminated. As a consequence, leakages are taken into account and the tourist income multiplier is lower. However, local inhabitants might change their buying behaviour due to the 'demonstration effect' of tourists (e.g. purchase imported products instead of local ones).

It is agreed that opportunity costs must be considered. If labour or land is used for tourism its social cost to an economy is its opportunity cost – or the cost of the opportunity of using it in the (presumably) next best activity. However, in most tourist countries or regions with a tourism vocation there is no full employment. The question is seldom 'manufacturing or tourism?' but very often 'tourism or unemployment?' Even when an alternative activity can be retained, a tourism region with valuable resources starts with the free raw materials as a main advantage. Is it not remarkable that many objective 1 regions of Southern Europe, eligible for European Regional Development Fund support, have opted for tourism as a strategic development path?

Over-dependence on tourism can be a danger. The sensitivity of tourism demand to all kinds of external factors has been emphasized above. Tourism is susceptible to changes from within (e.g. price changes and changing fashions) and outside (e.g. global economic trends in the generating markets, world financial crisis, terrorism, political situations, religious confrontations and energy availability). A good example is the negative impact of the financial crisis and the related world recession on the tourism activities of Hawaii.

'Tourism produces inflation' is a frequently heard saying, and a very dangerous slogan. The relationship between tourism and inflation is more complex, temporal and local. A high inflow of tourists during a season can provoke a rise in prices of many goods and services in the tourist region. Durand *et al*. (1994) assert that it is indisputable that in cities and tourist areas the prices for products and services are in general higher than in cities or regions where there is little or no tourism, and that in holiday resorts the prices for tourist services are higher in the peak season than in the rest of the year. This upswing of prices is presumably greater in poor regions than in richer ones. Tourists can afford to buy items at high prices, so retailers increase their prices of existing products and provide more expensive goods. This has two consequences: first, local residents have to pay more for their goods; and secondly, retailers selling to tourists can afford to pay higher rents and taxes, which are passed on to the consumer (Mathieson and Wall, 1982).

How far away is the impact noticed? Tourist demand is very often concentrated in a limited number of streets or areas. Local residents change their buying behaviour and move to other points of sale. Furthermore, tourists in general are only interested in a narrow range of goods and services, such as souvenirs, sport articles, clothes, beauty products, meals and special products (e.g. chocolates and lace in Bruges).

A different aspect is the price evolution of accommodation (hotels, rented apartments) and other facilities. In the short term, supply is inelastic and an upswing of mass tourism in a region may lead to higher prices. There is not always much discipline in the tourism sector.

A substantial increase in demand is followed by price increases. Regions very often forget that they are in competition with other regions, and the movement of demand from one Mediterranean country to another is a well-known phenomenon.

It is said that mass tourism makes land prices higher. The growth of tourism creates additional demand for land, and competition from potential buyers forces the price of land to rise. The local inhabitants are forced to pay more for their homes. Are the increasing land values to be considered negatively? All owners, land-owners and local residents profit from the additional value. From the macro-economic point of view, the final result is a benefit. Furthermore, this effect is quite local.

All in all, the impact of tourism on local residents should not be overemphasized. The costs are largely compensated for by the benefits: greater wealth, more jobs and higher land values. However, there can be situations – when tourism demand is very high – where inflationary tensions in tourism spill over into the economy at large and contribute to a rise in general inflation. In some countries tourism demand represents 10 per cent and more of the GDP, and inter-sectoral linkages of tourism are intensive.

Another question is: what are the factors responsible for inflationary pressure in the tourism sector? The French authors Durand *et al.* (1994) make a distinction between demand and cost inflation in the tourism sector. First of all there is demand inflation, which results in:

- Seasonal demand
- Inelastic supply
- An insufficient market reaction (certain resorts or firms profit from an economic rent)
- Imported inflation due to international arrivals (impact of hard currencies and increase of the money mass).

Cost inflation is a consequence of a number of factors:

- Peak management
- High taxes on some tourist products and services
- Rise of energy prices.

However, prices cannot be increased without considering the consumer – given the law of supply and demand, which stabilizes prices. Many tourists have changed their destination from France to Spain and from Spain to elsewhere because of price differentials.

Incidental costs of tourism

The costs emphasized by de Kadt, Krippendorf and many other authors are summarized very neatly by Frechtling (1994), and are covered by the term 'incidental costs' or detrimental externalities or external diseconomies.

Incidental costs, according to Frechtling, lead to quality-of-life costs and public or fiscal costs. Indeed, the local population of a region affected by external diseconomies of tourism can choose to deal with them in one of three ways:

1 They may have to accept a lower quality of life than they enjoyed without tourists.
2 They may redress the decline in their quality of life through public expenditure for which they pay taxes.
3 They may directly impose monetary costs on the tourists through taxes and fees.

Table 8.1 summarizes a number of important categories of incidental costs that are related to tourism import. It is not certain that a specific volume of tourists will produce costs in all categories. Besides direct incidental costs, Frechtling (1994) distinguishes secondary incidental costs. Additional visitors lead to new businesses, or the extension of existing ones, which in

Table 8.1 Possible direct incidental costs of tourism

Source: Frechtling (1994)

Life-quality costs	Fiscal costs
Traffic congestion	Highway construction, police services, public transportation, port and terminal facilities
Crime	Police services, justice system
Fire emergencies	Fire protection
Water pollution	Water supply and sewage treatment
Air pollution	Police services, public transportation
Litter	Solid waste disposal, police services
Noise pollution	Police services, zoning
Destruction of wildlife	Police services, park and recreation facilities, forestry maintenance, fish and game regulation
Destruction of scenic beauty	Park and recreation facilities, police services
Destruction of social/cultural heritage	Maintenance of museums and historic sites, police services
Disease	Hospitals and other health maintenance facilities, sanitation facilities, food service regulation
Vehicular accidents	Police services, justice system

turn require more employees and consequently a greater population. The latter imposes additional life-quality and fiscal costs on the community. Some of these costs for the additional residents are similar to those of additional visitors.

It is beyond the scope of this chapter to explore these indirect costs which are not generated directly by tourists, but indirectly. One example is very typical. Tourism demand is seasonal in many regions, and provides seasonal job opportunities. The region or country attracts a labour force that requires unemployment compensation and other income transfer programmes during the off-peak season.

Can tourism be a strategic vehicle in developed and less developed countries?

Can tourism play a strategic role in the development of a region or a destination in general? The answer to that question is not black or white. First, there is a preliminary condition. The basic requirement is the availability of tourism attractions, the necessary infrastructure and accessibility. However, not all attractions are able to mobilize a large group of visitors – tourists do not travel several thousands of miles to see what they have next door. Many inter-regional flows of tourists can be interesting, but insufficient to stimulate the development of a region. The degree of attractiveness of the tourism supply and the size of demand of the appealing factors are of vital importance.

Assuming that the necessary attractions are available in a country or destination, can tourism be a vehicle for development? From the international literature and my own experience, by and large the answer is positive. However, quite often a distinction is made between richer and poorer countries (Smeral, 2001; Sharpley and Telfer, 2002; Proença and Soukiazis, 2008).

Although any generalization should be avoided, there are doubts about the role of tourism as a vehicle of development in rich regions (Smeral, 2001). In developed economies the effects of the interaction between the expanding tourism industry and other industrial sectors must be taken into account. Tourism is lagging in productivity growth compared to other economic sectors. The productivity gap which is revealed by Smeral is manifested in so-called 'Baumol's disease'. This 'disease' refers to the fact that productivity in tourism is lower than in most other industries but the wages follow the level of most other sectors. Tourism is a very labour-intensive sector and cutting the cost of labour is very difficult. Croes and Rivera (2016) posit that the only way to survive is to increase prices in real terms in order to cover increases in labour costs. But this is far from evident. Dwyer *et al.* (2003) state: 'In a CGE model which incorporates a realistic set of economy-wide constraints, the effects of tourism growth on destination income and employment cannot be anticipated a priori.' We find a similar warning in Sahli and Nowak (2007): 'Policy makers should give due consideration to the general macro-economic equilibrium technique and CGE modeling when deciding on a tourism development strategy.' Furthermore, contributions of tourism to income generation, balance of payment effects and the international liquidity position are in most cases marginal, or in any case tourism has no dominant role. However, from the point of view of employment there are also several drawbacks. Indeed, tourism employment has a number of negative characteristics – although again, generalization is dangerous. In cities with business and/or cultural tourism, there are many jobs in hotels, restaurants, entertainment, and so on. Furthermore, in richer regions, tourism is a sector that offers job opportunities for unskilled people; these types of jobs are needed in all societies. It should not be concluded that tourism does not offer qualified jobs and does not employ highly qualified people.

The situation is very different in backward regions of developed countries with genuine tourism attractions. There is, in most cases, less competition with other sectors on the labour market, and unemployment is very often high. The advantages of tourism development (income generation, employment generation, tax revenue generation, encouragement of entrepreneurial activity, balance of payment effects and improvement of the economic structure), apply to this type of region (Williams and Shaw, 1998; Telfer, 2002a, 2002b; Vanhove, 2011).

Tourism as a vehicle for economic development is even more realistic for destinations in developing countries with interesting tourism attractions. Sharpley (2002) also cites several benefits. Most of them were highlighted above:

- Tourism is a growth sector, especially long-haul tourism.
- Tourism demonstrates high income-elasticity.
- Price-elasticity can do harm to tourism regions of rich countries.
- Tourism redistributes wealth.
- Tourism utilizes 'free' attractions such as climate, sea, beaches, mountains, monuments, way of life, architecture, etc. – in other words, resources are available and can in many cases be used in the tourism industry with marginal additional investments.
- There are no trade barriers to tourism.
- Tourism has backward linkages and stimulates entrepreneurial activity.
- Tourism is a guarantee for income stability.
- Tourism is a labour-intensive sector.

The next chapter, which is complementary to this chapter, should bring some evidence of the strategic role of tourism. Several cases illustrate the role of tourism in regional development.

Critical remarks

Four critical remarks should be made. First, many developing regions or countries have little choice in sector development, and frequently tourism is one of the few opportunities. There are many remote regions that have few alternatives for economic growth, due to the lack of a resource base or their distance from markets, their inimical climate or lack of water. Many of these countries or regions are suitable for tourism (Christie, 2002).

Secondly, many developing countries have a shortage of capital. To develop tourism, they need capital import. As such, this should not be considered to be a disadvantage. Tourism capital import increases the capital stock and strengthens the domestic economy. One can agree that the decision-makers are foreigners, with higher dependence from abroad. There is also the danger of repatriation of profits. But this phenomenon should not be exaggerated. Cash flows are in many cases used for extensions and modernization. If the returns on investment are sufficient, why should a group invest the profits abroad?

The third comment is more significant. In many developing countries import leakages are very high, but they are not higher, on average, than for most other sectors – on the contrary. There is a lot that can be done to reduce the import leakages with respect to food supply, construction, souvenirs, etc. Of course, the degree of development and the availability of natural resources will influence the success of reducing import leakages (see also Scheyvens, 2013, chapter 6).

Fourthly, and complementary to the preceding remark, there are strong linkages between tourism and other sectors. The case of handicraft is very instructive. In several countries there are real opportunities to develop their local handicraft industries using local materials. Kenya and Bali are very successful in that respect. In Mozambique there are interesting efforts in creating and enhancing handicrafts as well as marketing them. The program is called 'Aid to Artisans', and has the motto 'from maker to market'.

If 'tourism' is the right strategic development choice for the region, this is not yet a success in the sense of (a) value added creation for its population and (b) sustainable development. A tourism destination functions in a world of globalization and competition. A destination should respect a number of basic rules of competitiveness and create a competitive advantage by an efficient use of the resources. However, the practical cases from different parts of the world prove the existence of a tourism-led growth at least in less developed regions and less developed countries.

References and further reading

Archer, B. (1991). Tourism and island economies: impact analyses. In C. Cooper (ed.), *Progress in Tourism, Recreation and Hospitality*. London: Belhaven Press.

Ashley, C. (2006). Participation by poor in Luang Prabang trourism economy: current earnings and opportunities for expansion. *Working Paper*. London: Overseas Development Institute.

Bosselman, F., Peterson, C., and McCarthy, C. (1999). *Managing Tourism Growth*. Washington, DC: Island Press.

Brido, J.J., Punzo, L., and Risso, W. (2011). Tourism as a factor of growth – the case of Brazil. *Tourism Economics, 6*.

Briedenhann, J., and Wickens, E. (2004). Tourism routes as a tool for economic development of rural areas – vibrant hope or impossible dream? *Tourism Management, 1*.

Bull, A. (1995). *The Economics of Travel and Tourism*. Sydney: Longman.

Christie, I. (2002). Tourism, growth and poverty: framework conditions For tourism in developing countries. *Tourism Review, 1–2*.

Croes, R., and Rivera, M. (2016). *Poverty Alleviation through Tourism Development: A Comprehensive and Integrated Approach*. Oakville, ON: Apple Academic Press.

de Kadt, E. (1979). *Tourism Passport to Development*. Oxford: Oxford University Press.

Durand, H., Gouirand, P., and Spindler, J. (1994). *Economie et Politique du Tourisme*. Paris: Librairie Générale de Droit et de Jurispridence.

Dwyer, L., Forsyth, P., and Spurr, R. (2003). Inter-industry effects of tourism growth: implications for destination managers. *Tourism Economics, 2.*

Fletcher, J., and Westlake, J. (2006). Globalisation. In L. Dwyer and P. Forsyth (eds), *International Handbook on the Economics of Tourism.* Cheltenham: Edward Elgar.

Frechtling, D. (1994). Assessing the economic impacts of travel and tourism. In J. Ritchie and C. Goeldner (eds), *Travel, Tourism and Hospitality Research.* New York: John Wiley & Sons.

Guicheney, J., and Rouzade, G. (2003). *Le tourisme dans les programmes européens.* Paris: La Documentation Française.

Klaassen, L., and Van Wickeren, A. (1975). Interindustry relations: an attraction model. In H. C. Bos (ed.), *Towards Balanced Growth.* Rotterdam: North Holland Publishing Company.

Krippendorf, J. (1975). *Die Landschaftsfresser.* Ostfildern: Hallwag.

Krippendorf, J., Messerli, P., and Hänni, H. (eds) (1982). *Tourismus und Regionale Entwicklung.* Diesüsenhofen: Verlag Rüegger.

Mathieson, A., and Wall, G. (1982). *Tourism: Economic, Physical and Social Impacts.* London: Longman.

Mossé, R. (1973). *Tourism and the Balance of Payments.* Geneva: UIOTO.

Mshenga, P., Richardson, R., Njehia, B., and Birachi, E. (2010). The contribution of tourism to micro and small enterprise growth. *Tourism Economics, 4.*

Poon, A. (1993). Tourism, technology and competitive strategies. Wallingford: C.A.B. International.

Porter, M. (1985). *Competitive Advantage.* New York: The Free Press.

Porter, M. (1998). Clusters and the new economics of competition. *Harvard Business Review,* November/December.

Proença, S., and Soukiazis, E. (2008). Tourism as an economic growth factor: case study for Southern European countries. *Tourism Economics, 4.*

Ritchie, J.R.B., and Crouch, G. (2000). The competitive destination: a sustainability perspective. *Tourism Management, 21.*

Ritchie, J.R.B., and Crouch, G. (2003). *The Competitive Destination: A Sustainable Tourism Perspective.* Wallingford: CABI Publishing.

Sahli, M., and Nowak, J. (2007). Does inbound tourism benefit developing countries? A trade theoretic approach. *Journal of Travel Research,* May.

Scheyvens, R. (2013). *Tourism and Poverty.* New York: Routledge.

Sharpley, R. (2002). Tourism: a vehicle for development? In R. Sharpley and D. Telfer (eds), *Tourism and development: concepts and issues.* Clevedon: Channel View Publications.

Sharpley, R., and Telfer, D. (eds) (2002). *Tourism and development: concepts and issues.* Clevedon: Channel View Publications.

Shaw, G., and Williams, A. (1998). Tourism, economic development and the role of entrepreneurial activity. In A. Williams and G. Shaw (eds), *Tourism and Economic Development: European Experiences.* Chichester: John Wiley & Sons.

Smeral, E. (2001). Beyond the myth of growth in tourism. In P. Keller and T. Bieger (eds), *Tourism Growth and Global Competition.* St Gallen: AIEST.

Smeral, E. (2003). A structural view of tourism growth. *Tourism Economics, 1.*

Telfer, D. (2002a). The evolution of tourism and development theory. In R. Sharpley and D. Telfer (eds). *Tourism and Development: Concepts and Issues.* Clevedon: Channel View Publications.

Telfer, D. (2002b). Tourism and regional development issues. In R. Sharpley and D. Telfer (eds), *Tourism and Development: Concepts and Issues.* Clevedon: Channel View Publications.

Telfer, D., and Sharpley, R. (2008). *Tourism and Development in the Developing World.* London: Routledge.

Theuns, H. (1975). Enkele economische aspecten van internationaal toerisme in ontwikkelingslanden. *Maandschrift Economie, 7.*

Theuns, H. (1989). *Toerisme in ontwikkelingslanden*. Tilburg: Tilburg University Press.

UNCTAD (1971). *Elements of Tourism Policy in Developing Countries*. Geneva: UNCTAD.

UNWTO (2013). *Sustainable Tourism for Development*. Madrid: UNWTO.

Vanhove, N. (1977). Fremdenverkehr und Zahlungsbilanz der EG-Länder und der Mittelmeerländer. In R. Regul (ed.), *Die Europäischen Gemeinschaften und die Mittelmeerländer*. Baden-Baden: Nomos Verlagsgesellschaft.

Vanhove, N. (1986). Tourism and regional economic development. In J. Paelinck (ed.), *Human Behaviour in Geographical Space: Essays in Honour of Leo H. Klaassen*. Aldershot: Gower.

Vanhove, N. (1999). *Regional Policy: A European Approach*. Aldershot: Ashgate.

Vanhove, N. (2011). Tourism a Vehicle of Development? – A Regional approach. In P. Keller and T. Bieger (eds), *Tourism Development after the Crises*. Berlin: EVS.

Vellas, F., and Bécherel, L. (1995). *International Tourism*. London: MacMillan Press.

Violier, Ph. (2008). *Tourisme et développement local*. Paris: Belin.

Weber, S., and Tomljenovic, R. (eds) (2004). *Reinventing a Tourism Destination*. Zagreb: Institute of Tourism.

Williams, A., and Shaw, G. (1998). Tourism and uneven economic development. In A. Williams and G. Shaw (eds), *Tourism and Economic Development: European Experiences*. Chichester: John Wiley & Sons.

www.mindtools.com/pages/article/newSTR_66.htm#sthash.YeM9U109.dpuf

www.untwo.org/ebook/sustainable-tourism-for-development/

Chapter 9

Tourism export-led growth

Introduction

Do we find a confirmation of the conclusions of Chapter 8 in the tourism export-led models? Export-led growth can be defined as growth of an economy over time that is thought to be caused by expansion of the country's exports (Marin, 1992). In many countries inbound tourism represents a significant share of the exports. The link to tourism export-led growth (TLG) is quite evident: it is the growth of an economy over time that is due to an increase of a country's tourism export. In other words, 'tourism-led growth hypothesis' (TLGH) is a variant of the more general and well-known hypothesis of export-led growth (Balaguer and Cantavella-Jorda, 2002; Dritsakis, 2004). The TLG strategy remains the main reason for developing countries to allocate resources to tourism. The theoretical models that consider a causal relationship between tourism and economic growth are a phenomenon of the last two decades (Kim *et al.*, 2006).

Cortés-Jiménez *et al.* (2011) make a distinction between two different channels. The first channel is the tourism-led growth (TLG) hypothesis. According to this channel, tourism export expansion improves economy-wide efficiency in the allocation of inputs and leads to an increase in total factor productivity. The reasons are the same as those mentioned for the traditional export-led growth hypothesis (Bhagwati, 1978): competition on foreign markets leads to better management practices and forms of organization, to more labour training, to a pro-competitive effect on market structures, to increased capacity utilization, etc. By spilling over to the rest of the economy, these positive effects act as a technological improvement. Kim *et al.* (2006) speak of spillovers and other externalities.

The second channel is the so-called TKIG hypothesis. Tourism exports allow more capital goods imports which in turn leads to economic growth (see Nowak *et al.*, 2007). The reasoning runs as follows: tourism exports are viewed here as a source of foreign currency, and so as a means of financing imports of essential goods, especially imports of intermediate and capital goods. Thus, export expansion promotes capital accumulation and consequently economic growth through the expansion of the volume of inputs rather than through the increase in their efficiency. According to Cortés-Jiménez *et al.* (2011), the omission of capital goods imports from the analysis prohibits the detection of any TKIG mechanism and may either mask or overstate the effects of tourism expansion on economic growth.

Tourism is not only a significant foreign exchange earner allowing for the import of capital goods and other basic commodities, it also has a positive effect on the increase of long-run economic growth through several other channels (Schubert *et al.*, 2011):

- Tourism spurs investment in new infrastructure
- Tourism stimulates competition between local firms and firms in other tourist countries
- Tourism stimulates other sectors by indirect and induced effects (cfr tourism multiplier)

- Tourism contributes to an increase in income and creates employment (Dritsakis, 2004 and see Chapter 8)
- Expansion of the tourism sector may increase opportunities for local tourist firms to exploit economies of scale (Helpman and Krugman, 1985)
- Tourism is a factor of diffusion of technical knowledge and accumulation of human capital.

Dritsakis (2004) underlines two other benefits. Firstly, in areas with increased tourism there is a significant improvement in the cultural standards and facilities. Secondly, there is a fiscal aspect. Tourism activity has beneficial effects on public economics, especially at the local level.

Whether international tourism can lead to economic growth is an important question because the answer can lead to different policy directions. If tourism is an additional determinant of income growth, the policy implication is that 'all governments should commit to helping their tourism industry expand as much as possible' (Dritsakis, 2012). On the other hand, if the effect of tourism growth on economic growth works through the standard income determinants, the policy implication is that governments should help the tourism industry expand to the extent that it promotes growth in the standard income factors (e.g. capital accumulation). Why? Because investment in tourism that does not lead to growth in the standard income factors may be a less effective benefit for the economy in the long term (Du *et al.*, 2016). In their contribution 'Tourism and economic growth', Du *et al.* conclude:

> Policy makers need to decide where to invest public revenues and how to allocate incentives to encourage the long-term economic livelihood of citizens. While exceptions exist, previous studies have overwhelmingly supported the notion that there is a positive association between international tourism and economic growth. Since the late 1990s, those findings have been consolidated into the tourism-led growth hypothesis, which is widely accepted as a general concept by tourism boosters, and has been tested by tourism researchers using a variety of cointegration modelling approaches.

So far we have stressed the (causal) relationship between international (domestic) tourism earnings and economic growth. The relationship can also be bi-directional – economic growth stimulates tourism that generates GDP. We speak of 'economic-driven tourism growth'. Several authors (Dritsakis, 2004; Oh, 2005; Kim *et al.*, 2006) look at the relationship in the opposite direction. Does economic growth cause international tourism earnings? In other words, do tourism and economic development reinforce each other?

However, the tourism-led economic growth hypothesis does not always work (see Oh, 2005; Katircioglu, 2009). Oh investigated the causal relations between tourism growth and economic expansion for the Korean economy by using the Engle and Granger two-stage approach and a bivariate vector autoregression (VAR) model. The results of this research indicate that there is no long-run equilibrium relation between two series, while there is a one-way causal relationship of economic-driven tourism growth. We find a similar result with Cortés-Jiménez *et al.*, (2011) for Tunisia (see below):

> There seems to be no TLG mechanism in Tunisia, while the TKIG mechanism appears as a short-run phenomenon only. In total, tourism exports have contributed significantly towards financing the country's imports of capital goods, but they have not been the principal engine of long-term growth. On the contrary, the results support the hypothesis of a growth-led tourism in this country.

Economic-driven tourism growth can result in an expansion of the accommodation sector, airline sector and restaurants, thus increasing domestic demand.

Methodologies for measuring tourism's contribution to economic growth

Various methods are used to measure tourism's contribution to economic growth (Ivanov and Webster, 2013). The most popular methodology for investigating tourism's contribution to economic growth are cointegration and Granger causality tests (see Dritsakis, 2004; Durbarry, 2004; Oh, 2005; Katircioglu, 2009; Cortes-Jimenez et al., 2011; Seetanah, 2011, etc.). They belong to the family of econometric time-series techniques (Brida et al., 2011).

Wooldridge (2016) defines cointegration as follows: 'The notion that a linear combination of two series, each of which is integrated of order one, is integrated of order zero.' In the equation $Y = a + bX + \mu$, Y and X are cointegrated if the error term μ is stationary.

The methodological framework of Granger (1988) is based on a 'weak' concept of causality (Granger, 1969). When time series X Granger-causes time series Y, the patterns in X are approximately repeated in Y after some time lag. Thus, past values of X can be used for the prediction of future values of Y. A time series X is said to Granger-cause Y if it can be shown, usually through a series of t-tests and F-tests on lagged values of X (and with lagged values of Y also included), that those X values provide statistically significant information about future values of Y. According to this perspective, one variable causes a second variable if the second variable can be better predicted with all the available information on it and the past history of the first variable, than without using the past history of the first variable (Brida and Giuliani, 2013).

In the framework of the topic, it models changes in economic growth (e.g. GNP) as a function of a tourism development related proxy variable (e.g. international arrivals or international earnings). The goal of this method is to check the long-run correlation between changes in economic growth and changes in the tourism development proxy variable. The advantage of cointegration and Granger causality tests is that they determine the existence of correlation between tourism development and economic growth and the direction of causal relationship. However, Granger causality is not the same as true causality. In respect of this, Corrie et al. (2013) make the following observation:

> Granger causality is a statistical relationship between 'past' and 'current' variables; it is not a causal explanation of that relationship. Those who find evidence of Granger causality between tourism and gross domestic product (GDP) cannot conclude that tourism is causing growth in GDP; there may be some other factor that is causing growth in both tourism and in real GDP leading to a statistically observable relationship between the focal variables. In other words, modelling the relationship between tourism expenditure and GDP, alone, does not tell a complete story. One therefore expects results to vary depending upon the precise variables and timescales used. It is, as a result, important to take a broader perspective by, for example, seeking to determine if other related factors are having an effect on or driving the observed changes in tourism and economic growth.

A second methodology is the use of the Cobb–Douglas production function. In economics, the Cobb–Douglas production function is a particular functional form of the production function, widely used to represent the technological relationship between the amounts of two or more inputs, particularly physical capital and labour, and the amount of output that can be produced by those inputs. Some searchers employ a Cobb–Douglas production function at an industry or a national level (Capo et al., 2007), sometimes combined with a panel data analysis (Fayissa et al., 2008; Holzner, 2011). However, tourism is not an ideal application field. The tourism industry is not homogeneous but includes economic activities with different capital and labour requirements.

Cross-section analysis is a third method (see Figini and Vici, 2010; Narayan *et al.*, 2010). This method aims at identifying the correlation between tourism and economic growth over a cross-section of countries at a specific point in time. The main advantage of this technique over cointegration and Granger causality tests is the possibility of modelling different country characteristics (for example membership in an organization or trading bloc, least developed country status) and of investigating their impacts on economic growth (Ivanov and Webster, 2013). However, since the regression is applied over a single point in time, one cannot capture the dynamic aspects of the relationship between tourism and growth (Pablo-Romero and Molina, 2013).

To cope with this disadvantage several authors make use of 'dynamic panel data analysis' (e.g. Cortés-Jimenez, 2008; Fayissa *et al.*, 2008; Proença and Soukiazis, 2008). They overcome the cross-section analysis weakness by utilizing time-series data over a cross-section of countries. In a similar way to cross-section analysis, it allows the modelling of countries' specific characteristics.

Computable General Equilibrium (CGE) models are a fifth method (see Chapter 10). They have now received wide acceptance in tourism economic impact studies (for example, Dwyer *et al.*, 2004; Narayan, 2004; Blake *et al.*, 2008). They have been used to model potential external shocks and their impacts on the economy (for example, increase or decrease in tourism demand). According to Ivanov and Webster (2013) their main advantages are that they provide a comprehensive overview of the potential consequences of the shocks on country or industry levels and could be used for forecasting. However, this is also their major weakness – the CGE models identify potential *ex ante* but not actual *ex post* tourism impacts. Therefore, they cannot be used to measure the actual contribution of tourism to economic growth, but only to model the eventual consequences to economic growth of potential shocks in tourism demand, supply or government policy on tourism.

Finally, Ivanov and Webster (2013) refer to the growth decomposition methodology. It was initially developed by Ivanov (2005) and further refined by Ivanov and Webster (2007). In the field of tourism it has been applied to many countries (Ivanov and Webster, 2007; Brida *et al.*, 2011). The essence of the methodology is the decomposition of economic growth, expressed as real per capita GDP growth, into growth attributable to tourism and to other industries. Its major advantage (but also weakness) is the low data requirements – it requires only data on GDP, tourism GDP and mid-year population size. This method decomposes the growth but does not detect any causality.

Case studies of tourism export-led growth

CASE STUDY

The Proença–Soukiazis model: Mediterranean region

A good example of panel data analysis is the contribution of Proença and Soukiazis (2008). They show the importance of tourism – through international revenues – as a conditioning growth factor in Greece, Italy, Portugal and Spain.

They examine the role of tourism as a conditioning factor for improving the population's standard of living. The empirical analysis uses panel data techniques to estimate growth equations, combining time series and cross-sectional data for the four countries for the period 1990–2004. In their empirical analysis the model they estimate assumes the following form:

$$\Delta \ln y_{i,t} = \gamma_i + b \ln y_{i,t-1} + a_1 \ln (s)_{i,t} + a_2 \ln (n_i + g + \delta)$$
$$+ a_3 \ln T_{i,t} + a_4 D_{92-93} u_{i,t} \tag{9.1}$$

where

y = GDP per capita at PPP, constant prices γ
s = share of real investment to GDP
n = population; g = technology growth rates; δ = capital depreciation rate
T = international tourism revenues at PPP (cost prices)
d = dummy variable for 1992 and 1993 to capture instability effects EMS
$R^2 = 0.69$

The results indicate that tourism contributes significantly to the improvement of income and acts as a factor of convergence. Their research shows that every 1 per cent increase in international tourism revenues induces an increase of 0.026 per cent in per capita income in these countries.

CASE STUDY

The Fayissa–Nsiah–Tadase approach: Africa

The findings of Fayissa et al. (2008) are also very interesting. They analysed the impact of tourism on economic growth and development in Africa based on what they call a variant of a log linear Cobb–Douglas production. The equation takes the following form:

$$\ln PCI_{it} = B_0 + B_1 \ln TRP_{it} + B_2 \ln GCF_{it} + B_3 \ln EFI_{it} + B_4 \ln SCH_{it}$$
$$+ B_5 \ln FDI_{it} + B_6 \ln TOT_{it} + B_7 \ln HHC_{it} + \varepsilon_{it} \tag{9.2}$$

where:

PCI = real GDP Per capita
TRP = tourist receipts per capita in US$
GCF = gross fixed capital formation as a per cent of real GDP (proxy for investment in physical capital)

EFI = measure of the economic freedom index (political, economic, social, transparency and security)

SCH = secondary and tertiary school enrolment, as a measure of investment in human capital

FDI = foreign direct investment (net inflows) to capture the effect of foreign investment on growth

TOT = terms of trade for each country under consideration

HHC = household consumption expenditures

i = African countries 1–42

t = 1995–2004

$R^2 = 0.57$

The results of this model indicate that tourism (TRP) has a positive and statistically significant effect on the GDP per capita of African countries. They find that a 10 per cent increase in the tourism receipts of a typical African economy will result in a 0.4 per cent increase in the average per capita income (0.25 per cent with lagged GDP values). Croes and Venegas (2008) arrive at similar results with respect to Nicaragua.

CASE STUDY

The Seetanah model: island economies

Seetanah (2011) assesses the dynamic economic impact of tourism for 19 island economies for the period 1990–2007. He uses an augmented Solow growth model in which he incorporates tourism as one of the sources of growth. The model takes the following form:

$$Y = \dot{f}\,(IVTGDP, XMGDP, SER, EF, TOUR) \tag{9.3}$$

where:

Y = real GDP per capita

IVTGDP = physical capital (gross fixed capital formation as % of real GDP)

SER = human capital (secondary school enrollment)

XMGDP = openness of the economy: (X+M)/GDP

EF = economic freedom (economic freedom index based on ten economic freedoms)

TOUR = a measure of tourism development (tourism arrivals)

The econometric specification of the model can be written as follows:

$$y_{it} = \beta_0 + \beta_1\,ivtgdp_{it} + \beta_2\,xmgdp_{it} + \beta_3\,ser_{it} + \beta_4\,ef_{it} + \beta_5\,tour_{it} + \varepsilon_{it} \tag{9.4}$$

where the small letters denote natural logarithms of the variables implying a double log-linear specification to ease the interpretation of the results in percentage terms.

Furthermore, the author uses dynamic panel data regression and generalized methods of moments (GMM). He comes to the conclusion that the tourism development indicator implies that tourism has been an important factor in explaining economic performance in island economies. The coefficient of the tourism indicator varies from 0.12 to 0.14, indicating a positive short-term output elasticity of tourism. (The long-term elasticity might be higher; the tourism development indicator may take some time to have full potential effect on economic growth.)

CASE STUDY

The Brida–Punzo–Risso approach: Brazil

Brida *et al.* (2011) make use of cointegration analysis and of the dynamic data panel model. They formulate the hypothesis that growth could be tourism-led. They start from a recognized relationship between economic growth and international (and also domestic) tourism. They test in their contribution the rate of growth of per capita income and the growth rate of receipts from international tourism. They introduce the real exchange rate to take international competitiveness into account. They apply two econometric methodologies. Firstly, they use the cointegration technique for long country-level time series (1965–2007). Based on data for a shorter period (1990–2005), for the 27 Brazilian states, they apply in a second phase the Arellano and Bond dynamic panel data model.

In the case of the cointegration technique the authors specify the following autoregressive model in order to find a relationship among the vector of variables: YL, TT, RER. The dynamic panel model takes the following form:

$$\Delta \ln Y_{i,t} = \beta_1 \Delta \ln YL_{i,t-1} + \beta_2 \Delta \ln TT_{i,t} + \beta_3 \Delta \ln RER_{i,t} + \Delta \text{\euro}_{i,t,} \qquad (9.5)$$

where

Y = real income per capita
TT = international tourism expenditure
RER = the real exchange rate
i = 1–27 Brazilian states
t = 1990–2005
all the variables are in first differences
β_1 indicates to what degree current economic growth is determined by previous economic growth

As it is a dynamic model, estimated coefficients are short-run elasticities. They obtain long-term elasticities by dividing each of the coefficients by $(1-\beta_1)$. The authors show that the long-run elasticity of real income per capita with respect to tourism receipts amounts to 0.06. In other words, an increase of tourism receipts of 100 per cent produces an increase of 6 per cent in income per capita. An increment of 100 per cent in RER produces an increase of 27 per cent.

CASE STUDY

The Dritsakis approach: seven Mediterranean countries

Dritsakis (2012) examines the relationship between economic growth and tourism development in seven Mediterranean countries: France, Cyprus, Greece, Italy, Spain, Tunisia and Turkey. The purpose is to investigate empirically the long-run relationship between economic growth and tourism development. In pursuit of this objective, the tests of panel cointegration and fully modified ordinary least squares (FMOLS) are conducted, using panel data. The data used in this study are covering the period 1980–2007. The model includes real GDP, a tourism development variable (for the latter variable he uses two variants: TOUR 1 – real receipts and TOUR 2 – international tourist arrivals) and real exchange rate (EXR), which can be written as:

$$\ln GDP_{it} = \beta_{0i} + \beta_{1i} \ln TOUR_{it} + \beta_{2i} \ln EXR_{it} + e_{it} \qquad (9.6)$$

where:

GDP_{it} = the real GDP per capita
$TOUR_{1it}$ = real receipts per capita
$TOUR_{2it}$ = the number of international tourist arrivals per capita
EXR_{it} = the nominal effective exchange rate
e_{it} = the error term

Dritsakis estimates the coefficients of real GDP per capita by using the panel fully modified ordinary least squares method (FMOLS). Therefore, instead of a time-series or traditional fixed or random effect panel data approach, cointegration tests for a panel of countries are used. He applies panel cointegration tests for two models. In the first test he uses $TOUR_{1it}$ as the variable; in the second test he replaces $TOUR_{1it}$ by $TOUR_{2it}$.

The first model gives the better FMOLS results. The $\ln TOUR_{1it}$ shows an elasticity of 1.24 for the panel of seven countries. The β_2 value stands for the exchange rate elasticity and is significantly estimated at a positive value of 0.08.

The β_1 is significant and > than 1 for all Mediterranean countries (except Turkey). This allows Dritsakis to conclude:

> This means that tourist receipts affect the GDP for each country on a large scale. Also, β_2 parameter is positive and statistically significant for all countries (except Turkey), which means that real exchange rate also affects GDP. Moreover, because four of the seven countries' β_2 parameters are above one, the real effective exchange rate has a common scale impact on GDP. Therefore, with a higher exchange rate, the destination country has an increased number of foreign exchange tourism receipts. Apart from this, the tourism industry provided by the recipient or host country is more competitive in terms of price, which means it makes a more positive contribution to GDP.

CASE STUDY

The Brida and Giuliani model: Tirol–Südtirol–Trentino Europaregion

Brida and Giuliani (2013) apply the cointegration test in the empirical analysis of the tourism-led growth hypothesis (TLGH) for the regions Tirol (Austria), Südtirol and Trentino (Italy). For all three regions, the data applied in this study are annual time series, from 1980 to 2009, of regional real gross domestic product (GDP), number of international tourists visiting the regions (T) and the relative price index (RP) between the regions and Germany. For the three regions, Germany is the most important inbound market. Therefore the authors use German tourist arrivals and RP between Germany and the regions as indicators of international tourism and external competiveness. They try to detect the presence of a cointegrating relationship between lnGDP, lnT and $\Delta(\ln RP)$.

For South Tirol this leads to the following equation:

$$\ln GDP_t = 4.16 + 0.36 \ln T_t - 3.31 \, \Delta(\ln RP)_t \tag{9.7}$$

where

GDP = the regional GDP of South Tirol
T = German tourists visiting South Tirol
RP = the relative price index between Germany and the region
t = period 1980–2009

It is important to notice that the elasticity of lnGDP with respect to international tourist arrivals is positive. It takes the value of 0.36. The existence of a significant stable long-run relation between lnT and lnGDP is a necessary but not sufficient condition for causality between the two variables. In other words, one still needs to determine which variable is the cause and which is the effect. Therefore the Granger causality test is the next step. In the case of South Tirol the null hypothesis that international tourism does not Granger-cause real GDP is definitely rejected; instead, the null hypothesis that the real GDP does not Granger-cause international tourism cannot be rejected. These results allow us to infer that unidirectional Granger causality from international tourism to real GDP does exist.

The similar results for the Trentino region are:

$$\ln GDP_t = 5.94 + 0.25 \ln T_t - 1.82 \, \Delta(\ln RP)_t \tag{9.8}$$

In this case the elasticity of ln GDP with respect to international tourist arrivals is positive. It takes the value of 0.25, i.e. an increase in tourism arrivals by 100 per cent would potentially produce an increase of 25 per cent in the total local output. This means that the impact of increases in tourism demand is stronger in South Tirol (estimated elasticity of real output, 0.36) than in Trentino (estimated elasticity of real output, 0.25). Furthermore, based on the Granger causality test the TLGH can be validated.

Brida and Giuliani come to very different results for the Austrian Tirol region. Unlike the cases of South Tirol and Trentino, the cointegration tests for Tirol show that no cointegration exists between real GDP, international tourist arrivals and local relative inflation, since the null hypothesis of no cointegration relations cannot be rejected. Consequently, there is no convergence of the three variables to long-run equilibrium, and no causation exists between international tourist arrivals and real GDP, implying that the TLGH is not validated for the local economy of Tirol. The authors suggest two reasons for the lack of evidence in favour of TLGH. Firstly, the economy of Tirol is more complex and differentiated. Secondly, Tirol is less dependent on tourism than the two Italian regions.

CASE STUDY

The Holzner approach: cross-country analysis

Holzner (2011) starts with a cross-country analysis (134 countries). Later he seeks to check the main results of the cross-country analysis on the long-run relationship of tourism and economic growth with a panel data Cobb–Douglas production function. The first step is the application of a growth model in the context of a cross-county analysis. The cross-country regression equation is defined as (linear-log relationship):

$$g_i = \alpha_0 + \alpha_1 y_{oi} + \alpha_2 k_i + \alpha_3 h_i + \alpha_4 x_i + \varepsilon_i \tag{9.9}$$

where

g = average annual growth of output per labour unit (Holzner uses as a proxy for g the annual growth of the natural logs of real GDP per capita at PPP between the years 1970 and 2007)

y_o = the real GDP per capita at PPP

k = the average investment share of the real GDP for the period 1970–2007 depending on data availability

h = the average gross secondary school enrolment ratio for the period 1970–2007 depending on data availability

x = tourism dependency rate or the average share of travel services exports in GDP for the period 1970–2007 depending on data availability

ε = the error term

$\alpha_1 - \alpha_4$ are the regression coefficients of the respective explanatory variables

Holzner argues the use of the initial output level (y_o) as a development component as follows. Under the conditional convergence theory initially poorer countries have the possibility to grow faster as they learn, and they imitate and apply technology of developed countries in a short period of time. This is confirmed by the negative sign of α_1 as developed countries tend to grow at a slower pace than poorer countries. The application of the cross-country equation (134 countries) gives the following result:

Constant:	3.689 (2.72)***
Initial GDP per capita:	−0.663 (−3.61)***
Physical capital:	0.663 (2.21)**
Human capital:	0.026 (3.66)***
Tourism:	0.223 (2.59)**
R^2:	0.393

The symbols *, ** and *** following the t statistics represent a 10, 5 and less than 1 per cent significance level, respectively.

All growth variables have the expected signs and are highly significant. The tourism variable is significant at the 5 per cent level too. Given the linear-log relationship of the cross-country equation, an increase of the share of tourism exports in GDP by 10 per cent increases the growth rate of real GDP per capita by 0.02 percentage points.

As mentioned in the introduction to this case study, Holzner applies in a second step the panel data Cobb–Douglas production function as a trans-log production function. He estimates the following equation:

$$Y_{it} = y_t + \alpha y_{it-1} + \beta_1 k_{it} + \beta_2 h_{it} + \beta_3 x_{it} - \eta_i + v_{it} \tag{9.10}$$

where

y_t = productivity changes that are common to all countries

y_{it-1} = the lagged output variable which can be interpreted to measure conditional convergence

i takes values from 1 to 99

The above production function gives the following results:

Constant:	0.082 (1.48)
Lagged GDP per capita:	0.950(35.49)***
Physical capital:	0.035 (1.77)*
Human capital:	0.008 (0.83)
Tourism:	0.018 (2.84)***

The estimated coefficient (β_3) for the tourism variable is positive and very significant but the coefficient is not very high. A 1 per cent increase of the tourism share in GDP leads to a 0.02 per cent higher GDP per capita. The panel data analysis confirms the results of the cross-country analysis and Holzner concludes that tourism has a positive impact on the aggregate output of countries. Two more of Holzner's findings are interesting. Firstly, countries with a higher income from tourism tend to have higher levels of investment and secondary school enrolment. Secondly, taking into account the real exchange rate and manufacturing exports' share in the production function, tourism seems not to lead to a contraction of the manufacturing sector. He concludes that there is no danger of a 'Dutch disease effect'. In economics, the 'Dutch disease' is the apparent causal relationship between the increase in the economic development of a specific sector (for example tourism) and a decline in other sectors. The putative mechanism is that as revenues increase in the growing sector the given nation's currency becomes stronger compared to currencies of other nations (manifest in the exchange rate). This results in the nation's other exports becoming more expensive for other countries to buy, and imports becoming cheaper, making those sectors less competitive.

CASE STUDY

The Cortés-Jiménez–Nowak–Sahli approach: beach tourism in Tunisia

Cortés-Jiménez *et al.* (2011) reveal a much more complex relationship between economic growth and tourism exports. They examine the relationship between tourism exports, imports of capital goods and economic growth, with special reference to Tunisia over the period 1975–2007. The dynamic interaction between these variables is examined within a vector error correction model using the Johansen technique of cointegration with structural changes and the multivariate Granger causality test.

The authors consider that tourism may affect economic growth through two different channels, the tourism-led growth hypothesis (TLG) and what they call a TKIG hypothesis. In the TKIG hypothesis, tourism exports are a source of foreign currency that allows the financing of capital goods: 'Thus, export expansion promotes capital accumulation, and consequently economic growth, through the expansion of the volume of inputs rather than through the increase in their efficiency.'

The variables used are real gross domestic product (Y), real international tourism receipts (TOUR) and real imports of industrial machinery (IMP). The variables have been transformed into real terms by using the consumer price index (base 2000). Furthermore, all variables are transformed into natural logarithms. The Granger causality is based on the following equation:

$$\Delta \ln Y_t = \alpha_1 + \beta_{i1} \Delta \ln Y_{t-i} + \delta_{i1} \Delta \ln IMP_{t-i} + \varphi_{i1} \Delta \ln TOUR_{t-i}$$
$$+ \alpha_1 D88 + \gamma_1 ECT_{t-1} + \nu_{1t} \tag{9.11}$$

where

Y = real domestic product
IMP = real imports of industrial machinery
TOUR = real international tourism receipts
D = dummy variable
ECT = error correction term
β, δ and φ are the coefficients of the lagged explanatory variables
γ = parameter associated with ECT and represents the speed adjustment towards the long-run equilibrium

The results are surprising. The TLG hypothesis test reveals that both long-term and short-term unidirectional causal relationships from tourism exports to economic growth are not significant. This suggests that the TLG hypothesis cannot be inferred for the Tunisian economy. These findings are in line with earlier research by Hachicha (2003). This author found a weak sensitivity of economic growth to inbound tourism in Tunisia.

The TKIG hypothesis test indicates that there is a short-run causality from imports of capital goods (lnIMP), to economic growth (lnY). The results for the causality relationships between imports of capital goods, inbound tourism and economic growth provides evidence of the TKIG mechanism as a short-run phenomenon in Tunisia. Cortés-Jiménez *et al.* said:

> These results indicated that the foreign exchange made available by inbound tourism growth allowed the importation of capital goods which, in turn, increased the potential production of the Tunisian economy in the short run. However, over the long run, this positive impact of imports of capital goods on economic growth tended to die down, as attested by the insignificant coefficient of the ECT in the real GDP Equation.

What can a possible explanation for the absence of export led growth for Tunisia be? The authors give two possible explanations. A first factor could be the diversification of the economy in the early 1970s to textile, mechanical and electrical and other products. A second factor is related to the level of the tourism product. This product is to a large extent low-cost sun and beach tourism. This is probably responsible for a weak long-term growth. The TLG hypothesis implies growth through improvement of the efficiency of inputs induced by tourism exports. The policy conclusion for the authors is very clear:

> It is worth pointing out here that the above results merely suggest that the adoption of a 'coastal mass tourism' export expansion policy cannot always benefit economic growth. This cautionary note is important because there is a risk that too much emphasis being put on the establishment of more tourism and hospitality facilities (hotels, large coastal resorts, etc.), driven by quick profit returns, can lead in the long run to the reduction of the quality of the country's tourism product and its tourism earnings per capita in real terms. It is therefore imperative that government institutions, tourism planners and investors recognize the implications of their actions in the overall interest of the long-run economic sustainability of the tourism sector. The success of a strategy of tourism development ought not to be measured just in terms of increasing tourist numbers or revenues. Tourism should also be assessed according to its role in the broader development goals of the host country. In this context, it is recommended that the Tunisian government should not support the construction of new superstructure, such as hotels and restaurants, through monetary and fiscal policy incentives. Rather, they should encourage private and public bodies to improve the current tourism infrastructure and the image of the country in order to achieve higher room rates.

The case studies and the literature about tourism-led growth lead us to three major conclusions. Firstly, there is a clear empirical consensus that tourism promotes economic growth. The relationship between tourism and growth is mostly confirmed. The same conclusion is evident in Perles-Ribes *et al.* (2017). They found out that from a sample of 87 studies, 55 pointed to a univocal relationship and 16 other studies identified a bi-univocal relationship. Although the impact in relative terms is only moderate, there is a need for support in public and private sector in the development strategy of tourism growth. Allocation of resources to stimulate tourism is necessary to sustain tourism as a vehicle of growth development (Croes and Vanegas, 2008).

There is some evidence that the role of tourism in economic growth is larger for smaller developing countries than for the developed countries (Dritsakis, 2012). Also Eugenio-Martin *et al.* (2004) found that tourism was not universally growth-conducive in Latin America. They found that only in medium- and low-income countries was tourism likely to generate growth. We find a similar result with De Vita and Kyaw (2016). Based on a system generalized methods-of-moments estimation methodology with a large panel of 129 countries over 1995–2011, a 1 per cent increase in tourism expenditure leads to an increase in real GDP per capita of 0.3 per cent in low-income countries, 0.2 per cent in middle-income countries and 0.1 per cent for the high-income countries.

However, in the introduction to this section, we saw that the tourism-led economic growth hypothesis does not always hold (e.g. Oh for South Korea, Katircioglu for Turkey). Neither was the TLGH validated in the cases analysed above for Tirol (Brida and Giuliani, 2013) and Tunisia (Cortés-Jiménez *et al.*, 2011). This means that there is no significant cointegrating relation found between the time series of tourism demand and of local real GDP.

Secondly, several factors influence the relationship between tourism and economic growth, such as the economic development level of the country, the size of the country, the import leakages, the openness of the economy, the degree of dependence on tourism, tourism policy, tourism supporting infrastructure and the life cycle of the major tourism products of the destination (Kim *et al.*, 2006). Most probably we should also consider the poor level of reliability of available research data in many countries. In their publication 'Tourism-led growth hypothesis in the top ten tourist destinations', Shahzad *et al.* (2017) show that the relation between tourism development and economic growth is primarily positive for all top ten destinations but different from country to country:

> The heterogeneity among countries in terms of the tourism-economic growth nexus may be attributed to differences in the relative weight of the tourism industry in the overall economy of each country, the size and openness of each economy and its production capacity constraints, the relevance of local business in the tourism industry of each country and the possible negative externalities caused by tourism growth in some countries. In particular, the weakest relation between tourism and economic growth was noted for China and Germany, most likely because of the scant direct contribution of tourism to the respective economies of those two countries.

Surugiu and Surugiu (2013) put it that each destination has its own particularities, which should be observed and integrated in a wider socio-economic context. There is no generally valid recipe to confirm that TLGH applies in all tourism destinations. For Tugcu (2014), the possible explanation of the different relationships lies in the economic, political, sociological, environmental and ecological structures of the individual countries.

Thirdly, from the methodological point of view, most tourism-led growth studies can be classified under two strands. The first and most important strand includes studies based on cointegration and Granger causality tests. The second strand of research is composed of studies using cross-section or panel data.

Tourism and poverty reduction

The link between tourism-led growth and poverty alleviation is quite close. Croes and Vanegas (2008) expanded the tourism-led growth theory by introducing poverty to the relationship between growth and tourism. This relationship is a phenomenon of the last decade. The tourism-led growth strategy remains the main reason for developing countries to allocate resources to tourism (Croes, 2014). Tourism has several advantages over other economic activities. One of the characteristics of the tourism sector (see Chapter 1) is the fact that customers travel to places where the services are delivered. Once at the destination a tourist roams around and can make contact with the local people. The direct contact between local people and tourists supports the belief that tourism can reduce poverty. The tourist consumes many different products and services from several suppliers and creates a trickle-down effect.

Tourism development is not possible without attractions capable of attracting international tourists. Fortunately, many developing countries have many natural attractions at their disposal – sun and beach, mountains, etc. – as well as important heritage sites. According to Arezki *et al.* (2009), of the 48 least developed countries more than 50 per cent have world heritage sites within their borders.

Income inequality can be studied from two different points of view: personal income and regional income. Tourism has become an important economic activity for many developing countries and less developed regions in their search to lessen poverty and increase prosperity (Hawkins and Mann, 2007; Croes and Vanegas, 2008; Vanhove, 2014).

Croes, who did a lot of research on the topic 'tourism and poverty', suggests that there is little understanding of what impact tourism has on the poor in developing countries. Most tourism-led growth studies ignore the distribution of the benefits. The lack of understanding is a serious issue, although the World Tourism Organization (WTO) has identified tourism as a key driver to combat poverty. Many developing countries consider tourism as an important development trigger in their strategies to lessen poverty. The question arises to what extent tourism is a tool to alleviate poverty in less developed countries. According to Croes, empirical evidence supporting this assertion is lacking or weak. Efficiency is inherent to tourism-led growth. But if those who benefit from this efficiency are the upper class, then improved efficiency might lead to more inequality.

A basic question is, 'How do you define poverty?' Croes and Rivera (2016) make a distinction between four paradigms that investigate poverty: income poverty, the basic needs approach, the capabilities poverty paradigm (or deficiencies in many dimensions of human life such as education, health, command over resources and participation), and the subjective poverty paradigm (or the subjective well-being paradigm). For the relationship between tourism and poverty, only the first paradigm is useful.

The income poverty paradigm defines poverty in terms of the level of command of resources. Poverty is a situation wherein a person's resources fall below a certain minimum level of income, termed 'the poverty line'. Many researchers define this poverty line in absolute terms such as $1 or $2 a day per person. The millennium development goals define people living under $1 a day as extreme poor and $2 a day as poor. These development goals are very low. The income poverty concept is very helpful in defining the poverty ratio (see below) whatever the minimum income per day. This leads to the headcount poverty ratio or the proportion of a population that exists or lives below the poverty line.

Croes and Rivera posit that a tourism development strategy aimed at poverty reduction has unique advantages. They mention the following benefits:

- Higher stable employment
- Increased access to healthcare
- Increased access to education
- Stable export revenue
- Opportunity in remote areas
- Economic diversity
- Tangible and location-specific commodity value.

Income inequality from the personal income point of view

This is the background to the research by Croes (2014) on the relationship between tourism and poverty reduction. The application field is two poor developing countries: Costa Rica and Nicaragua. His study attempts to answer three interrelated questions. Firstly, does tourism development lead to poverty decline? Secondly, if the answer is positive, what is the nature of that relationship? Thirdly, what is the direction of the relationship? He examines the relationship between tourism and absolute poverty.

Croes employs the Kaldorian approach which asserts that foreign demand is the promoter of economic growth, and that growth reduces poverty. Kaldor (1966) articulated a set of long-run relationships between output, employment and productivity growth at the sectoral level of the economy, generally known as Kaldor's growth laws. Nowadays the services sector (e.g. tourism) is replacing traditional manufacturing. Many services are conceived as an 'engine of growth'. This approach applies an error correction model (ECM) to estimate and assess the empirical relationship between tourism and poverty reduction in Costa Rica and Nicaragua. Croes applied the following equation (for more details refer to Croes, 2014):

$$dP = \alpha_1 y \cdot + \alpha_2 dT + \alpha_3 t + \alpha_4 dt + \alpha_5 dNT + \alpha_6 dnt + \epsilon t \qquad (9.12)$$

where

dP = changes in the poverty rate (P = level of poverty)
y = real output
dT = total tourism growth
t = total tourism share of GDP
dt = total tourism share growth
NT = non-tourism export share of GDP
dnt = non-tourism export share growth
R^2 Nicaragua = 0.34
R^2 Costa Rica = 0.40

The dependent variable in this analysis is the first difference of the poverty headcount (the proportion of population that lives below the poverty line; in this case less than US$1 per day). The data employed for Costa Rica and Nicaragua are annual observations expressed in natural logarithms and cover the period 1980–2010.

What conclusions can be derived from the Croes study? The study entertains three propositions: (i) tourism matters for the poor; (ii) tourism does not have systematic effects on the poor; and (iii) tourism development matters most for the poor at lower levels of economic development.

The first proposition suggests that in Nicaragua and Costa Rica an increase in tourism receipts contributes to decreasing poverty as evidenced from a unidirectional Granger causality effect from tourism and poverty. In the case of Nicaragua, the growth elasticity of poverty was equal to 1.23. This means that a 1 per cent increase in tourism receipts reduces the poverty rate by 1.23 points. For Costa Rica, the results are quite different. While there is a long-run positive relationship with economic growth, the authors found a long-run positive relationship with poverty as well. This means that tourism in Costa Rica does not seem to benefit the poor in the long run.

The second proposition of the study is that tourism does not have systematic effects on the poor. In Costa Rica, tourism does not seem to matter for the poor. Unlike Nicaragua, job creation in Costa Rica is not the main catalyst against poverty. One additional international tourist to Costa Rica generates fewer jobs, which implies some diminishing returns. Salaries in tourism jobs in Costa Rica are comparatively lower than average salaries in the country and jobs are affected by seasonality.

Pro-poor growth means that tourism benefits the poor. Tourism development appears to provide benefits to the poor in Nicaragua and thus can be labelled as being pro-poor. The case of Costa Rica, on the other hand, does not pass the pro-poor test. Tourism development matters most for the poor at lower levels of economic development.

A few years later, Croes and Rivera (2017) examined the distributional effects of tourism growth in Ecuador applying a social accounting matrix (SAM) model. This study reveals three important findings:

> First, tourism development does help the poor increase their earnings, including those with the highest incidence of poverty, such as is the case for those in the first quintile. This finding is consistent with the first definition of pro-poor growth being that growth increases income levels of the poor regardless of inequality (the absolute pro-poor definition).

Second, the case of Ecuador also reveals that tourism development benefits the poor more than the non-poor (the relative pro-poor definition). And third, tourism development seems an effective strategy in addressing poverty issues in developing countries.

According to the authors the managerial implications are twofold:

> First, Ecuador should focus on increasing international tourism demand and promote tourist spending. The findings indicate that the income generated by tourism permeated to different groups, and if tourism is managed with a focus on poverty alleviation, tourism development can directly and indirectly (multiplier effects) benefit the poor. A demand focus will increase visits, length of stay, and spend per person, thereby increasing the size and performance of the tourism sector. Ultimately, this increase will spawn jobs of which many are potentially quite accessible to the poor as they require relatively few skills and little investment. Working together with the private sector is essential to spawn more wealth and distribution. In addition, the spending that reaches the poor should be promoted through actions that increase the direct and indirect participation of the poor in tourism. The demand focus requires that Ecuador as a destination should remain competitive and sustainable. And second, efforts should be undertaken to spread tourism offerings to rural areas in order to facilitate the participation of the poor in the tourism sector.

The two preceding analyses of Croes are focussed on individual countries. Two other research papers on the impact of tourism on poverty alleviation (Kim *et al.*, 2016; Alam and Paramati, 2016) are based on panel data for 69 and 49 developing countries respectively.

In an excellent piece of research work, Kim *et al.* (2016) suggest that it is very pertinent to question whether tourism can contribute to reducing the extreme poverty rate of a country. In order to improve our understanding of this issue, their study employs a panel data regression analysis to test whether tourism performance has a positive impact on poverty alleviation and, if so, whether this positive relationship varies according to a country's economic condition (i.e. the income level). They used panel data from 69 developing countries.

They set up the following panel regression equation (OLS model) to analyse the impact of tourism on the national poverty ratio:

$$\text{Poverty ratio}_{it} = \alpha + \beta . \text{Tourism}_{it} + X_{it} . \gamma + K_i + \phi_t + \text{€}_{ijt} \tag{9.13}$$

where

Poverty ratio$_{it}$ = the poverty head count ratio (%) at \$1.25 per day for country$_i$ in year$_t$ (very similar to Croes, 2014)
α = constant term
Tourism$_{it}$ = the log of tourism receipts in country$_i$ in year$_{t;}$ (two variants are tourism receipts per arrival and the log of the number of arrivals)
X_{it} = is a vector of variables, such as GDP per capita (GDPPC) and GDP growth
K_i = landlocked dummy, island dummy and distance from the equator but also country dummy variable or country fixed effects (e.g. country's culture) which is time constant
ϕ_t = dummy variable to catch external factors common to all countries
€_{ijt} = random error term

In this basic equation tourism receipts, GDP per capita and GDP growth are the key exogenous variables. But the authors also include geographical factors that influence a country's poverty ratio, such as a landlocked dummy and island dummy. These dummies capture the ease of communication and travel between countries. The distance from the equator is a proxy for a country's climate endowment, which influences development.

The above specification assumes that the impact on poverty is the same in all countries. But special characteristics of individual countries may influence the effects. Indeed, the level of development, measured in terms of GDPPC, may change the effect of tourism on the poverty ratio. Therefore the basic equation has been extended by including the interaction terms (see Alfaro *et al.*, 2004) for the tourism variable with the log of GDPPC:

$$\text{Poverty ratio}_{it} = \alpha + \beta_1 . \text{Tourism}_{it} + \beta_2 . \text{Tourism}_{it} \times \text{GDPPC}_{it}$$
$$+ X_{it.}\,\gamma + K_i + \phi_t + \epsilon_{ijt} \tag{9.14}$$

When including country fixed effects, the geographical dummies are dropped out because these time-invariant dummies are soaked up by country fixed effects. From the above regression equation, the net marginal effect of tourism on poverty is equal to:

$$\frac{\Delta \text{proverty ratio}_{it}}{\Delta \text{tourism}_{it}} = \beta_1 + \beta_2 . \overline{\text{GDPPC}}_{it} \tag{9.15}$$

The two independent variables β_1 (tourism) and β_2 (interaction term with GDPPC) show negative (– 24.214) and positive (+ 2.980) regression coefficients, respectively.

Further, it is very important that these two estimates indicate that the effect of (log) tourism receipts on the poverty ratio begins as negative and then shrinks with an increase in the level of a country's income per capita. Finally, the effect of tourism on poverty switches to being positive after a particular threshold of income level. In the present case the threshold of log GDPPC is 8.126 (in a log value) or about $3,400. This means that for countries with an income level less than 8.126, tourism contributes to reduce the poverty ratio; in countries with an income level more than 8.126, tourism increases the poverty ratio. If a country's GDPPC is about $5,000 (8.517 in log value) then the marginal effect of tourism on poverty is 1.167 (= 24.214 + 2980 × 8517), which means that a 1 per cent increase in tourism receipts leads to an increase in the headcount poverty ratio at $1.25 a day by 1.2 per cent.

Based on the empirical research, the main conclusions of Kim *et al.* (2016) are firstly, 'tourism expenditures do not have a significant effect on poverty reduction for all developing countries'. Secondly, by including the interaction term between tourism and income per capita:

> We find that the level of a country's economic development determines the pure effect of tourism on its poverty ratio, and that tourism has a heterogeneous effect on the poverty ratio in terms of the country's income level. Both the tourism variable and its interaction term with income per capita indicate that the effect of (log) tourism receipts on the poverty ratio starts negative, and the poverty reduction effect of tourism shrinks with an increase in the country's income per capita. The findings also suggest the effect of tourism on poverty reduction switches to become positive, and that tourism begins to exacerbate poverty after a particular income level threshold. Therefore, the results indicate that tourism development does not guarantee extreme poverty alleviation in all developing countries.

The most important conclusion of this study is undoubtedly that the positive effect of tourism on poverty alleviation switches to being negative after a certain threshold of a country's income level. In other words, only the least developed countries have benefited from tourism development in terms of reducing their poverty ratios. This result confirms the findings of Croes (2014), who also states that tourism development is an important factor for poverty reduction under a certain condition, namely, a lower level of economic development, as evidenced in

Nicaragua. On the other hand, in countries with relatively high economic development, tourism does not seem to make a difference for the poor. Croes' study of 2014 suggests that developing countries with GDPPC levels exceeding about international $7,500 will not enjoy poverty reduction through tourism.

The second piece of research work on the impact of tourism on poverty alleviation where several developing countries are involved is from Alam and Paramati (2016). They raise the question 'Does Kuznets curve hypothesis exist?' According to the Kuznets curve, the economic inequality theory suggests that as an economy develops, inequality first increases and then decreases, following an inverted U shape. This study is based on a panel data set of 49 developing countries from 1991 to 2012. Their empirical results confirm the long-run equilibrium relationship based on a modified OLS method between income inequality (measured through the Gini coefficient), foreign direct investment (FDI), trade openness, tourism revenue and GDP per capita. The results are interesting and surprising. The findings show that FDI inflows, trade openness and tourism revenue have a significant positive impact on income inequality; growth of GDP per capita decreases inequality. A 1 per cent increase of FDI inflows, trade openness and tourism revenue increases income inequality by 0.003 per cent, 0.009 per cent and 0.047 per cent, respectively.

But if the current level of tourism revenue doubles, it will significantly reduce the income inequalities in developing countries. The findings show that a 1 per cent rise in squared tourism revenues decreases inequality by 0.12 per cent. This confirms their Kuznets curve hypothesis. From a historical perspective, a growth in income levels causes increasing income inequality after a certain point. This result implies that further growth of tourism revenue in the future will lead to a reduction of income equalities in developing countries.

The results of Alam and Paramati do not contradict those of Kim *et al*. The panel of countries is not the same. The average development level of Kim's panel countries is higher than the one of Alam's panel countries. Furthermore Kim *et al*. focus more on the development level of the panel countries.

Income inequality from the regional point of view

Income inequality can also be studied from the regional point of view. Here a preliminary comment should be made. Many major tourism attractions are located in less developed regions and quite often tourism is the only development opportunity. But this does not imply that rich regions are not attracting many tourists. Bangkok, Beijing and Barcelona are only a few examples. A good example dealing with the relation between tourism and regional inequality is the research work by Li *et al*. (2016) with evidence from China. They examine the role of tourism development in reducing regional income inequality in China. They calculate the evolution of the Gini coefficient on the regional tourism and regional economic development of 31 provinces in China covering the period 1997–2010. The study supports the hypothesis that tourism can reduce regional income inequality in China. The results are consistent with an earlier study by Proença and Soukiazis (2008; see above) and Lee and Chang (2008). Based on a panel of OECD countries and non-OECD countries, Lee and Chang support the thesis that tourism contributes more significantly to the economic growth of developing countries or regions than to that of developed economies.

The European Commission recognizes the role of tourism in regional development. In the framework of the Structural Funds, the EU supports several regions in their efforts to develop tourism as a vehicle of change. In the objective 1 areas (the poorest regions of the EU), interventions of structural funds (SF) for the period 2000–2006 for tourism measures amount to 4,295 million euros, or 3.2 per cent of the total SF. (Retained codes or fields of intervention are: encouragement for tourist activities, tourism physical investment, non-physical investments, shared services for the tourism industry, vocational training.) In several European countries, tourism contributes to a redistribution of wealth between regions (see also Guicheney and

Rouzade, 2003). In several Eastern European EU countries this percentage was much higher for the period 2004–2006: Cyprus 21.0 per cent, Malta 15.4 per cent, Slovenia 12.3 per cent, Lithuania 8.3 per cent, Czech Republic 7.7 per cent, Latvia 6.1 per cent (Butowski, 2010).

Conclusion

'Can tourism be a strategic option for growth and sustainable development'? 'Is tourism a trigger for economic development and poverty alleviation'? Both questions are closely interrelated.

Referring to the many tourism-led growth studies, including those related to the nexus between tourism growth and poverty alleviation, there is a positive relationship between tourism development and economic growth. However, there is not always an unequivocal answer to these questions. It is important to recognize that those studies have been undertaken for several continents: Europe, Latin America, Africa, Asia and Oceania. This is confirmed by Pablo-Romero and Molina (2013). They examined a sample of 87 studies on the subject covering different time periods, countries and regions. They found that only four cases did not identify any relationship between tourism development and economic growth.

In the preceding chapter we saw that a net distinction should be made between developing countries and developed countries. Even within richer countries a distinction should be made between richer regions and backward regions. Two preliminary conditions should be underlined: the availability of tourism attractions with sufficient appeal to attract international tourists and competitiveness of the tourism destinations. Let us be clear that not all developing and developed countries comply with both conditions.

This and the preceding chapter suggest the following five conclusions. Firstly, tourism is a sector which can be a vehicle for economic development in LDCs. The analysed TLG studies contribute evidence for this thesis. However, there are exceptions. Several factors influence the relation between tourism and economic growth such as the availability of natural resources as one of the main sources of comparative advantage, the economic development level of the country, the import leakages, the openness of the economy, the degree of dependence on tourism, tourism demand, tourism policy, tourism supporting infrastructure and the type of tourism products. For the latter factor, the cheap 'sun and beach products' in Tunisia are a good example.

Secondly, tourism is not the best strategic development option for richer countries with full employment. This conclusion changes from the moment that a developed country is confronted with regions with high unemployment where real tourism attractions are available and without other development opportunities. This is the case for Sicily in Italy or Andalusia in Spain.

Thirdly, there is some evidence that a less developed country (LDC) can reduce its poverty ratio through tourism. But there is not a significant effect in all developing countries. Some authors attribute the exceptions to the high corruption in many developing countries.

Fourthly, the positive impact of tourism on poverty alleviation switches to become negative after some level of GDPPC. Kim *et al.* (2016) put that only LDCs with a GDPPC under about $3,500 to $7,500 (depending on which tourism indicator has been used: receipts, receipts per arrival or the number of tourism arrivals) really benefit from the tourism industry in terms of reducing their poverty ratios. In order to achieve the goal of pro-poor tourism (tourism benefiting the poor), policy makers should carefully consider their country's economic status before adopting tourism development policies. Kim *et al.* (2016) suggest that tourism competitiveness and its impact on the quality of life could vary across countries, depending on their respective economic conditions. Therefore, sustainable tourism development is of utmost importance.

Fifthly, tourism can also be an instrument to reduce regional disparities in a country. In the framework of its Structural Funds the European Union recognizes the role of tourism in regional development.

References and further reading

Alam, S., and Paramati, S. (2016). The impact of tourism income inequality in developing countries: does Kuznets curve hypothesis exist? *Annals of Tourism Research, 61.*

Alfaro, L., Chanda, A., Kalemli-Ozcan, S., and Sayek, S. (2004). FDI and economic growth: the role of local financial markets. *Journal of International Economics, 64 (1).*

Arezki, R., Cherif, R., and Piotrowski, J. (2009). *Tourism Specialization and Economic Development: Evidence from the UNESCO World Heritage List.* Washington, DC: IMF.

Balaguer, J., and Cantavella-Jorda, M. (2002). Tourism as a long-run economic growth factor: the Spanish case. *Applied Economics, 34 (1).*

Bhagwati, J.N. (1978). *Foreign Trade Regimes and Economic Development: Anatomy and Consequences of Exchange Control Regimes.* New York: National Bureau of Economic Research.

Blake, A., Arbache, J.S., Sinclair, M.T., and Teles, V. (2008). Tourism and poverty relief. *Annals of Tourism Research, 35 (1).*

Brida, J.G., and Giuliani, D. (2013). Empirical assessment of the tourism-led growth hypothesis: the case of Tirol-Südtirol-Trentino Europaregion. *Tourism Economics, 19 (4).*

Brida, J.G., Punzo, L.F., and Risso, W. (2011). Tourism as a factor of growth – the case of Brazil. *Tourism Economics, 17 (6).*

Butowski, L. (2010). Tourism in the EU economic and social cohesion policy in 1994–1999 and 2000–2006 budget programming periods. *Tourism Review, 58 (2).*

Capo, J.P., Riera, A.F., and Rossello, J.N. (2007). Tourism and long-term growth. A Spanish perspective. *Annals of Tourism Research, 34 (3).*

Corrie, K., Stoeckl, N., and Chaiechi, T. (2013). Tourism and economic growth in Australia: an empirical investigation of causal links. *Tourism Economics, 19 (6).*

Cortés-Jimenez, L. (2008). Which type of tourism matters to the regional growth? The cases of Spain and Italy. *International Journal of Tourism Research, 10.*

Cortés-Jiménez, I., Nowak, J.J., and Sahli, M. (2011). Mass beach tourism and economic growth: lessons from Tunisia. *Tourism Economics, 17 (3).*

Croes, R. (2014). The role of tourism in poverty reduction: empirical assessment. *Tourism Economics, 20 (2).*

Croes, R. and Rivera, M. (2016). *Poverty Alleviation through Tourism Development: A Comprehensive and Integrated Approach.* Oakville, ON: Apple Academic Press.

Croes, R., and Rivera, M. (2017). Tourism's potential to benefit the poor: a social accounting matrix model applied to Ecuador. *Tourism Economics, 23 (1).*

Croes, R., and Vanegas, M. (2008). Tourism and poverty alleviation: a co-integration analysis. *Journal of Travel Research, 47 (1).*

De Vita, G., and Kyaw, K.S. (2016). Tourism development and growth. *Annals of Tourism Research, 60.*

Di Meglio, G., and Gallego, J. (2016). Services for development? A Kaldorian approach, online reser.net/materiali/priloge/slo/95--di-meglio-gallego.pdf

Dongguk, N.K., Chai, H.S., and Pyun, J.H. (2016). The relationship among tourism, poverty, and economic development in developing countries: a panel data regression analysis. *Tourism Economics, 22 (6).*

Dritsakis, N. (2004). Tourism as a long-run economic growth factor: an empirical investigation for Greece using causality analysis. *Tourism Economics, 10 (3).*

Dritsakis, N. (2012). Tourism development and economic growth in seven Mediterranean countries: a panel data approach. *Tourism Economics, 18 (4).*

Du, D., Lew, A.A., and Ng, P.T. (2016). Tourism and economic growth. *Journal of Travel Research, 55 (4).*

Durbarry, R. (2004). Tourism and economic growth: the case of Mauritius. *Tourism Economics, 10 (4).*

Dwyer, L., Forsyth, P., and Spurr, R. (2004). Evaluating tourism's economic effects: new and old approaches. *Tourism Management*, 25 (3).

Dwyer, L., Forsyth, P., Spurr, R., and Ho, T. (2003). Contribution of tourism by origin market to a state economy: a multi-regional general equilibrium analysis. *Tourism Economics*, 9 (4).

Engle, R., and Granger, C. (1987). Cointegration and error correction: R, estimation, representation and testing. *Econometrica, 55.*

Eugenio-Martin, J., Morales, N., and Scarpa, R. (2004). Tourism and economic growth in Latin American countries: a panel data approach. *FEEM Working Paper No 26*, Fondazione Eni Enrico Mattei, Milan.

Fayissa, B., Nsiah, C., and Tadasse, B. (2008). Impact of tourism on economic growth and development in Africa. *Tourism Economics*, 14 (4).

Figini, P., and Vici, L. (2010). Tourism and growth in a cross section of countries. *Tourism Economics*, 16 (4).

Granger, C.W.J. (1969). Investigating causal relations by econometric models and cross-spectral methods. *Econometrica, 37 (3).*

Granger, C.W.J. (1988). Some recent developments in a concept of causality. *Journal of Econometrics, 39.*

Guicheney, J., and Rouzade, G. (2003). *Le tourisme dans les programmes européens.* Paris: La documentation Française.

Hachicha, N. (2003). Exports, export composition and growth: a simultaneous error-correction model for Tunisia. *International Economic Journal, 17 (1).*

Hawkins, D., and Mann, S. (2007). The world bank's role in tourism development. *Annals of Tourism Research*, 34 (2).

Helpman, E., and Krugman, P. (1985). *Market Structure and Foreign Trade.* Cambridge, MA: MIT Press.

Holzner, M. (2011). Tourism and economic development: the beach disease? *Tourism Management, 32.*

Ivanov, S. (2005). *Measurement of the macroeconomic impacts of tourism.* Unpublished PhD thesis, University of Economics – Varna, Bulgaria.

Ivanov, S., and Webster, C. (2007). Measuring the impact of tourism on economic growth. *Tourism Economics*, 13 (3).

Ivanov, S., and Webster, C. (2013). Tourism's contribution to economic growth: a global analysis for the first decade of the millennium. *Tourism Economics*, 19 (3).

Kaldor, N. (1966). *Causes of the Slow Rate of Economic Growth of the United Kingdom.* Cambridge: Cambridge University Press.

Katircioglu, S.T. (2009). Revisiting the tourism-led-growth hypothesis for Turkey using the bounds test and Johansen approach for cointegration. *Tourism Management, 30.*

Kim, H.J., Chen, M.-H., and Jang, S.C. (2006). Tourism expansion and economic development: the case of Taiwan. *Tourism Management, 27.*

Kim, N., Song, H., and Pyun, J.H. (2016). The relationship among tourism, poverty, and economic development in developing countries: a panel data regression analysis. *Tourism Economics*, 22 (6).

Lee, C.C., and Chang, C.P. (2008). Tourism development and economic growth, a closer look at panels. *Tourism Management*, 29 (1).

Li, H., Chen, J., Li, G., and Goh, S. (2016). Tourism and regional income inequality: evidence from China. *Annals of Tourism Research, 58.*

Marin, D. (1992). Is the export-led hypothesis valid for industrialized countries? *Review of Economics and Statistics, 74.*

Narayan, P. (2004). Economic impact of tourism on Fiji's economy: empirical evidence from the computable general equilibrium model. *Tourism Economics*, 10 (4).

Narayan, P., Narayan, S., Prasad, A., and Prasad, B.C. (2010). Tourism and economic growth: a panel data analysis for Pacific Island countries. *Tourism Economics*, 16 (1).

Nowak, J.J., Sahli, M., and Cortés-Jiménez, I. (2007). Tourism, capital good imports and economic growth, theory and evidence for Spain. *Tourism Economics, 13 (4)*.

Oh, C. (2005). The contribution of tourism development to economic growth in the Korean economy. *Tourism Management, 56*.

Pablo-Romero, M., and Molina, J. (2013). Tourism and economic growth: a review of empirical literature. *Tourism Management, 57*.

Perles-Ribes, J., Ramón-Rodríguez, A., Rubia, A., and Moreno-Izquierdo, L. (2017). Is the tourism-led growth hypothesis valid after the global economic and financial crisis? The case of Spain 1957–2014. *Tourism Management, 61*.

Proença, S., and Soukiazis, E. (2008). Tourism as an economic growth factor: a case study for Southern European countries. *Tourism Economics, 14 (4)*.

Schubert, F.S., Brida, J.G., and Risso, W.A. (2011). The impacts of international tourism demand on economic growth of small economies dependent on tourism. *Tourism Management, 32*.

Seetanah, B. (2011). Assessing the dynamic economic impact of tourism for island economies. *Annals of Tourism Research, 38 (1)*.

Shahzad, S.J.H., Shahbaz, M., and Ferrer, R. (2017). Tourism-led growth hypothesis in the top ten tourist destinations: new evidence using the quantile-on-quantile approach. *Tourism Management, 60*.

Surugiu, C., and Surugiu, M. (2013). Is the tourism sector supportive of economic growth? Empirical evidence on Romanian tourism. *Tourism Economics, 19*.

Tugcu, C.T. (2014). Tourism and economic growth nexus revised: a panel causality analysis for the case of the Mediterranean Region. *Tourism Management, 42*.

Vanhove, N. (2014). Tourism a strategic option for regional development of less developed regions. In H. Pechlaner. and E. Smeral (eds), *Tourism and Leisure: Current Issues and Perspectives of Development*. Wiesbaden: Springler Gabler.

Wooldridge, J. (2016). *Introductory Econometrics: A Modern Approach*, 6th edn. Boston: Cengage Learning.

Chapter 10

The economic impact of tourism

Introduction

Tourism can have a great impact on regions and, obviously, destinations. The dimension of tourism worldwide has an economical, social, cultural and environmental influence on tourism destinations (Mathieson and Wall, 1982), and the influence can be positive and/or negative. This chapter focusses on the economic impact. Some sociological, cultural and environmental impacts will be dealt with as cost elements here and in Chapter 12.

What are the main aspects of an economic impact? They can be classified into seven major groups:

1 Income generation
2 Employment generation
3 Tax revenue generation
4 Balance of payment effects
5 Improvement of the economic structure of a region
6 Encouragement of entrepreneurial activity
7 Economic disadvantages (see Chapter 8).

On the occasion of the twentieth anniversary of IAST (International Academy for the Study of Tourism), Frechtling and Smeral (2010) gave a broader significance to 'the economic impact of tourism':

> According to the tradition of tourism economic studies, 'the economic impact of tourism' is a term that covers one, some or all of the following economic changes resulting from the presence of visitors in an area, their activities or their expenditures:
>
> ● Business receipts
> ● Value added contribution to gross domestic or regional product
> ● Employment (jobs, persons employed)
> ● Labour earnings
> ● Other factor earnings (dividends, interest, rent, profits)
> ● Government tax revenue
> ● Other government revenue (e.g., user fees, fines, receipts of government enterprises)
> ● Distribution of income
> ● Government spending
> ● Externalities and public goods
> ● Multiplier effects on transactions, output, income, employment or government
> ● Revenue

- New business formation
- Real property and other asset values
- Business investment in plant and equipment
- Price levels
- Interest rates on borrowed funds and return on capital
- Foreign exchange rates
- Imports and exports
- International Balance of Payments.

This is a long list with all possible impacts of the presence of visitors in a destination. Some impacts are very direct, others are more indirect. All in all, this enumeration is not fundamentally different from the point of view of Mathiesen and Wall. When one talks of the economic impact of tourism, income and employment generation always come first. Six major factors govern the magnitude of the economic impact:

1 The nature of the main facility and its attractiveness
2 The volume and intensity of expenditure
3 The level of economic development in the destination
4 The size of the economic base of the destination
5 The degree to which tourist expenditures recirculate within the destination
6 The degree to which the destination has adjusted to the seasonality of tourist demand (Mathieson and Wall, 1982).

In tourism literature there always was a great interest in balance of payment effects. A special section of this chapter will show that these effects are much more than inbound and outbound expenditures.

In tourism it is quite common to speak of direct and indirect effects, and most measurement methods make a distinction between each group of effects. To allow a better understanding of those effects, the underlying mechanism will be explained. This brings us to the famous and magic 'tourism multiplier'. In fact, there is a whole variety of multipliers. Some clarification and demystification of the multiplier concept is necessary.

The main part of this chapter focusses on the measurement of income and employment generation. Special aspects concern tax-revenue generation, the impact of events, the qualitative aspects of employment in tourism, improvement of the economic structure of a region, and encouragement of entrepreneurial activity. Most of these aspects are interwoven with topics dealt with in other sections of this chapter and Chapter 8.

Balance of payments and tourism

For a long time, earning foreign currencies was considered to be the main benefit of international tourism. For many developing countries earning hard currencies has a vital significance, and tourism is a welcome source of the foreign currencies they need to finance necessary imports. The relative importance of tourism with respect to foreign currencies is far less important for developed countries.

Nevertheless, in many western countries in the 1950s and 1960s tourism was considered to influence the international liquidity position. It is not so long ago – in the 1960s – that France and the United Kingdom took the decision to restrict their citizens taking holidays abroad in order to support their balance of payments and, more particularly, to protect the value of their own national currency. This was a kind of tourism import quota. The impact of these restrictive measures could be serious for some destinations (e.g. the Belgian Coast suffered from the British and French decision in 1967), but the overall effect on the balance of payments for the generating countries was rather limited. Some governments overestimated the role of international tourism on the value of the local currency. To get a better understanding of the role of tourism in the international liquidity position, we must define the place of the sector in the balance of payments. This is not limited to the travel account. This section should make it clear.

The balance of payments is 'an account which shows a country's financial transactions with the rest of the world. It records inflows and outflows of currency' (Tribe, 1997). It is a statement that takes into account the value of all goods, all services, all foreign aid, all capital loans and (in former days) all gold coming in and going out, and the interrelations underlying all these items (Samuelson, 1964; Bull, 1995).

The structure of the balance of payments

The basic convention applied in constructing a balance of payments statement is that every recorded transaction is represented by two entries with equal values. One of these entries is designated a credit (positive), while the other is designated a debit (negative). In principle, the sum of all credit entries is identical to the sum of all debit entries, and the net balance of all entries in the statement is zero. In practice, however, the amounts frequently do not balance. Data for balance of payments estimated are often derived independently from different sources, and as a result there may be a summary net credit or net debit (i.e. net errors and omissions in the accounts). A separate entry, equal to that amount with the sign reversed, is then made to balance the accounts.

A balance of payments (IMF presentation) is composed of two main parts:

1   The current account, which includes

- goods
- invisibles or services (travel, transportation, other services)
- income (compensation of employees, investment income)
- current transfers (e.g. workers' remittances)

2   The capital and financial account, which refers to capital transfers and acquisitions/disposal of non-produced, non-financial assets, and financial assets and liabilities

- capital account (e.g. migrants' transfers, debt forgiveness)
- financial account
- direct investment abroad, direct investment in the country
- portfolio investment (assets, liabilities)
- financial derivatives
- other investments (trade credits, loans, etc.)
- reserve assets (e.g. foreign exchange).

As described above, there is generally a third and minor part: net errors and omissions.

Let us illustrate all this with a practical case – the balance of payments for Spain, a typical tourism destination. In 2015 Spain's current account was positive thanks to the services element (Table 10.1). Travel is a component of services. That is the reason why the tourism exports and imports are put into brackets. It is clear that the surplus on the current account is due to the travel account.

Table 10.2 shows the travel balance of EU countries, Australia, Japan, Canada, the USA and a number of developing island countries specializing in tourism. For a good interpretation of the ratio tourism exports/exports of goods and services (a/d), the term 'travel' covers business and personal travel (tourism) as well.

Table 10.1 The balance of payments for Spain, analytic presentation, 2015 (billions US$)

Source: IMF, *Balance of Payments Statistics Yearbook* (2016)

	Exports/credits	Imports/debits	Balance
A. Current account *			16
Goods	277	301	−24
Services	118	65	53
Travel	(56)	(17)	(39)
Primary income	58	59	−1
Secondary income	15	27	−12
B. Capital account*	9	1	8
C. Financial account*			22
Direct investment	58	25	33
Portfolio investment	96	85	11
Financial derivatives			−1
Other investment	24	44	20
D. Net errors and omissions			4
E. Reserves and related items			6

* Excludes components that have been classified in the categories of reserves and related items.

The share of tourism exports in total exports of goods and services of the countries in Table 10.2 varies in the EU countries from 27.6 per cent for Greece and 20.8 for Cyprus to only 2.1 per cent for the Netherlands and 1.4 per cent for Ireland. All Mediterranean countries show a share of 10 per cent or more except Italy (7.1 per cent) and France (6.0 per cent); all these countries register a positive net travel balance. Notice further the dominant position of tourism in island destination such as the Bahamas, Fiji and the Seychelles.

The net positive travel balance of the USA is striking; this is largely due to personal travel and not business travel. The weak US dollar in 2015 attracted many foreign tourists to the USA (see Chapter 3; Figure 3.1). US personal inbound tourism increased from $88 billion in 2008 to $162 billion in 2015.

A travel deficit in itself is not bad; it must be seen in the framework of international trade theories. Many factors can be responsible for such a deficit: tourism supply, the exchange rate, climate, and the economic health of the country. The thesis of a balance in the travel account, which is sometimes put forward, is a dangerous one. I am in agreement with Gray (1970) when he posits:

> The idea of the desirability of balance in travel account f.o.b. might seem to argue for balance in all sub accounts of the balance of payments or particularly in the current balance. That this is a spurious doctrine which would contravene all mechanisms whereby nations gain from the exchange of goods and services needs no detailed investigation here. Such a concept, carried out to its ultimate, would debar trade in all categories except those in which two-ways trade takes place and would be even more constraining than insistence upon bilateral balancing of trade with each individual trading partner.

Table 10.2 Travel balance in EU countries and reference countries, 2015

Source: IMF, *Balance of Payments Statistics Yearbook* (2016)

Country	Travel credit (a)	Travel debit (b)	Travel balance (c)	Goods and services credit (d)	(a/d) × 100
Austria	18	9	9	200	9.0
Belgium	12	19	−7	368	2.7
Luxembourg	4	3	1	113	3.5
Denmark	7	9	−2	158	4.4
Finland	3	5	−2	86	3.5
France	47	46	1	752	6.0
Germany	37	77	−40	1573	2.5
Greece	16	2	14	58	27.6
Ireland	5	6	−1	351	1.4
Italy	39	24	15	547	7.1
Netherlands	13	18	−5	619	2.1
Portugal	13	4	9	82	15.8
Spain	56	17	39	396	14.1
Sweden	11	14	−3	223	4.9
United Kingdom	45	63	−18	777	5.8
Cyprus	3	1	2	12	20.8
Czech Republic	6	9	−3	154	3.9
Estonia	1	1	0.0	18	7.8
Hungary	5	2	3	110	4.5
Latvia	1	1	0.0	16	6.2
Lithuania	1	1	0.0	31	3.2
Malta	2	1	1	14	10.0
Poland	10	8	2	236	4.2
Slovak Republic	2	2	0.0	81	2.5
Slovenia	3	1	2	33	7.6
Bulgaria	3	1	2	32	9.7
Romania	2	2	−0.0	72	2.8
Australia	29	23	6	238	12.1
Japan	25	16	9	784	3.2
Switzerland	16	16	0.0	416	4.2
Canada	16	−29	−13	489	2.8
United States	204	113	91	2261	9.0
Morocco	6	1	5	33	18.2

Country	Travel credit (a)	Travel debit (b)	Travel balance (c)	Goods and services credit (d)	(a/d) × 100
Mexico	18	10	8	404	4.4
Thailand	45	8	37	276	16.3
Bahamas	2	0.0	2	3	75.0
Fiji	1	0.0	1	2	33.3
Seychelles	0.0	0.0	0.0	1	30.8

* Travel excludes passenger services, which are included in transportation

The real tourism external account

As noticed earlier, the travel account is only part of the story (see also the TSA in Chapter 2). To find out what tourism is worth to a country, we should include all international transactions that are in some way necessary because of tourism (Baretje and Defert, 1972; Durand *et al.*, 1994). These include not only final tourism payments, but also international payments for goods and services needed for investment in and operation of the tourism industry. The result can be termed the 'real tourism external account'. Baretje and Defert were the first to develop such a real tourism account (see Table 10.3). Later the WTO (1988) developed a standard model (see Table 10.4). Both tables give a totally different view than the traditional balance of payments of the real significance of international tourism transactions. However, it is not so simple to estimate all the different items.

In line with the preceding paragraphs, Airey (1978) divided the effects of tourism on the balance of payments into three categories: primary, secondary and tertiary effects. The primary effect refers to tourism receipts from abroad and payments of residents abroad. Secondary effects are the effects on the balance of payments of the direct tourist expenditures as they percolate through the economy. Secondary effects, therefore, do not require the initial

Table 10.3 Tourism external account according to Baretje and Defert

Credit	Debit
Tourist receipts from abroad	Tourist expenditures abroad
Exports of goods	Imports of goods (food and equipment)
Transportation (payments by foreign companies)	Transportation (payments to foreign companies)
Foreign tourism investments	Tourist investment abroad
Dividends, interest and profit received	Dividends, interest and profit paid out
Training of foreign staff	Payments for training abroad
Income from national workers abroad	Salaries repatriated abroad
Promotion	Promotion
Other services	Other services
Balance: deficit	Balance: surplus

> **Table 10.4** A model of a real tourism external account
>
> Source: Adapted from WTO (1988)

Tourism accounts	Credit	Debit	Balance
A. Service accounts			
A.1. international travel			
1. pleasure			
2. professional			
3. other purposes			
A.2. tourism services			
1. restaurants, bars, cafés			
2. hotels, etc.			
3. international transport			
4. other tourism services			
B. Income accounts			
B.1. earnings from work in tourism			
B.2. earnings from tourism investments			
C. Transfer accounts			
C.1. private tourism sector			
C.2. public tourism sector			
I. Current account balance (A + B + C)			
D. Capital account			
D.1. direct tourism investment			
D.2. portfolio tourism investment			
D.3. investment in tourism property (real estate)			
D.4. other tourism investment			
D.5. commercial credits related to tourism			
D.6. loans to tourism enterprises			
II. Basic tourism balance = (I + D)			

visitor expenditure to have taken place in another country (Mathieson and Wall, 1982). They may appear in a number of different forms:

- Direct secondary effects (import hotels, marketing expenditure abroad, dividend payments to overseas investors, etc.)
- Indirect secondary effects (imports of subcontractors)
- Induced secondary effects (expenditures permeate through the economy and this creates a multiplier effect).

Tertiary effects are flows of currency not initiated by tourist expenditures (purchase of travellers' requisites, export stimulus of foreign products – such as the purchase of ouzo at home after a visit to Greece). The distinction between primary, secondary and tertiary effects is interesting from the theoretical point of view, but difficult to identify in practice.

Finally, the travel account is drawn up according to two possible approaches. The first is the 'survey method', and is based on periodic surveys to measure tourist receipts and expenditures. This is the case in the UK and the USA. France, Germany and many other European countries, however, practise the *méthode bancaire* or bank method (Durand *et al.*, 1994). This method is based on financial regulations and exchange figures from banks and other financial institutions (Bull, 1995). Both methods have pros and cons, but the bank method has the big disadvantage that the purpose of a financial transaction is not always clear. Furthermore, in a monetary zone such as the eurozone there are no longer exchange transactions by the individual tourist.

The magic tourism multiplier

The basics of the tourism multiplier

Mathieson and Wall (1982) define the tourist multiplier 'as a number by which initial tourist expenditure must be multiplied in order to obtain the total cumulative income effect for a specific time period'. This is a dangerous definition, as it is presented as a black box process. In reality there is a variation in multiplier values; the income multiplier is one of them. A more precise description can be found in Fletcher and Archer (1992). It is based upon the recognition that the various sectors that make up the economy are interdependent. In addition to purchasing primary inputs such as labour, imports, etc., each sector will purchase intermediate goods produced by other establishments within the local economy. Therefore, any autonomous change in the level of final demand (domestic expenditures, inbound tourism or investments) will not only affect the industry that produces that final good, but also that industry's suppliers and suppliers' suppliers, etc.

Owing to this sector interdependence, any change in final demand will bring about a change in the economy's level of output, income employment and government revenue. The term 'multiplier' refers to the ratio of the change in one of the above variables to the change in final demand that brought it about. We can illustrate the mechanism with the following scheme (see Figure 10.1).

Taking the expenditure in a hotel as a starting point, to whom does this expenditure accrue? One part creates value added or factor remuneration in the hotel. It is direct income within the region concerned. A second part leads to local business transactions – a hotelier must restock inventories to provide for future sales (bread, meat, vegetables, fruit, etc.). A third part of the expenditure is used to pay profit taxes, local taxes, etc. to local, regional or national governments. A fourth part is spent on leakages such as imports of goods (e.g. whisky) and payment of profits to people and organizations outside the region or country.

Purchases of meat, bread and vegetables provoke, in turn, the same above-mentioned effects – income creation, intermediate purchases, public transfers and import leakages – for the butcher, the baker and the farmer. This process continues with a third and a fourth round. Following each round, the national or regional effects become smaller. The income created in successive rounds is called the indirect income, and the degree of magnitude of these indirect effects is governed by the extent to which business firms in the nation or region supply each other with goods.

However, a second derived impact can be noted. The more wages and profits (direct and indirect) due to the hotel expenditure rise, the more consumer expenditure increases – and this provides a further impetus to economic activity. Additional business turnover occurs, and this generates income. These are the so-called induced effects.

The indirect and induced effects together (called secondary effects – but note that this must not be confused with secondary expenditure) can be quite considerable in the absence of

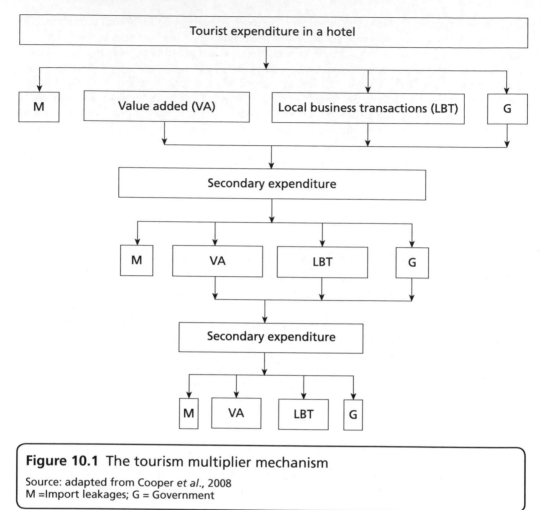

Figure 10.1 The tourism multiplier mechanism

Source: adapted from Cooper et al., 2008
M =Import leakages; G = Government

important leakages, such as savings (assuming that sufficient resources are available). In Figure 10.1, indirect and induced effects are presented together.

To summarize, there are three different effects:

1 The direct effect of a change in final demand refers to first-round effects.
2 The indirect effect recognizes the need for an industry – subject to a change in final demand for its product – to make purchases from other industries within an economy in order to produce its output.
3 The induced effect occurs as income levels rise throughout the economy as a result of the initial change in final demand, and a portion of the increased income is re-spent on final goods produced within the local economy. This additional local expenditure, arising from increased income, will generate further repercussive effects. The addition to total output, income, employment and government revenue caused by this re-spending of local income is known as the induced effect.

Two important observations should be made. First, the supplying firms should have enough resources and spare factors of production. (See Computable General Equilibrium models, page 299.) Secondly, there are few arguments to suggest that induced effects in tourism are different from the same effects in other sectors. The consumer behaviour of tourism earners cannot be so different from that of textile earners or those in other economic sectors.

There are several factors which determine the size of the multiplier. The first factor is the size of the destination – the smaller the size of the region, the bigger the leakages. The second factor concerns inter-sector linkages. A mono structure, by definition, leads to high imports (see next section). This brings us to the third factor, or possible leakages. There are three well-known leakages:

1 The saving quota of the population of the destination
2 The import quota, or the share of tourism expenditure that is spent to imported products
3 The tax quota, or the share going to the public sector.

A fourth possible factor is the supply constraints in the economy (see page 284).

Types of multipliers

There is a lot of confusion about the term 'tourism multiplier'. In reality there are several types, each with its own meaning.

The most interesting is the *tourism income multiplier* (TIM). It shows the relationship between an additional unit of tourist spending and the changes that result in the level of income in the economy. However, in theory, any income accruing to non-nationals resident in the area is usually extracted from the sum.

With respect to the income multiplier, a further distinction is made between the orthodox income multiplier (also called 'ratio' multiplier) and the unorthodox income multiplier (see Mathieson and Wall, 1982; De Brabander, 1992; Mihalic, 2002). For both income multipliers, two types are distinguished:

1 Orthodox income multipliers

   type I – (direct + indirect income)/direct income
   type II – (direct + indirect + induced income)/direct income

2 Unorthodox income multipliers

   type I – (direct + indirect income)/change in final demand (additional expenditures)
   type II – (direct + indirect + induced income)/change in final demand (additional unit of spending).

These orthodox multipliers are of little value, although they can give an idea of the degree of internal linkages in the local economy. Much more emphasis should be given to the two types of unorthodox income multipliers. The multiplier with the greatest practical value and that makes the most sense is undoubtedly the *unorthodox income multiplier type I*.

Table 10.5 lists the values of the orthodox and unorthodox multipliers of type II of a number of sources; these statistics give an idea of the great differences in function of the destination and accommodation forms.

Looking at Table 10.5, an expenditure of 100 euros in Edinburgh leads to a direct income of only 19 euros, and the sum of direct, indirect and induced effects amounts to 28 euros; these effects are of course higher from the point of view of Scotland or the United Kingdom – the larger the region, the lower the leakages. Notice the very different effects per accommodation type.

It is obvious from Table 10.5 that the larger the area, the higher the corresponding tourism multiplier value. The value of the multiplier is determined by the structure of the economy, the inter-sector relations, the import content, and the nature of the tourism product, etc.

Table 10.5 Values of various type II multipliers

	Direct income	Orthodox multiplier	Unorthodox multiplier
Gwynedd case (Archer et al., 1974)			
● Hotel	0.23	1.43	0.32
● Bed and breakfast	0.57	1.10	0.63
● Caravan	0.14	1.49	0.21
● Composite	–	1.34	0.37
Seychelles (Archer)	0.34	2.87	0.88
Edinburgh (Vaughan, 1977)			
● Hotel	0.20	1.43	0.29
● Bed and breakfast	0.14	1.80	0.26
● Caravan	0.16	1.38	0.22
● Composite	0.19	1.47	0.28
Flanders (Vanhove, 1993 – type I)			
● Composite	–	1.30	0.57
Antwerp province (Yzewijn and De Brabander, 1989 – type I)	–	1.36	0.57

As stated above, the greatest interest is in the unorthodox income multiplier of the type I (direct + indirect income creation)/tourist expenditure. With the knowledge of the expenditure and the tourism income multiplier, direct and indirect income creation can be estimated. The crucial point is the knowledge of TIM, which is unknown. However, TIM-values can sometimes be used for countries and/or destinations with similar products and general economic circumstances.

One precaution should be mentioned. There is quite often confusion between the terms 'multiplier' and 'multiplicand'. The quantity of expenditure is basically the multiplicand. However, not all the expenditure is available to create income in the destination; some tourist expenditure never enters the economy at all (e.g. a rented camper van in Spain, but the camper van owner lives in Paris and thus the rental charges do not enter Spain). The same applies to package tours; a large proportion of the money paid by the holidaymaker accrues to airlines from outside the destination.

A second multiplier is the *employment multiplier*. This multiplier describes either the ratio of the direct and indirect (secondary) employment generated by additional tourism expenditure to the direct employment alone, or the amount of employment generated by a given amount of tourist spending. As with the income multiplier, a distinction can be made between orthodox and unorthodox types. The tourism sector is characterized by many part-time workers, and therefore all jobs should be converted into full-time equivalent job opportunities.

Any tourism employment multiplier starts from three assumptions:

1 Each productive sector fully utilizes its current labour force
2 There is spare capacity in the labour force
3 There is no change in the capital/labour mix.

The next two multipliers are very similar to each other. Because most tourism products are not 'stocks', the terms 'sales' and 'output multipliers' are more or less synonyms.

The sales or transactions multiplier measures the effect of an extra unit of tourist spending on economic activity within the economy; the multiplier relates tourism expenditure to the increase in business turnover that it creates. The *output multiplier* relates a unit of tourist spending to the resultant increase in the level of output in the economy (this is very similar to the sales multiplier; see Fletcher and Archer, 1992). While the sales multiplier considers only the level of the sales that result from the direct and secondary effects of tourism spending, the output multiplier takes into account both the levels of sales and any real changes that take place in the level of stocks. The sales multiplier in the Archer study for the county of Gwynedd, North Wales, was 1.46; the corresponding income multiplier was 0.32 (Archer, 1991). A sales multiplier, after all, is not of such great importance. Indeed, a clear distinction should be made between value added and turnover; value added (income creation) is a part of turnover creation. A destination is only interested in the generated value added and employment. However, during the 1960s the turnover effect of Clement (1961) was considered to be the real multiplier in many tourism circles. Clement's transaction multiplier was equal to 3.48, and several tourism experts and politicians used this multiplier whether it was relevant or not. The strangest thing was that in many tourism circles, this was considered to be the same in all countries and all destinations.

The government revenue multiplier demonstrates how much government revenue is created by each additional unit of tourist expenditure (taxes, charges, etc., less grants).

The import multiplier demonstrates the value of imported goods and services associated with each additional unit of tourist expenditure.

It must be clear that the various types of multipliers are intrinsically linked. Let us take an example:

Tourist expenditure	€1,000
Output generation	€2,500
Direct income generation	€350
Indirect income generation	€200
Induced income generation	€200

In this case, the Keynesian multiplier (see below) is 0.75, the ratio multiplier (total income generated to direct income) equals 2.14, and the output multiplier is 2.5.

How can the TIM values be defined?

This section is devoted to the income multiplier – the orthodox multiplier and the unorthodox multiplier (see Bull, 1995). The traditional Keynesian multiplier formula is equal to:

$$k = \frac{1}{1 - c + m} = \frac{1}{1 - MPC} \tag{10.1}$$

where

k = income multiplier
MPC = marginal propensity to consume
1 = the additional unit of tourism expenditure (leakages are the proportion of this expenditure which goes into savings (1 − c) and imports (m))

In equation (10.1) we assume that all the original tourism expenditure turned straight into direct and indirect income. This is not always the case. Account must be taken not only of the savings quota, but also of the taxation on income and the expenditure on imports.

These are two additional leakages from extra local consumption-income circulation. Equation (10.1) therefore becomes:

$$k = \frac{L}{MTR + MPS + \{[1 - MTR - MPS]MPM\}}$$ (10.2)

where

MTR = marginal tax rate
MPM = marginal propensity to import

With an MPS value of 20 per cent; an MTR equal to 30 per cent and an MPM on consumption expenditure equal to one-third, the multiplier k equals 1.5.

So far the assumption has been that all the original tourism expenditure turned directly into direct and indirect income, but this may not be the case. Very often some of the food and drink in a hotel is imported. There is even tourist expenditure that never enters the economy – for example, payments for transport operated by foreign carriers, foreign-owned lodging, etc. In this case, equation (10.2) becomes:

$$k = \frac{1 - L}{MTR + MPS + \{[1 - MTR - MPS]MPM\}}$$ (10.3)

or

$$k = \frac{1 - L}{\text{leakages}}$$

where L = the immediate leakage attributable to tourist spending not entering the economy, or the need to import goods, services and factors to provide directly for tourists' needs.

With the same parameters as for equation (10.2) and L equal to 40 per cent, the tourism multiplier k is not higher than 0.9.

The developed equation (10.3) is far too simplistic, and is unable to measure variations in the form and magnitude of sectoral linkages and leakages out of the destination's economy during each round of transactions (Cooper et al., 2008). Cooper et al. posit that 'Even the most complex and comprehensive Keynesian models developed for some studies are unable to provide the level of detail that is required for policy making and planning'. Therefore they suggest using *ad hoc* models.

Ad hoc models

Ad hoc models are similar in principle to the Keynesian approach. They are suited to regional analysis, where it may be impractical or too expensive to undertake a full input–output analysis.

The simplest *ad hoc* model is shown in equation (10.4):

$$A \cdot \frac{1}{1 - BC}$$ (10.4)

where

A = the proportion of additional tourist expenditure remaining in the economy after first-round leakages – i.e. A equals the (1 – L) expression in the Keynesian model
B = the propensity of the local people to consume in the local economy
C = the proportion of expenditure by local people that accrues as income in the local economy

More advanced models have been developed to calculate tourist multipliers to estimate the effect of expenditure on income and employment. One of these models was developed by Archer and Owen (1971):

$$\sum_{j=1}^{N}\sum_{i=1}^{n}Q_{j}K_{ji}V_{i}\cdot\frac{1}{1-c\sum_{i=1}^{n}X_{i}Z_{i}V_{i}} \tag{10.5}$$

where the first part of equation (10.5) is direct and indirect income generated:

j = each category of tourists, j = 1 to n
i = each type of business establishment, i = 1 to n
Q_{j} = the proportion of total tourist expenditure spent by the jth type of tourist
K_{ji} = the proportion of expenditure by the jth type of tourist in the ith category of business
V_{i} = direct and indirect income generated by unit of expenditure by the ith type of business

and the second part includes the additional income generated by re-spending of factor earnings by the resident population:

X_{i} = the proportion of total consumer expenditure by the residents of the area in the ith type of business
Z_{i} = the proportion of X_{i} that takes place within the area
c = the marginal propensity to consume

The multiplier and input–output analysis

Input–output analysis provides a general equilibrium approach to measuring economic impacts, rather than the partial equilibrium approach used in the methods discussed above. The input–output approach is very often used to estimate the income and employment generation; the corresponding multiplier is a derived product. It can be considered to be the best method to estimate income and employment multipliers. Input–output analysis is concerned with interrelations arising from production; the main function of inter-industry accounts is to trace the flow of goods and services from one production sector to another. Table 10.6 shows the structure of a traditional input–output table. This table, which is called a transactions matrix, covers all the goods and services produced in an economy (country, region, destination). It is distinguished by the fact that production activities are grouped together into a number of sectors. Tables in actual use range in size from about 25 to 100 or more productive sectors.

Each sector appears in the accounting system twice, as a producer of outputs (by row) and as a user of inputs (by column). The elements in each row of the table show the disposition of the output of that sector during the given accounting period. It is composed of two parts: the intermediate deliveries (x_{12} shows the deliveries from sector 1 to sector 2), and the final use. With respect to tourism, the final use relates to domestic consumption, inbound tourism (or exports), tourism investment and government expenditures.

The role of a sector as a purchaser of inputs is shown in a column. Each column is composed of three elements:

1 Purchases from other sectors (e.g. x_{12} means that sector 2 purchases from sector 1)
2 Primary inputs (wages, capital returns, taxes); this comprises the value added of the sector
3 Imports.

Table 10.6 A basic input–output table

Sales to	Intermediate demand sectors					Final demand Y	Output
	1	2	3	4	... n		
Purchases from							
Sector 1	X_{11}	X_{12}	X_{13}	X_{14}	... X_{1n}	Y_1	X_1
Sector 2	X_{21}	X_{22}	X_{23}	X_{24}	... X_{2n}	Y_2	X_2
Sector 3	X_{31}	X_{32}	X_{33}	X_{34}	... X_{3n}	Y_3	X_3
Sector 4	X_{41}	X_{42}	X_{43}	X_{44}	... X_{4n}	Y_4	X_4
...	...	...	...	...	...	...	...
...	...	...	...	...	...	...	...
Sector n	X_{n1}	X_{n2}	X_{n3}	X_{n4}	... X_{nn}	Y_n	X_n
Remuneration of factor labour	W_1	W_2	W_3	W_4	... W_n	W	W
Profits/dividends	P_1	P_2	P_3	P_4	... P_n	P	P
Taxes	T_1	T_2	T_3	T_4	... T_n	T	T
Imports	M_1	M_2	M_3	M_4	... M_n	M	M
Total inputs	X_1	X_2	X_3	X_4	... X_n		X

where:
x_{ji} = all intermediate deliveries
X = output
Y = final demand composed of private consumption, investment, government expenditure and exports
M = imports

Transactions are usually recorded at the producer's price rather than at the purchaser's cost, which means that trade and transport margins are ascribed to the using sectors. The separation between intermediate and final use and between produced and primary inputs leads to four types of transactions, which are shown in four sections of Table 10.6.

● Section 1 comprises the main part of the inter-sector accounts. Each entry xij indicates the amount of commodity i used by sector j.
● Section 2 contains the final use of produced goods and services; in practice broken down by major types of use (consumption, investment, export and government).
● Section 3 (the bottom left-hand section) shows each sector's purchases of primary inputs (W, P and T) and imported goods and services.
● Section 4 contains the direct input of primary factors to final use (e.g. government employment and domestic service).

It is very important to notice that the 'tourism sector' is never registered as a single sector in an input–output table; tourism consumption is spread over several sectors (see Chapter 1). The relationship between the different parts of an input–output table can be written in algebraic terms (to ease the presentation, all types of final demand are represented by a column vector Y):

$$X = AX + Y \qquad (10.6)$$

$$X - AX = Y$$

$$(I - A)X = Y$$

$$X = (I - A)^{-1}Y$$

$$\Delta X = (I - A)^{-1}\Delta Y \tag{10.7}$$

where

X = vector of total sales of each sector
Y = vector of final demand
A = a matrix of inter-sector transactions and $(I - A)^{-1}$ is the inverse matrix of the transaction coefficients
I = unit matrix

A change in the level of Y (ΔY) will create an increase in the level of activity in the economy (ΔX) (see output multiplier). With respect to the income multiplier, we are only interested in income generation.

Direct income creation can be calculated using the formula:

$$Y_d = \hat{B}_k \cdot b \tag{10.8}$$

where

Y_d = direct income generation
$\hat{B}_k$ = diagonal matrix of income coefficients (value added at market prices sector j/ production value sector j)
b = column vector of tourist expenditure after elimination of imports and VAT.

In the next step, the indirect income generation is calculated:

$$Y_t = \hat{B}_k (1 - A)^{-1} \cdot b \tag{10.9}$$

where

Y_t = direct and indirect income creation
$(1 - A)^{-1}$ = inverse matrix

Indirect income generation is the result of subtracting direct income (equation 10.8) from the total income generation (equation 10.9).

Now we have all the ingredients to calculate the orthodox and unorthodox income multiplier type I. We have only to apply the definition. To avoid any misunderstanding, income is sometimes only one part of the total value added; in most cases it comprises all items of value added. The same exercise can be applied for all aspects of value added and tax revenue. For the Seychelles, Archer calculated an average tourism multiplier for all value added components (direct + indirect + induced) of 0.88; the government revenue amounted to 0.28 per cent of tourism expenditure.

It is important to be aware that Table 10.6 and the above-mentioned formulae are a simplification of a normal presentation and application of input–output analysis. Nevertheless, they give the basic principles. More refined methodology is beyond the scope of this publication.

An example of the use of input–output analysis to calculate the income and employment multiplier, can be found in Table 10.7. It is an application by the Austrian Institute of Economic Research applied to Austria (Smeral, 2011).

This table is interesting for two reasons. Firstly, the value added multiplier (an unorthodox income multiplier) is quite high (0.78) and higher than the one of three other components of

Table 10.7 Value added and employment multipliers for Austria for the year 2005

Source: WIFO – Smeral (2011)

Sector	Value added multipliers per unit of net expenditure	Employment multipliers per €100,000 net expenditure*
Residents' consumption	0.71	1.1
Non-residents' consumption (tourists)	0.78	1.5
Government	0.89	1.6
Equipment investments	0.57	0.9
Exports	0.54	0.8

*= without VAT and imports

the final demand. Secondly, the employment multiplier amounts to 1.5 or one job is created per €100,000 net tourism expenditure. The employment multiplier resulting from tourism demand is higher than the multipliers of most other components of final demand.

Some remarks

Additional production of tourism services requires the commitment of resources that could otherwise be used for alternative activities (Cooper *et al.*, 2008). If labour is in abundance, there is no problem. The situation changes when labour or other resources are not abundant (see page 295, Computable General Equilibrium models). In the latter case, meeting the tourists' demands may involve the transfer of labour from other activities to the tourism sector. This provokes an opportunity cost or income foregone (see Chapter 12) which is often not considered in the estimation of the economic impact (Archer, 1991). When there is a real shortage, there may be the need to import labour. This will result in higher import leakages, as income earned from this imported labour may, in part, be repatriated. There can be a similar situation with the use of capital resources.

A second comment is linked to the first. It concerns the displacement effect. According to Cooper *et al.* displacement can take place when tourism development occurs at the expense of other economic activities and is referred to as the opportunity cost of the development. Displacement is more commonly referred to when a new tourism investment is seen to take away tourism demand from existing firms – for example, a successful big new hotel complex may reduce the turnover of existing hotels. As a consequence, the overall tourism activity may not (or may only partly) have increased (see Chapter 12).

A third remark is of a completely different nature. The use of input–output analysis poses the problem of insufficient correspondence between the sector in an input–output table and the data derived from visitor expenditure surveys. As a consequence, the tourist expenditure has to be deconstructed to fit the sectors defined in the existing input–output table. A loss of accuracy is the logical result.

A fourth comment concerns the static character of most multiplier methods. They assume that production and consumption functions are linear, and that inter-sector expenditure patterns are stable (Cooper *et al.*, 2008). Furthermore, they assume that all sectors are able to respond to additional demand (supply capacity condition; availability of factor resources). The models are also based on constant relative prices, and they suppose no change in technology (Archer, 1991).

It must be clear that multiplier analysis does not measure the long-term benefits for a destination due to the growth of tourism (Archer, 1991; Cooper *et al.*, 2008).

As a last remark we want to avoid any confusion between linkage analysis and tourism impact analysis. The first analysis is a complement to the second (Cai *et al.*, 2006). Linkage analysis examines the strengths of the inter-sectoral forward (FL) and backward relationships (BL) between the tourism sector and the non-tourism industries. The FL measures the relative importance of the tourism sector as supplier to all other industries. The BL measures its relative importance as demander. The Leontief supply-driven multiplier is considered as the measure for backward linkage whereas the Ghosh supply-driven multiplier is a measure of forward linkage. The latter is based on a matrix with output coefficients (distribution coefficients) and a primary input vector (W = V $(1-S)^{-1}$; S is a matrix with output coefficients). Directly applying conventional linkage analysis to tourism is not straightforward because tourism in not an industry in an input–output table. Cai *et al.* developed an adapted methodology to apply the linkage analysis and applied it to Hawaii.

Measurement of income generation

The preceding section is a good introduction to measuring the impact of tourism on income. The two basic driving forces for the tourism sector are expenditure and investment, both of which are essential elements of final demand in an input–output table. Receipts in foreign exchange are a component of expenditure, and as such the export element of final demand. Foreign exchange earnings in tourism can be of great importance in certain countries – Spain is a good example.

The key elements of the final demand, tourism expenditure (tourism export included) and tourism investment, are the basis of two major benefits: income and employment. In other words, what does tourism create in terms of income and employment generation? As such, there is a relationship between the four key variables in the tourism sector: expenditure and investment on the one side, and income and employment on the other. Between these four key variables there are special links. For example, investments depend on the expenditure in the present and the future. In turn, investments can stimulate expenditure. There is also a linkage of the key components with other aggregates. Government receipts in tourism are a derivative of expenditure and investments. In principle, each economic activity yields returns to the public sector, such as direct taxes, VAT, company taxes, social security receipts, etc. These returns are a function of the key variables, as is the case for any other economic sector.

To measure income generation, different methods have been developed. Depending on the methods applied and the specification of income components, income generation can be defined in terms of GDP, NNI (Net National Income), and income of the different production factors (e.g. labour earnings). The most commonly applied methods are:

- The national accounts method (simplified)
- The Henderson–Cousins method
- The input–output approach
- The multiplier method
- The Computable General Equilibrium (CGE) models.

Each of these methods has pros and cons; the choice of a method is very often influenced by the availability of data or instruments (e.g. an input–output table for the destination) and the financial resources. The best-performing method is undoubtedly input–output analysis. However, all methods start from expenditure and investments, and all but one are related to the multiplier mechanism.

All these methods have one drawback in common: they assume that factors of production (such as labour) flow freely to the tourism sector. These resources are assumed not to be used elsewhere (see Chapter 12 and Dwyer *et al.*, 2004). This is the case in most developing countries. In destinations where there is full employment, the net effect can be lower. This applies to all possible economic effects, such as income, value added and employment. Therefore Dwyer *et al.* suggest the use of Computable General Equilibrium (CGE) models. At the end of this chapter a special section deals with CGE models.

The national accounts method (simplified)

The national accounts method is used when the destination cannot make use of an up-to-date input–output table and does not have a TSA. In this case, a 'simplified national accounts method' can be a substitute. The application requires several steps:

1 The available expenditure data are broken down into subgroups which are very close to sectors of the national accounts, such as food, drinks, accommodation, transport, etc.
2 VAT is eliminated from the gross receipts and these adjusted expenditures are the basis to measure the gross value added creation for each subgroup, based on ratios derived from national accounts.
3 Indirect income generation is the next step.

As we saw in the previous section, indirect value added generation is linked to intermediate deliveries. The latter are equal to:

$$\text{Intermediate deliveries} = \text{turnover} - \text{VAT} - (\text{imports} + \text{direct income}) \qquad (10.10)$$

All the elements of this equation are known or can be derived via national accounts ratios. Intermediate deliveries in turn are composed of value added, imports and inter-sector deliveries, and can be measured via average national accounts ratios. This provides the first round indirect value added, and first round intermediate deliveries. The latter are the starting point of second, third, fourth and possibly fifth rounds. We have only to total all the calculated indirect value added in the successive rounds to obtain the total indirect value added. Gross value added (direct and indirect) less depreciation provides us with net value added. This method is not the most refined one, but it is after all logical in its conception, and is quite simple to apply.

The Henderson–Cousins method

The original version of this method was developed by Archer and Owen (1971) and improved by Henderson and Cousins (1975) in the well-known Greater Tayside study. The method requires a tremendous volume of fieldwork, and is therefore only applicable for small destinations.

The starting point of this method is an injection of tourist expenditure. It has the further practical advantage that the multiplicand depends upon the number of days spent in the destination by tourists and their daily expenditure, the number and size of which are estimable by survey methods. The business unit is taken as the basic element of this analysis, and the objective is to measure for each business the contribution to regional income (and employment) out of receipts from tourism. Furthermore, the method is built on the principles of the tourism multiplier.

The multiplier process may be expressed as follows:

$$k = a + b + c \qquad (10.11)$$

where

k = multiplier
a = direct regional income generation per € of tourist expenditure, i.e. factor incomes generated within businesses which directly receive tourist expenditure

b = indirect regional income generation per € of tourist expenditure, i.e. factor incomes generated in other businesses whose turnover is indirectly augmented with purchases made by the original businesses

c = induced regional income generation per € of tourist expenditure, i.e. factor incomes generated as the result of expenditure by residents of the region whose income has previously been increased through direct or indirect income generated by tourism

For a better understanding, the following may be helpful:

*j*th type of tourist	*i*th type of business		
	Accommodation	Restaurant	Shopping
Hotel			
Camping			
Holiday village			
Rented apartment			

More formally:

$$a = \sum_{j=1}^{n}\sum_{i=1}^{n} K_{ji} Y_{di} \tag{10.12}$$

where

a = direct regional income generation

K_{ji} = the proportion of €1 expenditure spent by the jth type of tourist in each type of business

Y_{di} = the increase in factor incomes in the region per €1 of turnover to the ith type of business generated exclusively within that type of business which directly receives tourist expenditure

If b = indirect regional income generation:

$$b = \sum_{j=1}^{n}\sum_{i=1}^{n} K_{ji} (Y_i - Y_{di}) \tag{10.13}$$

where Y_i = the increase in factor incomes per €1 of turnover to the ith type of business generated within that type of business and in all other types which participate in the subsequent flow of transactions

If c = induced income generation:

$$c = (a + b) \frac{1}{1 - L \sum_{i}^{n} X_i Z_i Y_i} \tag{10.14}$$

where

L = average propensity to consume with disposable income (see former c in Keynesian expression)

X_i = the proportion of total consumer spending by residents in the ith type of business

Z_i = the proportion of consumer spending by residents in the ith type of business within the region

The complete model to measure regional income generation can be expressed as follows:

$$G_r = \sum_{j=1}^{n}\sum_{i=1}^{n} N_j Q_j K_{ji} Y_i \left(\frac{1}{1 - L \sum_{i=1}^{n} X_i Z_i Y_i} \right) \tag{10.15}$$

where

G_r = total income generation
N_j = the numbers of days in the region spent by the jth type of tourist
Q_j = the total daily expenditure by the jth type of tourist.
N_j and Q_j together represent the multiplicand, while the remainder of the expression specifies the consequent multiplier

The input–output approach

Earlier in this chapter we dealt with the structure of an input–output table and how it can be used to measure various multipliers. However, the main function of input–output analysis with respect to tourism is to calculate the value added and employment generation.

In the application of the procedure, five steps are crucial:

1 First, determine whether the destination has an up-to date input–output table or a useful reference table. This is a preliminary condition.
2 Next, the final demand or net tourism expenditure must be defined – this implies corrections for VAT and imports.
3 The tourism expenditure must then be broken down in such a way that the expenditure can be attributed to the sectors contained in the available input–output. This step is far from straightforward. Tourism expenditure is spread over different sectors, and several typical tourism sub-sectors (such as accommodation and retail trade) are not used in national input–output tables. Furthermore, the transactions are expressed in producers' prices and not market prices. On the other hand, tourist expenditure is defined in market prices. The differences between consumption price and producers' prices are called distribution margins (distribution and transport). Therefore it is necessary to define the corresponding distribution margins for each product and/or service group. The margins are in fact the output of the retail trade and transport sectors, and the corresponding amounts should therefore be attributed to the retail trade and different transport sectors. In a number of cases, the distribution margin is equal to zero. This applies when the producing sector sells directly to the consumer (e.g. repair of cars, hotel and restaurant).
4 Direct income generation is estimated by multiplying the real production of the different sectors with the corresponding income coefficient, defined as NVA_{mpj}/P_j. In input–output notation:

$$Y^d = \hat{B}_k \cdot b \tag{10.16}$$

where

NVA_{mpj} = net value added at market prices of sector j
P_j = output sector j
Y^d = direct income generation
$\hat{B}$ = diagonal matrix of income coefficients
b = column vector of tourist expenditure (final demand f_j) after elimination of imports and VAT

$$b_j = f_j - f_j^{imp} - VAT_j \tag{10.17}$$

5 Next, the indirect income generation is estimated:

$$Y^t = \hat{B}_k (1 - A^n)^{-1} \cdot b \tag{10.18}$$

where

Y^t = direct + indirect income creation
$(1 - A^n)^{-1}$ = inverse matrix based on national inter-sector relations

To obtain the indirect income generation, Y^d is subtracted from Y^t.

It is possible to go one step further and relate the induced effects. This is possible by including an additional column and row in the matrix of production coefficients. This column is that part of the final demand that constitutes consumer expenditure; the row is income payments to the personal sector (Archer and Fletcher, 1996).

The multiplier method

The final method is the multiplier method. This consists of a simple multiplication of tourism expenditure with the income multiplier (type II). The problem is that this multiplier is unknown. Sometimes, the multiplier of a similar region is applied. This can only be justified when the economic structure of the reference region is very similar to and of the same size as the region concerned. However, such a situation is exceptional, and the result can only be a very approximate estimation of the income generation.

Measurement of employment generation

Employment is, together with income generation, the most important benefit of tourism development. The measurement of the employment impact can be divided into two groups:

1   The supply approach

-   tourism-related sectors
-   minimum requirement method

2   The demand approach

-   the national accounts method
-   the Henderson–Cousins method
-   the input–output approach
-   the multiplier method.

The application of these approaches leads to a number of full-time job equivalents, either employed or self-employed.

The supply approach

In tourism research, two supply approaches are quite often applied. The first can be called 'employment in tourism-related sectors', and is simply an addition of the employment (self-employed and employee) in sectors that are considered to be tourism-related, such as accommodation, restaurant, cafés, etc. The result is an overestimation of the number of jobs. Many of the firms working in these sectors supply not only tourists but also, and sometimes almost only, local residents. Therefore this method has neither a scientific nor a practical value.

The second supply approach, the minimum requirement method, can be more relevant, particularly in smaller areas or destinations. It should be implemented in different steps. First, the relevant sectors for tourism must be defined. The choice of the sectors is less important (e.g. retail trade) than in the preceding supply approach, and the reasons will become clear as we advance to the next steps. Once the relevant sectors have been defined, the employment in those sectors can be registered.

In the following stage, a region without tourism activities and without regional distribution function is defined; this is known as the reference region. In the reference region, the employment in the relevant sectors per 1,000 inhabitants should be noted. This ratio is considered to be the 'minimum requirement'. Finally, the tourism share in the relevant sectors of the tourism destination of step 1 is calculated. This is the total employment per sector minus the minimum requirement based on the ratios obtained in the reference region.

With respect to this method, two points should be noted. First, there might be underestimation of the tourism employment due to unregistered jobs in the tourism destination. Second, the tourism destination itself should be free of any distribution function outside the region.

Most measurements of employment generation are based on the demand approach. The methods are the same as for the calculation of the income impact. Therefore, the following paragraphs have been restricted to the essential items, and the TSA approach and the Henderson–Cousins method have been omitted. Currently, the TSA procedure for the employment table is not available (see also Heerschap, 1999). The Henderson–Cousins method is not suitable for the measurement of employment.

The national accounts method

The use of the national accounts method is quite simple. Based on income (value added) generation, we can derive the employment by dividing the income generated by the average gross salary of the employed and self-employed (gross income plus the employer's social security contribution). This leads to the number of 'standardized' employed persons. This approach can lead to an underestimation owing to the fact that the salaries in the tourism sector are below the national average. On the other hand, an overestimation can be the result of neglecting profits in the tourism firms. This approach – and this applies to all demand methods – does not take into account employment in the public sector related to tourism.

Sometimes a destination authority is only interested in the direct effect. In this case, it is sufficient to divide the income generated, adjusted for VAT, by the average gross salary of an employed person.

The input–output approach

Employment generation can be calculated, based on the input–output approach, in a similar way to income generation:

$$E_d = \hat{A}k \cdot b \tag{10.19}$$

$$E_t = \hat{A}k\,(1 - A^n) \cdot b \tag{10.20}$$

where

E_d = column vector of direct sectoral employment
E_t = vector of direct and indirect employment
$\hat{A}k$ = diagonal matrix of employment coefficients; the employment coefficient or labour coefficient is defined as the employment in sector i divided by the production in sector i
b = column vector tourist expenditure

The application of this approach to Flanders (Vanhove, 1993), with a tourism expenditure of €3.98 billion, resulted in direct income generation of €1.86 billion, €0.65 billion in indirect income, direct employment of 54,900 and indirect employment of 19,000 people (reference year, 1990). This employment effect is of the same magnitude as in the most important industrial sectors in Flanders.

With the same method, it was relatively easy to calculate the direct and indirect government receipts for Flanders:

	Direct + indirect effects (billions of euro)
Direct taxes	0.17
Profit taxes	0.14
Indirect taxes	0.10
Related to production VAT	0.35
Social security	0.27
Total	1.03

In other words, an expenditure of €3.98 billion created €1.03 billion in government receipts.

A similar and interesting piece of research was carried out by Archer and Fletcher for the Seychelles (Archer and Fletcher, 1996), also based on the input–output method. However, in their application, induced effects were also retained. This study proves how important tourism is in terms of income and employment creation. The reference year was 1991, and the case is relevant for the impact tourism might have on a country.

The major data of economic impact for the Seychelles were:

Visitor arrivals	97,668
Tourist nights	938,000
Tourism expenditure	527 million SEYRs (or 99 million US$)
Income creation	466 million SEYRs (direct, indirect and induced)
Government revenue	148 million SEYRs
Direct employment generated	3,772
Total employment generated	8,312 (direct, indirect and induced)

The contribution of tourism to the GDP was 18.4 per cent. With the secondary effects resulting from the multiplier effect, tourism contributed approximately 23.5 per cent to the GDP.

About 24 tourists created one direct job, but with secondary jobs (indirect and induced) taken into account as well, only 10.8 tourists were needed to support one job. In terms of nights, 248 nights contributed to a direct job and with secondary jobs 113 nights were sufficient for one job. A similar figure for Bruges (948 nights for a direct job; reference year 1992) shows the very labour-intensive character of tourism in the Seychelles.

Archer and Fletcher (1996) also calculated the number of tourists needed in the Seychelles to create one job for a number of countries of residence:

	Direct	Direct, indirect and induced
UK/Eire	22.4	10.3
France	25.5	11.6
Germany	18.7	8.4
Italy	22.4	10.0
Switzerland	20.8	9.2
Africa	29.3	13.5

These data stress the relative importance of German tourists for the Seychelles. The impact on employment of these tourists is about one-quarter greater than that of tourists from Africa.

Another interesting case is Asturias (Valdés *et al.*, 2007). Tourism expenditure in Asturias (a region in Spain) for the year 2005 was estimated at €1.782 million. The direct, indirect and induced income (GVA) and employment effects per sector are given in Table 10.8. With respect to this table, two points draw our attention. Firstly, the unorthodox income multiplier for Asturias is much higher than the one for Flanders (0.80 versus 0.63). Secondly, although many sectors are directly or indirectly involved, more than two thirds of income generation takes place in the sectors horeca and trading and repair (purchases of food and sundry purchases). This percentage amounts to 72 per cent for employment generation.

Of course, the results for Asturias, Flanders and the Seychelles cannot be generalized to any country or region. It all depends on leakages, economic structure, tax systems, etc. Nevertheless, by and large the impact of tourism on income and employment generation is important. This conclusion also holds for most developing countries.

The multiplier method

Above, the employment multiplier was defined either as the ratio of the direct and indirect (secondary) employment generated by additional tourism expenditure to the direct employment alone, or as the amount of employment generated by a given amount of tourist spending. The latter formulation has the greatest practical value.

$$E_k = (\text{direct} + \text{indirect employment})/\text{expenditure} \tag{10.21}$$

Table 10.8 Income and employment effects per sector of tourism expenditure in Asturias, 2005

Source: Valdes *et al.* (2007)

Sector of activity	Income (in €million)				Employment (in 1,000)			
	Direct	Indirect	Induced	Total	Direct	Indirect	Induced	Total
Agriculture and fisheries		19	5	24		2	1	3
Food		26	5	32		1	0.0	1
Other industries		20	7	27		1	0.0	1
Energy and water		23	6	29		0.0	0.0	0.0
Construction		14	4	18		1	0.0	1
Trading and repair	232	89	52	373	8	3	2	13
Horeca	700	7	27	734	25	0.0	1	26
Transport	94	34	19	147	2	1	0.0	3
Business services	–	148	56	204		3	1	4
Other services	11	11	30	43	0.0	0.0	1	2
Total	1,037	390	213	1,640	36	11	7	54

For the province of Antwerp, E_k amounted to 0.54 jobs per million Belgian francs expenditure; in the Flanders study, E_k was equal to 0.49.

As for the income generation, this method is only valuable if one makes use of an employment multiplier of a region with more or less identical characteristics. It is important to be aware that knowledge of direct and indirect employment per million expenditure in similar regions leads to a rough estimation.

Special characteristics of employment

So far the quantitative employment effect of tourism has been emphasized, but attention should also be paid to the qualitative aspects. First, tourism is a growth sector, and all predictions for the next decade (EIU and UNWTO) are promising. Even in developed countries, tourism is a sector with promising job opportunities. However, Thomas and Townsend (2001) warn against having too optimistic a perspective. The exceptionally rapid growth of the 1980s, relative to employment in all other sectors, was no longer the case in the 1990s. Smeral (2001) sounds the same warning.

Secondly, tourism is a sector with a high degree of semi-skilled and so-called unskilled workers. This can be seen as an opportunity for the large number of unskilled workers without jobs, especially in developing countries (Cucker, 2002; Stacey, 2015). Tourism is also a sector with a high percentage of part-time jobs. Hudson and Townsend reveal that in Great Britain, 38 per cent of the men and 56 per cent of the women working in the horeca sector (hotel, restaurant and cafes) are part-time workers (Hudson and Townsend, 1992). According to Wood, there is a tendency in advanced industrialized societies towards increased part-time employment and the casualization of work (Wood, 1992). Thomas and Townsend (2001) show that in 1998, UK hotels and restaurants employed as many part-time workers (not standardized) as full-time ones.

A fourth characteristic of employment in tourism is the high share of female workers. According to Hudson and Townsend, in Great Britain women account for 45 per cent of full-time workers and take 73 per cent of the part-time jobs. The study for the Antwerp province reveals that 50 per cent of part-timers are female workers (Yzewijn and De Brabander, 1989).

The sector also has many small firms and self-employed workers. For the Antwerp province, in the horeca sector the ratio of employee to employer is no higher than two. Moreover, British sources indicate the increasing number of young workers in the tourism sector (The Host Consultancy, 1991; Wood, 1992).

A final characteristic is the seasonality of employment. The intensity of seasonality is different per country and tourism region, but where it exists it makes tourism employment less attractive.

We find a confirmation of these characteristics in an OECD study (Stacey, 2015) in Table 10.9.

All in all, employment in tourism is growing, but most characteristics indicate that the sector has a poor image (Smeral, 2004).

The impact of events: special features

The demand methods dealt with in the two preceding sections can be applied to events; however, cost–benefit analysis (see Chapter 12) is a better approach. In economic impact studies of events, expenditure is the key element. Therefore it is important, especially with major events, to define expenditure in the right way. Furthermore, it is necessary to make a distinction between the result for the event organizer and that for the host city (Baade and Matheson, 2004).

> **Table 10.9** Characteristics of tourism employment* in selected OECD countries, 2013
>
> Source: Stacey (2015)

% share	Tourism	Total economy
Part-time jobs	31.1	20.7
Temporary jobs	21.9	14.1
Persons working with the same employer for less than 2 years	45.3	24.9
Youth (15–24 years)	20.6	9.4
Women	55.9	43.2
Self employed	23.9	19.3
Persons with 3rd level education	13.8	31.3
Persons working in micro enterprises (1–9 persons engaged)	47.5	31.2

*= Accommodation and food service activities

Only event-related 'new' expenditure can be taken into account. This implies in the first place a setting of the boundaries of the host region. This can be local, regional or national. Adjustments are necessary for expenditure of local residents, expenditure by 'casuals', expenditure by 'time switchers' or direct imports (event-related goods and services sourced outside the destination) (Dwyer *et al.* 2010).

Major events always involve 'crowding-out' effects, expenditure switching and retained expenditure. Big events are very often confronted with crowding-out effects, when traditional visitors prefer not to visit the region where the event takes place for reasons of over occupation, higher prices, etc. (Scherly and Breiter, 2002). These effects can take different forms:

● Geographical diversion – people avoid the place of the event and visit another region; locals leave the region (e.g. many local residents of Monaco leave the area during the Monaco Grand Prix; another well known example was the fall in the number of Japanese tourists visiting South Korea due to the World Cup in 2002 – down 50 per cent)
● Temporal substitution – traditional visitors come before or after the event
● Monetary substitution – visitors abstain from coming to the region and spend the money on other products or services.

Cost–benefit analysis takes these crowding-out effects into account through the application of the 'with and without' and not the 'before and after' principle (Vanhove, 1976).

Mules and Faulkner (1996) cite several examples of what they call expenditure 'switching':

● Local people might participate in the event and reduce their expenses for other goods and services. This is a pure substitution effect. Ryan (1998) uses the term 'displaced expenditure'.
● Visitors may switch their expenditure in time. They planned a trip to the region regardless, and simply arrange the timing of their visit to coincide with the event. Their expenditure cannot be attributed (or only partially) to the event (see also Dwyer and Forsyth, 1997).
● Visitors may switch their expenditure in terms of location within a country.
● Local, regional or national governments may switch public expenditure from other public works to infrastructure in favour of the event.

A special case is retained expenditure (Ryan, 1998), which occurs when residents strongly support the event and would have travelled out of the city or region anyway in order to attend it. In other words, the spending is not lost to other destinations. In that sense, the event does contribute to the economy of the destination.

Many tourism destinations organize several events per year to improve the tourism attractiveness. Public support for events is never far away. The allocation of event subsidies by public authorities needs to respect different stakeholders and interests – economic, social and ecological effects. Events with the greatest expenditure for the destination are not always the most interesting. Therefore the 'Event Performance Index' (EPI) was developed by Bandi and Künzi (2017). It is a holistic valuation tool as a guideline for public support of cultural and sports events. The EPI consists of seven key criteria:

- Size of the event
- Economic value
- Touristic value and image
- Innovative strengths
- Value of networking
- Value of participation and social exchange
- Relative ecological burden of the event.

These criteria are operationalized and measured on appropriate quantitative or qualitative scales. The aggregation of the different indicators results in the EPI. The authors developed a special formula including a special weighting system. The design of the EPI allows account negative impacts such as the ecological burden to be taken into account. Needless to say, such an index can be helpful for tourism destinations and municipalities in general to allocate event-related grants.

Computable General Equilibrium models

Why Computable General Equilibrium models?

Following a great deal of thought about where to put the discussion of Computable General Equilibrium (CGE) models in this chapter, it seemed best to deal with them at the end. It will become clear why.

In the preceding sections several techniques and methods to evaluate the economic impact of tourism have been discussed. In the last decades, several authors (Blake, Dixon, Dwyer, Forsyth, Pratt, Sinclair and others) have underlined a number of limitations of the prevailing methods. Dwyer *et al.* (2004) refer to Input–Output analysis. They state:

> The fundamental problem with input-output analysis is that it is incomplete; it ignores key aspects of the economy. It effectively assumes that there is a free, unrestricted flow of resources to these parts of the economy. The effects which come about because of resource limitations, the workings of the labour and other markets, the interactions between the economy and the rest of the world, are all ignored. A good example is the expenditure of local citizens for a big event such as the World Cup. What one spends for the event can not be used for other goods and services. In such case we are confronted with a substitution effect. As a result, Input-Output analysis does not capture the feedback effects, which typically work in opposite directions to the initial change.

Input–output ignores the presence of constraints in the economy on the availability of resources and consequently the competition among the sectors for the resources, the economic relationships among the sectors and the role of price adjustments (exchange rate included). In other words indirect and feedback mechanisms are not taken into account (Sahli and Nowak, 2007).

Alternative techniques have been developed to address the problems. CGE models are now extensively used. Gradually, CGE also made its entry into tourism, especially in Australia, the UK, the USA and Canada. But what does CGE mean? Let it be clear that CGE is not new. The literature on CGE analysis stems from developments of the Walrasian general equilibrium (GE) framework.

It is not easy to define CGE models. Wing (2003) refers to the Walrasian general equilibrium theory and describes CGE as follows:

> Computable general equilibrium (CGE) models are simulations that combine the abstract general equilibrium structure formalized by Arrow and Debreu with realistic economic data to solve numerically for the levels of supply, demand and price that support equilibrium across a specified set of markets. CGE models are a standard tool of empirical analysis, and are widely used to analyse the aggregate welfare and distributional impacts of policies whose effects may be transmitted through multiple markets, or contain menus of different tax, subsidy, quota or transfer instruments.

Examples of the use of CGE models may be found in areas as diverse as fiscal reform and development planning, international trade and, increasingly, environmental regulation. Among tourism related authors, we find one of the best descriptions in Blake *et al.* (2006). They define CGE models as follows: 'CGE models are based on the GE framework and consist of a set of equations, characterizing the production, consumption, trade and government activities of the economy which are solved simultaneously'. They distinguish four types of equations:

- Market equilibrium conditions ensure that supply is equal to demand. This applies for goods, services, production factors and currencies.
- Income-expenditure equations.
- Behavioural relationships which give the reaction of economic agents to changes in incomes and prices, determining consumers' demand for each good and service.
- Finally, production functions determine how much is produced for any given level of factor utilization.

The number of equations is different from country to country. It depends on many factors: number of sectors, number of consumer demands, availability of data, etc. In the Fiji CGE model (Narayan, 2004) there are 35 domestic industries (agricultural, industrial and service sector industries), 34 commodities and two occupational types. The equations are classified into five groups:

1 Those that describe households and other final demands for commodities
2 Those that describe industry demands for primary factors and intermediate inputs
3 Price equations
4 Market-clearing equations for factors of production and commodities
5 Other equations, such as those defining GDP, employment, consumer price index, etc.

Frechtling and Smeral (2010) describe CGE models according to three characteristics (see also Adams and Parmenter, 1995):

1 The assumption of competitiveness in CGE models. This describes a competitive world that includes utility maximization in consumption, cost minimization in production, zero pure profits, and market clearing.
2 CGE models simulate an economy with efficient markets. In the CGE world, each market has an equilibrium solution for a set of prices and levels of production.

3   The core database of a CGE model is usually a set of input-output accounts showing the flows of commodities and factors between industries, households, governments, importers and exporters. These tables are normally supplemented by numerical estimates of various elasticity parameters.

> CGE models go beyond input-output models by linking industries via economy-wide constraints. With these constraints in place, the economy-wide implications of stimulating one industry can be negative and a positive impact for some industries may be generated at the expense of others. For example, contrary to input-output analysis, CGE models do not assume that resources, such as labour, land and capital, flow freely to tourism-related industries, and they generally include feedback effects from other markets.

In general terms, CGE models are a class of economic models that use actual economic data to estimate how an economy might react to changes in policy, technology or other external factors. CGE models are also referred to as AGE (applied general equilibrium) models. A full description of CGE is beyond the objective of this book. The models can be simple or complicated. It differs from case to case. They can contain constraints and rigidities. For more information it is necessary to refer to the specialized literature. Early CGE models were often solved by a program custom-written for that particular model. Models were expensive to construct, and sometimes appeared as a 'black box' to outsiders. Today most CGE models are formulated and solved using one of the GEMPACK or GAMS software systems. In the Victorian Formula 1 Grand Prix (Victorian Auditor-General, 2007), the CGE model was the MONASH Multiregional Forecasting model that is maintained by the Centre of Policy Studies at Monash University.

Some criticism has been made of CGE analysis. The main objection is the fact that CGE is time consuming and complicated to apply. Another basic point concerns the general equilibrium nature of CGE analysis. Indeed one of the assumptions is market clearing, or what we call market efficiency. There are, however, forces or rigidities that prevent an equilibrium outcome. A more fundamental concern is whether CGE models describe economic reality. Frechtling and Smeral (2010) warn that in some cases the parameters of CGE models are calibrated by values not derived from valid statistical processes related to the variable. Sometimes the application of CGE models is questionable. This can be the case when there is rather high unemployment in the destination.

Static and dynamic CGE models

The CGE may be static or dynamic. Many CGE models are comparative-static: they model the reactions of the economy at only one point in time. A good example is the economic impact of international tourism due to the Olympics during the two weeks of the Beijing Olympic Games (Li and deHaan, 2007). For policy analysis, results from such a model are often interpreted as showing the reaction of the economy in some future period to one or a few external shocks or policy changes. That is, the results show the difference (usually reported in percentage change form) between two alternative future states (with and without the policy shock). The process of adjustment to the new equilibrium is not explicitly represented in such a model, although details of the closure (for example, whether capital stocks are allowed to adjust) lead modellers to distinguish between short-run and long-run equilibria.

By contrast, dynamic CGE models explicitly trace each variable through time – often at annual intervals. These models are more realistic, but more challenging to construct and solve. They require, for instance, that future changes are predicted for all exogenous variables, not just those affected by a possible policy change. The dynamic elements may arise from partial adjustment processes or from stock/flow accumulation relations: between capital stocks and investment, and between foreign debt and trade deficits (wikipedia.org/wiki/Computable_general_equilibrium, 12.3.2010).

In reality, static models may be appropriate for much of the analysis that is undertaken, where inter-temporal allocation is not the major concern (Blake *et al.*, 2006).

Input–output analysis versus CGE

The utility of CGE becomes clearer when one compares CGE models to the theoretical output of other techniques. Let us start with I–O analysis. Indeed, the core database of a CGE model is usually a set of input–output accounts. Dwyer *et al.* (2010) formulate the limitations of the I–O approach as follows:

- Resource constraints do not exist. In other words, additional resources are assumed to be unemployed with no constraints on their availability. It is assumed that factors of production are not being used elsewhere and do not result in a decrease of output in other activities. With respect to labour in tourism regions, we should not overemphasize this limitation. Most tourism regions show a high percentage of unemployment (see also Li and deHaan, 2007).
- Prices and costs remain fixed as economic activity expands. This means that I–O analysis excludes changes in factor and product prices which may affect employment and output of other sectors. This assumption also applies to the price of the local currency in the case of an inbound tourism boom (Dwyer *et al.* 2004). This is correct when the tourism sector is dominant and the change of final demand due to additional tourism expenditure is relatively very high.
- There are constant ratios between inputs and output, between value added and output, and there is the assumption of constant labour productivity. In the short term and for minor changes of final demand, constant ratios can be justified. For middle- and long-term projections combined with a serious shift of tourism demand, the I–O results might be biased.
- Spending on new tourism products (e.g. an event) by the local population does not lead to a diversion of spending away from other goods and services. In theory there should be a diversion. The question is how important is the reduced production.

The four limitations can lead to the conclusion that the I–O approach overestimates the impact of additional tourist spending on the economy (Blake *et al.*, 2006; Pratt and Blake, 2007). All depend on the magnitude of tourist expenditure changes, the situation on the factor markets and the time period considered. CGE is assumed to consider the above-mentioned limitations. Dwyer *et al.* (2010, and referring to previous publications of Dwyer *et al.*, 2006a, 2006b) write:

> For the purpose of estimating the impacts of an injection of new money into an economy such as might be associated with an event, CGE models can make specific assumptions about the availability of factors of production, such as to what extent their supply can be increased, and to what extent there is an excess of some factors (as with unemployment of labour). The behaviour of agents in a CGE model is assumed to be sensitive to changes in relative prices as well as quantity variables. Price rises will limit the extent of economic expansion associated with the event, and may even lead to contractions in economic activity in some sectors.

There are many other possible situations. Government spending on infrastructure to support tourism must be financed. The necessary additional taxes may moderate private consumption and indirectly lead to a reduction of the output of sectors related to consumption. CGE models are now at our disposal and represent the whole economy in which resource constraints and feedback effects are explicitly recognized. For measuring changes in the overall economy or in a specific aspect (e.g. employment, imports) I–O analysis has its limits. There is, however, a clear link between a CGE model and an I–O model. The latter is embedded in a CGE model, but links to other aggregates and markets are explicitly modelled (Dwyer et al., 2004). For more details about the choice between I–O and CGE, refer to 'Economic evaluation of special events' (Dwyer et al., 2006a).

Cost–benefit analysis versus CGE

Most of the limitations of the I–O approach also apply to cost–benefit analysis or CBA (see Chapter 12). An essential difference between both techniques is the following. CBA is primarily a partial equilibrium technique. It focusses on direct impacts of a project. CGE techniques are general equilibrium. Furthermore, CBA is very detailed. Unpaid and underpaid costs and benefits and side effects on complementary and competitive firms are taken into account. CGE techniques are general equilibrium but less detailed (Dwyer et al., 2010). A CBA takes into account several costs and benefits which would not be considered in a CGE model. Dwyer and Forsyth refer to non-priced effects (e.g. noise of an event or traffic congestion) which do not get included in the markets which are modelled.

CBA and CGE are complementary techniques. One technique picks up items that are not taken into account by the other. One of Dwyer and Forsyth's conclusions is very relevant:

> The two techniques focus on different aspects of the evaluation problem. CBA is the established technique for assessing the benefits and costs of a project, and as such, it is appropriate for an event. CGE models are the preferred technique for assessing the impact of an event on economic activity, and its various dimensions such as GSP/GDP and employment.

Use of CGE modelling in tourism

Five interesting cases can be used to illustrate CGE modelling in tourism. Three of the cases relate to important events and the two other cases concern important interventions in the economy of Fiji – a famous tourism destination.

- Qantas Australian Grand Prix 2000
- 2005 Australian Formula 1 Grand Prix
- A Chinese CGE model of the Beijing Olympic Games
- Economic impact of tourism in Fiji
- Economic impact of a devaluation on tourism in Fiji.

Dwyer et al. refer to several applications of CGE models in tourism. Most of the references relate to Australia. But we find applications for tourism projects and events in many other countries. Blake et al. (2003) used this technique to measure the effects of Foot and Mouth disease on inbound tourism and its consequences for the UK economy. There are many more applications. Blake et al. refer to Canada (taxation), Spain (taxation), Mauritius (tax reform), Cyprus and Malta (effects of EU membership and associated changes in tourism demand). Li and deHaan (2007) apply the CGE analysis to the international tourism of China and the Beijing 2008 Olympic Games. Dwyer et al. (2004) give some types of issues which can be explored using CGE analysis:

- What impact will a change in domestic or inbound tourism have on economic activity (national or regional)?
- What impact will an increase in outbound tourism have on the national economy?

- What impact has a special event (e.g. Olympic Games) on the national or regional economy?
- How will a tourism tax affect economic activity?
- How will a Value Added Tax impact on the tourism sector and GDP? (Gooroochurn and Sinclair, 2005; Gago *et al.*, 2009)
- How will tourism crises such as September 11 or the Sars epidemic impact on the economy?

CASE STUDY

Case 1: Qantas Australian Grand Prix 2000

Dwyer *et al.* (2006a) compare the assumptions under the spinning I–O model and the CGE model with respect to the Qantas Australian Grand Prix in 2000.

Assumptions of I–O model

- All final demand components are exogenous; in other words, consumption, exports, etc. are not explained within the model.
- Production factors are endogenous, which implies a very high elasticity of labour, capital and land.
- No price-induced substitution effect, which means that no price changes affect consumers and suppliers. Real wages and exchange rate are fixed.
- Government expenditure remains constant and is given exogenously.
- State employment is flexible, which implies that sufficient additional labour is available.
- Fixed nominal exchange rate and world price of imports.

Assumptions of CGE model

- All main final demand components are endogenous. The model provides theories to explain the behaviour of these final demand components following an expenditure shock to the system.
- Capital and land use are given exogenously. There is an assumption of fixed public investment and fixed capital.
- Price-induced substation effects occur and real wages and private investment are flexible.
- Government expenditure is variable and tax rates are fixed.
- State employment is regarded as fixed (zero elasticity) or flexible (perfect elasticity). Both simulations were undertaken and the results were averaged.
- Fixed nominal exchange rate and world price of imports.

The starting point is the additional expenditure. The event created an injection from interstate and overseas sources of A$51.25 million. Both models resulted in the following results for Australia:

Table 10.10 Comparison of I–O and CGE macro-economic results for the Qantas Australian Grand Prix event on the Australian economy, 2003 (millions A$)

Source: Dwyer *et al.* (2006a) p. 325

Macro variables	I–O	CGE
Change in real output ($m)	120.1	24.46
Change in real GDP	43.3	8.8
Change in employment	592	129

Although the final conclusion goes in the same direction for the two approaches, the differences are in the projected impacts of the event on real output, GDP and employment. They confirm the thesis that in normal circumstances CGE analysis shows lower impacts than the I–O approach.

CASE STUDY

Case 2: 2005 Australian Formula 1 Grand Prix

The second case concerns the 2005 Australian Formula 1 Grand Prix (Victorian Auditor-General, 2007). It is a comparison of a CBA and a CGE approach. For the application of CBA to the GP, refer to Chapter 9.

Formula 1 is recognized as the highest class of motor racing. It attracts large crowds, worldwide television coverage and media attention and a large amount of corporate and government sponsorship. One rationale for government support is that Formula 1 generates substantial economic benefits (e.g. spending by visitors on hotels, restaurants and entertainment).

Inherent in CGE models is the assumption of optimizing behaviour by households and producers in the context of the capacity constraints in the economy. The Victorian study gives in its introduction the characteristics of CGE models:

- Prices and quantities are determined within the model
- The equilibrium allocation of production factors between alternative uses
- Competitive product and factor markets
- Supply and demand are equalized at equilibrium prices

- Household decisions over demand for products and the supply of factors are based on utility maximization subject to price and income constraints
- Supply of products and demand for factors by producers are based on the objective of profit maximization, subject to constraints of technology.

The CGE model used in this case is the MONASH Multi Regional Forecasting (MMRF) model that is maintained by the Centre of Policy Studies at Monash University. The above-mentioned study gives the mechanics of MMRP. The description is very interesting, so the full mechanics as written in the report is quoted below:

> In principle, increased demand for locally produced goods and services associated with a major event such as the Grand Prix affects the Victorian economy in a variety of ways. First, there are the direct demand effects experienced by the producers of final goods and services purchased by the additional spending. A good example is the restaurant industry in the context of the Grand Prix.
>
> These direct effects are followed by a succession of indirect demand effects. These are first felt when the producers of the additional goods purchased as part of the Grand Prix demand more intermediate inputs from other industries, and construct and install new plant and equipment. The initial indirect demand effects set in train further rounds of indirect effects as firms supplying the intermediate inputs and supplying the new investment spending raise their own production levels in order to meet the increased demand, and so on.
>
> At each stage of the process, induced income effects may augment the direct and indirect demand effects. These induced income effects occur when the households supplying the additional labour, and the owners of the newly utilised fixed capital, spend their increased incomes on final goods and services. As before, this spending sets off further successive rounds of indirect demand effects, and consequently further induced income effects.
>
> The sequence of demand effects described above arises from the linkages between industries in the chains of production and distribution of goods and services. An I-O model is designed to capture these inter-industry linkages. The MMRF model, however, builds on the I-O framework by allowing for the inclusion of the constraints absent from the I-O calculations, including general specifications about the behaviour of agents (consumers, producers and investors).
>
> Substitution possibilities are incorporated in the MMRF model so that the behaviour of agents in the model is sensitive to changes in relative prices as well as to quantity variables. For example, if prices in one state rise relative to the prices of goods produced in another state, then purchasers will substitute interstate goods for local goods. Similarly, if wages rise relative to the cost of employing capital, then capital-labour ratios tend to rise.
>
> An implication of including the additional constraints together with an active price mechanism is that the expansion effects of increased spending

in one area tends to be offset by crowding out of other elements of demand. For example, suppose the economic activity associated with the grand prix pushes up the demand for skilled labour in Melbourne. In the presence, of a constraint on labour supply of certain skills, this will bid up wage rates, increasing the production costs of all industries. Those industries facing international competition will be unable to pass on these cost increases and will be forced to cut back output and employment.

Another example is that spending at the Grand Prix by overseas visitors could put upward pressure on the real exchange rate. This encourages imports and forces domestic import-competing industries to cut back output and employment. By contrast, 10 models do not incorporate the possibility of crowding out and instead assume that the economic factors necessary to respond to any increased demand do not come from existing production.

The key MMRF modelling assumptions in the analysis of GP are the following:

- Labour markets: the model assumes that the GP has no effect on national employment, with the national real wage rate adjusting to ensure that national employment does not change. This is a standard long-run modelling assumption. At the state level, it is assumed that labour is mobile between state economies. As a consequence, a state that is favourably affected by the GP – in this case Victoria – will experience increased employment.
- Public expenditure, tax rates and government budgets. Real public consumption expenditure is assumed to move with real private consumption expenditure. Government budget balances are held fixed in the model via endogenous changes in lump-sum payments to households. As a consequence any increase in taxation receipts arising from the GP will be immediately passed on to households.
- Real consumption is assumed to change in line with changes to real income available to residents (the MMRF model takes account of direct income from labour, capital, government welfare payments and income tax).
- In MMRF rates of return on capital are defined by unit costs of investment. For the long-run results reported here, the rates of return are fixed in the model via endogenous capital adjustments.

The results of the MMRF modelling are given in Table 10.11. In the MMRF approach there are two scenarios. In the same table we also give the impacts based on the NIEIR (National Institute of Economic and Industry Research) model (for more details, refer to the report (NIEIR, 2005)).

The two types of modelling lead to different results. They are the consequence of the structures of the two models and differences in inputs to the models (e.g. induced tourism and the increase of Victorian expenditure on the GP financed from domestic savings are not retained in the MMRF model). One NIEIR result seems unrealistically high. The full-time employment effect is not in proportion to the increase of the expenditure of visitors.

Table 10.11 Economic effects of the 2005 Grand Prix to Victoria (millions A$)

Source: Victorian Auditor-General, State Investment in Major Events, 2007

	MMRF 1	MMRF 2*	NIEIR
Gross state product	101.8	64.2	165.7
GSP plus induced tourism	110.9	62.4**	174.8
Private investment	24.1	12.7	54.0
Private consumption	56.8	16.1	78.6
Public consumption	12.6	3.6	–
State tax receipts	11.9	3.5	15.2
Full time employment positions (no)	600	400	3,650

* Based on more strict assumptions about direct impacts
** No induced tourism

CASE STUDY

Case 3: A Chinese CGE model of the Beijing 2008 Olympic Games

Li and deHaan (2007) used the CGE technique to measure the economic impact of international tourism on the Chinese economy. Their starting point is the China 2002 I–O model and an estimation of international visitor spending (foreign tourists, athletes, officials, media visitors and sponsor visitors) during the Beijing 2008 Olympic Games (low, central and high scenario). The model assumptions are:

- There are different economic agents in the economy, 122 sectors, representative of households and government. The 122 sectors are aggregated into 13 industries: primary, secondary, ten tourism-related sectors and other services.
- Two factors of production: labour and capital.
- On the demand side, utility maximization subject to the resource constraints leads to demand functions.
- On the supply side, profit maximization subject to the resource constraints leads to supply functions.

- Prices are adjusted to make all excess demands equal to zero.
- The Leontief function, Cobb–Douglas function, the Constant Elasticity of Substitution (CES) function and Constant Elasticity of Transformation (CET) function are applied to production and demand functions.
- The representative household receives revenues through offering factors of production to produce domestic and export goods, and it receives government transfers.
- The government receives taxes on production and income, and consumes public goods. Foreign investment is assumed to be fixed, which leads to a fixed current account balance.
- Finally, the Armington assumption is used in the model. This assumption specifies that domestic goods and imports cannot be perfectly substituted.

The international tourism impact of the Beijing 2008 Olympic Games on the Chinese economy is summarized in Table 10.12. As in any CGE model the results are influenced by the choice of magnitude of some key parameters (e.g. price elasticities, expenditure per day)

Table 10.12 The economic impact of international tourism of Beijing 2008 Olympic Games on Chinese economy (millions $)

Source: Li and deHaan (2007)

	Low	Central	High
Change in real GDP	97.5	147.5	199.5
Change in international tourism demand	600.8	899.4	1199.2
Change in real tourism consumption	376.4	567.3	763.8
Percentage change of price of foreign consumption (%)	0.04	0.06	0.08
Change in GDP per change in international tourism demand	0.16	0.16	0.17

The impact of the foreign visitors to the Olympic Games is rather limited. According to the central scenario, the ratio of increased international visitor spending due to the Olympics to total international tourism receipts in 2008 (Games excluded) is only 0.02 per cent. More striking is the conclusion of the authors that the increase in welfare ($147.5 million in the central scenario) would be brought to households by holding the Beijing Olympic Games. During the period 2000–2005 the average annual real GDP increase in China amounted to about $200 billion. They conclude that 'the absolute value of welfare increase ($147.5) related to the Beijing Olympics seems big but the relevant value of welfare increase (0.07 %) is very small'. Compared to the size of the Chinese economy, the stimulus of the Olympics on international tourism is relatively very small.

CASE STUDY

Case 4: Economic impact of tourism in Fiji based on the Fiji CGE model

Narayan (2004) describes the structure of the Fiji CGE model. It is based on the ORANI model of the Australian economy. It gives an answer to the question: 'What are the long-run macro-economic effects of a 10 per cent increase in tourist expenditure in Fiji?'

Table 10.13 Macro-economic effects of a 10 per cent increase in tourist expenditure in Fiji

Source: P. Narayan (2004), Economic impact of tourism on Fiji's economy: empirical evidence from the computable general equilibrium model, *Tourism Economics*, p. 426

Variable	Percentage change
Private savings	1.9
Private consumption	1.9
Balance of payments surplus	540.1*
Private investment expenditure	1.3
Total government savings	860.0*
Imports	1.1
Exports	1.6
Consumer price index	1.2
Investment price index	0.8
Private disposable income	1.9
Income tax revenue	2.4
Company tax revenue	1.9
Production tax revenue	1.6
Tariff revenue	0.8
Excise tax revenue	1.7
VAT revenue	2.5
Real aggregate private investment	0.4
Real GDP	0.5
Real consumption	0.7
Real national welfare	0.7
Net after tax rural wage rate for unskilled labour	1.8
Net urban wage rate for unskilled labour	1.7
Wage rate for informal sector labour	5.8
Aggregate demand for informal unskilled labour	−2.9

* indicates in 1,000 Fiji $

The major results of this study are:

- Real GDP increases only by 0.5 per cent.
- Real consumption increases by 0.7 per cent.
- Private disposable income goes up by 1.9 per cent.
- The increase in total exports (1.75 per cent) outweighs the increase in total imports and contributes to an improvement in the balance of payment by F$540,000.
- There is a substantial gain in tax revenue (income tax; company tax; production tax; tariff revenue; excise tax and VAT revenue).
- Wage rates for unskilled labour in rural and urban areas increase by 1.8 per cent and 1.2 per cent respectively. The wage increase in the informal sector is even higher.

This Fiji case is a good example of the broad application field of CGE models. Fiji is also the application area of the full economy-wide study of the impact of a devaluation of the local currency. The choice of Fiji is interesting as a well-known tourism destination with an open economy.

CASE STUDY

Case 5: Economic impact of a devaluation on tourism in Fiji

In 2009 the Reserve Bank of Fiji announced a devaluation of the Fijian dollar by 20 per cent. The Fijian dollar is linked to a basket of currencies of its five major trading partners – Australia, Japan, New Zealand, the UK and the USA. This is the background of the study of Pratt (2014) on the impact of this devaluation on tourism and the Fijian economy in general.

A currency devaluation means that the price of a country's exports, denoted in foreign currency, will decrease, hence increasing the purchasing power of origin countries. Exports will be less expensive on the world market and tourism is expected to increase as the destination becomes more competitive. Alternatively, imports will be more expensive at the destination. A devaluation has an impact on both the demand and supply sides of the economy.

Regression analysis is the classical method used to estimate the impact of a devaluation on tourism inbound, tourism outbound and GDP. This method does not capture the interrelationship between tourism and other sectors. The research objectives of Pratt (2014) go much further. He estimates the impact of a devaluation of the Fijian dollar on the economy using a static CGE model. CGE models show both macro-economic and sector effects and take into account the full workings of an open economy. Pratt describes the possible impacts as follows:

A devaluation impacts both the demand and supply sides of the economy. It might result in higher prices, which could generate a negative real balance. This could lead to lower aggregate demand and output. Alternatively, a devaluation can have a negative effect on aggregate demand through income distribution. For example, aggregate demand and output may decline if income is redistributed from income groups with low propensity to save to income groups with a high propensity to save. Also from the demand side, if the price elasticities of imports and exports are sufficiently low, the trade balance may worsen (expressed in domestic currency). From the supply side, the benefits that accrue to a country that devalues its currency will depend on the extent to which the capital used in production is imported as well as the extent to which goods and services used in intermediate consumption are imported or domestically produced. The interactions between the exchange rate, real output, real income and employment are diverse and complex and the direction of impacts are ambiguous.

CGE models are a standard tool of empirical analysis, and are widely used to analyse the aggregate welfare and distributional impacts of exogenous shocks or policies whose effects may be transmitted throughout the economy. A crucial factor in any CGE application is the chosen elasticities. Therefore Pratt applied a sensitivity analysis for the elasticity of tourism demand and for elasticity of transformation. It should be said that in this case, the macro-economic variables remain qualitatively the same under the various chosen elasticities.

The 'shock' to the Fijian economy of a 20 per cent devaluation of the Fijian dollar was important. The estimated macro-economic results are shown in Table 10.14. As expected the devaluation makes Fiji more competitive in terms of inbound tourism. Tourism consumption increases by 5.3 per cent, which is rather low. The elasticity of demand has been set at 0.5 per cent. The exports in general increase by 9.5 per cent. A devaluation should also lead to a decrease of imports. In the Fijian case the import reduction is spectacular. Imports are estimated to decrease by 38.8 per cent.

But the devaluation also has other negative effects on the national economy. Domestic production sees a fall of 9.6 per cent. Of greater concern are the large estimated decreases in consumption (–20.7 per cent) and investments (–21.3 per cent), two components of final demand.

Pratt concludes: 'Results from a computable general equilibrium model of Fiji indicate that, while devaluation will increase tourism consumption, the overall effect on the economy will be contractionary, as household consumption, investment and domestic production will all decrease'. The overall impact is negative. The net value added decrease was 5 per cent; in other words, the benefits gained from an increase of exports (tourism included) do not outweigh the negative effects in other sectors of the economy.

The results are robust for different values of elasticities of tourism demand, the elasticity of substitution and the elasticity of transformation. The results confirm other research conducted on devaluations. Pratt attributes the negative results to:

Table 10.14 Macro-economic impacts of a 20 per cent devaluation of the Fijian dollar

Source: Pratt (2014)

Economic variable	Percentage change
Tourism consumption	5.3
Price of tourism	−0.6
Welfare	−14.3
Consumption	−20.7
Investment	−21.3
Price of investment	0.7
Labour	3.0
Wage rate	−5.2
Capital	−0.7
Return to capital	−6.5
Domestic production	−9.6
Exports	9.5
Imports	−38.8
Net value added	−5.0

Welfare changes depend on (a) how much exporting versus non-exporting sectors contribute to the economy, and (b) linkages between exporting and non-exporting sectors, and consequently the multiplying effect of exporting sectors. Fiji's exports are mainly driven by the exports of tourism, which have the effect of stimulating economic growth. However, the increase in exports of tourism and other sectors comes at the expense of deteriorating terms of trade and the weaker power of imports, which results in a decrease in GDP and welfare.

Some time passed between Pratt's research and the devaluation of the Fijian dollar. It is important to notice the impacts *ex post*. 'Data published by the Reserve Bank of Fiji (RBF, 2011) show that the results obtained using the CGE model in this paper align qualitatively with the official statistics.'

References and further reading

Adams, P., and Parmenter, B. (1995). An applied general equilibrium analysis of the economic effects of tourism in a quite small, quite open economy. *Applied Economics, 27.*

Airey, D. (1978). Tourism and balance of payments. *Tourism International Research-Europe*, third quarter.

André, F., and Cardenete, A. (2009). Designing efficient subsidy policies in a regional economy: a Multicriteria Decision-Making (MCDM) – Computable General Equilibrium (CGE) approach. *Regional Studies, 8.*

Archer, B. (1991). The value of multipliers and their policy implications. In S. Medlik (ed.), *Managing Tourism.* Oxford: Butterworth-Heinemann.

Archer, B. (1995). Importance of tourism for the economy of Bermuda. *Annals of Tourism Research, 4.*

Archer, B. (1996). The economic impact of tourism in the Seychelles. *Annals of Tourism Research, 1.*

Archer, B., and Fletcher, J. (1996). Tourism: its economic importance. In M. Quest (ed.), *Horwath Book of Tourism.* London: MacMillan.

Archer, B., and Owen, C. (1971). Towards a tourist regional multiplier. *Regional Studies, 5.*

Archer, B., Shea, S., and de Vane (1974). *Tourism in Gwynedd: An Economic Study.* Cardiff: Wales Tourist Board.

Baade, R., and Matheson, A. (2004). The quest for the Cup: assessing the economic impact of the World Cup. *Regional Studies, 4.*

Bandi, M., and Künzi, A (2017). Event Performance Index. A holistic valuation tool as a guideline for public support of cultural and sport events. Paper presented at the 52nd TRC meeting. Lisbon: TRC.

Baretje, R., and Defert, P. (1972). *Aspects économiques du tourisme.* Paris : Berger-Levrault.

Baum, T. (1995). Trends in international tourism. In *Insights.* London: English Tourist Board.

Blake, A. (2007). *The Economic Impact of Tourism in Static and Dynamic CGE Models.* Palma: IATE conference.

Blake, A. (2009). The dynamics of tourism's economic impact. *Tourism Economics, 3.*

Blake, A., Gillham, J., and Sinclair, M. (2006). CGE tourism analysis and policy modelling. In L. Dwyer and P. Forsyth (eds), *International Handbook on the Economics of Tourism.* Cheltenham: Edward Elgar.

Blake, A., Sinclair, M., and Sugiyarto, G. (2003). Quantifying the impact of foot and mouth disease on tourism and the UK economy. *Tourism Economics, 4.*

Bonham, C., Edmonds, C., and Mak, J. (2006). The impact of 9/11 and other terrible global events on tourism in the United States and Hawaii. *Journal of Travel Research, 45.*

Bosselman, F., Peterson, C., and McCarthy, Cl. (1999). *Managing Tourism Growth.* Washington, DC: Island Press.

Bull, A. (1995). *The Economics of Travel and Tourism.* Sydney: Longman.

Cai, J., Leung, P., and Mak, J. (2006). Tourism forward and backward linkages. *Journal of Travel Research, 45,* August.

Clement, H. (1961). *The Future of Tourism in the Pacific and the Far East.* Washington, DC: US Department of Commerce.

Cooper, A., and Wilson, A. (2002). Extending the relevance of TSA research for the UK: general equilibrium and spillover analysis. *Tourism Economics, 1.*

Cooper, C., Fletcher, J., Fyall, A., Gilbert, D., and Wanhill, S. (2008). *Tourism: Principles & Practice,* 4th edn. London: Prentice Hall.

Croes, R., and Severt, D. (2007). Research report: evaluating short-term tourism economic effects in confined economies – conceptual and empirical considerations. *Tourism Economics, 2.*

Cucker, J. (2002). Tourism employment issues in developing countries: examples from Indonesia. In R. Sharpley and D. Telfer (eds), *Tourism and Development: Concepts and Issues*. Clevedon: Channel View Publications.

De Brabander, G. (1992). *Toerisme en Economie*. Leuven: Garant.

Durand, H., Gouirand, P., and Spindler, J. (1994). *Economie et Politique du Tourisme*. Paris: Librairie Générale de droit et de Jurisprudence.

Dwyer, L., and Forsyth, P. (1997). Impacts and benefits of MICE tourism: a framework for analysis. *Tourism Economics, 1*.

Dwyer, L., and Forsyth, P. (eds) (2006). *International Handbook on the Economics of Tourism*. Cheltenham: Edward Elgar.

Dwyer, L., Forsyth, P., and Dwyer, W. (2010). *Tourism Economics and Policy*. Bristol: Channel View Publications.

Dwyer, L., Forsyth, P., and Spurr, R. (2003). Inter-industry effects of tourism growth: implications for destination managers. *Tourism Economics, 2*.

Dwyer, L., Forsyth, P., and Spurr, R. (2004). Evaluating tourism's economic effects: new and old approaches. *Tourism Management, 3*.

Dwyer, L., Forsyth, P., and Spurr, R. (2006a). Economic evaluation of special events. In L. Dwyer and P. Forsyth (eds), *International Handbook on the Economics of Tourism*. Cheltenham: Edward Elgar.

Dwyer, L., Forsyth, P., and Spurr, R. (2006b). Assessing the economic impacts of events: a computable general equilibrium approach. *Journal of Travel Research, 45*.

Dwyer, L., Forsyth, P., and Spurr, R. (2007). Contrasting the uses of TSAs and CGE models: measuring yield and productivity. *Tourism Economics, 4*.

Dwyer, L., Forsyth, P., and Spurr, R. (2009). Economic assessment of events: the role of CGE analysis. In J. Spindler and D. Huron (eds), *L'Évaluation de L'Événement touristique*. Paris: L'Harmattan.

Dwyer, L., Forsyth, P., Spurr, R., and Van Ho, T. (2003). Tourism contribution to a state economy: a multi-regional general equilibrium analysis. *Tourism Economics, 4*.

Eurostat, OECD, WTO and UN Statistics Division (2001). *Tourism Satellite Account: Recommended Methodological Framework*. Luxembourg: Eurostat.

Ferri, J. (2004). Evaluating the regional impact of a new road on tourism. *Regional Studies, 4*.

Fletcher, J., and Archer, B. (1992). The development and application of multiplier analysis. In C. Cooper (ed.), *Progress in Tourism, Recreation and Hospitality Management, Vol. 3*. London: Belhaven Press.

Forsyth, P., Dwyer, L., and Spurr, R. (2007). *State Investment in Major Events: Integrating Economic Impact Modelling with Cost Benefit Analysis*. Palma: IATE conference.

Franz, A., Laimer, P., and Smeral, E. (2001). *A Tourism Satellite Account for Austria*. Vienna: Statistik Austria and WIFO.

Frechtling, D. (1994). Assessing the economic impacts of travel and tourism. In J. Ritchie and C. Goeldner (eds), *Travel, Tourism and Hospitality Research*. New York: John Wiley & Sons.

Frechtling, D. (2011). *Exploring the Full Economic Impact of Tourism for Policy Making*. Madrid: UNWTO.

Frechtling, D., and Smeral, E. (2010). Measuring and interpreting the economic impact of tourism: 20:20 hindsight and foresight. In D. Pearce and D. Butler (eds), *Tourism Research: A 20–20 Vision*. Oxford: Goodfellow Publishers Limited.

Gago, A., Labandeira, X., Picos, F., and Rodriguez, M. (2009). Specific and general taxation of tourism activities. Evidence from Spain. *Tourism Management, 30*.

Getz, D. (1991). *Festivals, Special Events and Tourism*. New York. Van Nostrand Reinhold.

Ghadimi, H. (2007). *Computable General Equilibrium (CGE) Models: A Short Course*. Regional Research Institute, West Virginia University.

Gooroochurn, N., and Sinclair, M. (2005). Economics of Taxation. Evidence from Mauritius. *Annals of Tourism Research, 2.*

Gray, H.P. (1970). *International Travel International* Trade. Lexington: Heath Lexington Books.

Hall, M., and Page, S. (2006). *The Geography of Tourism & Recreation.* London: Routledge.

Heerschap, N. (1999). The employment module for the Tourism Satellite Account of the OECD. *Tourism Economics, 5.*

Henderson, D., and Cousins, R. (1975). *The Economic Impact of Tourism: A Case Study in Greater Tayside.* Edinburgh: Tourism and Recreation Research Unit, University of Edinburgh.

Hudson, R., and Townsend, A. (1992). Tourism employment and policy: choices for local government. In P. Johnson and B. Thomas (eds), *Perspectives on Tourism Policy.* London: Mansell Publishing.

Keller, P., and Bieger, T. (eds) (2003). *Sport and Tourism.* AIEST Congress, Athens, 2003. St-Gall: AIEST.

Kim, H., Gursoy, D., and Lee S. (2006). The impact of the 2002 World Cup on South Korea: comparisons of pre- and post-games. *Tourism Management, 27.*

Klaassen, L., and Van Wickeren, A. (1975). Interindustry relations: an attraction model. In H.C. Bos (ed.), *Towards Balanced International Growth.* Rotterdam: North Holland Publishing Company.

Li, S., and deHaan, C. (2007). *The Economic Impact of International Tourism on the Chinese Economy: A Computable General Equilibrium Analysis of the Beijing 2008 Olympic Games.* Palma: IATE conference.

Mathieson, A., and Wall, G. (1982). *Tourism: Economic, Physical and Social Impacts.* London: Longman.

Michael, E. (2003). Tourism micro-clusters. *Tourism Economics, 2.*

Mihalic, T. (2002). Tourism and economic development issues. In R. Sharpley and D. Telfer (eds), *Tourism and Development: Concepts and Issues.* Clevedon: Channel View Publications.

Mules, T., and Faulkner, B. (1996). An economic perspective on special events. *Tourism Economics, 2.*

Narayan, P. (2004). Economic impact of tourism on Fiji's economy: empirical evidence from the computable general equilibrium model. *Tourism Economics, 4.*

NIEIR (2005). *Economic Evaluation of the 2005 Foster's Australian Grand Prix.* Melbourne.

NRIT (2003). *De macro-ekonomische betekenis van toerisme en recreatie in Nederland in 2001.* Breda: NRIT.

OECD (2000). *Measuring the Role of Tourism in OECD Economies: The OECD Manual on Tourism Satellite Accounts and Employment.* Paris: OECD.

Polo, C., and Valle, E. (2008). An assessment of the impact of tourism in the Balearic Islands. *Tourism Economics, 3.*

Pratt, S. (2014). A general equilibrium analysis of the economic impact of a devaluation on tourism: the case of Fiji. *Tourism Economics, 20 (2).*

Pratt, S., and Blake, A. (2007). *The Economic Impact of Hawaii's Cruise Industry: The Love Boat or the Titanic.* Palma: IATE conference.

Ryan, C. (1998). Economic impacts of small events: estimates and determinants – a New Zealand example. *Tourism Economics, 4.*

Ryan, C., and Lockyer, T. (2001). An economic impact case study: the South Pacific Masters' Games. *Tourism Economics, 3.*

Saarinen, J. (2003). The regional economics of tourism in Northern Finland: the socio-economic implications of recent tourism development and future possibilities for regional development. *Scandinavian Journal of Hospitality and Tourism, 2.*

Sahli, M., and Nowak, J-J. (2007). Does inbound tourism benefit developing countries? A trade theoretic approach. *Journal of Travel Research, 45.*

Samuelson, A. (1964). *Economics.* New York: McGraw-Hill.

Scherer, R., Strauf, S., and Bieger, T. (2002). Die wirtschaftlichen Effekte von Kulturevents. Das Beispiel Lucerne Festival. In *Schweizerische Tourismuswirtschaft, Jahrbuch 2001/2002.* St Gallen: Universität St Gallen.

Scherly, F., and Breiter, M. (2002). *Impact économique des grandes manifestations sportives en Suisse. Etude de cas 'Athletissima' Lausanne 2001.* Lausanne: HEC Lausanne.

Schmidhauser, H. (1979). *The Employment Effect of Tourism in the Tertiary Sector, Demonstrated by the Example of Switzerland.* Bern: AIEST.

Smeral, E. (2001). Beyond the myth of growth in tourism. In T. Bieger and P. Keller (eds), *Tourism Growth and Global Competition.* St-Gall: AIEST.

Smeral, E. (2002). *A Tourism Satellite Account for Austria: The Economics, Methodology and Results.* 37th TRC Meeting, Barcelona 2002.

Smeral, E. (2004). Quandaries of the labour market in tourism exemplified by the case of Austria. *Tourist Review, 3.*

Smeral, E. (2009). The impact of the financial and Economic crises on European Tourism. *Journal of Travel Research, 1.*

Smeral, E. (2009). Methods for measuring the incremental economic impact of a temporary event: a critical assessment. In J. Spindler and D. Huron (eds), *L'Évaluation de L'Événement touristique.* Paris: L'Harmattan.

Smeral, E. (2011). *Public financing of Tourism Organisations: A Conceptual Approach.* Paper presented at the 61st AIEST-Conference. Barcelona: AIEST.

Smeral, E., and Wüger, M. (2008). Methods for measuring the effects of the EU presidency on international tourism. *Tourism Economics, 2.*

Stacey, J. (2015). *Supporting Quality Jobs in Tourism.* Paris: OECD Publishing.

The Host Consultancy (1991). *Jobs in Tourism and Leisure: A Labour Market Review.* London: ETB.

Theuns, H. (1989). *Toerisme in ontwikkelingslanden.* Tilburg: Tilburg University Press.

Thomas, B., and Townsend, A. (2001). New trends in the growth of tourism employment in the UK in the 1990s. *Tourism Economics, 3.*

Tisdell, C. (ed.) (2000). *The Economics of Tourism, Vol. 2, Part 1.* Cheltenham: Edward Elgar Publishing.

Tribe, J. (1997). *The Economics of Leisure and Tourism.* Oxford: Butterworth-Heinemann.

Tribe, J. (2005). *The Economics of Recreation, Leisure & Tourism,* 3rd edn. Elsevier: Amsterdam.

UNCTAD (1971). *Elements of Tourism Policy in Developing Countries.* Geneva: UNCTAD.

VAGO (2007). *State Investment in Major Events.* Melbourne: Victorian Government.

Valdés, L., Aza, R., Banõs, J., Torres, E., and Valle, E. (2007). *A Methodology to Evaluate the Economic Impact of Tourism in a Region: The Case of Asturias.* Palma: IATE congress.

Vanhove, N. (1976). Cost–benefit analysis: theory and techniques applied to tourism. In S. Wahab (ed.), *Managerial Aspects of Tourism.* Turin: Salah Wahab.

Vanhove, N. (1986). Tourism and regional economic development. In J. Paelinck (ed.), *Human Behaviour in Geographical Space: Essays in Honour of Leo H. Klaassen.* Cheltenham: Gower.

Vanhove, N. (1993). Sociaal-economische betekenis van het toerisme in Vlaanderen. In U. Claeys (ed.), *Toerisme in Vlaanderen.* Leuven: Acco.

Vanhove, N. (1997). Mass tourism – benefits and costs. In S. Wahab and J. Pigram (eds), *Tourism, Development and Growth.* London: Routledge.

Vanhove, N. (2003). Externalities of sport and tourism investments, activities and events. In P. Keller and T. Bieger (eds), *Sport and Tourism.* AIEST Congress, Athens, 2003. St-Gall: AIEST.

Vaughan, R. (1977). *The Economic Impact of the Edinburgh Festival*. Edinburgh: Scottish Tourist Board.

Williams, A., and Shaw, G. (eds) (1988). *Tourism and Economic Development: Western European Experiences*. London: Belhaven Press.

Wing, I. (2003). *Computable General Equilibrium Models and Their Use in Economy-Wide Policy Analysis: Everything You Ever Wanted to Know (But Were Afraid to Ask)*. Boston, paper (Wikipedia).

Wood, R. (1992). Hospitality industry labour trends: British and international experience. *Tourism Management, 3*.

WTO (1988). *Economic Review of World Tourism*. Madrid: WTO.

WTO (2000). *Tourism Satellite Account, Measuring Tourism Demand*. Madrid: WTO.

Yzewijn, D., and De Brabander, G. (1989). *De economische betekenis van het toerisme en de recreatie van de Provincie Antwerpen*. Antwerp: Provincie Antwerpen.

Zhang, J., Madsen, B., and Jensen-Butler, C. (2007). Regional economic impacts of tourism: the case of Denmark. *Regional Studies, 6*.

Chapter 11

Micro-evaluation of projects in the tourism and hospitality industry

Introduction

So far we have dealt with various aspects of demand and supply in tourism, and the impact of tourism on value added creation, employment generation and the balance of payments. There is still one economic aspect missing. There cannot be a tourism industry without projects. These projects can take different forms, such as development of attractions, accommodation, entertainment, transport, congress centres, events, etc. They all involve serious investment. The investor – public or private sector – always has a great financial responsibility, and therefore a preliminary investment appraisal is a must.

Long experience in the tourism sector has demonstrated that many investment decisions are very emotional; sometimes projects by physical planners are taken for granted, wrong investment appraisal methods are applied and/or the right method is used incorrectly.

Therefore, giving special attention to investment appraisal has its place in a book dealing with various economic aspects of tourism. To a large extent, the methods dealt with in this chapter are not unique for the tourism sector. However, any responsible person in tourism should have knowledge of the right approach to evaluating a tourism project. Probably the responsible person – public or private – will not carry out the investment appraisal; nonetheless, he or she should be able to understand the results of such a study.

Most projects in the tourism sector are the initiative of individuals or companies – tourism or financial – and here the classic investment appraisal methods apply. However, in tourism, more than in any other sector, the investor (or what we call the 'paymaster') is often not a company or a tourism entrepreneur but the public sector. Indeed, many projects belong to the general tourism infrastructure, and the benefits do not only accrue to the paymaster, who may not consider the negative effects. In other words, externalities must be taken into account. In such a case, the classic methods of investment appraisal are insufficient.

The latter consideration justifies the title of this chapter. A project can be appraised from the micro point of view or from the macro point of view. In the first case, only benefits (receipts) and costs for the investor (private or public) come into the picture. In the second case, the benefit and cost items are large in number and of different natures. The total impact of the project for the destination should be taken into account. Application of cost–benefit analysis is the correct method (see Chapter 12).

This chapter focusses on three topics. First, there is a focus on the nature of investment appraisal and an exploration of the difference between micro and macro approaches. A second section deals with the conventional and the more scientific methods of investment appraisal, while the third section looks at the content of a feasibility and business plan related to the hotel sector.

The nature of a tourism investment appraisal

This section focusses on two major topics: the basics of investment appraisal, and an exploration of the difference between micro- and macro-evaluation.

An investment comprises a planned series of capital expenditures undertaken in anticipation of their generating a larger series of cash flows at various times in the future. The main problem of investment appraisal is quite clear from this definition: it is the evaluation of uncertain future cash flows in relation to cash outlays (possibly also uncertain) in the immediate or near future. The solution of this general problem involves an understanding of the basic techniques of discounting and compounding.

The basic assumption of discounting and compounding is that money has a time value, i.e. a given sum of money now is normally worth more than an equal and certain sum at some future date. Why? Because it permits profitable investment or consumption in the interval. This means that a given sum today is worth more than the same sum in ten years, because it can be invested and earn additional money in the intervening period. For this reason, economists have learned to discount receipts expected in the future. The opposite side of the coin is the time preference of individuals for present consumption over present savings (or future consumption). For postponing consumption, people need to be rewarded. The reward per unit of savings, in the form of interest, will depend on several factors, and we shall deal with this further in this chapter.

Discounting is the ascertainment of present values; compounding is the ascertainment of terminal values. The basic equations are:

$$S = P(1+r)^n \tag{11.1}$$

$$P = \frac{S}{(1+r)^n} \quad \text{or} \quad S(1+r)^{-n} \tag{11.2}$$

where

P identifies a sum at the present time
S identifies a sum arising in the future
r = rate of discount
n = year 1 to n

Most investment problems involve more than the comparison of a future sum with a present sum; usually the problem is relating a series of future cash flows to a present investment outlay or a series of outlays. Equation (11.2) becomes:

$$P \sum_{i=1}^{i=n} \frac{A_t}{(1+r)^n} \tag{11.3}$$

where A_t = cash flow in year t

In a case where the cash flows vary from year to year in an irregular manner, there is no formula that will enable the present value of the series to be computed in one embracing calculation. Where the series of cash flows follows a regular pattern, shortcut formulations can be used. Three situations arise in practice. The first is constant periodic cash flows or annuities. In this case, equation (11.3) can be transformed into:

$$P = \frac{A[1 - (1 + r)^{-n}]}{r} \qquad (11.4)$$

when A = 1

$$a_{n/r} = \frac{1 - (1 + r)^{-n}}{r} \qquad (11.5)$$

and $a_{n/r}$ = present value of an annuity of €1 a year for n years at r per cent per annum.

The second case is constant periodic cash flows – perpetuity. A perpetuity is an annuity that goes on for ever. If in equation (11.5) n goes to infinity, so that the annuity becomes a perpetuity, then the $(1 + r)^{-n}$ term becomes zero, and the present value of the perpetuity equals 1/r (Bierman and Smidt, 1990).

The third possible situation is when cash flows grow at a compound rate. The shortcut formula becomes:

$$P = \frac{A_{a_{n/r_o}}}{1 + b} \qquad (11.6)$$

where

$r_o = (r - b)/(1 + b)$
b = growth rate of the cash flows

An investor is after all interested in the return on an investment project. Therefore, we return to equation (11.3) to define the yield rate, which is the solution r in equation (11.3); it is the rate that equates capital outlays and their resultant cash flows. The yield rate is that rate of interest that discounts future cash flows to the present value.

Although the ascertainment of the terminal values is of less importance with respect to investment appraisal, two formulae should be mentioned. The first relates to a series of cash flows:

$$S = \sum_{i=1}^{i=n} A_i (1 + r)^{n-1} \qquad (11.7)$$

In the case of constant periodic cash flows, a shortcut formula can be applied:

$$S = \frac{A[(1 + r)^n - 1]}{r} \qquad (11.8)$$

Where A is a series of 1, equation (11.8) becomes:

$$S_{n/r} = \frac{[(1 + r)^n - 1]}{r}$$

where $S_{n/r}$ is the conventional symbol for the terminal value of an annuity of €1 per year, for n years at r per cent per annum.

These basic notions and formulae are the fundamentals of the discounting (or scientific) methods of investment appraisal that are dealt with in the third section of this chapter.

The difference between micro- and macro-evaluations has been explained. The discounting methods mean that we take into account the revenues and cash costs over the life of the project, discounting them to a base year and subtracting the capital costs of the project (also discounted).

The discounted cash flow approach takes account only of the advantages of the project to the investor (i.e. it is a micro-evaluation).

For many tourism projects, the discounted cash flow approach is insufficient. Social cost–benefit analysis (CBA) is more useful. Referring to Prest and Turvey (1967), CBA can be defined as:

> A practical way of assessing the desirability of projects, where it is important to take a long view (in the sense of looking at repercussions in the further as well as in the nearer future) and a wide view (in the sense of allowing for side effects of many kinds on many persons, industries, regions etc.) i.e. it implies the enumeration and evaluation of all the relevant costs and benefits.

In addition to the cash flows, the calculations take account of all the changes in social benefits and social costs that result from the project, reducing them to monetary terms and discounting them to a present value from which the capital cost may be subtracted in order to obtain the net present value. CBA is by definition a macro-approach. We set the macro-economic costs and benefits against each other. Costs are defined in a special way – what level of output would have been reached if the factors of production were utilized in the rest of the economy? In other words, the costs of the project are measured in terms of its opportunity costs. Benefits are the additional benefits to the community that result from the realization of the project. The fundamental objective of a CBA is to complete the private economic calculations with figures for the economic benefits and costs of a project to its consumers and the society as a whole (see Chapter 12).

The discounting methods

The unscientific conventional methods of investment appraisal

Before dealing with the discounting methods, the conventional methods that are very often applied in tourism will be briefly discussed. The most conventional method is undoubtedly the 'rate of return method', or the 'average-profit method'. This method can be defined as the ratio of profit, net of depreciation, to capital. This method has three significant shortcomings:

1 It fails to allow for the incidence of capital outlays and earnings. In other words, this method neglects one of the basic principles of investment appraisal: money has a time value.
2 It neglects the pre-production period. The latter has a great impact on the results of big projects with a long preparation and construction phase.
3 It strongly discriminates against short-term projects and projects that pay off more heavily in the early than the later years.

A variant of the rate of return method is the 'peak-profit method'. The basis of this method is to take the level of profit in the best year and express it as a rate of return on the sum invested. The assumption behind this method is that the peak-profit rate of return is in some way a guide to the average profitability of the project. It is evident that the same shortcomings apply to this variant. Furthermore, having similar profit streams every year is an additional assumption.

A third, and quite often applied, conventional method is the 'payback method'. This method does not calculate a return, but the time period it takes (T) for an investment to generate sufficient incremental cash to recover the initial incremental capital outlay in full. If A (cash flow) is constant:

$$T = \frac{C}{A} \tag{11.9}$$

This method is applied for sectors and projects subject to rapid technological changes, and is useful in assessing risk and liquidity.

Owing to the significant shortcomings or the special character of the conventional methods, discounting methods are far more suitable in appraisal of tourism projects. There are three basic discounting methods:

1 The net present value method (NPV), which has two derived methods:

- Benefit–cost ratio (B/C)
- NPV per unit of outlay

2 The yield method, or the internal rate of return (IRR)
3 The annual capital charge method (ACC).

Taking into account the fact that the underlying conditions of the ACC method are never fulfilled in tourism, it is the other discounting methods that will be discussed in the following paragraphs.

Net present value method

The NPV can be defined as the sum of the annual net benefits (gross benefits minus gross costs) of an investment discounted by the opportunity costs of capital. The latter is the rate of return that capital can earn on its best alternative uses. In other words, it is the sum of the present values of the cash flows for all the years during the project's life. Cash flows can be categorized into positive and negative.

Positive cash flows (receipts) can take different forms:

- Gross receipts (or net profit)
- Rent
- Net changes in working capital
- Net residual asset values
- Depreciation provision less replacement expenditure.

Negative cash flows (expenditures) are:

- Capital outlays
- Operational expenditure (or operating losses)
- Terminal expenditure.

In mathematical terms, NPV can be written as:

$$\text{NPV} = \sum_{i=1}^{i=n} \frac{A_i}{(1+r)^i} \quad \text{or} \quad \sum_{i=1}^{i=n} \frac{B_i}{(1+r)^i} - \sum_{i=1}^{i=n} \frac{C_i}{(1+r)^i} \qquad (11.10)$$

where

A_i = net cash flow at the end of year i
B_i = positive cash flows
C_i = negative cash flows
r = cost of capital or discount rate
n = project life

The minimum NPV value acceptable for an investor is zero; a value lower than zero means that the present value of the costs exceeds the present value of the benefits.

Three important points should be noted with respect to the application of equation (11.10):

1 The NPV value is strongly influenced by the value of the discount rate; the higher the r value, the lower the NPV.
2 Although depreciation is a cash flow, depreciation is never included as a cost in discounted cash flow (dcf) analysis. Its function in conventional accounting – to allow for recovery of the initial capital outlay – is taken care of in the dcf techniques by entering the original capital outlay into the cash flow.
3 Financial charges such as interest and repayment of capital (amortization) are not normally taken into account in the cash flow because the discounting techniques themselves allow for the return on capital as well as the return of capital – assuming the capital outlay has been entered into the cash flow as a cost item, which is the normal practice.

Internal rate of return

The IRR of a tourism investment project is defined as the rate of 'interest' which discounts the future net cash flows of a project into equality with its capital cost; it is the r value that results in a zero NPV.

$$IRR = \sum_{i=1}^{i=n} \frac{A_i}{(1+r)^i} - C = 0 \quad \text{or} \quad \sum_{i=1}^{i=n} \frac{B_i}{(1+r)^i} - \sum_{i=1}^{i=n} \frac{C_i}{(1+r)^i} \tag{11.11}$$

Without using software the calculation of IRR can be time consuming, owing to the successive discounting approximations (successive interpolations). A shortcut formula can be helpful:

$$IRR = L_r + (H_r - L_r) \frac{\text{NPV at } L_r}{|\text{NPV at } L_r + \text{NPV at } H_r|} \tag{11.12}$$

where

L_r = an interest rate that results in a positive NPV
H_r = an interest rate that results in a negative NPV

The expression $|\text{NPV at } L_r + \text{NPV at } H_r|$ is the absolute difference between the two NPVs.

Benefit–cost ratio

A variant of the NPV, often used in project appraisal, is the 'benefit–cost ratio' – or the present value of the benefits over the present value of the costs:

$$\frac{B'}{C'} = \frac{\displaystyle\sum_{i=1}^{i=n} \frac{B_i}{(1+r)^i}}{\displaystyle\sum_{i=1}^{i=n} \frac{C_i}{(1+r)^i}} \tag{11.13}$$

Any B/C ratio over 1.00 should be accepted. However, the ratio can vary as a function of the degree of 'grossness' (i.e. lack of detail) in the project presentation. A simple example may be an illustration. Table 11.1 presents the same project in three different forms of 'grossness'.

In other words, the same project can be presented with several B/C ratios and all ratios are correct. Needless to say, this means that a project evaluator can present the same project in a more positive or a less positive way. This method also makes it difficult to compare different projects because each project can have a different degree of 'grossness' of the cost items.

Table 11.1 The benefit–cost ratio for the same project presented with different levels of detail, A, B and C

	A	B	C
Present values			
● Capital outlay	100	100	100
● Marketing costs	100	–	100
● Administrative costs	100	100	–
● Maintenance	1,000	1,000	–
● Other costs	1,500	–	–
Total costs	2,800	1,200	200
Benefits	3,100	1,500	500
NPV	300	300	300
B/C ratio	1.11	1.25	2.50

Net present value per unit of outlay

The NPV per unit of outlay is simply the NPV divided by the total investment outlay, with the latter being discounted at the same rate used to get the NPV. In the context of a fixed development budget, this is considered by many authors of cost–benefit analysis to be the best approach for the ranking of projects. We start first with the project with the highest NPV per unit of outlay; then comes the project with the second highest ratio, etc. If the budget is limited, the project with the lowest ratio should be dropped first.

However, the definition of 'investment' itself contains some arbitrary elements. In some projects, 'current' outlays may be just as important as 'capital' outlays. For this reason, it is probably desirable to define the denominator in this measure to include all outlays subject to the rationing process, rather than just the 'investment' expenditure alone. The formula can be written as:

$$R = \frac{NPV}{C'} = \frac{B' - C'}{C'} \tag{11.14}$$

where

R = NPV per unit of outlay
B' and C' are expressed in present values

In relating NPV or dcf to total costs, we automatically arrive at the most acceptable criteria to be applied.

Accept/reject decisions

As a formal accept or reject criterion, NPV and IRR lead to the same selection of single projects. However, the ranking can be different (see Figure 11.1).

What are the advantages and disadvantages of the NPV and IRR methods? The advantages of IRR are threefold:

1 It is most familiar to people.
2 There is no dispute about the cost of capital; nevertheless, *ex-post* the IRR should be related to a reference base.
3 There is no discussion about what to include in the denominator.

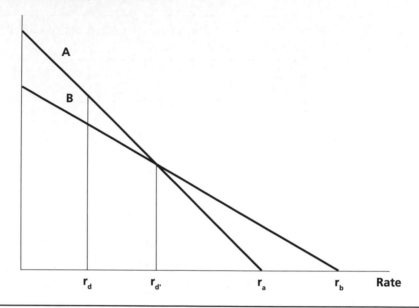

Figure 11.1 Comparison of NPV and IRR methods

The IRR also has a number of disadvantages:

1 The rate of discount cannot be changed during the lifetime of the project (this disadvantage has only theoretical significance).
2 It works in favour of short-term projects.
3 It can yield multiple and meaningless results.
4 It may provide a different project ranking to the NPV approach.
5 There is the explicit assumption that the expected cash flows throughout the project are received by the investor and can be reinvested at the IRR (de Keijzer and Renaud, 2017).

In Figure 11.1, the IRR of project A is equal to r_a and of project B is equal to r_b. As long as the discount rate is lower than $r_{d'}$, project A is superior to project B; beyond the $r_{d'}$ rate we reach the inverse situation.

The NPV method has one major drawback. NPV is an absolute quantity – a money value expressed in absolute terms – and as such it is difficult to interpret the result. What is the meaning of an NPV of 100 million euros? This value can be high, but also rather marginal. Comparison of the result with the amount of investment is necessary, which gives the NPV per unit of outlay.

The necessity for a feasibility study

A project evaluation is more than an application of a discounted cash flow method. It is necessary to investigate in advance the possibility of selling the tourism products and the cost of their production, so that the anticipated profit may be foreseen before taking a decision in favour of or against the venture. The detailed process of this investigation and measurement is known as a feasibility study. Pandit (1986) describes a feasibility study as follows:

> The literal meaning of the word feasibility is possibility, practicability etc., but its application in the present context covers a wider range. Feasibility in this case would

cover necessity, practicability and profitability, based on which a decision can be taken on the justifiability of the investment.

According to Ward (1991), 'a feasibility study might be defined as an appraisal of a development proposal providing a measurement of the return on investment'.

In these descriptions there are three basic elements. First, *necessity* means there is a demand in the market. In the case of a hotel project, this implies the following demands:

● General market conditions (e.g. geo-economic situation)
● Project market conditions (the performance of existing hotels, sales composition)
● Specific demand factors (type of economic activities, characteristics of existing hotels)
● A segment of customers and growth perspectives.

Secondly, *practicability* indicates that the implementation of the project is technically practicable. Many facets should be considered and investigated, including:

● Architecture (what will make the hotel superior to the ones in the competing market, attractive and acceptable to the guests, suitable for efficient operation, etc.)
● Basic architectural plans (site plans, typical floor plan, etc.)
● Budgetary constraints, quality level and size
● Available sites – examining them and evaluating their suitability (suitability of location and various aspects of the plot of land such as size, soil conditions, visibility of the site, shape of the site, availability of water, electricity and other public utilities, etc.)
● Factors relevant to the preference of the clientele (e.g. entrance, size of the bedrooms, view from the rooms, facilities, garden and landscape)
● Investment costs.

Thirdly, *profitability* relates to the NPV or IRR and financial obligations – in other words, will the project meet all its operating expenses, debt refunding, depreciation and tax payments, and earn profit? All this implies that attention should be paid to the tariff structure, pricing system, and how and by whom the hotel will be run (e.g. franchising, management contract or owner). Once these three elements have been defined, we can prepare a business table.

A business table: a practical example

The principles of a feasibility study were applied to a family hotel at the Belgian Coast in the mid-1990s. The market possibilities were investigated and a variety of occupancy rates were applied. The practicability was analysed and translated into investment costs. The third step is the profitability. We start from the following characteristics:

1 A hotel with 100 rooms
2 An investment of €17 million, divided as follows

   ● land €1 million
   ● hotel €10 million
   ● restaurant €2 million
   ● recreation €3 million
   ● shops €1 million

3 Equity €10 million and loan capital €7 million
4 Construction period one year
5 Average room rate, €120
6 Interest rate, 5 per cent

Table 11.2 Business table for a family hotel, 2017 (in €10,000)

Year	1	2	3	4	5	6	7	8	9	10	11
Investment											
Land*	100										
Hotel	1,000										
Horeca	200										
Recreation	300										
Shops	100										
Receipts											
Hotel		175	219	263	263	263	263	263	263	263	263
Restaurant		16	16	16	16	16	16	16	16	16	16
Recreation		36	36	36	36	36	36	36	36	36	36
Shops		5	6	8	8	8	8	8	8	8	8
Total		232	277	322	322	322	322	322	322	322	322
Running costs											
Hotel		105	131	158	158	158	158	158	158	158	158
Recreation		12	12	12	12	12	12	12	12	12	12
Total		117	143	170	170	170	170	170	170	170	170
GOP./Ebitda*		115	134	153	153	153	153	153	153	153	153
Financial costs											
Depreciation		82	82	82	82	82	82	82	82	82	82
Interest		35	32	28	25	21	18	14	11	7	4
Grants		75	75								
Total		42	39	110	107	103	100	96	93	89	86
Ebta**		73	96	43	47	50	54	57	61	64	68
Taxes		22	29	13	14	15	16	17	18	19	20
Net profit		51	67	30	33	35	38	40	43	45	47
Amortization		70	70	70	70	70	70	70	70	70	70
Cash flow		133	149	112	115	117	120	122	125	127	129
Cash in/out	−1,700	190	209	153	153	153	153	153	153	153	153
Residual value											880
IRR	6.0 %										

* Ebitda: Earnings before interest, taxes, depreciation and amortization
** Ebta: Earnings before taxes and amortization (debt payments)

7 Depreciation in € million

	30 years	10 years
● land	–	–
● hotel	7.5	2.5
● restaurant	1.2	0.8
● recreation	2.0	1.0
● shops	1.0	

8 The hotel had a tax rate of 30 per cent
9 The residual value after ten years of operation is expected to be €8.8 million

Based on these assumptions, it is possible to forecast the annual results and the NPV and IRR of the project (see Table 11.2). The calculation is restricted to ten years with a residual value at the end of the tenth year of operation. To a certain extent the procedure is unusual; a 30-year period of operation is more common.

Table 11.2 provides a lot of useful information with respect to the profitability of the hotel and the financial side of the project. First, the NPV equals €1.025 million and the IRR amounts to 6.0 per cent. Compared to the prevailing interest rate for investments and the inherent risks of any investment project, this result is not very profitable.

Secondly, the project shows a net profit throughout the whole lifecycle considered. As a consequence, the cash flow or the sum of net profit (losses) and depreciation is positive for every year of operation.

Thirdly, the cash flow is sufficient each year to finance the annual debt payments.

Fourthly, the ebitda shows the gross operational profit. It is very often the basis for evaluating a takeover price of a company or a project. Seven to nine times the ebitda is a rule of thumb to define a takeover price.

Finally, notice that the calculation of the NPV or IRR is not based on the cash flow but on the row cash in/out of Table 11.2 (see definition of positive and negative cash flows in the application of dcf methods). The amount of €1.899 million for the first operational year is the sum of the GOP (gross operational profit) of €1.149 million and the grants (0.750 million) to support the hotel investments.

References and further reading

Bierman, H., and Smidt, S. (1990). *The Capital Budgeting Decision: Economic Analysis of Investment Projects*, 7th edn. New York: Macmillan Press.

de Keijzer, P., and Renaud, J. (2017). *Financieel management en financiering. Waardering, financiering en risicobeheersing*, 2nd edn. Amsterdam: Noordhoff Uitgevers.

DeFusco, R., McLeavey, D., Pinto, J., Runkle, D., and Anson, M. (2016). *Quantitative Investment Analysis*, 3rd edn. CFA Institute.

Deloof, M., Manigart, S., Ooghe, H., and Van Hulle, C. (2012). *Handboek Bedrijfsfinanciering*, 4th edn. Gent: Intersentia.

Lengkeek, J.W. (2016). *De investeringsanalyse in recreatie en toerisme*. Breda: Letters en Bits.

Pandit, S.N. (1986). *Hotel Project: Feasibility Evaluation*. Vienna: Schriftenreihe für empirische Tourismusforschung und Hospitality Management.

Prest, A., and Turvey, R. (1967). Cost–benefit analysis: a survey. *Surveys of Economic Theory*, Vol. II. London: Macmillan.

Robinson, T., Henry, E., Pirie, W., and Broihahn, M. (2015). *International Statement Analysis Workbook*. CFA Institute.

Sweers, J., and de Graaf, I. (2013). *Hospitality Benchmark 2013*. Amstelveen: KPMG.

Ward, T.J. (1991). The hotel feasibility study – principles and practice. In C. Cooper (ed.), *Progress in Tourism, Recreation and Hospitality Management*. London: Belhaven Press.

Chapter 12

Macro-evaluation of projects in the tourism and hospitality industry

Foundations of CBA

Cost–benefit analysis (CBA) is a practical way of assessing the desirability of projects, where it is important to take a long view and a wide view – i.e. it implies the enumeration and evaluation of all relevant costs and benefits. In CBA, we try to consider all the costs and benefits to society as a whole. That is the reason why some people refer to CBA as social cost–benefit analysis. For Boardman *et al.* (2001), cost–benefit analysis is 'a policy assessment method that quantifies in monetary terms the value of all policy consequences to all members of society. The net social benefits measure the value of the policy. Social benefits minus social costs equals net social benefits.' The broad purpose of CBA is to help in social decision-making.

The foundations of CBA are the Pareto efficiency, willingness to pay (see consumer surplus) and producer surplus. An allocation is Pareto-efficient if no alternative allocation can make at least one person better off without making anyone else worse off. An allocation is inefficient, therefore, if an alternative allocation can be found that would make at least one person better off without making anyone else worse off. Boardman *et al.* (2001) state that 'one would have to be malevolent not to want to achieve Pareto efficiency – why forgo gains to persons that would not inflict losses on others?' These writers make the link between positive net benefits and Pareto efficiency. If a policy has positive net benefits, then it is possible to find a set of transfers, or side payments, that makes at least one person better off without making anyone else worse off. A full understanding of this link requires some knowledge of how to measure costs and benefits in CBA. It is necessary to consider willingness to pay as the method for valuing the outputs of the policy, and opportunity costs as the method for valuing the resources required to implement the policy.

The costs are measured in terms of its opportunity costs, or what level of output would be reached if the factors of production were utilized in the rest of the economy. Benefits are the additional benefits to the community that would result from the realization of the project. Costs and benefits of a project are the time streams of consumption forgone and provided.

In a CBA, there are four important steps:

1. Identification of the cost and benefit items
2. Quantification of the cost and benefit items
3. Valuation of the cost and benefit items
4. Calculation of net present value (NPV) and/or internal rate of return (IRR).

Cost and benefit items in an CBA scheme are to a large extent based on the existence of externalities. In the next section we make a distinction between positive and negative externalities.

Externalities in tourism

Macro-evaluation or CBA is directly related to the externalities. 'External benefits' is a frequently used term in tourism. What do we understand by external benefits, and are there also external costs?

'Externalities' is one of the vaguest and most ambiguous terms in economic science. Webster's Dictionary defines 'externality' as 'the state or quality of being external'. This definition is of course not very helpful. We find a more useful description in Boardman *et al.* (2001), who describe an *externality* as an effect that production or consumption has on third parties – people not involved in the production or consumption of a good. It is a by-product of production or consumption for which there is no market. 'No market' is not an essential part of the definition, and in my view is not always correct.

Other authors use the expression 'external effects' instead of 'externalities' (Sugden and Williams, 1988; Mishan, 1994). They consider the social costs and benefits of a (private or public) project rather than the financial outlays and receipts that would be considered by decision-makers in private (or public) firms. There are several reasons for expecting social costs and benefits to be different from private (public) outlays and receipts. Indeed, externalities or external effects may occur for a wide variety of reasons. Some result because a particular type of technology is used (e.g. deterioration of the landscape caused by transport of electricity). Others result because of interdependencies or synergies between producers and consumers of different groups of producers (e.g. my neighbour is a beekeeper who provides pollination services for the fruit in my orchard). A third group of externalities occurs because of networking (e.g. a convention centre stimulates the turnover of hotels and restaurants). Others arise because of negative effects on competitive projects, companies or events.

It is clear from the above that there are positive and negative externalities. The first group produces benefits, while the latter imposes social costs.

'Externalities' is a generic term that is used, rightly or wrongly, to justify many projects. Furthermore, in many studies several terms are used to cover externalities – indirect effects, spillover effects, induced effects, stemming effects, pecuniary effects, side effects, etc. Many consultants in the tourism sector abuse externalities to inflate the so-called benefits of a project. Therefore, to avoid such abuses it seems appropriate to start with identification of the types of externalities.

In this section a distinction is made between three types of negative and three types of positive externalities: 'unpaid' costs and benefits; 'underpaid' costs and benefits; and positive and negative side effects.

Negative externalities

The first category of negative externalities is *unpaid costs*. Any project or event is the initiative of a person, firm or public body. Who pays for or finances the project is not important; we call the investor the paymaster. At this level the paymaster is responsible for the investment costs and the running costs of the project, but he also cashes in the direct payments of the consumer (e.g. entrance fees to participate in an event, the use of a ski-lift, etc.). We call this the 'project' or 'micro-' level. It does not matter if the investor belongs to the private or the public sector. However, in most cases the paymaster does not pay for all the costs of the project or event. Many projects provoke a lot of economic, social and/or environmental costs for which the investor does not pay. There is no free lunch. A third party will pay the bill or suffer inconvenience (Vanhove, 2003).

Typical examples of unpaid costs include:

- Water pollution
- Air pollution
- Noise pollution
- Traffic congestion
- Security costs of events
- Destruction of landscape
- Extension of an airport
- Sight pollution of windmills.

In the case of *underpaid costs*, some costs are taken into account, but not at the full price. A typical example is the expropriation of land for a big event at a price below the market value – in other words, the price of the land retained in the investment costs at the micro-level is lower than the real value. This brings us to the notion of opportunity costs. Cost should be measured at opportunity costs.

'Opportunity costs' is another economic term that leads to a lot of interpretation problems and misunderstanding. Any tourism project (e.g. an event) requires resources that could be used to produce other goods or services instead. Tourism projects such as festivals, sporting events, theme parks, winter sports infrastructure, for example, require labour, land, capital and/or equipment. The resources used for these purposes cannot be used to produce other goods or services. Almost all public or private projects incur opportunity costs. Conceptually, these costs equal the value of the goods and services that would have been produced had the resources used in carrying them out been used instead in the best alternative way (Boardman *et al.*, 2001). In other words, production elsewhere is forgone.

As stated, cost items should be measured at the opportunity costs. In efficient markets, opportunity costs are equal to market prices. However, markets are not always efficient. Let us suppose that the Olympic Games is to take place in a region or country with very high unemployment. In the construction phase of the necessary infrastructure (e.g. new stadia, new sport infrastructure) and in the running of the games, hundreds or thousands of unemployed find jobs. All of them are paid a normal salary. These salaries are included in the investment and running costs at the micro-level.

However, costs should be measured at opportunity costs. It is the value of resources employed in their most productive alternative use. What are the opportunity costs of an unemployed person? His or her best alternative is probably unemployment. The corresponding contribution of unemployed people to the national product is zero (unemployment benefit is a pure transfer). There is no production (goods or services) forgone. This type of underpayment of costs is quite often a very important item in project appraisal from a macro point of view. This might be even more the case in a tourism than in an industrial region. Many tourism regions have high unemployment.

A third group of negative externalities relates to *side effects* on competitive projects or events. We all know of situations where a new tourism project is competing with an existing production unit in the same region – for example, a seaside resort with a famous beach festival is confronted with a similar new production in a neighbouring resort, or a new congress centre is built in a place close to a city which already has good congress facilities. In such circumstances, a reduction in the turnover of the existing product can be expected. The corresponding reduction of value added should be considered as a cost item for the new event or congress centre.

Positive externalities

Again, *unpaid benefits* are the first category of positive externalities. The paymaster does not pay all the costs of a tourism project and, similarly, not all benefits of a project or an event accrue to the investor. In tourism there are many possible unpaid benefits, such as:

- Image effect
- Promotion effect
- Improvement of international liquidity position
- Increase of property value
- Free fees.

However, in other cases the consumer does not always pay the full price of a product or service, or we are confronted with *underpaid benefits*. If the consumer pays less than the market price for a service (e.g. a performance) – benefits are measured in terms of market prices – it seems obvious that there is an underpayment of benefits. The situation becomes more complicated when we consider the consumers' willingness to pay. This brings us to the notion of consumer surplus. The latter is one of the foundations of CBA (Pearce, 1983; Boardman *et al.*, 2001). It is the benefit to consumers over and above the price they pay for a good or service.

A demand curve indicates the quantities of a good or service that individuals purchase at various prices. In Figure 12.1, a downward-sloped demand curve is illustrated as line P_1F.

The key is the link between demand schedules and the willingness to pay (WTP). Figure 12.1 illustrates that there is at least one consumer who is willing to pay a price of P_1 for one unit of service X. Similarly, there is at least one person who would pay a price of P_2 for the second unit of X, and there is someone who would pay P_3 for the third unit of X, and so forth. The message from this exercise is that the area under the demand curve, or the sum of all the unit-wide rectangles, closely approximates the WTP for X by all members of society. In other words, the triangle P_1P_4C and the rectangle P_4CX_3O in Figure 12.1 approximate society's WTP for a given amount of X, in this case the amount X_3. Thus, the sum of the triangle and the rectangle approximates the total gross benefits society would receive from consuming X_3 units of service X. The consumers pay P_4 to the producers of the tourism service. In this case, the net benefits from consuming X_3 units equal the area below the demand curve but above the price line P_4C. This triangle P_1P_4C is called the consumer surplus. When demand curves are known, consumer surplus is one of the basic concepts in CBA to value impacts. The reason why consumer surplus is so important to CBA is that changes in consumer surplus can be used as reasonable approximations of society's WTP policy changes (Boardman *et al.*, 2001).

To show how the concept of consumer surplus can be used in CBA, consider a project that results in a price change. We take a price reduction in Figure 12.1 from P_4 to P_5. This would result in a benefit to consumers equal to the area of the trapezoid P_4CFP_5. It follows both because consumers gain from paying a lower price for the X_3 units they previously purchased, and because they gain from the consumption of $X_3 - X_4$ additional units.

If there is an increase in the price, there is a loss of consumer surplus. However, if the price increase results from an imposed tax, there is no loss but a simple transfer – money is transferred from consumers to the government. From the perspective of society as a whole its net impact is zero. Changes in consumers' surplus are measures of the effects on the welfare of individuals of changes in the prices of goods that they consume. Individuals may be affected in a very similar way if there are changes in the costs of 'factor prices' (such as labour, the use of capital and land) that they supply. Such changes are said to lead to changes in producers' surplus (Sugden and Williams, 1988). Producer surplus is the supply-side equivalent to consumer surplus. To define producer surplus, we refer to Figure 12.2. At a price of P_1, the producers receive revenues equal to the area represented by the rectangular area OP_1BX_1. The difference

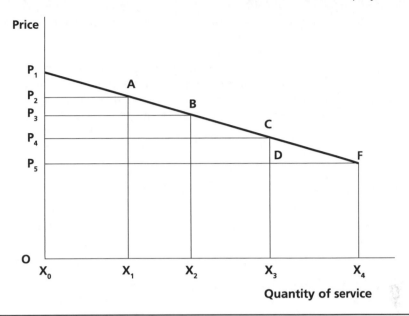

Figure 12.1 Consumer surplus

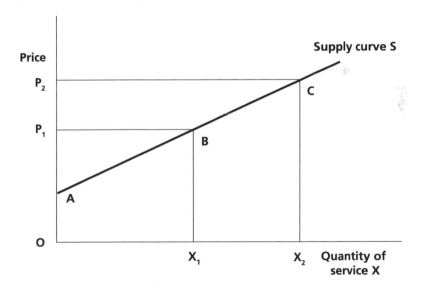

Figure 12.2 Producer surplus

between this rectangular area and the area of the rectangle under the supply curve S, that is the area AP_1B, is called producer surplus. Indeed, some producers are willing to produce at a price lower than P_1.

Thus, producer surplus equals the revenues from selling X_1 less the variable costs required to produce X_1 – or the sum of total producer surplus and opportunity costs (that is areas AP_1B + $OABX_1$) corresponds to total revenues.

Price changes that are due to a project result in impacts on producers that can be valued in terms of changes in producer surplus. An increase in price to P_2 increases producer surplus (or economic profits) by P_1P_2CB (Boardman *et al.*, 2001).

Most tourism projects or events have a positive impact on the turnover of many other production units such as hotels, restaurants, pubs, souvenir shops, etc., known as the *side effects* on complementary activities. It is not the turnover that counts but the additional value added created. Quite often the additional value added in complementary activities is many times greater than the value added at the micro-level. Those complementary activities have in their turn an impact on intermediate deliveries. We call them indirect effects (indirect income).

Care must be taken with secondary effects due to spending of earned direct and indirect income, or induced effects (induced income). Should we take into account the portion of incomes resulting from an event spent by the recipients? This brings us to the famous multiplier effects, in particular the induced effects (see page 276). These induced effects need to be treated with caution.

Identification of cost and benefit items

The identification of cost and benefit items is directly related to the externalities dealt with earlier in this chapter. Table 12.1 might be helpful in identifying the cost and benefit items from the viewpoint of society as a whole. We distinguish four levels of costs and benefits. The first level is the micro-level, also called the project or paymaster's level – in other words, relating to who pays for the project. The other three levels are related to the externalities dealt with earlier in this chapter. Table 12.1 can be applied to the identification of possible cost and benefit items of a big event (see Table 12.2).

Table 12.1 Cost–benefit scheme

Level	Costs	Benefits
Project or paymaster's	Ca: investment Cb: running costs	Ba: direct receipts
'Unpaid' level	Cc: unpaid use of factors of production	Bb: unpaid satisfaction of needs
'Underpayment' level	Cd: underpayment of factors of production	Bc: underpayment of products and services
Side effects	Ce: side effects on competitors	Bd: side effects on complementary sectors, firms or projects

This is not the only possible cost–benefit scheme. Another possible scheme is described by Scherly and Breiter (2002). Their approach is thematic and applied to a sports event. They make a distinction between:

1 Economic impact (based on national accounts)

- direct economic impact
- indirect economic impact

2 Ecological aspects

- transport
- energy, air and climate
- waste
- landscape

3 Social aspects
4 Image (perception of the organization, visitors and local population).

In reality this approach is closer to a general impact analysis than a genuine CBA. The sub-title of the study, *Economic impact of major sports events in Switzerland*, indicates this.

Table 12.2 Cost–benefit scheme for an event

Level	Costs	Benefits
Micro-level	• infrastructure costs • running costs of the event	• receipts from consumers • support from sponsors
'Unpaid' level	• public security costs • increased garbage collection • deterioration of site • social effects on local population or inconvenience costs to local people (circulation, noise, lost time, property damage, etc.)	• image-building • improvement of international liquidity position • improvement of infrastructure of the region
'Underpaid' level	• opportunity costs • employment of unemployed labour (negative cost)	• consumer surplus • improvement of infrastructure of the region in case of local financial contribution

Side effects on competitive and complementary activities	• possible effect on a competitive event	• additional value added creation in:
		  – hotels and other lodgings
		  – restaurants, pubs, etc.
		  – shops
		  – other tourism activities
		• indirect effects and/or multiplier effects
		• induced effects
		• creation of new economic activities

Quantification of cost and benefit items

The next step is to express the items of Table 12.1 in quantitative terms – arrivals, nights, meters, cubic meters, volumes, etc. We can be confronted with two possibilities: either the cost and benefit items are measurable, which is the normal situation, or the items cannot be expressed in a quantitative unit; in that case they are called intangible items. A typical intangible cost item is the destruction of the natural beauty of a landscape.

With respect to the quantification of cost and benefit items, a number of principles should be respected. The first is quite evident – it is important to avoid double counting. The cost–benefit scheme can be very helpful in avoiding one or more cost or benefit items being counted twice, but even so double counting is not impossible. The development of a camping area cannot lead to higher land value of the area and to additional value added created in the accommodation firms on the site; it should be either higher land value or additional value added.

More important is the application of the 'with and without' principle rather than the 'before and after' principle. The first principle compares the tourism development of the project with the situation that would occur without the project – in other words, it is an evaluation in terms of the difference it makes (also called the base case situation). The 'before and after' principle attributes to a project effects that are not caused by it, but which occur because of the passage of time or for other irrelevant reasons (e.g. what were the costs before the new facility was implemented, and what will they be afterwards?).

An example makes it clear. The construction of a congress centre in a city will boost the number of nights stayed. It would be incorrect to attribute all additional nights to the congress centre; the number of nights would still probably have increased without the congress centre. The 'with and without' leads in this case to a lower benefit than the 'before and after'. However, there are cases where we have the opposite situation (e.g. a declining trend of nights in the city where the congress centre is built).

It is furthermore important to emphasize that in Table 12.1 technological spillovers should be taken into account insofar as they alter the physical production possibilities of other producers or the satisfaction that consumers can get from given resources. On the other hand, pecuniary spillovers should not be taken into account if the sole effect is via prices of products or factors. There are cases involving transfers of resources from one group in the economy to another.

The comments made in Chapter 10 concerning crowding-out effects, expenditure switching and retained expenditure should be considered in the quantification of the different items.

Valuation of cost and benefit items

A third step in CBA is the valuation of the quantified items; the latter must be expressed in monetary units for each period of time over the economic life of the project.

In general, market prices are considered to be a proxy of the social valuations; market prices of final outputs indicate the 'proper' valuation of benefits, and market prices of resources the 'proper' valuation of costs.

> The prices placed on goods and services through the exchange process afford a means of measuring the value attached to those goods and services by those who participate in the exchange, and provide a basis for evaluating project effects in monetary terms.
> (US Government, Federal Inter-Agency River Basin Committee,
> Subcommittee on Benefits and Costs, 1950 – *The Green Book*)

In evaluating costs, attention should always be fixed on estimating the social opportunity cost of the resources used in the project; in other words, the social value of goods and services that would have been produced if the resources had been employed in the next best alternative public or private use. For most goods and services bought by public authorities from commercial firms, as well as for labour hired in competition with the private sector, the market price is an adequate measure of social opportunity cost.

In practice, there is not always a market price. In these cases, a shadow price or accounting price can be used (Sassone and Schaffer, 1978; Mishan, 1994; Boardman *et al.*, 2001). This is the price an economist attributes to a good or a factor on the argument that it is more appropriate than the existing price, if any. So, the price of a water purification plant down the river can be the shadow price for the waste water from a big tourism project discharged into the river, and for which the tourism project is not charged. Many writers reserve the term 'shadow price' for outputs that are not sold in a direct market. However, shadow prices may also be used to correct the underestimation or overestimation of the value of a particular resource.

Other price standards in the absence of market prices include:

● The alternative production cost
● Individuals' willingness to pay (see next section)
● Surrogate prices based on the behaviour of economic agents
● The prices of similar things elsewhere.

There are still items that are incommensurable (see Figure 12.3), such as the improvement of a landscape by a park (in the opposite case, the value of destruction of a landscape) or increase or decrease in the rate of juvenile delinquency due to tourism development. Another example is the saving of lives due to a better infrastructure. Although the number can be measured, for ethical reasons no value is given to saving a human being.

Sometimes there is opposition to the application of CBA because of the existence of intangible and/or incommensurable cost or benefit items. This is not a sufficient argument. We should recognize that some items cannot be expressed in monetary terms, without saying that those items should be neglected. Therefore we recommend adding (beside the table of quantifiable items) a qualitative table with costs and benefits that are intangible and/or incommensurable. We call this an itemization of the incommensurable physical benefits and costs associated with the project. It is suggested that a short description of the expected intangible effects should be added. This itemization can be helpful for the decision-makers of the project.

Very often the question is raised as to what should be done in case of price inflation and relative price changes. As a rule, we recommend the application of constant prices. For convenience, this will usually be the price level in the first year. Adjustments need not be made for inflation or general price increases. Uniform change in all prices can be ignored, and have no influence on the value of NPV or IRR. Adjustments need to be made for relative price changes. If some prices are likely to change relative to others, this should be reflected in the CBA.

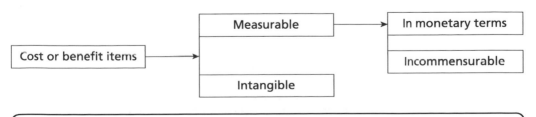

Figure 12.3 Various types of cost and benefit items

A special case is when there are adjustments to the market prices relative to taxes and subsidies. Indirect taxes are a cost to those who pay them, but it does not necessarily reflect economic costs to the country or the region as a whole in the sense that an increase of tax does not mean that more economic resources are required. From the viewpoint of the economy, taxes and subsidies must be viewed as transfer payments which normally should be excluded in evaluating the costs of a project. Thus, an import tax on beef consumed in the tourism sector should not be regarded as a cost to the economy, since it merely represents a transfer from the hotelier to the government. Conversely, a grant on vegetable growing is clearly a benefit to the farmer but is not a benefit to the economy.

On the benefit side, an indirect tax on final output should be deducted as a cost by the producer paying it, but it should not be deducted from the valuation of the benefits for social cost–benefit analysis. In practice, market prices (including VAT) are the rule to evaluate benefits based on the principle of 'willingness to pay'. Indirect taxes are part of the price people are willing to pay. In any case, indirect taxes paid by foreigners are a net benefit for the country; in tourism, the share of inbound tourism can be very important. All purchases must be cleared of VAT and other sales taxes. A tax paid to the government is a tax paid to society. This can lead to a real difference in profitability between a social cost–benefit application and a pure financial assessment.

This rule cannot be applied in all circumstances. A higher tax for pure budgetary reasons has nothing to do with willingness to pay. Thus, a higher tax on fuel leads to higher transport cost savings in a CBA of a new highway project, but in this case the tax has a pure transfer effect and does not contribute to any increase of welfare.

Willingness to pay and consumer surplus

Consumer surplus is an important item in many CBA applications. This is the case for many recreation projects and events with no (or a low) entrance fee. This brings us to the question of valuation of non-priced or non-market tourism resources. The following line of thought of Reynisdottir *et al.* (2008) is very inspiring and helpful:

> A natural attraction with free access is a non-market good. However, it is possible to assess its value to consumers in monetary terms. One way of doing this is to measure the consumers' WTP (willingness to pay) for the good, should a market exist for that good. In the same context as in a market situation, WTP for a non-market good is based on the assumptions of rational choice and utility maximization. If a change occurs in a non-market good (for example environmental improvement) by which the person believes he or she is better off in some way, that person, may wish to pay some money in order to secure this change, and so the WTP reflects a person's economic valuation of the good in question.

The estimation of the WTP for a natural attraction or any other attraction is the basis of social cost and benefit analysis (CBA), which relies on the Kaldor–Hicks criterion; that is, if the total net value (social benefit less social costs) of the natural attraction increases, the total welfare will also rise because winners could in principle compensate the losers for any losses involved in the society (Tisdell, 2006).

How does one cope with the valuation of non-priced resources? In the literature we find two methods that in many cases can bring a solution: (a) the travel cost method (TCM) and (b) the contingent valuation method (CVM). The TCM is based on market behaviour or revealed preference, while CVM methods provide a stated preference framework by asking respondents about their willingness to pay (WTP) or willingness to accept (Greiner and Rolfe, 2004).

Travel cost method

The TCM method is based on the premise that the costs of using a tourist area (e.g. a recreational site) can be considered as a proxy measure of visitors' willingness to pay and thus their valuation of that site. Let us suppose that visitors do not pay to gain entry to a recreation site, which is often the case, but they have incurred expenditure implicitly or explicitly to travel to it. This can be used as a measure of the valuation of that site (Tisdell, 2006). It involves the travel costs incurred by visitors to a tourist site (e.g. a museum) plus any entry fee as a proxy for their effective price for visiting the area.

The TCM has two different forms: individual and zonal. The first variant (ITCM) concerns trips generated by individuals. Visitors from different origins bear different travel costs depending on the distance from the destination (e.g. an event). This results in differences in total costs and differences in the rates of visits they induce. Both elements are the basis of estimating a demand curve. Of course, other factors are also important such as income, price, taste, etc. Price is more than the admission fee; it includes all travelling costs to and from the destination.

The second variant relates to trips on a zonal basis and is called the zonal travel cost method (ZTCM). In this case one uses the number of trips to a site, relative to the population of a particular zone. The operational core of the ZTCM is the trip generation function (Boardman *et al.*, 2001). This measures the relative frequency of visits to a recreation site from the different zones in relation to the travel cost involved in visiting the recreation site. In other words the ZTCM is based on actual visitors rather than potential visitors. The ZTCM implies the specification of the zones from which users of the site originate (concentric rings or isotime lines around the recreation site on a map). Based on a purely theoretical example, Figure 12.4 gives the relation between average total cost per person (TC) and average visits per person (V) for five zones A through E visiting a museum, for example.

Suppose that people from zone C make on average six visits per person. Actually they pay only $65 for each visit (based on the Boardman example). The consumer surplus for someone from zone C is obtained by summing the consumer surpluses associated with each visit across all trips ($90 – $65 = $25 for the first visit, $85 – $65= $20 for the second visit, and $15, $10, $5, and $0 for the third, fourth, fifth, and sixth visits respectively), which equals $75. This amount is represented by the area of the shaded triangle in Figure 12.4.

The data for average total cost per person (TC) and average visits per person (V) are represented graphically in Figure 12.4 for five different zones A through E. The equation TC = 95 – 5V (inverse demand curve) fits the data perfectly in the purely theoretical example. In practice, OLS would be used to fit a line to data points that would not all lie exactly on the line. It shows how much a person is willing to pay for a visit to the museum or other attraction. In the case represented by Figure 12.4, $90 for the first visit, $85 for the second visit, $80 for the third visit . . . and $20 for the fifteenth visit.

Knowing that the consumer surplus per person from zone C equals $75 and with the knowledge of the population of each zone, it is very simple to calculate the total consumer surplus per year and the average consumer surplus per visit for that zone. The consumer surplus for zone C is obtained by multiplying the consumer surplus per person by the population of zone C. Adding across all five zones gives us the total consumer surplus for the museum. Dividing the total consumer surplus by the total number of visits gives the average consumer surplus per visit.

An application of the TCM: Mount Buffalo National Park

An interesting application of the ZTCM can be found in Herath and Kennedy (2004). They use the TCM to estimate the economic value of Mount Buffalo National Park, the oldest national park in Victoria, Australia. In the ZTCM, the area surrounding the recreation site is

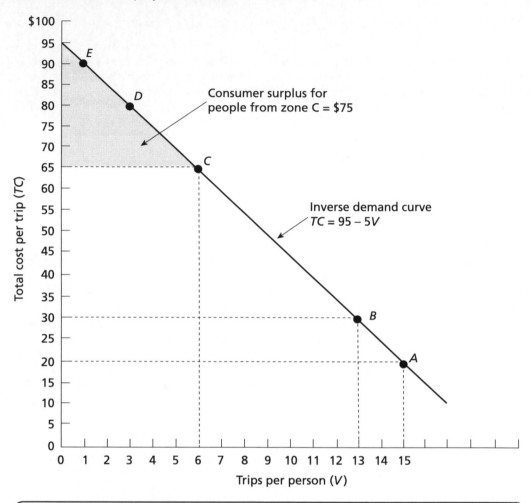

Figure 12.4 ZTCM and consumer surplus

Source: Boardman *et al.*, 2001

divided into 13 zones for which resident populations and distances from the site are estimated. Visitors from any given zone will incur similar expenses in visiting the site. The dependent variable in the ZTCM is visits per 1,000 resident population per year:

$$V_i = [(v_i/n) \times N \times 1000]/P_i \qquad (12.1)$$

where

V_i = visitation rate/1,000 population zone i
v_i = number of visitors from zone i per year
n = number of visitors interviewed
N = total number of visitors per year
P = the total population of zone i

The zonal visitation rate is regressed against the average zonal travel cost (first-stage demand curve). A distinction is made between average travel costs without travel time cost and another with travel time cost included. This leads to two regression equations. The first-stage demand curve for Mount Buffalo without travel time costs is given in the following equation (double-log function has the highest R^2):

$$\ln V = 11.01 - 1.57 \ln TC \qquad (12.2)$$

This equation is the basis to simulate the visitation rate from each zone that would occur under different entry fees (see also Boardman *et al.* 2001). Entry fees are treated in the same way as other costs. Herath and Kennedy (2004) simulated a fee increase by raising the costs by A\$5 and repeated the process up to A\$100. The total visitation rate from each zone was computed by summing the predicted rates from each zone at each price level. The summed visitation rates at each price level provide the demand curve for travel to Mount Buffalo National Park at various price levels. The demand curve is based on regression analysis (linear, double log, log-linear and linear-log). The best fit obtained without travel time costs is given by the equation:

$$\ln Q = 12.432 - 0.0015P \qquad (12.3)$$

The area under the demand curve gives the consumer surplus enjoyed by the visitors to the park. It is calculated by integrating the function between upper point A\$100 and lower point A\$0.

For the pure linear function [$Q = 246,014.07 - 1,407.24P$] the calculation of the consumer surplus is rather simple knowing that the demand curve cuts the Q axis at 246,014 and the P axis at 174.8 (in this case $246,014.07 - 1,407.24P$ equals a zero value). The corresponding consumer surplus equals ($246,014 \times 174.8$)/2 or A\$21.5 million. The calculated CS are very sensitive to the type of the chosen function (double-log, log-linear or linear-log).

The travel cost method has a number of limitations. A first question is how we measure the time involved in travel. Is 'income forgone' the right approach? Sometimes the opportunity cost of time is multiplied by 1/2 or 1/3, which is contestable. Not all TCM applications take travel time costs into consideration. But this attitude is also debatable.

This is not the major limitation. More important is a situation where a visitor enjoys multiple attractions during his trip. In this case visits may not be attributable to one but several reasons. The difficulty lies in determining what part of the costs should be assigned to a specific reason. This can lead to a strange situation where people living close to an attraction (e.g. a museum or an event) pay more than those who live farther away.

In a large natural area, one cannot avoid the fact that multiple tourist experiences have to be considered. TCM is inappropriate when the total experience consists of several experiences. In such a case a bundle of experiences may motivate the trip (Armbrecht, 2014).

Contingent valuation method

The contingent valuation method (CVM) is a well-established stated preference technique for estimation of the economic value of non-market resources. The underpinning of the method is the assumption that individuals can be induced to reveal their true willingness to pay for non-monetary goods through their behaviour in hypothetical markets (see Boardman *et al.*, 2001; Herath and Kennedy, 2004; Greiner and Rolfe, 2004; Tisdell, 2006; Asafu-Adjaye and Tapsuwan, 2008).

The CVM has been used in a wide variety of fields such as security, education, environmental protection, global warming, water quality (Farr *et al.*, 2016), water supply, tourism and recreational projects/events (Greiner and Rolfe, 2004; Herrero *et al.*, 2011; Armbrecht, 2014; Saayman *et al.*, 2016).

This method has several variants. The most frequent used models are:

- The open ended model: respondents are asked to state their maximum WTP, but no values are suggested.
- The iterative bidding model: posits a series of amounts until respondents reveal their maximum WTP – increasing or decreasing.
- The dichotomous choice model: respondents are asked whether they would participate in an activity if it were to cost them €X. The €X bid amount offered to any given respondent is randomly chosen from a predetermined set of bid amounts distributed over the survey sample. Only 'yes' or 'no' are required for these pre-specified bid amounts.
- Double-bounded dichotomous choice format (Greiner and Rolfe, 2004; Asafu-Adjaye and Tapsuwan, 2008; Herrero *et al.*, 2011) is similar to the dichotomous choice model but depending on the first response given by the interviewee, a second closed question is posed. Amounts immediately below being offered if a negative answer was given initially; or immediately above if a positive answer was given initially. Furthermore, all interviewed persons are posed a final question, 'What is your maximum WTP?'

My preference is for the dichotomous choice model. This model focusses directly on a precise bid price. This approach presumes a sufficient number of respondents per bid class. Figure 12.5 shows a histogram of dichotomous-choice responses (see Boardman *et al.*, 2001). The histogram shows the distribution of responses to bid prices. On the horizontal we find the bid prices ranging from the lowest price offered to the highest. The vertical axis gives the percentage of respondents who answer 'yes' to the bid price offered.

The fitted curve in Figure 12.5 may be viewed as the demand curve. The area under the curve provides an estimate of the individual's willingness to pay. If the values of X are evenly spread, then the histogram can be used to obtain an estimate of the average individual's WTP by applying the formula:

$$\text{WTP} = v \sum_{k=0}^{n} (\text{probability of acceptance at price kv}) \qquad (12.4)$$

where

v = the interval between prices (width of the individual bars)
n = number of values of X (number of bars)

Boardman *et al.* (2001) underline that researchers rarely work directly from the histogram of accepted bids. Estimates are usually made by estimating a statistical model for predicting the probability that an individual with specific characteristics will accept paying a particular bid price.

Prudence is always called for in applying CVM, especially in case of sensitive (political) matters. WTP is not always a reality. Never apply CVM for projects or topics which are being considered in a tense atmosphere. Furthermore CVM and TCM do not always lead to the same result (see Herath and Kennedy, 2004; Armbrecht, 2014), especially when tourists are faced with a bundle of experiences: the direct experience related to the main purpose of the visit and experiences on the site before and after (dining, going for a walk, possibly a visit to the beach). This can lead to a higher WTP (consumer surplus + travel costs and entrance fee).

Nevertheless the contingent valuation method is very useful to estimate the WTP and the corresponding consumer surplus. Very often they are the only alternative. In case of very different results it is possible to work with variants and to see to what extent the CBA is sensitive to the variants.

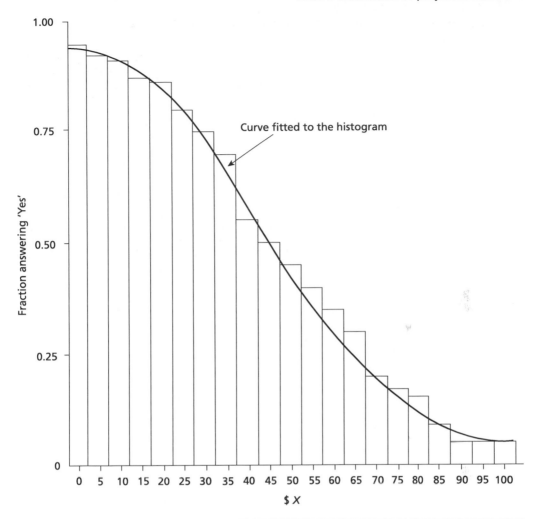

Figure 12.5 Histogram of dichotomous-choice models

Source: Boardman *et al.*, 2001

An application of the CVM: music festival Santiago de Compostela

This case study deals with the Santiago de Compostela Contemplative Music Festival (CMF), taken as a prototype of a cultural good which seeks to boost and diversify the city's tourist appeal (Herrero *et al.*, 2011). The CVM was applied to this case study to provide an economic valuation thereof by estimating the WTP declared by tourists or residents of the city attending the concerts. The CMF is always held during Holy Week. The 2007 festival, our case study in this work, comprised eight concerts, held in different churches and venues. The ultimate goal is to estimate an individual demand curve and the value of consumer surplus, in this case the intrinsic valuation of the tourism good analysed.

The authors describe their approach in the following terms. They used the double-bounded dichotomous choice format in the valuation exercise, with a final open question, as pointed out previously. Initial bids were offered to interviewees through a closed question and were different in each case, having been allocated randomly so as to avoid any possibility of anchoring bias in the estimations. The initial bids were €15, €30 up to €250. The amounts proposed in the first question were based on a previous comparison of season ticket costs at the main music (religious) festivals in Spain. Depending on the first response given by the interviewee, the second closed question was subsequently posed, amounts immediately below being offered if a negative answer was given initially, or immediately above if the answer was affirmative. The aim of this bidding game was to find the best fit for the individual's valuation, although all those interviewed were posed a final open question in which they were asked to express their maximum WTP.

The survival function (Figure 12.6) is the demand curve of direct users of the CMF in Santiago de Compostela. It indicates the probability of existing consumer intensity for the various valuation bids. The consumer surplus is the area enclosed between the demand curve and the axes of the coordinates. The bids on the horizontal axis vary between €0 and €320. (The bids take the values 0, 8 15, 30, 45, 60, 80 up to 320 euros, etc.) For a bid price of €8 the survival rate is 0.91, for €15 the rate is still 0.80 but for a bid price of €320 nobody is willing to pay that price. The area below the demand curve represents the WTP and in this case is easy to measure. It is the sum of the values of the individual bars (see Figure 12.6). For the CMF the mean WTP amounts to €45.89. This is the mean for all those attending the festival. When the sample is large enough it is possible to calculate the WTP results for different segments. In the case of CMF, the young people have a WTP mean of €42.7 and the elderly of €64.5.

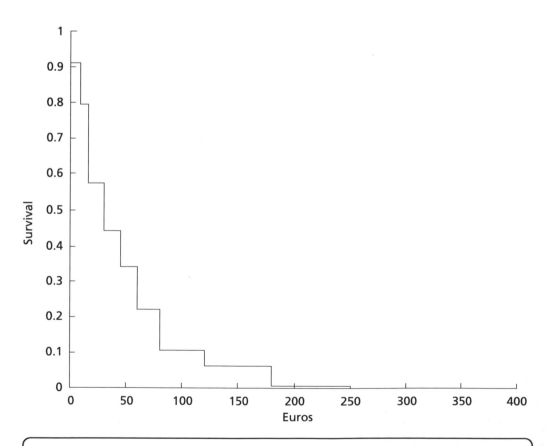

Figure 12.6 WTP survival function or CMF demand curve

Source: Herrero et al., 2011

Application for coastal tourism management

A completely different application field of contingent valuation is coastal tourism management. An interesting study relates to three Turkish beaches of Kizkalesi, Yemiskumu and Susanoglu near Mersin (Birdir *et al.*, 2013). Mersin is the provincial capital of the eponymous Mersin Province in the South of Turkey. A similar study concerns the coastal line in Central Greece – Volos (Halkos and Matsiori, 2012).

Beaches are not only considered as public domain, but also as a source of income. Economic benefits can be derived from their recreational use. That is the reason why beach management is so important.

In the Turkish case, three areas – Kizkalesi, Yemiskumu and Susanoglu, all located along the southern coast of Mersin – were selected for the study to improve the management of the beaches. More than 400 beach visitors were involved. Washed-up litter and man-made debris were stated as the prime dislike at all three beaches. Based on a contingent valuation, two thirds were willing to pay for improved beaches, the amounts ranging from €0.40 to €7.94. Mean values found were €2.33 for Kizkalesi, €2.22 for Yemiskumu and €1.77 for Susanoglu beaches. With this study it was seen that approximately €1.70–2.30 can be applied to the beaches as a fixed price per visit for maintenance and improvement.

Calculation of NPV and/or IRR

Now we have all the elements to calculate the NPV or IRR. Table 12.1 can be transformed into the form of Table 12.3. The latter is a calculation table. For each cost and benefit item, a column is provided (there can be more than one column for each generic cost and benefit item).

Table 12.3 Calculation table in CBA

Year	Ca	Cb	Cc	Cd	Ce	ΣC	Ba	Bb	Bc	Bd	ΣB	Σ (B – C)
1												
2												
3												
4												
5												
6												
7												
8												
9												
10												
.....												
30												
NPV												

ΣC = sum of all cost items for year 1 to 30
ΣB = sum of all benefit items for year 1 to 30
Σ (B – C) = sum of benefits minus costs for year 1 to 30

Table 12.3 also contains special columns for the sum of the costs, the sum of the benefits and finally for the sum of (B – C). This allows us to calculate the NPV and the IRR.

A crucial point in the NPV calculation is the choice of the discount rate. The role of the discount rate is two-fold. First, it makes costs and benefits accruing at different points of time commensurable. Secondly, in considering the net benefits achieved by an investment project attention has to be paid to its costs, which means the opportunity forgone. The role of the discount rate is to help to ensure that these opportunities forgone, which are themselves time streams of costs and benefits, are properly taken into account. The opportunities forgone can be in:

1 The public sector

   ● consumption
   ● investment

2 The private sector

   ● consumption
   ● investment.

In other words, the discounting is necessary to allow for the time factor and the cost of capital.

In theory, the social time preference or the social opportunity cost as social rate of discount can have several foundations. It is not the intention to explore this aspect in this publication – the literature on that topic is immense, sufficient to fill up many shelves of a library. In reality, four different schools of thought can be distinguished (Dasgupta and Pearce, 1972; Mishan, 1994). The first is the 'social time preference' (STP) school of thought. This means that consumption in the near future is preferable to consuming something of the same market value in the more distant future. This school argues that the social discount rate should reflect society's preference for present benefits over future benefits. STP expresses the social substitution ratio of actual and future consumption. STP can be expressed in real terms and in nominal terms; the difference between them is the depreciation of the money.

The second is the 'social opportunity cost' (SOC) school of thought. The SOC of a project (in the public sector) is the present value for society of the best alternative project that at the same time is excluded by the project. SOC is the present value of the consumption flows that would arise without the project. The second school of thought suggests that the social discount rate for use should reflect the rate of return foregone on the displaced project.

Others prefer to apply the government's borrowing rate or the average rate of return of long-term treasury bonds. Although this third alternative is quite often used, this approach is sometimes considered as a second-best solution. Indeed, people neglect more productive investment for bonds without risk (underestimation of SOC), and interest rates are influenced by market imperfections (influence of monetary and fiscal policy).

The fourth school of thought advocates the rate of return on private investments. Public projects should earn a rate of return equal to good private projects, and hence the interest rate equal to private rates of return can be used in the CBA.

If benefits and costs are expressed in constant prices, it is recommended that the real interest rate should be used. The market interest rate is in theory the sum of the real interest rate and inflation; however, the reality is quite often different. The real interest rate R can be deduced from the following formula:

$$(1 + r) = (1 + R)\,(1 - i) \tag{12.5}$$

$$R = [(1 + r)/(1 + i)] - 1 \tag{12.6}$$

where

R = real interest rate
r = market interest rate
i = inflation rate

Risk and uncertainty

In the application of CBA, we can be faced with a number of special problems. The first is risk and uncertainty. Here we take the two terms as synonyms, although this is not completely correct. Risk is inherent in all investment projects, but for some projects the uncertainty might be bigger. In the tourism sector there are many projects with uncertain factors. How do we tackle risk and uncertainty? In the literature, several procedures are proposed (see US Government, Federal Inter-Agency River Basin Committee, Subcommittee on Benefits and Costs, 1950 – *The Green Book*). Two have little value:

1 Risk premium to the discount rate
2 Shortening of project life.

These procedures have little value because nobody can tell us what risk premium should be taken, or by how many years a project should be shortened. We prefer to recognize that there are risks, and thus recommend that two or three variants be taken for one or more cost or benefit items. The consequence of this approach is a multitude of NPVs or IRRs. However, it cannot be the intention to present 50, 100 or 200 results. Therefore, we propose to stick to three combinations:

1 The most pessimistic approach. In this case, the highest value is taken for each cost item and the lowest for each benefit item. If the NPV > 0, we get a positive sign, in favour of the project.
2 The most optimistic approach. This uses a combination of all the lowest cost and all the highest benefit alternatives. An NPV < 0 is a negative indication, against the project.
3 The most likely result. Here, NPV or IRR is based on a combination of all the most likely estimations of cost and benefit items.

This brings us to the sensitivity analysis (Boardman *et al.*, 2001), with worst- and best-case analysis, the most plausible estimates and partial sensitivity. The latter is most appropriately applied to what the analyst believes to be the most important and uncertain assumptions. It can be used to find the values of numerical assumptions at which net benefits equal zero. The partial sensitivity analysis can also be applied with respect to the right choice of the discount rate.

Another approach of risk analysis is 'component analysis', based on the composition of the cost components as well as the composition of the benefit components of the NPV. Here, we refer to the composition of the last row of Table 12.3. It must be reassuring for an investor if one cost component represents 60 per cent of the NPV of the costs and there is not much uncertainty about the estimation of that item; similarly if a benefit component has a high share in the NPV of benefits and shows little risk.

Limitations in space and time

Any project is influenced by the definition of space and time. The NPV or IRR of a project can be calculated for a resort, destination, region, county or country. The result will most probably be different with respect to the space (or area) level. Two examples make this clear. A major event, financed by the destination, can lead to important side effects (see Bd items in Table 12.3) which do not accrue to the inhabitants of the destination and as such cannot be considered as a benefit for the destination. However, from the national point of view these benefits should be taken into account. Another relevant example is the building of a congress centre in a city subsidized by the national government. For the city the grant means a reduction of the investment and/or operation costs, but from the national point of view the subsidy should be disregarded.

Limitations in time are of a different nature. The question arises as to how long a period we should take into account in order to get a reasonable estimate of the total effect of the investment. The answer depends on many elements. The first factor is the height of the social discount rate. A high discount rate leads to a negligible NPV of a benefit accruing in 30 years or more. Other important elements include physical length of life, technological changes, emergence of competing products or projects, and shifts in demand.

Three case studies of CBA

The theory of CBA can be illustrated with three case studies. The first one concerns an investment project for a new congress centre in Bruges with a life time of 30 years. I was responsible for that study project. Although the project dates from the 1970s, the application procedure is still up to date. Unlike in the USA, many convention centres in Europe are supported by the public sector. The second case is quite different. It relates to the 2005 Australian Formula 1 Grand Prix. This is an event that takes place in one particular year. This is also the case for the third case study: the Australian CBA for the 2022 FIFA World Cup.

CASE STUDY

Case 1: Congress centre in Bruges

At the beginning of the 1970s, a feasibility study was commissioned for a new congress centre in Bruges. The study started from the important assumption that 50 per cent of the cost could be transferred to a cultural function. In the town there was at that time a need for a cultural centre and a congress centre, and it was assumed that the new project could fulfil both functions. As a consequence, part of the project was eligible for grants from the national government.

The first part of the study dealt with the market possibilities for attracting conferences to Bruges. In the second part, investment costs and running costs were estimated. The two main parts analysed the micro- and macro-profitability. This case is a good example for showing the difference in profitability between a micro- and a macro-approach.

From the micro-profitability point of view, the congress centre showed a very negative result during each year of operation. The first, second, sixth and tenth years of operation showed the following losses:

- First year: €–130,000
- Second year: €–111,000
- Sixth year: €–57,000
- Tenth year: €–40,000

Table 12.4 Cost–benefit scheme, congress centre, Bruges

Level	Costs	Benefits
Project	Ca: investment congress centre	Ba: direct receipts congress centre
	Cb: running costs	
'Unpaid' level	Cc: security costs, reception costs	Bb: prestige and promotion value
'Underpayment' level	Cd: transfer of investment and running costs to the cultural function	Bc: none
Side effects		Bd: additional value added hotels, restaurants and shops

The application of Table 12.1 to the Bruges case resulted in cost and benefit items as listed in Table 12.4.

With a discount rate of 8 per cent, the project resulted in an NPV of €5 million or an IRR of 33.5 per cent. This macro-profitability is in sharp contrast to the micro-profitability.

From the composition of the macro-benefits it can be deduced that less than one-fifth of the present value of the receipts accrue to the investor of the congress centre:

- Ba: €1.247 million or 18.0 per cent
- Bb: €1.800 million or 25.6 per cent
- Bd: €3.949 million or 56.4 per cent.

It is quite remarkable that more than half of the benefits of the project accrue to hotels, restaurants and shops. This case shows that a very negative micro-profitability can be paired with a more than acceptable macro-profitability. This can be a sufficient argument for a local authority to finance the losses at the micro-level in order to harvest the benefits at the macro-level for the local community.

CASE STUDY

Case 2: 2005 Australian Formula 1 Grand Prix

A second CBA case concerns the Australian Formula 1 Grand Prix. In Chapter 10 we dealt with a CGE case relative to the Australian Formula 1 Grand Prix. The Victorian Auditor General's Office commissioned (alongside the CGE study) a cost–benefit study (CBA) to estimate the level of net benefits to Victorians (Victoria being a region in Australia). It should be noticed that CBA and CGE are quite different in their purpose, method and application. The results of both studies are not directly comparable to each other. CGE seeks to establish economic effects such as the increase in Victoria's GDP and employment. CBA estimates the net benefits (benefits minus costs) to the Victorians. The study estimates the welfare effects of the GP on households in Victoria (Victorian Government and business included) and not the welfare effects to Australia.

Table 12.5 gives a general overview of the costs and benefits retained in the CBA for the Australian Grand Prix. Due to the particular character of some items,

---

Table 12.5 Benefits and costs to Victoria from the Australian Formula 1 Grand Prix in millions A$, 2005

Source: Victorian Auditor-General (VAGO), State Investment in Major Events, 2007

Benefits	Amount
• Visitor payments to AGPC (Australian Grand Prix Corporation)	41.5
• Sponsor payments to AGPC	10.9
• Consumer surplus	3.4
• Attendance free GP related events	1.9
• Business surplus accruing to businesses	3.7
• Labour surplus	1.7
Total benefits	63.1
Costs	
• GP construction and operation costs	68.1
• GP related government costs	0.5
• Loss of park uses and amenity	0.4
• Transport congestion	0.5
• Noise costs	0.2
Total costs	69.8
Net benefit (using the most reliable data and best estimates for B and C)	−6.7

more explanation is necessary. In Table 12.6 we put the benefit and cost items into our theoretical scheme (see Table 12.1).

Visitor and sponsor payments to AGPC (see Table 12.5) speak for themselves. The study distinguishes between visitor origins: Melbourne, other Victoria, interstate and international. The other benefit items are less clear but justified. The authors make a distinction between two types of consumer surplus. The first consumer surplus relates to the ticket price. The gross consumer benefit of a good or service is valued at the maximum amount that consumers are willing to pay for it (see Department of Finance, 2006). Ticket prices may not reflect the maximum that many consumers may be willing to pay for the Grand Prix. The practice of ticket scalping is an indication that people are willing to pay more than the official ticket price. In other words consumer surplus exists; there is a difference between what consumers are willing to pay and what they actually pay. Based on a study of the Centre for Tourism Research in Canberra about price sensitivity, the consumer surplus was estimated at 10.8 per cent of Grand Prix ticket revenue from sales to Victorians. Any consumer surplus of non-Victorians is not relevant.

The second group of consumer surplus concerns local people attending events related to the Grand Prix, such as the F1 parade and Federation Square activities. These events are free of charge. This consumer surplus was estimated at A\$10 per person attending related events.

There are also benefits to Victorian businesses and labour. The basic assumptions are: (a) there are sufficient unemployed or part-time workers available to meet the additional demand and (b) there is spare capacity in capital and land in businesses in the region to meet additional demand. Businesses such as hotels are assumed to be able to generate a surplus because of the potential for spare capacity and unemployed or underemployed workers who can be employed on a casual basis to meet the extra demand. Business and labour surplus resulting from increase in tourism in the region of New South Wales is based on a former CGE study of Dwyer *et al.* (2005). According to this study 16.9 per cent of additional tourist expenditure accrues to business in the region; the corresponding figure for labour surplus amounts to 41.5 per cent.

The business surplus for the GP is calculated in the following way:

- Estimate of the additional expenditure by international and interstate tourists (air fares are excluded because most overseas visitors use foreign airlines and grand prix tickets are not taken into account because they accrue to the AGPC).
- 20 per cent accrues to non-Victorians.
- There is no crowding out.

$$BS = (E - \Delta EO) \times (BR) \qquad (12.7)$$

where:

BS = business surplus
E = additional expenditure by tourists
BR = per cent additional expenditure which accrues to business (16.9 per cent)

ΔEO = per cent additional expenditure which accrues to non-Victorians (20 per cent)

or:

$$BS = (A\$55 - A\$11) \times 16.9 = A\$7.4$$

Only half of BS is retained given that conventional CBA would allocate a zero value to the surplus on the basis of assuming full employment of factors of production. The authors take a prudent position by taking the average position between the two perspectives.

Labour surpluses are calculated based on the following formula:

$$LS = E \times A \times B \times C \tag{12.8}$$

where:

LS = labour surplus
E = additional expenditure by tourists
A = per cent of E spent on labour
B = per cent of A that is done by extra labour employment
C = per cent of wage that represents a surplus to the additional labour employed

or:

$$LS = A\$55 \times 0.415 \times 0.5 \times 0.15 = A\$1.7$$

Cost items need less explanation. Capital expenditure is included in a CBA, but depreciation is not as this would involve double counting. The AGPC construction and operating costs relate to:

● Event management and staging (e.g. payments to the department of infrastructure, loss of income of tenants of Albert Park)
● Recurrent engineering such as assembling, dismantling, etc.
● Marketing/promotion and catering
● Administration.

The other government costs concern expenses to agencies (e.g. police, State Emergency Service, St John Ambulance, etc.) reporting net expenses in excess of recoverable amounts to AGPC. Due to the Grand Prix, visitors (visits for sporting and informal recreational use) cannot use Albert Park Reserve during several weeks. The estimate of lost uses is based on the travel cost method (Lansdell and Gangadharan, 2002). This method is used to infer the surplus value that each user derived from the use of the park. The underlying idea is that those who travel a long way have high travel costs and, hence, very little surplus value from using the park. Those who have low travel costs have higher surplus value. In the Grand Prix CBA study the Lansdell and Gangadharan figure is A\$13.30 for lost uses and an amount of half this for reduced amenities.

Transport congestion is another concern (traffic diversion and traffic congestion). In the Grand Prix week, about 15,000 vehicles are diverted out of the park each day for seven days. Each vehicle takes an additional three minutes and the travel time cost was estimated at A$22 per vehicle hour.

Noise costs are inherent to a Grand Prix. The question is how many people reside within a particular dB line. Some are severely affected and others are less affected. The cost of noise disamenity is estimated from the negative effects on property values. For the Grand Prix the authors assume that noise impacts would cause weekly rentals (actual or imputed; A$500 a week) of the 2,500 severely affected properties to fall by 20 per cent and the rents of the 3,300 other affected properties to fall by 10 per cent for one week.

How can we now put the above-mentioned costs and benefit items in the theoretical cost–benefit scheme of Table 12.1?

It should be noticed that this Grand Prix is an event that takes place in a particular year. Calculation of a NPV or IRR does not apply. All costs and benefits accrue to the year 2005.

Table 12.6 Cost–benefit scheme for the Australian Formula 1 Grand Prix, 2005

Source: Victorian Auditor-General, State Investment in Major Events, 2007

Level	Costs	A$ mln
Micro level	● GP construction and operation costs	68.1
	● GP related government costs	0.5
Unpaid level	● Loss of park uses and amenity	0.4
	● Transport congestion	0.5
	● Noise costs	0.2
Underpayment level	● pm	
Side effects	● pm	
Total costs		69.8
	Benefits	
Micro level	● Visitor payments to AGPC	41.5
	● Sponsor payments to AGPC	10.9
Unpaid level	● pm	
	● Consumer surplus	3.4
Underpayment level	● Attendance free GP related events	1.9
Side effects	● Business surplus accruing to businesses	3.7
	● Labour surplus	1.7
Total benefits		63.1
Net benefit		(6.7)

CASE STUDY

Case 3: Australia and the 2022 FIFA World Cup

In 2010 Football Federation Australia (FFA) was bidding for Australia to host the FIFA World Cup. The Australian government had committed $45.6 million in financial support. A cost–benefit analysis was commissioned by the Department of Resources, Energy, and Tourism from Deloitte Access Economics. The aim of the study was to examine the economic benefits and costs of Australia hosting the 2022 World Cup. The study in itself is interesting. The results of the report strongly influenced the Australian government's courageous decision not to support the World Cup in Australia. The 2022 FIFA World Cup was finally awarded to Qatar.

The Australian proposal included 12 stadia across 10 host cities nationwide and would see World Cup matches played across six states and territories. In the framework of the analysis the authors (Access Economics) of the report evoke a number of typical benefits and costs. A FIFA World Cup typically confers a range of important economic benefits. These include additional tourism activity and improved infrastructure and transport systems. Tourism legacy benefits (based on the experience of the Sydney Olympics) from the World Cup were estimated to continue for two years: 1 per cent of international visitors in 2023 and 0.5 per cent in 2024. More indirect benefits are also potentially available through showcasing a city or country as a business and tourism destination and building a sense of community pride and cohesiveness. But there are also major costs and risks involved in hosting such an event. They involve the actual costs of constructing necessary infrastructure and providing security, the risk of significant cost overruns and underutilization of facilities following the event (see the South African situation after the 2010 World Cup). Further costs can arise through displacement of non-event visitors and added inconvenience for residents during the period of the World Cup. The analysis focusses on the direct financial aspects of the 2022 World Cup. This means that some important social costs and benefits have not been quantified.

In the analysis a distinction is made between three scenarios:

1   Scenario 1 – full stadia costs. All stadium construction costs, upgrades and overlay costs associated with the 12 stadia are allocated to the World Cup.
2   Scenario 2 – partial stadia costs. Stadia costs incurred directly as a result of the World Cup, especially upgrades of stadia in some host cities and new stadia in two host cities. It includes all overlay and temporary costs for other stadia required to become FIFA compliant.
3   Scenario 3 – overlay costs. Overlay costs for the 12 stadia.

The statement that the three scenarios considered reflect the likelihood of those stadium works being developed irrespective of Australia staging the World Cup is very important.

Table 12.7 Net benefits of hosting the 2022 World Cup in Australia (in millions $ and NPV terms)

Source: Access Economics, 2010

Benefit/Cost	Scenario 1	Scenario 2	Scenario 3
Benefits			
Tourism	726	726	726
Local organization committee	173	173	173
Television broadcasting	46	46	46
Other World Cup related (e.g. consumer surplus; goods and service tax on sold tickets)	114	114	114
Total benefits	1,059	1,059	1,059
Costs			
Bidding	46	46	46
Infrastructure	1,948	776	204
Transport	50	50	50
Security	333	333	333
Cost of government	97	97	97
Other World Cup related (e.g. cost of upgrading and building training facilities)	62	63	63
Total costs	2,536	1,364	792
Net benefit	−1,477	−305	+266

For the interpretation of Table 12.7, two points should be taken into account. Firstly, a NPV method is utilized to discount ($r = 4.5$ per cent) future costs and benefits to a present value. Secondly, tickets sales are a FIFA receipt and do not accrue to Australia.

There are significant differences in net benefit between the three scenarios in Table 12.7:

- Scenario 1: net cost of $1,477 million
- Scenario 2: net cost of $305 million
- Scenario 3: net benefit of $266 million.

These differences are driven by the allocation of stadia costs, with all other aspects of the tournament common to each scenario. The significant difference between scenario 1 and 2 is due to around $1.6 billion of stadium construction being allocated away from the World Cup.

Referring to the cost–benefit scheme in Table 12.1, which cost and benefit items are not taken into account in Table 12.7?

Let us start with the unpaid costs and benefits. An example of unpaid costs are the inconvenience for the local population during the event. A World Cup gives short-term positive feelings of well-being (national pride – 'halo effect'). Such effects can be experienced broadly across the Australian community. We agree they are not tangible and not measurable.

At the level of underpaid costs and benefits, one possible item might have been underestimated. Due to the assumption about the labour market, no negative underpaid costs were retained. But it is important to notice that a full employment assumption was a condition to be taken into account. According to the authors, relaxing the full employment assumption improves the net result by $680 across all three scenarios. However, the consumer surplus based on the number of Australians that would have travelled overseas to attend the World Cup but now stay in Australia is well taken into account.

There are also residents who leave the country due to the event. The authors believe that this is compensated for by the residents who give up a holiday abroad to remain in Australia for the event.

A major event also has an impact on complementary activities such as hotels, restaurants and other tourism business. They are included in the tourism benefits as welfare revenue (and not revenue). The economic welfare is measured in a Computable General Equilibrium (CGE) model by real gross domestic product (GDP). It is the contribution of the additional spending to national income, or the net impact on earnings by labour, capital and tax revenue that contributes to the welfare of Australians.

Impact on competitive activities was also considered but not retained in the final CBA. Hosting the World Cup affects other professional sports in Australia due to restricted access to major sporting venues and changes to normal operating schedules. They call it 'Impact on other sporting codes'.

The conclusion of the report is important:

> The fundamental conclusion drawn from this analysis is that, except under the most favourable cost conditions, the expected financial benefits from tourism, team and media spending are not sufficient to outweigh the significant costs of stadium construction and operational services required to host the event.

This conclusion must have been taken due to the long period between the moment of the CBA and the year the World Cup takes place. This creates a lot of uncertainties about the costs of the stadium infrastructure. Security costs were estimated based on the current environment. Due to international factors those costs might be much higher. Another factor that might have influenced the conclusion is the fact that for major events governments are often required to provide a range of guarantees to the relevant governing bodies (in this case FIFA).

Final remarks

In many applications of CBA there is confusion between the costs and receipts of the project on the one hand, and the public expenditure and tax receipts on the other. A clear distinction must be made between the macro-evaluation of a project and the financial account of the public sector. The financial account of the public sector relates to the expenses and taxes, both reduced to a present value. Taxes are a transfer, and can never be considered in a CBA.

A special problem is the comparability of the profitability of a project with other projects. In most cases this is a theoretical problem; in practice, there is no similar project. A comparison of a project in one field with one in another field does not make much sense. A choice between a tourism project and an education project cannot be based on the difference in IRR; the choice is purely a political decision.

References and further reading

Access Economics (2010). *Cost Benefit Analysis of the 2022 Fifa World Cup*. Sydney: Department of Resources, Energy and Tourism.

Armbrecht, J. (2014). Use value of cultural experiences: a comparison of contingent valuation and travel cost. *Tourism Management, 42*.

Asafu-Adjaye, J., and Tapsuwan, S. (2008). A contingent valuation study of scuba diving benefits: case study in Mu Ko Similan Marine National Park, Thailand. *Tourism Management, 29*.

Baade, R., and Matheson, A. (2004). The quest for the Cup: assessing the economic impact of the World Cup. *Regional Studies, 4*.

Beritelli, P., Bieger, T., Müller, H. *et al.* (2004). *Assessing the Economic Impacts of Hallmark Sport Events: The Case of the World Ski Championship 2003 in St Moritz-Engadine*. Paper presented at TRC Meeting in Guildford, 2004 (unpublished).

Birdir, S., Ünal, Ö., Birdir, K., and Williams, A. (2013). Willingness to pay as an economic instrument for coastal tourism management: cases from Mersin, Turkey. *Tourism management, 36*.

Boardman, A., Greenberg, D., Vining, A., and Weimer, D. (2001). *Cost–Benefit Analysis: Concepts and Practice*, 2nd edn. Upper Saddle River, NJ: Prentice Hall.

Bull, A. (1995). *The Economics of Travel and Tourism*. Sydney: Longman.

Burgan, B. (2001). Reconciling cost–benefit and economic impact assessment for event tourism. *Tourism Economics, 4*.

Dasgupta, A., and Pearce, D. (1972). *Cost–Benefit Analysis: Theory and Practice*. London: Macmillan.

Department of Finance (2006). *Handbook of Cost-Benefit Analysis*. Canberra: Commonwealth of Australia.

Dwyer, L., Forsyth, P., Spurr, R., and Van Ho T. (2005). *The Economic Impacts and Benefits of Tourism in Australia: A General Equilibrium Approach*. Technical Report, CRC for Sustainable Tourism.

Farr, M., Stoeckl, N., Esparon, M., Larson, S., and Jarvis, D. (2016). The importance of water clarity to Great Barrier Reef tourists and their willingness to pay to improve it. *Tourism Economics, 22 (2)*.

Ganchev, O. (2000). Applying value drivers to hotel valuation. *Cornell Hotel and Restaurant Administration Quarterly*, October.

Greiner, R., and Rolfe, J. (2004). Estimating consumer surplus and elasticity of demand of tourist visitation to a region in North Queensland using contingent valuation. *Tourism Economics, 10 (3)*.

Halkos, G., and Matsiori, S. (2012). Determinants of willingness to pay for coastal zone quality management. *Journal of Socio-Economics, 41*.

Harman, F., and Clarke, H. (2007). *State Investment in Major Events*. Melbourne: Victorian Government.

Hawkins, C.J., and Pearce, D.W. (1971). *Capital Investment Appraisal*. London: Macmillan.

Hefner, F. (2001). The cost–benefit model as applied to tourism development in the state of South Carolina, USA. *Tourism Economics*, 2.

Herath, G., and Kennedy, J. (2004). Estimating value of Mount Buffalo National Park with the travel cost and contingent valuation models. *Tourism Economics, 10 (1)*.

Herrero, L., Sanz, J., and Devisa, M. (2011). Measuring the economic value and social viability of cultural festival as a tourism prototype. *Tourism Economics, 17 (1)*.

Klaassen, L.H., and Botterweg, T.H. (1974). *Projectevaluatie en imponderabele effecten: een schaduwprojectenadering*. Rotterdam: NEI.

Klaassen, L., and Vanhove, N. (1971). Macro-economic evaluation of port investments. In R. Regul (ed.), *The Future of the European Ports*. Bruges: College of Europe.

Lansdell, N., and Gangadharan, L. (2002). Comparing travel costs models and the precision of their consumer surplus estimates: Albert Park and Maroondah Reservoir. *Australian Economic Papers, 42(4)*.

Layard, R., and Glaister, S. (eds) (1994). *Cost–Benefit Analysis*, 2nd edn. Cambridge: Cambridge University Press.

Mintel (2003). Hotels in Australia. *Travel & Tourism Analyst*, August.

Mishan, E.J. (1994). *Cost–Benefit Analysis*. London: Routledge.

Pearce, D.W. (1983). *Cost–Benefit Analysis*, 2nd edn. London: Macmillan.

Prest, A., and Turvey, R. (1967). Cost–benefit analysis: a survey. *Surveys of Economic Theory, Vol. II*. London: Macmillan.

Raybould, M., and Mules, T. (1999). A cost–benefit study of protection of the northern beaches of Australia's Gold Coast. *Tourism Economics*, 5.

Reynisdottir, M., Song, H., and Agrusa, J. (2008). Willingness to pay entrance fees to natural attractions: an Icelandic case study. *Tourism Management, 29*.

Rushmore, S. (1992). Seven current hotel-valuation techniques. *Cornell Hotel and Restaurant Administration Quarterly*, August.

Saayman, M., Krugell, W., and Saayman, A. (2016). Willingness to pay: who are the cheap talkers? *Annals of Tourism Research, 56*.

Sassone, P.G., and Schaffer, W.A. (1978). *Cost–Benefit Analysis: A Handbook*. London: Academic Press.

Scherly, F., and Breiter, M. (2002). *Impact économique des grandes manifestations sportives en Suisse, Etude de cas 'Athletissima' Lausanne 2001*. Lausanne: HEC Lausanne.

Sinclair, T., and Stabler, M. (1998). *The Economics of Tourism*. London: Routledge.

Smith, S. (1997). *Tourism Analysis: A Handbook*, 2nd edn. Edinburgh: Longman.

Spindler, J., and Huron, D. (eds) (2009). *L'Évaluation de L'Événement Touristique*. Paris: L'Harmattan.

Sugden, R., and Williams, A. (1988). *The Principles of Practical Cost–Benefit Analysis*. Oxford: Oxford University Press.

Tisdell, C. (2006). Valuation of tourism's natural resources. In L. Dwyer and P. Forsyth (eds), *International Handbook on the Economics of Tourism*. Cheltenham: Edward Elgar.

United Nations (1993). Feasibility study on the Arona Valley Tourism Development Project. *Escap Tourism Review, 12*.

United Nations (1999). *Guidelines on Integrated Planning for Sustainable Tourism Development*. New York: UN.

US Government, Federal Inter-Agency River Basin Committee, Subcommittee on Benefits and Costs (1950). *Proposed Practices for Economic Analysis of River Basin Projects (The Green Book)*. Washington, DC: US Government.

VAGO (2007). *State Investment in Major Events*. Melbourne: Victorian Government.

Vanhove, N. (1978). Tourism planning: economic instruments–an evaluation at the project level. *Tourism Planning for the Eighties*, 28th AIEST Congress, Cairo. Bern: AIEST.

Vanhove, N. (1997). Mass tourism: benefits and costs. In S. Wahab and J.J. Pigram (eds), *Tourism Development and Growth*. London: Routledge.

Vanhove, N. (2003). Externalities of sport and tourism investments, activities and events. In P. Keller and T. Bieger (eds), *Sport and Tourism*. 53rd AIEST Congress, Athens. St-Gall: AIEST.

Van Rompuy, V., and Vertonghen, R. (1982). *Sociaal-economische kosten-batenanalyse*. Leuven: Acco.

WES (1971). *Micro and Macro ekonomische rendabiliteit van een kongresgebouw te Brugge*. Brugge: WES.

Witt, S., Brooke, M., and Buckley, P. (1991). *The Management of International Tourism*. London: Unwin Hyman.

Yolal, M., Gursoy, D., Uysal, M., Kim, H., and Karacaoglu, S. (2016). Impacts of festivals and events on residents' well-being. *Annals of Tourism Research*, 61.

Index

Index